PROPERTIES OF EMPIRE

PROPERTIES OF EMPIRE

Indians, Colonists, and Land Speculators
on the New England Frontier

IAN SAXINE

New York University Press

NEW YORK

NEW YORK UNIVERSITY PRESS
New York
www.nyupress.org

Library of Congress Cataloging-in-Publication Data

Names: Saxine, Ian, author.
Title: Properties of empire : Indians, colonists, and land speculators on the New England frontier / Ian Saxine.
Other titles: Early American places.
Description: New York : New York University Press, [2019] | Series: Early American places | Includes bibliographical references and index.
Identifiers: LCCN 2018041757 | ISBN 9781479832125 (cl : alk. paper)
Subjects: LCSH: Abenaki Indians—Land tenure—Maine. | Abenaki Indians—Maine—Treaties. | Indians of North America—First contact with Europeans—Maine. | Maine—History—Colonial period, ca. 1600–1775.
Classification: LCC E99.A13 S29 2019 | DDC 974.004/9734—dc23
LC record available at https://lccn.loc.gov/2018041757

For Mom, Dad, and Meghan

Contents

Wabanaki Glossary

The Wabanakis were not a unitary political or even linguistic entity but rather a group of culturally and linguistically similar peoples—often intermarrying with one another—who cooperated in trade, diplomacy, and war when it suited them. Around 1700, they formalized that relationship by forming the Wabanaki Confederacy. The various nations all spoke different branches of the Abenaki language, which is part of the larger Algonquian language group. These "tribal" affiliations remained fluid from a modern perspective, as overlapping kinship networks encouraged families to shift locations (and therefore, from a European viewpoint, "tribal" identity) due to political differences, marriage choices, or other reasons.

After a period of mid-seventeenth-century turbulence (discussed in chapter 2), the following major Wabanaki nations discussed in this book were sorted as follows, from west to east:

The *Pigwackets* lived primarily along the Saco River

The *Amarascoggins* lived along the Androscoggin River

The *Kennebecs* lived along the river of that same name

The *Penobscots* resided along a river of that same name

The *Wulstukwiuks* (also known as the Maliseet) lived along the St. John River. To the south, along a bay that bears their name, lived their close relatives, the *Passamaquoddies*, who, however, are not mentioned as a distinct people in most written records until the 1760s.

Other Abenaki speakers, many of whom were related to the above groups, lived in mission villages along the St. Lawrence River, called St. Francis (Odanak) and Becancour (Wowenock). Finally, the *Mi'kmaqs*, also members of the Wabanaki Confederacy, lived in present-day Nova Scotia and Cape Breton Island.

Names, Places, and Dates

A few words about names, places, and dates are in order. While acknowledging the uses of the "settler colonial" framework, I agree with those scholars who have pointed out that calling the Europeans who arrived in the Dawnland "settlers" is misleading. The impact of the newcomers on the human and physical geography of the land was profoundly *un*settling. Therefore, unless referring to Europeans "settling" in a long-established town in which they were invited to live, I call them what they were: colonists, newcomers, and sometimes trespassers or squatters. The newcomers hailed from across the British Isles, and also included French Huguenots, German Protestants, and a scattering of (usually) unfree Africans. When referring to them in general, I shall use the political label "English" before 1707, and "British" after the political union of England and Scotland that year. Most of the nomenclature normalized in historical accounts like this one comes from the colonizers, so I also use the Wabanaki word *Bostoniak*—"Boston people" to refer to the speculators originating in that place.

The term "Wabanaki" embraces both a constellation of linguistically and culturally similar groups and a political confederacy that formed sometime in the early or mid-eighteenth century (see glossary). Unfortunately, much remains unclear about the extent of the confederacy's influence, so in this book, "Wabanaki" will be used as a general name for the Indigenous Algonquian-speaking inhabitants of present-day Maine and the Canadian Maritimes. Documentary evidence allows for more precise political nomenclature of the different Wabanaki tribes by the last quarter of the seventeenth century, and where possible, I use it. To avoid repetition, I also use the terms Native American, Indian, Indigenous, and, as an adjective, Native, interchangeably. When referring to individual Wabanakis, I have tried to use the names those people used for themselves.

Unless accompanied by the qualifier "present-day," the terms "Maine" "Acadia," and "Nova Scotia" refer only to the area within the physical extent of European control. I will call the rest of the Northeast what the people living there did: the Dawnland. I refer to the region between them as the eastern frontier (a glance at a map shows that Maine lies east of Massachusetts), the Maine or Dawnland frontier.

Except in cases where it would impede understanding (such as idiosyncratic abbreviations) I have left the spelling and style of the original sources unchanged. So, too, are the dates. Until 1752, British sources used the Julian calendar, which was by then eleven days behind the rest of Europe, which followed the Gregorian calendar. French sources are dated according to the Gregorian calendar throughout. Until 1752, the English began the New Year on March 25 on their "Old Style" calendar, before switching to the "New Style" on January 1, 1752. To prevent confusion, dates between January 1 and March 25 were often recorded as: February 2, 1733/4. In the text, all dates are adjusted for a New Style start of the year on January 1.

Properties of Empire

Introduction: Power and Property

The one thing everyone agreed was that the 1736 encounter along the St. Georges River should not have happened. The Penobscot Indians who carried out the orderly eviction of frightened Scots-Irish colonists along the river in present-day Maine had never authorized the intrusion onto their lands. Led by Arexis, a sagamore (chief) fresh from a visit to Boston to complain about the trespassers, a "considerable number of Indians . . . Sett up a Mark" near the river, according to witnesses, and ordered all the colonists living above it to pull down their houses and leave.[1] Thomas Gregg and his neighbors had answered advertisements from wealthy land speculator Samuel Waldo, promising that he held "indisputable" title to the area.[2] None of them expected to be thrown out of their new homes by Indians acting with the approval of Massachusetts authorities (who then claimed the region), even as a province garrison nearby did nothing to interfere. When the Penobscots sent a delegation to Boston in June 1736, Waldo had not expected the legislature and the governor to side with the Indians and agree that his title—based on a controversial 1694 deed—was void because the Penobscots had never acknowledged it. The legislators asked to judge the affair did not want Waldo to provoke a confrontation in the first place that threatened to undermine the foundations of their own frontier investments, which relied on deeds recognized by the Penobscots and other linguistically and culturally similar peoples in the region who called themselves Wabanaki. Not least, the entire situation does not square with how most people today think about conflicts between European colonizers and Indigenous nations in North America over questions of landownership.

What happened on the St. Georges River in 1736 was the product of a complicated relationship between Native power and the Anglo-American quest for landed property on the New England frontier in present-day Maine. That relationship is the subject of this book. *Properties of Empire* traces the rise and fall of an Anglo-Wabanaki relationship based—for different reasons—on Indigenous land rights. Over the long run the arrival of large numbers of land-hungry colonists was catastrophic for the Wabanakis. But on the Maine frontier the logic of empire did not lead inexorably to a land without Native people. Instead, a confluence of factors—including Wabanaki decisions—led to the rise of an elite within colonial society committed to a system of landownership that depended on Indian deeds. This system did not last, but its destruction—like its creation—was far from inevitable.

Explaining why this was so requires exploring the multiple cultures of ownership at work in the region along with the dynamic relationship that emerged among them. Wabanakis, elite Boston-based land specu-lators, and hardscrabble colonists all articulated different understand-ings of landownership. Contests between colonists and Indians over land have usually been portrayed as centering on the question of *who* had a just claim to a particular area. In this framing, Euro-Indian land disputes become a matter of borders. On the Maine frontier, Wabana-kis and newcomers did struggle over where to draw boundaries. But disagreements over fundamental questions on the nature of landown-ership complicated what could have been a straightforward exercise in drawing a line in the dirt. What actions demonstrated possession? How could possession be transmitted between individuals or groups? What, if any, responsibilities to one's neighbors did possession entail? Indians and colonists (who arrived first from England and later else-where in the British Isles) answered these questions in different ways, but more than two cultures of ownership collided in the place the Wabanakis called the Dawnland. Colonists were themselves divided to the extent that using catchall terms like "British" can risk glossing over important differences between ordinary colonists and the absentee land speculators who rose to prominence during the eighteenth cen-tury. Ongoing Wabanaki resistance to British incursions exacerbated tensions within colonial society by forcing land companies to choose between maximizing profits and financing stable communities on a sometimes dangerous borderland.

Properties of Empire offers a different way to frame the meeting of early modern empires and Indigenous peoples in North America, as a prolonged contest to define the nature of landownership involving people at all levels of society in communities from Norridgewock to North Yarmouth. This contest took place in town meetings and county courts, in formal treaties, village councils, and face-to-face confrontations over fences and fishing rights. At times participants attempted to impose their ideas of ownership onto each other, while at others they sought to employ the logic of strangers to persuade them of the justness of their claims. The continual struggle to construct a commonly agreed-upon culture of landownership shaped diplomacy, imperial administration, and matters of law.

This contest was not unique to this thinly populated corner of Britain's Empire, but Maine's frontier featured a phenomenon to a greater degree than elsewhere that forms the heart of this book: the extended *re*interpretation of initial land sales between Indians and English newcomers. The last consensual Wabanaki sales to the English occurred before 1688. Yet Wabanakis, colonists, and land speculators continued to offer new interpretations of these exchanges well into the eighteenth century. Whatever the intentions of their architects, these initial transactions did not retain a fixed meaning. Instead, different groups of Indians and newcomers advanced their own readings of the old agreements in a contest lasting well into the eighteenth century.

While not by itself exceptional, the colonial Maine frontier is exceptionally well suited for a study of landed property. The leaders, courts, and municipal bodies in the Province of Massachusetts Bay (which claimed Maine until 1820) had few peers as record keepers in the early modern world. Not even remote York County—which encompassed all of Maine until 1759—escaped their attentions. In addition, the balance of power between the Wabanakis and Massachusetts in the region remained competitive until 1763, after around 150 years of sustained contact, providing a much longer period of time to study than most North American border zones.[3] The French presence nearby along the St. Lawrence and in Acadia contributed both to a bolstering of Wabanaki power (in the form of supplies and occasionally direct military assistance) and to the historical record (through the correspondence of Jesuit missionaries living in some Wabanaki villages, and of French officials preoccupied with using the Indians as a cudgel against New England). Despite these features that distinguished Maine from its Anglophone neighbors, its government and people were more like neighboring colonies than not. The same can be said for the Wabanakis, who—while hunting more and farming less than neighbors to the south—shared language and culture with other Algonquian-speaking nations in eastern North America.

Although contemporaries regarded Maine as a rude, often-dangerous backwater (a new pastor arriving from Harvard in 1725 considered his flock there "mean animals"), Maine has enjoyed a renewed surge of interest among early American historians.[4] It was, they reveal, a vibrant religious frontier where the Puritans' strict brand of Calvinism collided with Catholicism, Anglican practice, and Indigenous beliefs.[5] Maine was also an arena where different attitudes about gender met, diplomatic cultures interacted, and empires clashed.[6] In this imperial struggle, the lives of Maine residents often entwined with diverse inhabitants of present-day Maritime Canada, as well as the network of French and Indigenous communities dotting the St. Lawrence River.[7]

Properties of Empire does not seek to relitigate their findings but instead to center the question of landownership in its exploration of what one scholar has called the "texture of contact" between cultures on a turbulent frontier.[8] It does so because the participants involved believed that landownership mattered a great deal. For example, proprietors among a Massachusetts delegation to Canadian Wabanaki villages on the St. Lawrence in 1725 took the trouble to bring along bundles of deeds on their arduous winter journey, hoping to find the proper Indians to show the documents.[9] The proprietors wanted these conversations with Indians over the veracity of old land deeds to be over. But as this book makes clear, that did not happen. Far from being relegated to a distant past, early land deals in the region remained the subject of unending disputes to define their meaning.

Scholars have added greatly to our understanding of those seventeenth-century Anglo-Indian land transactions in Maine, New Hampshire, Long Island, and elsewhere.[10] They have attempted to discern whether the Indigenous participants intended to alienate land to the newcomers, if the written records are an accurate rendition of the actual events, and if they received a "fair" price for parting with particular tracts. Their findings have tended to comport with parallel work on Native American history, concluding that the Indians were far too savvy to be duped and too powerful to be bullied off of their land by early buyers. Although they did not like to admit it, British colonizers had to accommodate local ideas about property and diplomacy as they built communities in the Wabanaki Dawnland. Purchasers took care to involve all the necessary Wabanaki claimants to desired land because outnumbered colonists could not hope to survive as trespassers. The resulting agreements reserved significant rights for the Indians. Even when the balance of power in the region equalized and then began to tilt away from the Wabanakis, proprietors knew that the Indians retained the ability to reduce new homes and barns to kindling.

This book examines how different actors on a contested borderland tried to repurpose those old agreements to meet new demands. The ensuing clashes reveal that Indigenous ideas about the relationship between land use, diplomacy, and reciprocity continued to shape the contours of debate. Eighteenth-century Massachusetts leaders did their best to keep questions surrounding individual deeds (which they insisted were private, binding economic transactions) removed from wider political negotiations subject to Wabanaki expectations of reciprocity. As the proprietors' 1725 winter slog undertaken to "prove" proprietors' title to the appropriate audience of Indians (a process bound up in wider negotiations to end an Anglo-Wabanaki war) shows, they failed.

They failed in part because Wabanaki military power remained too formidable to ignore down to 1763. But they also failed because by the early eighteenth century, most of the major proprietors with Maine land titles based their claims on Indian land deeds. The proprietors faced competition, however, in the form of other speculators, frontier squatters, and from rival claimants on behalf of the Crown. As a result, major proprietors of Maine lands—usually well-connected men—pushed for Massachusetts to acknowledge the reality of Wabanaki land rights.[11]

In contrast to the divided newcomers, the Wabanakis maintained a united front on the question of property. This was no small achievement for a decentralized confederacy of villages and extended family groups without a coercive system of government. These diverse communities made different choices about adopting the religion of various European missionaries, where to live, and what extent to participate in periodic imperial wars that raged around them. But in numerous councils and private conversations—all but a handful unrecorded by outsiders—the Wabanakis hammered out a consensus strategy for discussing the question of land with Massachusetts. They settled on a policy of refusing any additional land sales and policing a clear boundary with the newcomers, abandoning seventeenth-century hopes to integrate the colonists into Indigenous networks of land use. Maintaining consensus required constant effort, as speculators and their backers in the Massachusetts government made repeated efforts to pry even one faction's endorsement of unacknowledged or fraudulent old land deeds. Wabanaki success in maintaining unity made it impossible for Massachusetts to ignore Native interpretations of both property and diplomacy.

Questions of sovereignty—of Wabanaki subjugation to the British or French Crowns—often mingled with questions of property, and scholars have tended to either treat them as indistinguishable or to focus their attention on sovereignty.[12] But linking sovereignty and property fails to explain their divergent paths. Beginning in 1693, Massachusetts leaders took the official position that the Wabanakis had become subjects of the Crown. But their denial of Wabanaki sovereignty in theory did not result in an erosion of actual Native sovereignty and in fact preceded a redoubled emphasis on Wabanaki property rights.

Properties of Empire therefore probes the relationship between Native power and the question of landed property in early America by highlighting the drawn-out contest to grapple with those issues in Maine. In doing so, it finds a British Empire characterized by uncertainty, confusion, and even incompetence. The ad hoc system of land tenure that developed on the eastern frontier of Massachusetts owed at least as much to a reluctant series of compromises, personal opportunism, and petty rivalries as to any overarching imperial logic. Of course, as other recent histories show, empires do not need to be well run to make a lasting impact.[13] By focusing on the extended debate over the meaning of early land transactions, *Properties of Empire* shows the transfer of ideas about property and diplomacy was far from a one-way process. Although Massachusetts leaders wished to impose their own ideas about both matters onto their interactions with the Wabanakis, Native unity and power in the face of divisions within colonial society made that impossible. As a result, Wabanaki values not only influenced the early land transactions but also shaped subsequent reinterpretations of them.

The extended and diffuse nature of this conversation, while sometimes informed by the initial justifications for empire and possession offered by elites in European centers of power during the early years of contact (itself the focus of a great deal of scholarship), more often echoed with the voices of Wabanaki speakers, ambitious land speculators, and humble farmers and loggers pursuing their own agendas.[14] Although many of those voices went unrecorded or come down to us through unsympathetic narrators, this book tries to recapture them. At the same time, it takes seriously the reminder that in some cases "actions speak much louder than thoughts" as Jared Hardesty reminds us in his study of slave life in eighteenth-century Boston.[15]

The conversation occurring in the American Northeast had parallels elsewhere around the world, especially where "settler colonial" empires sought to replace Indigenous peoples on the land they desired.[16] So, too, did what historian Allan Greer called the "thoroughly unsystematic property 'systems'" that emerged from them.[17] In Australia and New Zealand, the same factors at work in the Dawnland—the balance of power between the Indigenous residents and British colonizers, and what sort of Britons arrived in the early years—shaped the history of those places. In New Zealand, as in Maine, private companies played a major role in establishing the first colonists and missionaries. The outnumbered British conducted negotiations and land purchases from the powerful Maoris that British officials found it difficult to overturn later. At the same time, the Colonial Office found recognizing Maori land title useful because it enabled them to exert far greater control over wayward colonists. In contrast, Australia began as a state-run colony. The small enclave established by the first Britons did not need to buy land from the outnumbered Aboriginals recently devastated by smallpox. When colonists began arriving in large numbers after 1822, they overwhelmed the Aboriginals and spread across the landscape. By the mid-1830s, concludes one scholar, unabashed theft "had come to be regarded as the law of the land."[18] As in the nineteenth-century United States, the racialization of difference, and even the entwining of whiteness with possession itself, played an important role in shaping the plans of the colonizers but nevertheless varied according to local circumstances.[19]

It is those local circumstances, *Properties of Empire* contends, that shaped both the character of Britain's colonial project and how different groups of Indians and newcomers articulated and implemented ideas of landownership in early America.

This book takes a chronological approach. Chapter 1 examines Wabanaki and English cultures of landownership and community at the time they began sustained contact during the early seventeenth century. Chapter 2 traces the turbulent history of seventeenth-century land purchases on the coast of present-day Maine, and the process by which Massachusetts elites came to believe in the superiority of Indian land deeds for securing title at very same time that Anglo-Wabanaki diplomatic relations descended into open warfare. By 1713, Massachusetts had—in defiance of imperial officials in Whitehall—embedded Indian deeds into the never precisely defined mix of acceptable sources of title in Maine. Massachusetts elites, especially land investors, hoped these deeds would bring order to a frontier that was home to a hodgepodge of previous claims. That administrative chaos worked to Wabanaki advantage.

The next two chapters explore the period (1713–27) when Wabanakis, frontier colonists, and an emerging group of Boston-based land speculators all sought to resettle the war-torn frontier. Chapter 3 argues that Massachusetts and Wabanaki leaders both desired peace, but their interpretations of the Treaty of Portsmouth (1713) ending the previous era of warfare rested on divergent understandings of landownership. Realizing the colonists could not be incorporated into Indigenous networks of land use, the Wabanakis turned to a strategy of containment, selectively acknowledging coastal sales while disavowing unacknowledged or fraudulent seventeenth-century deeds. Theoretical Massachusetts respect for Native land rights did not translate into respect for actual Indian understandings of landownership, however, leading to the renewed outbreak of war in 1722. This Fourth Anglo-Wabanaki War and subsequent agreement (an extended process known as Dummer's Treaty) resulted in a diplomatic coup for the Wabanakis, and forms the subject of chapter 4. At Dummer's Treaty the Wabanakis succeeded in attaching Native expectations of reciprocity and diplomatic protocol with their acknowledgment of many (but not all) seventeenth-century deeds, eventually convincing many major land speculators to treat the treaty itself as a form of deed. After 1727, the Wabanakis lacked the military strength to defeat Massachusetts forces without French aid (which they had enjoyed between 1689 and 1713). Henceforth, Wabanaki power depended on a combination of military ability to hinder (but not defeat) British attempts to colonize the Dawnland, and their capacity to endanger shaky speculator claims by disavowing the treaty that effectively guaranteed them.

The next three chapters trace the factors contributing to the success of Dummer's Treaty after 1727, and why Wabanaki and Massachusetts leaders alike continued to value it. Chapter 5 turns to the postwar threats to the land speculators' titles coming from ambitious imperial officials and frontier townspeople. This ongoing instability made the speculators more dependent on Indian land deeds. Chapter 6 investigates how and why the Wabanakis were able to successfully invoke Dummer's Treaty during the 1730s to ward off one land company's attempts to exploit the fraudulent 1694 Madockawando land cession. Chapter 7 examines new stresses placed on Dummer's Treaty by a combination of imperial events and the arrival of Governor William Shirley, who held a financial stake in companies without recognized Indian deeds.

Chapter 8 explains the demise of Dummer's Treaty in the early 1750s. It argues that the decisive event in its destruction was the arrival of a powerful new land company in the Kenenebec River region. Deriving their title largely from a vague, long-lost royal patent rather than Indian deeds, the Kennebeck Proprietors devoted their energies to challenging the legitimacy of Indian deeds, bought the friendship of Governor Shirley, and played an important role in pushing the frontier into the Seven Years' War between Britain and France, which ultimately destroyed most of the Wabanaki ability to influence the wider discussion of landownership in the region, although the Wabanakis themselves endured.

The conclusion traces the ambiguous legacy of this contest of meanings into the twenty-first century on both sides of the international border. Although 1763 marked a decisive break with the past—ending Wabanaki military power and evicting their French backers from the continent—the struggle over the nature of landed property in the region cast a long shadow. Questions about the relationship between property and belonging—and what responsibilities it entailed—lingered in the United States and Canada. Nor did Indigenous people vanish. Instead, later generations of Wabanakis and their neighbors discovered ways to resurrect the promises made in the old treaties and begin to work toward the true reciprocity envisioned by their ancestors.

1 / Networks of Property and Belonging: Land Use in the Seventeenth Century

Over the course of the seventeenth century, divisions within Massachusetts society over the legitimacy of various claims to landownership became closely entwined with questions over the place of Indian land rights within the English imperial system. That process cannot be understood without examining the distinct Wabanaki and English ideas about land use and property, each shaped by their respective environments, culture, and political structure, around the time of sustained contact between them after 1600. For both Wabanakis and English people, the early seventeenth century was a time of wrenching transformation. As a result, present-day New England was the site of an encounter between multiple systems of property entering a period of instability.

The Land

More than just a stage, the land itself was an actor in the unfolding drama. Both Indians and colonists had to adapt their strategies for survival in modern Maine. Farmers struggled with rocky, acidic soil and short growing seasons, but water proved as important as the soil in shaping life in the region. Waterways provided essential sources of food and the quickest transportation routes for all residents until after the American Revolution. North and east of Casco Bay (beyond today's Portland), New England's smooth coastline becomes dotted with hundreds of islands creating countless harbors, bays, and inlets. Several large rivers—the Saco, Androscoggin, Kennebec, and Penobscot—slice their way across the landscape before spilling into the Atlantic Ocean. When long winters depleted food stores and hunting failed, many residents depended on fish and clams during the lean months of early spring. As the seventeenth century progressed, winters grew harsher, while all seasons grew less predictable as part of a trend known as the Little Ice Age. The difficulty of agriculture and unpredictability of other food sources meant the region could not support large numbers of people year-round. As a result, both absolute numbers and population density remained low in the region throughout the colonial era. Before a series of epidemics drove down their numbers, perhaps 10,000 Indians lived within the boundaries of present-day Maine in 1600. The region's total human population did not reach 10,000 again until around 1730.[1] Practicing more intensive agriculture and bringing livestock allowed the colonists to feed more people per acre than the Wabanakis, but eighteenth-century Maine's largest town—Falmouth (now Portland)—could only feed itself with supply ships from Boston by the 1730s. With 2,400 inhabitants in 1749, Falmouth was not large even by the standards of colonial America, but its residents nevertheless suffered periodic food shortages the surrounding communities could not alleviate.[2] Writing for a Massachusetts audience in 1715, a minister from the town of York tried to brag about his neighbors' Spartan lifestyle, claiming "we in the Borders of the Country are glad of Barley Cakes," in contrast to his readers' "White Bread."[3]

English newcomers called themselves "settlers," the language revealing their intent to tame a landscape that was—even apart from how they viewed its Wabanaki inhabitants—wild. They failed. Moose, bears, and other large animals remained common well into the eighteenth century.[4] When winter abated, clouds of insects rose up to torment the unprepared. Certain times of year were bad enough that colonial authorities scheduled repairs on Maine's Fort Richmond around them during the 1740s.[5] Travel remained difficult after over a century of British occupation. Boston attorney Daniel Farnum learned for himself just how unsettled the Maine frontier remained in 1750. Tasked with collecting evidence for a sensational murder trial that took place near the coastal hamlet of Wiscasset, Farnum spent a week in February 1750 carrying out his task. To gather evidence and notify witnesses in the several hardscrabble communities on Casco Bay's northern coastline, Farnum had to travel by open whaleboat in the "exceeding cold."[6]

The landscape in question that Indians and colonists called home remained sparsely populated and—in terms of human settlement—lightly touched. Most homes were small. Aside from a handful of meetinghouses and a few chapels Wabanaki Catholic converts put up, the only sizeable structures in the region were forts. The two-story, box-shaped block houses studding the colonial towns on the frontier served as grim testimony that questions of land use, even among small numbers of people, frequently turned violent.

Community in the Dawnland

Before Europeans arrived, the people and the land shared a name: "Wabanaki" meant people of the "land of the dawn," or "Dawnland."[7] This shared name captured how the people thought about their relationship to where they lived. In eighteenth-century conferences with colonial leaders, Wabanaki speakers said they "belonged" to rivers or stretches of land.[8] In contrast, early modern English people "belonged" to towns or other human communities rather than to the land itself.[9] To belong to a place—or person—implies a relationship, and the early modern English usage of the term to describe a person's residence in those terms was no accident, reflecting the web of privileges and obligations bound up in town life.[10] The Wabanaki claims to belong to land or rivers stemmed from their view that their community privileges and obligations extended beyond the human occupants. Like other Eastern Algonquian speakers, the Wabanakis often described the land as "Wlô-gan": the Common Pot.[11]

The "common pot" metaphor captured the Wabanaki worldview, which recognized they shared the land with other animals and people. As a result, the Wabanakis managed available resources in cooperation with animals and otherworldly beings rather than wielding dominion over them, as European Christians believed their God had directed them to do in the Book of Genesis.[12] Instead, the Wabanakis lived in what scholars call an "animate" world, in which in which people, animals, and even some nonliving things had a spirit or force, and they were conscious of sharing a network of relations with humans and others. Wabanakis told stories of an earlier mythical age when humans and animals had similar characteristics. Individuals who were adept at tapping into spiritual power could still blur these distinctions, such as a war chief who could escape foes by transforming into a fish and swimming to safety.[13] Tales about Gluskap, a mythic figure who served as an ideal for Wabanaki men, emphasized the importance of conserving game and fish for future generations.[14] Numerous stories warned about resource hoarding and selfishness.[15]

The Wabanaki belief system reflected their lived reality of sharing an ecosystem with limited resources. Wabanakis pursued a seasonally varied subsistence strategy refined over time to make the most of their environment. Some groups practiced maize horticulture, which had spread from the Southwest and had reached the Saco River by 1400, and the St. John River by 1690. Despite this, a short growing season made the plant an unreliable staple east of the Kennebec, and the poor soil in many locations encouraged the Wabanakis to rely on diverse food sources.[16] Before 1600, most evidence of maize production north of the Saco exists at inland village sites, while coastal residents exploited marine resources.[17] With the exception of some larger villages in the south, which could number up to a thousand inhabitants, Dawnland residents spent much of the year in family bands of between fifteen to twenty-five people, living in easily constructed wood and bark homes called wigwams suited to their mobile subsistence strategy.[18] During the winter, family bands hunted moose and deer inland, using snowshoes to pursue their prey. In spring and autumn, Families gathered in larger villages for spring planting and harvest in autumn, with some southern villages growing beans and squash along with corn. In between planting, weeding, and harvesting, the people traveled to gather wild plants, nuts, and berries, catch fish and shellfish in the rivers and seacoast, and take seabirds and seals where available.[19]

Rooted in these environmental and religious realities, Wabanaki concepts of property emphasized relationships bound by reciprocity and mutual obligation. Control of resources was intimately tied together with social relations. Family bands headed by a male hunter served as the basic economic and social unit. These bands grouped into lineages claiming a shared male ancestor, with fluid membership shifting due to marriages, changes in subsistence patterns, or political disagreements. Gatherings of multiple lineages into one or more villages formed what Europeans labeled a "tribe."[20] These tribes were in a state of flux during the early and mid-seventeenth century, as epidemics and wars with rival nations sparked migrations and consolidations in response (discussed in chapter 2). Dawnland residents did not fully coalesce into the political alignments discussed in this book until after 1650, in a sense mirroring events in the British Isles, where England and Scotland finally formed the United Kingdom of Great Britain in 1707.

Although the precise size and structure of political groupings changed over time, the Wabanakis were a consensus-based society. Leaders, called *sagamores*, ruled through example and exhortation rather than coercion. European observers from the earliest years of contact until the late eighteenth century from Casco Bay to the St. Lawrence River agreed on this fact.[21] "Their Sagamors are no Kings," Captain Christopher Levett wrote of Casco Bay Indians he met in 1623, "for I can see no Government or Law amongst them but Club Law: and they call all Masters of Shippes Saga-more, or any other man, they see have a commaund of men."[22] Joseph Aubery, a Jesuit missionary who lived among the Wabanakis of Meductic and Odanak, reported in 1710: "Nothing of great importance is discussed or decided except . . . in a numerous Council. The notables—that is to say, the elders—and the captains of war-parties assemble. A speaker rises in their midst, and pronounces a discourse. If he perorate aptly, eloquently, or cleverly, he wins his cause; if timidly, hesitatingly, inelegantly, his cause is lost."[23]

A consensus-based society did not mean the Wabanakis lacked social distinctions. Several seventeenth-century European observers noted sagamores and other "principal men and young women" distinguished themselves by certain dress and manners.[24] Individuals wielded different amounts of personal power derived from their performance as providers, speakers, shamans, or warriors. Wabanakis did not seek power to dominate but rather to achieve prestige and independence. Like property, power depended on the acknowledgment of others. Wabanakis associated the two by honoring those who gave rather than amassed wealth. Both Wabanaki men and women had to demonstrate power throughout their lives. Dawnland residents recognized differences based on age, gender, and ability.[25] Women and men performed distinct yet complementary tasks, with men hunting and women preparing and storing meat, men clearing the fields and women planting corn. Unlike Iroquoian-speaking Indians in the American Northeast, most Wabanaki women lacked formal political power. Wives, sisters, and daughters of powerful men did enjoy higher status, however.[26] Wabanaki women had a say in community decisions, to which their participation in complementary patterns of gender-specific labor entitled them. The indirect (and, to Europeans, often invisible) nature of Wabanaki women's influence meant that clashing ideas of gender roles did not complicate Wabanaki relations with Europeans to the degree that occurred in many other parts of the Americas.[27]

With few exceptions, only adult men who had reached full status as successful hunters—indicating they held both earthly and spiritual power—contributed to decision-making in formal councils.[28] These councils deliberated on how to conduct trade, diplomacy, and war. When negotiating with Europeans, sagamores frequently interrupted proceedings to confer with their councils. Sometimes large numbers of people

assembled for important treaties. When one Massachusetts land speculator met with Penobscot leaders in 1735, he counted sixty-four men,
"with a considerable Number of Squaws and Children" gathered for the
talk. If wives and children accompanied all the men, then more than
three hundred Indians, or almost half of the Penobscots, had shown up
for the conference.[29] For sagamores, bringing large numbers of people
to a treaty gave proof that they indeed spoke for numerous followers. It
also meant that if new topics arose during discussions that the village
had not authorized their leaders to act upon, they could more quickly be
consulted.

Wabanaki decisions about use and distribution of land occurred
in this context of consensus and reciprocity. Although scholars agree
the Wabanakis—like other Native Americans—exercised control over
distinct territories, little evidence survives indicating how Wabanakis
determined which individuals and groups could use which land before
1600.[30] Early European observers, busy sizing Wabanakis up as potential
trading partners, allies, or enemies, devoted little attention to the matter. Most later, better-documented conversations between Wabanakis
and British colonists focused on questions of political identity of Indian
landholders rather than distinguishing *which* Penobscots or Kennebecs
used a particular place.

However obscure the details, surviving evidence proves the Wabanakis recognized distinct use rights for different groups of people. After
meeting with a Massachusetts commission in 1753, some Kennebecs
promised, "We will inform the Relations and Friends to the Owners of
these Lands what has been said."[31] Judging from seventeenth-century
agreements with English colonists, these rights included access to hunting and fishing in certain areas.[32] Wabanakis articulated these claims
to residents of Brunswick during the early eighteenth century. In 1737
prominent residents there wrote to the Massachusetts General Court to
complain locals "conversant among them" knew the Wabanakis "look
upon us as unjust usurpers and intruders upon their rights and priviledges. . . . They claim not only the wild beasts of the forest, and fowls of
the air, but also fishes of sea and rivers."[33] Because the Wabanakis farmed
adjoining plots in common villages that moved once soil and other local
resources were exhausted, distribution of farmland did not pose a social
problem among them.

Difficulties in translating concepts of ownership, disruption of
established communities, and European observers' unfamiliarity with
Indigenous diplomatic and cultural protocols combine to make all

eighteenth-century evidence about Wabanaki landownership particularly suspect. A 1720 diary kept by a land speculator named Thomas Fayerweather provides the most detailed surviving description of a Wabanaki approach to land distribution, inheritance, and transfer to outsiders. Fayerweather and several of his associates in the Muscongus Proprietors visited the Penobscot Wabanakis that year, seeking Native ratification of the company's land deed, which descended from a controversial 1694 Indian sale. Through an interpreter, the proprietors told Nimquid, the local sagamore (who probably led a lineage of several related family bands) about their mission. Nimquid denied the validity of the 1694 sale and put off the proprietors. According to Fayerweather's account, "The land was entirely his from Madonquod on Ramsim point the Eastern side of Muscongus bay to Penobscott Falls," but Nimquid told his guests "he could not in prudence dispose thereof until he consulted the other Sagamores."[34]

Because the Muscongus Proprietors based their claim on a disputed sale by the Penobscot sagamore Madockawando, they took the unusual step of asking Nimquid how he obtained his land rights. They learned Nimquid inherited them from his grandfather "Essagaigoneit," who in turn granted it to "his Eldest son John Hart who gave it to Nimquid (his brother's son) s[ai]d Hart being yet alive in co[mpany] with . . . us on board our sloop." Furthermore, Nimquid said, John Hart's grandsons Actson and Joseph stood to inherit the land next.[35] The Muscongus Proprietors later spoke with Actson and his brother Honestus, who confirmed what Nimquid had told them, adding that "Actson was Sagamore of Penobscot and own'd from Massawesskeage to Penobscott."[36] Temporarily rebuffed, Fayerweather and his associates returned to the area two months later, where they received an invitation to meet with all the leading Penobscots in a coastal village on the Muscongus River Fayerweather recorded as "Agemoggan." After a private council, the sagamores informed the proprietors the Penobscot lands "belong to their young men and they c[oul]d not dispose of them from 'Em besides they did not care to have the English settle among 'Em," wishing to avoid "difficultys and inconveniency" experienced by other Wabanakis living near colonists.[37] The Muscongus Proprietors were clumsy diplomats, mistaking Penobscot politeness for an eagerness to invite colonists onto their land (the opposite was true),[38] but they nevertheless created the most detailed surviving evidence of Penobscot land use in the early modern period.

Fayerweather's diary indicates the Penobscots practiced what anthropologists call a "paternal" system of land use, in which family bands recognized a male head of an extended family's right to use land but not to alienate it.[39] Sons who hunted with their fathers from a young age obtained a claim to continue doing so when he died. Nimquid's insistence that the land was "his" exclusively should be read less as an indication of private ownership and instead viewed in the context of the sagamore's need to disavow the 1694 Madockawando claim. Even though Nimquid, as local sagamore, claimed the exclusive use of a discrete territory for his lineage, and his neighbors (such as his cousin and fellow sagamore Actson) recognized those boundaries, Nimquid's rights did not extend to inviting strangers onto the territory without consulting the rest of the Penobscots.[40] Nimquid had inherited these rights from a previous lineage leader related to him, and his younger male kin would succeed him. Thus Nimquid's proprietorship placed him in the role of manager of the land's resources, as well as a provider for his extended family, a responsibility his immediate male relatives shared with him. All of these rights, however, relied on periodic acknowledgment from neighboring lineages and should not be confused with permanent ownership passed down among families. A 1730 letter from New Hampshire's Lieutenant Governor David Dunbar relating a conversation with a Penobscot leader whom the British called Nathaniel echoed this arrangement. According to Dunbar, Nathaniel told him all Penobscots had "an interest in every individual spot of ground, and that it is unalienable, but they agree for peace and order among themselves, to have certain rivers, ponds, and tracts of land for their particular fishing and hunting."[41] This arrangement was similar to those of the Algonquian-speaking Indians on present-day Long Island.[42]

Some anthropologists have argued that the late eighteenth-century Penobscot practice of dividing hunting territories by family band around particular rivers or streams, the families then claiming it in severalty, originated in the precontact era.[43] However, profound political and demographic disruptions of the seventeenth century render such stability unlikely, as well as impossible to determine. Scholars arguing for this "riverine" model have tended to rely on uncritical readings of several eighteenth-century European accounts. For example, in 1710 the intendant of New France, Antoine-Denis Raudot, claimed the Wabanakis divided their hunting territories with each family band leader (*chief de famille*) taking a river or stream.[44] Raudot did not attribute these claims to any Indians or travelers, nor did he visit the Wabanaki villages he discussed, although he could have spoken with Indians and French travelers.[45]

A half century later, in 1764, a group of Penobscots told Massachusetts governor Francis Bernard "that their hunting grounds and streams were all parceled out to certain families, [implying private ownership] time out of mind."[46] Although late eighteenth-century Penobscots did parcel out their beaver-hunting territories, gradually shifting to a form of individual ownership of hunting rights, the Penobscot claims of timelessness reveal less about their long-standing land allotment than they do about Penobscot thoughts regarding British notions of property. The Penobscots made this statement while trying to persuade Governor Bernard—then on a surveying expedition—they had a valid claim to their land. Great Britain had just defeated the Penobscots' French allies in the Seven Years' War, seizing Canada in the 1763 Peace of Paris. With their powerful ally removed from North America, the Penobscots made their case to Bernard from a position of weakness. Before they talked about parceling land out to families, the Penobscots said "they supposed themselves to have a right to enjoy their lands in common with the inhabitants of Canada by the Capitulation," meaning that they wished to remain on their lands just as the defeated French colonists did.[47] The Penobscots had often heard Massachusetts leaders telling them that they could not interfere with the private property rights of British subjects, while trumpeting the importance of old land deeds. Several scholars have seized on these statements as evidence for a long-standing Penobscot practice rather than as justifications given to a conqueror.[48] A strong probability exists that the Penobscots who spoke in 1764 of an ancient practice did so with the same motive as the early twentieth-century anthropologist Frank Speck, who popularized the argument, proving to a skeptical Anglo-American audience that Indians were in fact "civilized" enough to own land.[49]

It was not only in 1764 that the Penobscots invoked tradition to get what they wanted from Europeans. In seeking out lower trade prices in 1749, a number of Penobscots at Fort St. Georges insisted, "It is our Custom when things are Cheepest there to Trade."[50] For the Penobscots, like other Eastern Woodlands Indians, their "custom" was to incorporate trade into diplomacy, and therefore a notion like "cheap" was in itself a novelty.

The purpose of Wabanaki group control over land use would contrast with English intent as much as the methods. European observers, whatever their other differences, agreed the Wabanakis did not seek to amass wealth. Sometimes Europeans admired or even idealized this quality, but often they did not. Residents of Brunswick, after describing their Indigenous neighbors' claims of usufruct rights to surrounding lands, decried their "idle way of living."[51] In his 1749 overview of the *Present*

State of British Settlements in America, Boston physician William Douglass sniffed, "Like the wild Irish, [the Indians] dread Labour more than Poverty."[52] Moral fulminations aside, European observers were correct in observing the Wabanakis did not see acquisitiveness as a virtue. Like other societies of hunters, fishers, and gatherers, they did not store large amounts of food for extended periods.[53] As a society the Wabanakis valued leisure over stockpiling material goods, and this outlook shaped their strategies of resource use.[54]

The Wabanakis remained steadfast in defending their system of land use and its accompanying system of reciprocity with other people, animals, and spiritual beings, even when confronted by newcomers. Between 1600 and 1763, European traders and missionaries flooded Wabanaki villages with a torrent of new material goods and religious practices. Dawnland residents accepted some eagerly, others with reservations. Even as they incorporated many of these innovations into their lives, the Wabanakis adhered to their system of land use and reciprocity. Native resilience in defending this system—coupled with their enduring political power—forced the arriving English colonists to adjust their own practices accordingly.

New England Cultures of Landownership

In direct contrast to the Wabanakis, the prevalent early modern English ideal of landownership centered on individual proprietors' *lack* of dependency on others as much as possible. In the wake of the decline of feudal relationships, growing numbers of early modern Britons practiced commercial farming. Some worked the land as tenants while others owned freeholds. The latter situation became the focus of English (later British) aspirations on both sides of the Atlantic. Above all, ordinary people strove to achieve "competency," meaning a degree of economic and social self-sufficiency.[55] By 1600, England had already moved toward a legal and economic system oriented toward individual autonomy to a greater extent than anywhere else in Europe.[56]

English law, custom, and even ritual prized possession of land through agriculture to a degree unmatched by the other early modern European arrivals in the Americas. English law—unlike the French or Dutch—granted title to a person who built a fixed dwelling on unused land and continued to occupy it. The early and sustained drive to establish private ownership over American land also distinguished the English imperial project from its rivals.[57] Sir Edward Coke's influential texts, published between 1628 and 1644, rooted men holding land as property in Psalm 115:16.[58]

The quest for competency fit well with the religious worldviews held by many colonists entering the Dawnland. Although not as Calvinist (or "Puritan") as early arrivals to other parts of New England, plenty of godly colonists in the region shared a Puritan ethic balancing individual gain and communal responsibility.[59] "Tho' a Man has but a Competency," wrote Samuel Moody, a pastor in York, Maine, "necessary Food and raiment, plain and homely fare, but still his own, 'tis Comfortable, 'tis Honorable."[60] Most New England colonists sought this honorable comfort as landowners rather than tenants or laborers. As late as 1747, a Maine landowner warned a would-be absentee landlord, "If you should not like to live [here], you cannot Rent it for one cent Interest, the poorest people here if they have been any time in the Country, makes shift to get land of their own either by takeing up or buying."[61] The powerful drive to acquire land even crept into Puritan theological exhortations. Samuel Sewall, a Massachusetts judge and large-scale landowner, wrote to his brother in 1687 expressing the hope that "The Lord give you and me skill and oportunity [sic] to take up a Lot in Heaven where every Inhabitant will rejoice in the strength of our Title, and our great Landlord will demand but Thanks for our Quit-Rent."[62]

Colonists' aspirations toward competency based on individual freeholds nevertheless involved recognition of various overlapping use rights. In much of seventeenth-century England, a form of farming called "open field" prevailed. Each community pastured its cattle, swine, and sheep on common land in common herds and flocks, watched by townsmen paid for the job. In this system, every freeholder had certain rights, such as how many of each type of animal they could pasture, called a "stint," proportioned by the number of acres held. Some manorial lords granted landless individuals customary rights to pasture several animals and collect firewood. Each farmer tilled narrow slices of land according to a collectively agreed upon program coordinating the village pattern of sowing, reaping, and laying fallow. In some regions, especially East Anglia, landowners consolidated their holdings into one or more large fields through purchase, enclosed them with fences or hedges, and made decisions about planting depending on their individual sense of the market.[63] New England colonists implemented similar measures as towns filled up.

Like their compatriots elsewhere in New England, colonists making a home in Maine struggled to balance individual acquisitiveness and social harmony. Seventeenth-century English Puritans in pursuit of godly community at times punished individuals for business practices that modern audiences would find quite ordinary. In 1637, Bostonians fined the merchant Robert Keayne £200 for overcharging his customers, and his church forced him to make a public apology or face excommunication, an experience from which he never recovered.[64] By the early eighteenth century, merchants such as Samuel Waldo engaged in far more blatant manipulations while incurring little more than grumbling.[65] Numerous historians have argued that by 1700, many New England colonists decoupled their pursuits of prosperity from their pursuit of salvation.[66]

Even as New England colonists developed growing ties to the transatlantic economy, producing and consuming a multiplying array of goods, they embraced these changes with unequal enthusiasm.[67] At the same time merchants and large-scale landowners increased their wealth, the numbers of tenants and poor smallholders rose.[68] As the principal source of both security and prosperity in New England, land became a focal point for both social and economic anxieties.

Although New England colonists all viewed land as a commodity to be owned, divisions emerged as to the extent to which community norms could—or should—temper individual acquisition. Maine was no exception to this general rise in tensions, which local conditions aggravated. In the portions of Massachusetts farthest from Boston—the Connecticut River towns and Maine frontier—large-scale proprietors exerted outsize influence from the earliest years of colonization. Along the Connecticut River, several prominent families, called the "River Gods," founded and led town governments from the mid-seventeenth century until the American Revolution.[69] In Maine, men like Ferdinando Gorges and Joshua Scottow performed this role.[70] Even after colonists founded towns on the frontier, absentee proprietors retained control over much of the land around them.

The communities that colonists formed in Maine—the New England town—were not only clusters of residents but also legal and political entities with changing relationships to landed property around them. The physical cluster of buildings and their residents making up Maine towns like Falmouth and Brunswick contained distinct—though overlapping—legal entities. The *inhabitants* of the town of Falmouth were the people who lived there who also had the right to vote in municipal affairs, concerning matters such as selecting minor officeholders for tasks like inspecting local fences or minding hogs. The *proprietors* owned shares in the undivided land that made up Falmouth. Some lived in Falmouth; others did not. Proprietors decided when and how the undivided land (commons) should be allotted, as well as whether to admit new proprietors. The inhabitants and proprietors both had the authority to admit (or exclude) new members, the former in town meetings, the latter in their separate proprietors meetings. The term "inhabitant" did not encompass all the people who resided within the bounds of a New England town. Many communities also contained individuals or families often called "sojourners," who were permitted to reside there but had limited political or economic rights.[71] In contrast, inhabitants could, by law, lay claim to relief from the town, "in case through sickness, lameness, or otherwise."[72] In theory, the inhabitants and proprietors held separate meetings to conduct their affairs, but in practice many seventeenth-century towns combined the two, especially as membership closely overlapped during the first decades of colonization.

Sorting out confusion over the proper prerogatives of proprietary and town bodies became the arena for a drawn-out clash between elite and popular conceptions of law and property. The Massachusetts legislature acted to formalize the distinct role of proprietary and town bodies in the wake of imperial tensions and the arrival of a new charter (discussed in chapter 2) in several acts in the 1690s. From 1692 onward, proprietors— wherever they lived—voted according to shares held in the commons, met separately, and held final say over admitting new members. Town meetings, in contrast, were open to all landowners or "inhabitants of each town ratable at £20 estate" and were empowered to choose their own officers annually and pass laws as they saw fit on all municipal matters.[73] In many Maine (and Massachusetts) communities, the people living in town clashed with absentee proprietors who claimed much of the community real estate over the boundaries of ownership and authority.

This struggle between frontier residents and absentee land speculators persisted throughout the colonial era. As various groups of English people arrived in the Dawnland, they debated how to best transfer Indigenous land into the network of towns and proprietary companies that constituted the essential features of England's emerging Atlantic empire. In Maine, as in the rest of New England, the process was marked by confusion, experimentation, and frequent flouting of metropolitan directives, all while the newcomers grappled with the realities of Indigenous power and landownership.

Much as they may have wished otherwise, English patterns of residence and landownership in seventeenth-century Maine (like elsewhere in North America) developed in response to Native actions toward the newcomers. Like so many other imperial pretentions, English assumptions that they would impose their vision of ownership on the land foundered upon the reality of Wabanaki presence and power. When more numerous Indian communities articulated clear claims of possession on the landscape, early English arrivals had no choice but to respond. Indigenous land claims and diplomatic protocol therefore exerted a major influence on patterns of English colonization in the region. In a series of seventeenth-century agreements, the English entered into reciprocal relationships with Wabanaki proprietors in exchange for territory. English colonists violated those relationships—both intentionally and not—over time for a number of reasons, but one difference between Wabanaki and English ideas about landed property lay at the heart of the problem. The English viewed land use as a way to gain independence, with frontier colonists in particular viewing freeholds as a way to avoid entangling, unequal relationships with outsiders. In contrast, Wabanaki land use sought to manage and exploit a web of reciprocal relationships between human and nonhuman groups. Although the Wabanakis tried to incorporate colonists into this network, the English refused to adjust their own land use practices accordingly.

Even as growing numbers of colonists violated these relationships—inaugurating a period of intermittent warfare between 1675 and

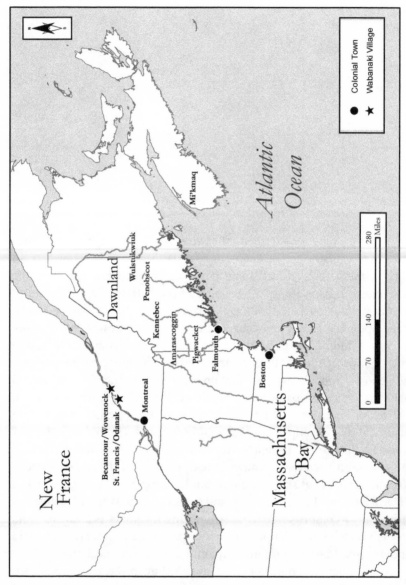

MAP 2.1. Seventeenth-century Maine frontier.

1713—New Englanders discovered that Indian deeds were the most reliable form of land conveyance. These deeds were more precise than vague royal patents and proved useful in warding off metropolitan attempts to interfere in colonial affairs. Paradoxically, by the turn of the eighteenth century, Massachusetts placed a mounting emphasis on the importance of Indian land deeds—and corresponding Native rights to unsold land—even as the Bay Colony's political relationship with the Wabanakis continued to worsen. Subsequent Wabanaki military victories combined with growing Massachusetts acceptance of Native land rights (however self-serving) to lay the foundation for a renewed peaceful relationship by 1713. Other factors—Anglo-French imperial rivalry, the rise of Jesuit influence in some Wabanaki communities, and friction over the fur trade—all influenced decisions for war and peace on the Dawnland frontier, but by the late seventeenth century, the relationship between Native power and colonial land rights loomed large in shaping the nature of Anglo-Wabanaki diplomacy.

Chaos and Accommodation

Wabanakis and English newcomers managed to reach a number of mutually beneficial agreements over land use during the seventeenth century, maintaining a mostly amicable coexistence until 1675. Frontier residents forged these relationships amid turbulence rocking both of their political communities. Buffeted by uncertainty, Wabanakis and English alike hoped to build stable relationships with their new neighbors. The seventeenth-century Maine frontier revealed the possible means—and limits—of coexistence between different cultures of ownership.

Beginning around 1600, a series of political and demographic shocks rippled across the Dawnland, sundering old political organizations and fostering new ones. Rival confederacies dominated by the present-day Mi'kmaq (living in modern Nova Scotia) and a farming people living on the coast of today's Maine called Almouchiquois by the French began a large-scale war around 1600. The Mi'kmaqs, who had access to English, French, and Basque traders since the early sixteenth century, enjoyed a decisive military superiority and crushed the Almouchiquois by 1615.[1] As the survivors feuded among themselves, famine descended onto the unsettled region, weakening the inhabitants just as European traders triggered a devastating pandemic of an unknown disease in 1616, lasting until 1619.[2] The first large-scale outbreak of smallpox in North America struck the survivors in 1633.[3] Lacking immunity to the diseases sweeping through their villages, Dawnland residents died in droves, with fatalities exceeding 90 percent in some places. Among the present-day Wulstukwiuk and Passamaquoddy, according to the most thorough study, the population plummeted from approximately 7,600 people in 1600 to perhaps 2,500 survivors in 1650.[4] Along the southern Maine coast, the Almouchiquois and their neighbors dissolved as political entities. Survivors merged with neighboring groups or fled the region, some eventually settling along the St. Lawrence.[5] The epidemics wreaked cultural havoc along with causing shattering population losses, erasing knowledge of tribal history and traditional skills, and prompting dramatic changes in kinship networks as survivors built new family units.[6] Among their descendants, according to one Abenaki historian, the catastrophe is "still remembered with a prohibition to discuss it in detail."[7]

Other Indians and Europeans moved to fill this void. By the 1640s, Abenaki-speaking people moved from their inland villages toward the coastal areas around the drainages of the Saco, Kennebec, and Penobscot Rivers, absorbing remnants of earlier groups.[8] After numerous exploratory voyages and a failed attempt at colonization in 1607, English adventurers returned to the Dawnland coast on a more permanent basis during the 1620s.[9] Arriving at the site of present-day York, Maine, in 1623, Christopher Levett observed, "There I think a good plantation may be settled," with much land "already cleared, fit for planting of corne and other fruits, having heretofore ben planted by the Salvages who are all dead."[10] Levett received a warm welcome from survivors around Casco Bay, who were eager for allies.[11] Similar encounters occurred up and down the Maine coast in subsequent years.[12] Dwindling populations and a surfeit of unused land made Dawnland residents disposed to welcome the newcomers. Facing challenges of their own, the English colonists sought good relations with the Wabanakis.

Throughout the seventeenth century the English colonists entering the Dawnland endured a dizzying succession of political and proprietary overlords, inaugurating a pattern of disputed, overlapping claims to the region that lasted into the nineteenth century. Following King James I's grant of his claim in 1620 (by right of discovery) to the Council of New England, claim to the region the English called the Province of Maine passed from one English gentleman (Sir Ferdinando Gorges was the first) to another over several decades. As if to ensure maximum confusion for Maine colonists (and everyone else involved), Massachusetts Bay Colony seized the area for itself twice, in the 1650s and again in 1668, only to be thwarted each time by another English monarch (Charles II).

Finally, the Bay Colony purchased Maine in 1680, but then a new English king (James II) revoked the Massachusetts charter and incorporated it into the more centralized Dominion of New England. Bridling at the changes imposed by their new governor, Sir Edmond Andros, Bay Colonists overthrew the Dominion government in 1689 and received a new charter in 1692, as well as control over Maine.[13]

The English policy on Indian land purchases during the turbulent seventeenth century was a bundle of contradictions. Officially, the king of England claimed New England by right of discovery. As restated by a later colonial agent of Massachusetts, the king (through his subjects) could take "possession of a desert, uncultivated and uninhabited . . . or of a Country inhabited by Salvages, who are without Laws and Government."[14] Although successive monarchs adhered to this political and legal fiction throughout the seventeenth and eighteenth centuries, colonists in America faced the reality that this land was in fact held by people who lived under laws and governments of their own. John Winthrop, the second governor of Massachusetts Bay, advanced several challenges to Native American land claims that became popular among English colonists and their advocates, including John Locke.[15] "That which is common to all is proper to none," he insisted. Without grants of individual title, or permanent dwellings, fences, and livestock to mark their holdings, the Indians could not lay claim to most of their territory. Unaware of the complex networks of Indigenous land use, Winthrop called the rivers and forests (often managed by the Indians to promote certain types of plant and animal resources) "wastelands," fit for occupation by English people, "leaving [the Indians] such places as they have manured for their corn."[16] In any case, Winthrop claimed, "there is more than enough for them and us," and "we shall come in with good leave of the natives."[17] In the short term, Winthrop's prediction was correct. As long as enough land remained for both Natives and newcomers, the colonists tended to enjoy the Indians' "good leave."

Most aspiring English landowners in the Dawnland obtained this "good leave" by entering into mutually beneficial agreements with the Wabanakis. Whether they were in Maine by the permission of Ferdinando Gorges or as squatters, many English colonists compensated local Indians for their land. In turn, most coastal survivors of the seventeenth-century wars and epidemics were happy to enter into negotiations with the English. Far from being swindles, the evidence suggests most early land transactions in what became northern New England were consensual, and the Indians knew what they had agreed to in numerous written deeds.[18]

The phrasing of most seventeenth-century deeds, subsequent Wabanaki actions and words, as well as the circumstances of their creation all point to their legitimacy. In many deeds, aside from initial payments, the Wabanaki signers received annual payments in the form of various goods. When Nanuddemaure, "proprietor of these lands" around Pejepscot (near present-day Brunswick) sold them to fisherman John Parker in 1659, he received "one Beaver Skin" on the spot and "the yearly rent of one Bushell of Corn and a quart of Liquor to be paid unto the said Nanuddemaure his heirs for ever." Nanuddemaure and his heirs also retained the right "to fish fowl and hunt also to set Otter Traps without Molestation."[19] The local sagamore, Rawandagon—called "Robin Hood" by the English—also signed the deed, indicating that the entire community of Wabanakis nearby had agreed to allow Nanuddemaure to sell the tract to Parker.[20] Like most deeds signed along the coast, the Nanuddemaure deed contained multiple Native signatures.[21] Further indicating he had not been duped, Rawandagon acknowledged the deed again before a justice of the peace in 1666.[22] In another example, "Mr. Roles . . . the Sagamore of Newichawanuke" sold a half mile of land between two rivers and his fishing rights "Right of the Ware" to Humphrey Chadbourne in 1643 but reserved both a tract for himself, and, among other rights, half of the "great Alewifes that shall be taken at that Ware from Time to Time for Ever."[23]

Wabanaki reaction to a deed signed without their consent in 1694 provides an instructive contrast. The unilateral cession by a sagamore named Madockawando of a large tract of land on both sides of the St. Georges River destroyed his influence among his people, who backed a new leader. A year later Madockawando had moved to present-day New Brunswick to live among the Wulstukwiuks.[24] The Wabanakis continued to repudiate the sale for the next seventy years. When protesting the Madockawando deed, Wabanaki speakers seldom extended their condemnations to other agreements.

Alongside one category of consensual agreements and another of coerced or fraudulent deeds exists a third: seventeenth-century agreements that later Massachusetts speculators willfully distorted to justify eighteenth-century land grabs. Mostly signed between 1649 and 1665, these deeds between various Wabanakis and two competing groups of English fur traders appeared to grant the newcomers title to wide swathes of land on both sides of the Kennebec River. The first English arrivals from the Pilgrim Plymouth colony opened a trading post in the area of present-day Augusta in 1629, which remained operational until 1676, along with several others at still-unknown locations.[25] Beginning in 1649, Boston merchant Thomas Lake (joined in 1654 by Thomas Clarke) began erecting trading posts of his own along the

Kennebec. Both Plymouth and the Clarke & Lake Company signed deeds with various Wabanakis. These documents constitute perhaps the most puzzling of Dawnland transactions.[26] (The destruction of many Clarke & Lake records during the eighteenth century makes them among the more elusive land companies to study, as well.)[27] As written, they granted title to tracts extending ten to fifteen miles on each side of the Kennebec River. These deeds granted far larger tracts than those along the coast and were measured in miles or leagues rather than by reference to specific geographic features, indicating either willful or accidental misunderstandings.[28] Transactions like Abecaduset's and Konebris's 1649 deed to a Clarke & Lake agent did not reserve any use rights for the Indians in the ten-mile tracts extending on either side of the Kennebec River, which may indicate the sellers never imagined the English planned to do anything more than set up trading posts.[29] At the time, these and Wabanaki "sales" in the region were probably no more than invitations to spread out trading operations (which the English had been operating in the vicinity for decades), allowing locals to obtain more coveted merchandise. During the eighteenth century, the Kennebec River Indians never acknowledged anything but a trading post in the area, whereas they and other Wabanakis recognized other early deeds.[30] Whatever their original intent, eighteenth-century Wabanaki statements indicate they believed their military victories in the wars of 1675–77 and 1688–1713 nullified these agreements.[31] Perhaps sensing this, the Clarke & Lake heirs to inland Kennebec River claims did not press the issue for a century.

Viewed from a seventeenth-century perspective, Indigenous consent to most early sales (apart from the Kennebec River transactions) made sense. Because the Wabanakis reserved rights to hunt and fish on the ceded land, the agreements may have appeared advantageous. The Indians attracted potential allies and trading partners at the cost of some unused farmland. The Wabanakis did not then realize European-style agriculture, pasturing, and residence would destroy the land's usefulness for the Indians. Eighteenth-century Wabanaki statements reveal that once the Indians learned what effect colonists had on the land, they refused to sell any more.[32] During the mid-seventeenth century, the reduced Wabanaki population faced a growing military threat from the Iroquois Confederacy to the west, which launched a series of raids into the Maritime Peninsula. As they allied with other Algonquian speakers against the Iroquois, the Wabanakis made land grants to the English to obtain further assistance against a powerful foe.[33]

On the coast, some Indian signers received a different form of support than an alliance. A scattering of isolated families received guarantees of portions of their land while obtaining new neighbors and trading partners. Romanascho, mother of a sagamore near the town of Wells, even obtained "constant recourse to" buyer John Wadleigh's house, "and several gifts she continually receiveth, to a greater value, than the thing is worth, as she supposeth."[34] Although Romanascho's prominence garnered her greater consideration than the typical Wabanaki woman, arrangements like hers underscore the varied motivations of seventeenth-century Indians signing over their land to the English.

For the Wabanakis, the value of what they received in exchange for their lands extended beyond the annual gifts of corn or other goods. Although the Englishmen who wrote the deeds often described a payment of "yearly rent"—as did the Nanuddemaure deed—the Wabanakis understood it as gifts or tribute, part of an ongoing, reciprocal relationship.[35] In the Dawnland, gifts—whatever their form—served a vital diplomatic function, opening and initiating ties between communities.

Early English views of these agreements were equally complex. The deeds had no legal standing in England, as they clashed with royal claims of sovereignty. In addition, proprietors like Ferdinando Gorges knew that colonists' Indian land purchases could challenge their own titles. However, the English lacked the strength to bully the Indians into submission. Although diminished by war and disease, thousands of Wabanakis still lived between the Saco and the St. John Rivers, far outnumbering the English. Bowing to this reality, Gorges directed his agents in Maine to first sign contracts with incoming colonists, then to "give some what to the Adjacent Sagamore or Native, for their Consent" provided "it be no considerable Sum," justifying the payment as a goodwill gesture that would distinguish the English from their European rivals and facilitate the spread of Christianity and "civilization" among the Indians.[36] The practice resembled the custom of quieting in England, by which manor lords paid squatters or other occupants a sum of money for their land without acknowledging they held a valid title to it.

English colonists who traveled to the Dawnland without proprietary permission left few written traces of their thoughts on Native land rights besides the deeds and later depositions, in part because of the low literacy rates among the hardscrabble fishermen and farmers who constituted the first generation of Maine colonists.[37] Whether or not they agreed with John Winthrop that Indians had no legal claim to lands not being farmed, early colonists soon discovered they could obtain large estates at a lower cost by dealing directly with the Indians. Many never registered their deeds in the county court at York, which could indicate a disregard for the validity of Indian land sales or an unwillingness to make an arduous journey.[38] Some colonists regarded Massachusetts law as too rigid and impersonal, and avoided resorting to the courts whenever possible.[39] These colonists—often poorer and less educated than their neighbors— were more likely to try their luck on a remote frontier like Maine. During the eighteenth century some Maine colonists continued to display indifference to recording deeds from sources they mistrusted—in that case, absentee land speculators.[40]

Enterprising individuals like fisherman John Parker, who bought up tracts along the mid-Maine coast and up the Kennebec River, may have engaged in their own forms of subtle manipulation when making agreements with the Wabanakis. Although Nanuddemaure and Rawandagon reserved certain use rights in their 1659 deed to John Parker, indicating their equal role in the negotiations, Parker or one of three English witnesses chose the date for annual payment. By stipulating the Indians would come to Parker's house on Christmas Day, the Englishman may have tapped into a contemporary Yuletide custom in which landlords would treat their tenants, the wealthy would care for the poor, and traditional authority would be inverted for a brief time. In scheduling his annual rent on Christmas, Parker could symbolically transform his Native hosts into guests and mark his payment as an aberration in their usual relationship.[41] Some other English renters also scheduled their payments on Christmas.[42]

Whatever Parker and other early Maine colonists thought of Native land rights, they—and growing numbers of Massachusetts residents— came to realize the advantages of Indian land deeds. Provided a competent interpreter could be secured, Indians gave more accurate grants than Englishmen who had never seen the land in question. Although misunderstandings sometimes led to overlapping claims, Indian deeds caused fewer problems than royal patents. The deeds also better corresponded to the political reality on the ground. Since the Indians *were* in physical possession of the territory many colonists had to pay them for, it made sense to accord these transactions the weight of law. Colonists also found Native deeds useful for circumventing distant English claims. Ferdinando Gorges realized that fact from across the Atlantic when he warned an agent in 1664 that Indian land deeds were "Derogatory to the Grant to me made by his sd late Majesty."[43]

As powerful Englishmen on both sides of the Atlantic struggled to ensure colonists showed due deference to their claims to property and authority, Indian deeds rose in importance. Ironically, the English failure to respect the reciprocal obligations contained within those deeds pushed the Dawnland frontier into a maelstrom of violence even as the value of those deeds rose.

Restoring the Balance

Maine colonists caused the first war on the Dawnland frontier by destroying the reciprocal relationship the Wabanakis had built with them. Unlike the later wars that would roil the region with depressing regularity, the First Anglo-Wabanaki War of 1675–78 (also known as King Philip's War, for a prominent leader in southern New England) did not stem from clashes over land. Instead, paranoia on the part of the English that the Wabanakis were in league with the Algonquians of southern New England led them to end a generation of relative—though far from idyllic—peace on the Maine frontier. Before 1675, colonists and Wabanakis had traded with and even visited one another on occasion, a circumstance not surprising given that a scattering of Indians remained on the coast.[44] As late as 1688, New England chronicler Cotton Mather noted that many Wabanakis "dwelt in the Indian manner among" the Maine towns.[45] John Josselyn, a resident of Black Point (future Scarborough) recalled in 1648 "Certain Indians coming to our house . . . desired leave to lodge all night in our kitchin, it being a very rainie season, some of them lay down in the middle of the Room, and others under the Table, in the morning they went away before any of the people were up."[46] A 1688 deposition in North Yarmouth noted a similar event without fanfare.[47]

Full-scale war erupted when the English demanded the Wabanakis turn over all their firearms, fearing they were plotting to join the Wampanoag King Philip's war against the colonies.[48] For the still friendly Wabanakis, the demands—levied by both Massachussetts leaders and frontier towns alike—were both insulting and dangerous, as the Indians depended on guns to hunt by 1675.[49] On top of these demands, some colonists killed the infant son of the sagamore Squando, tipping over a canoe containing the child, ostensibly to see if Indian children could float, as was rumored among the colonists.[50]

Treated like enemies, the Wabanakis gradually assumed that role, moving to restore balance to what appeared to them a broken relationship. Wabanaki warriors, skilled forest fighters, wreaked havoc on the Maine frontier. In a matter of months, they reduced English Maine to a thin southern coastal strip consisting of the towns of Wells, York, and Kittery. Although the New England colonies defeated King Philip's allied Algonquian tribes in 1676, Massachusetts suffered repeated set-backs against the Wabanakis in a grinding conflict marked by ambushes, betrayals, and rising bitterness.[51] In a final peace treaty in April 1678, the Indians released their captives and allowed English colonists to return to their homes. In exchange, they demanded promises of reciprocal justice, with English submitting complaints about Wabanakis to sagamores, and Indians directing complaints about colonists to English authorities. The Wabanakis also demanded an annual tribute of a peck of corn for every colonial household living in Maine, terms the defeated English, Cotton Mather noted, "might think, not very Honourable."[52]

English failure to fulfill the terms of the treaty, coupled with their first sustained encroachments on unsold land, signaled that they did not share the Wabanaki ideal of a reciprocal relationship. Following the treaty of 1678, Thomas Danforth, the newly appointed president of Maine, began issuing land grants around what became the town of North Yarmouth on unceded land. Colonists began to trickle in despite Indian protests. Other Wabanakis along the Saco and Androscoggin Rivers complained of English nets stopping fish from traveling upriver, and allowing colonial livestock to roam free, devouring Native corn.[53] By making land around their towns inhospitable for Wabanaki subsistence practices, the colonists violated, at the very least, the spirit of all the agreements guaranteeing the Wabanakis continued use of the land they sold.

As the Wabanakis confronted their aggressive New England neighbors, their increasing ties to New France provided them with a potential ally and alternative to the English weapons and trade goods on which they had come to depend. French traders, soldiers, and explorers had been a regular feature in the Dawnland throughout the seventeenth century, establishing the colony of Acadia in Mi'kmaq and Wulstukwiuk territory in present-day Nova Scotia. Proselytizing Jesuits, beginning with Gabrielle Dreuilletes in 1646, traveled to Wabanaki villages throughout the Dawnland, attracting a number of converts.[54] Families of Wabanakis from the Connecticut River to the St. John moved to mission villages along the St. Lawrence, some attracted by the Jesuits, many others fleeing war-torn communities.[55] Several Jesuit and Capuchin priests moved to Wabanaki villages on the Androscoggin, Penobscot, and St. John Rivers, establishing missions there.[56] Although even Catholic Wabanakis remained politically independent of the French, the presence of missionaries and kinship ties with the St. Lawrence mission villages among the Wabanakis bolstered French influence in the Dawnland.

As the English continued to violate the Wabanaki vision for the Common Pot, the Indians resorted to violence to redraw new boundaries with the aggressive newcomers. Wabanaki warriors began to strike Maine towns in the autumn of 1688, sparking the Second Anglo-Wabanaki War (1688–99). Clandestine French supplies and encouragement became overt once England and France declared war in Europe during 1689 in a conflict Anglophone colonists called King William's War, after their sovereign. Franco-Wabanaki forces drove the English out of every town and fortification northeast of Wells by 1696, flooding Massachusetts with refugees and reclaiming much of the Dawnland for the Indians. Massachusetts signed a peace agreement with the Wabanakis in 1699, but hostilities resumed in 1703, and the Third Anglo-Wabanaki War (blending into yet another Anglo-French imperial conflict that New England colonists called Queen Anne's War) lasted until the combatants signed the Treaty of Portsmouth in 1713.

The Consequences of War

The violence of 1688–1713 consumed entire communities, destroying old relationships forever. The destruction also paved the way for new ones to grow from the wreckage. The English population of Maine plummeted from a prewar peak of 6,000 to fewer than 2,000 people by 1713, most of them clustered around the three southernmost towns of Wells, York, and Kittery. The war also increased the influence of large absentee landowners in Maine, who were able to buy numerous family claims from poor refugees who had given up on returning. A group of wealthy speculators living in Boston snapped up many of the refugee titles, then waited for the time when the frontier could again be safe for British colonization.

Wabanaki communities also experienced profound changes during the war years. The Treaty of Portsmouth ended a long period of political and demographic turmoil, and by 1713 Dawnland inhabitants coalesced into political groupings still recognizable today. From east to west, the Wulstukwiuks, Penobscots, Kennebecs, Amarascoggins, and Pigwackets occupied the major river drainages of the St. John, Penobscot, Kennebec, Androscoggin, and Saco, respectively. These tribes allied with the French during the warfare of 1688–1713, with many villages housing Jesuits, and all containing Catholic converts. Although they scored a number of victories, often with French assistance, the Wabanakis also endured immense suffering. Frequent raids by New England militia forced the Wabanakis to abandon many of their villages and disrupted seasonal subsistence patterns. Massachusetts commissioners meeting with the Wabanakis in 1698 received reports of Indians and their captives starving to death. Disease also scythed Native ranks, particularly an outbreak in 1697–98, which "consumed them wonderfully," according to Cotton Mather.[57] Many Wabanakis spent the 1703–13 war years in the Canadian villages of St. Francis (Odanak) and Becancour (Wowenock) to avoid New England forces, relying on the French for trade goods and even food, which their new allies struggled to provide.[58] Their wartime experience soured many Wabanakis on their French allies. Around 1700, the various Wabanaki tribes also formed a political confederacy in concert with Iroquoian-speaking Mohawks and Hurons living in Canada. Over time, the confederacy formalized already occurring cooperative relationships between northeastern tribes. Little information survives about the confederacy's operation before the mid-eighteenth century, however, rendering discussion of its precise influence before then little more than speculation.[59] Nevertheless, the trend after 1713 remains clear: the Wabanakis grew disenchanted with their erstwhile French allies at the same time they forged tighter bonds among themselves.

Alongside disease and hunger, another wartime misfortune befell the Wabanakis that would only reveal itself in the fullness of time. Massachusetts governor William Phips managed to get a pair of prominent Wabanakis to make a massive land cession without consulting their people. The disaster had its origins in 1693, when a number of war-weary sagamores signed a cease-fire with Phips. As written, the treaty included pledges of "hearty subjection and obedience unto the Crown of England" by the assembled Indians, and turning over several high-profile hostages to Massachusetts as a pledge of sincerity.[60] Phips probably made verbal promises to the Indians that the English omitted from the written document, as he later claimed, "All things on my part have been duely observed," and French reports mentioned promises of "trade and amity."[61] But Phips did not return the hostages, who had included a brother of Kennebec sagamore Egeremet, and a cousin of both Egeremet and Penobscot sagamore Madockawando.

As the Kennebecs and Penobscots—who had been divided over the peace treaty—debated the proper response, Madockawando and Egeremet met Phips on an English vessel in May 1694. After spending two hours with Phips in the ship's cabin, Madockawando signed a deed selling off a large land tract on both sides of the St. Georges River.[62] Unlike most seventeenth-century deeds, this one made no mention of the sagamore speaking on behalf of other occupants or obtaining their consent, instead describing Madockawando as the "Only true and lawful Owner" of the land. For an unspecified "valuable Consideration" (this wording was in itself not unusual in English deeds—Sir William Blackstone's seminal *Commentaries on the Laws of England* specified a legal deed alienating land had to be for "valuable" consideration, meaning a fair price),[63] Madockawando surrendered all claims to the lands around the St. Georges, including the standard hunting and fishing rights.[64]

Madockawando left no explanation for this land cession, which had been conducted without the consent of most Penobscots. Perhaps Phips did not tell the sagamore what the cession entailed.[65] Madockawando had publicly expressed a desire for peace in Penobscot councils, along with a return of the hostages, which included his cousin, and may have believed the land cession was the only way to achieve these aims.[66] The Jesuit missionary to the Penobscots at this time observed that the ongoing war with the English presented the Indians in the vicinity with an unpleasant dilemma—they would either have to confront Phips and a force of five hundred soldiers rebuilding a fort in the heart of their country or withdraw and face "unavoidable" hunger and destitution.[67] Peace with the English would enable Madockawando to escape that choice. A Wabanaki eyewitness to the negotiations on board Phips's vessel reported seeing Madockawando and Egeremet throw their hatchets into the sea in a gesture intended to symbolize a lasting peace.[68]

The meeting had the opposite effect. An overwhelming majority of the Penobscots denounced the cession as soon as word of it leaked out. Their outrage doomed the associated 1693 peace treaty in short order. Encouraged by the French governor of Acadia, who ritually adopted their leader, the antitreaty party soon grew to include most of the Penobscots, who jeered at Madockawando's rump faction as they held a great council to prepare for war.[69] A chastened Madockawando eventually joined the raiders who broke the peace, who, in the usual Wabanaki fashion, desired consensus. Madockawando's meeting with Phips brought the political career of the most powerful Penobscot sagamore of the seventeenth century to an abrupt end. The sagamore's unauthorized decision highlighted the limits of individuals' power within Wabanaki political culture. Sagamores' authority rested on their ability to build and maintain consensus on important matters. Leaders like Madockawando who acted outside these bounds soon found their influence gone. In 1695, a broken Madockawando moved with a handful of relatives to settle among the Wulstukwiuks on the St. John River, where he died in 1698.[70]

Phips and Madockawando's meeting cast a long shadow over Anglo-Wabanaki relations. Phips had acted outside of his official capacity in purchasing Indian land, a move that provoked controversy in Massachusetts. (Unlike Madockawando, however, Phips faced unemployment for other reasons, stemming from charges of illegal trade and violation of the Navigation Acts. He died in London defending his administration in 1695.)[71] Successive governors followed Phips's example in using their official position to advance their interests as Maine landholders when dealing with the Wabanakis.

Rejection of Madockawando's cession became a lodestar of Penobscot diplomacy for the next sixty years. When they invited the English to return to "their former rights of Lands" in 1699, the Penobscots specified a number of locations from Pemaquid to the Piscataqua River, but never the St. Georges River. They also insisted on retaining their hunting and fishing rights, as specified in all other agreements except for Madockawando's.[72] In addition, the Penobscots continued to express their relationship to the English king in the abstract terms of other seventeenth-century agreements, stating "King William Englishman's King is their King," in keeping with frequent Native pronouncements that they stood on an equal footing with English colonists in relation to a distant European monarch.[73] When the Wabanakis signed the Treaty of Portsmouth with Massachusetts and New Hampshire leaders in 1713, they repeated these terms, inviting the British to reoccupy their "antient Plantations," making no mention of the disavowed Madockawando sale.[74]

Future Massachusetts governors interpreted the 1693–94 agreements in a different light. Every one of them used the 1693 "submission" to claim the Wabanakis as subjects to the Crown, and all future treaties repeated pro forma declarations of sovereignty over the Indians.[75] As long as the Wabanakis remained powerful, Bay Colony leaders did not attempt to make these pretensions a reality and inserted them (unbeknownst to the Indians) for the benefit of imperial officials in London.

The 1694 Madockawando deed—a separate document from the 1693 treaty—followed a different historical course. In 1719, William Phips's adopted son, Spencer, sold the claim to John Leverett, founder of the Lincolnshire Company, formed to take advantage of a dormant claim in the region, which became known as the Muscongus Patent.[76] In pressing its claims, the company at times relied upon the contested cession, with deleterious consequences for Anglo-Wabanaki relations. However, other wartime changes in the Bay Colony created the potential for greater cooperation.

Creating a New Property Regime

During the 1680s, escalating clashes with a newly appointed governor drove many Massachusetts colonists to endorse Native land rights as a way to preserve both property and independence. Reacting to years of Massachusetts intransigence, King Charles II revoked the Bay Colony charter in 1684, and his brother and Catholic successor, James II, appointed Sir Edmond Andros to administer Massachusetts as part of the newly created Dominion of New England, encompassing New York and all colonies eastward. Alongside other controversial decisions, Andros sparked a firestorm of protest by refusing to recognize any land titles that did not originate from the king's patent.[77] Andros and his council justified their actions by asserting, as Judge John Palmer wrote, "'Tis a Fundamentall Point consented unto by all Christian Nations that the First Discovery of a Countrey inhabited by Infidells, gives a Right and Dominion of that Countrey to the Prince in whose Service and Employment the Discoverers were sent."[78] Viewing the hodgepodge of town, colony, and Indian deeds prevalent in the Bay Colony, Andros and his supporters insisted these claimants apply to the government for new titles for their lands.

Many Massachusetts colonists reacted to these developments with outrage, insisting that Indian land rights had always formed the foundation of the Bay Colony's proprietary regime. Edward Rawson, a colony secretary before the Andros regime, issued a point-by-point rebuttal to Palmer, quoting the arguments of the Reverend John Higginson in defense of Native land rights. According to Higginson and Rawson, colonists held their lands "By a right of purchase from the Indians who were Native inhabitants, and had possession of the Land before the English came hither."[79] Rawson accused Andros of responding to Higginson by "vilifying the Indian title, saying They were Brutes etc," to which Higginson responded the land had belonged to the Indians and was therefore not the king's to grant, and this was "a standing Principle in Law and Reason."[80] Rawson also appended a complaint from John Lynde of Charlestown, who claimed to approach Andros, "shewing him an Indian Deed for Land, [Andros] said, that their hand was no more worth than a scratch with a Bears paw, undervaluing all my Titles, though every way legal under our former Charter Government."[81]

Extolling the virtues of Indian land titles allowed Massachusetts colonists not only to shield their land and government from royal interference but also to fashion a flattering image of the Bay Colony as a moral exemplar in its dealings with Native neighbors. During the heat of the confrontation with Andros, one anonymous pamphleteer asked rhetorically, "whether no Indian Lands, nor Indian Rights, have been Patented away" by the regime? Rejecting the argument "that the Indians, because [they are] Pagans, have no Title to any Lands at all in this Countrey," the writer insisted "the World will . . . judge us the juster, and more righteous of the two, who own they have . . . a Just Right to all their Lands but those, which they have by fair Contract or just Conquest parted with."[82]

During a second period of uncertainty over the Massachusetts charter between 1715 and 1721, Jeremiah Dummer, the Bay Colony's agent in London, refined these arguments in his official *Defence of the New England Charters*.[83] Dummer's tract embodied the orthodox position of Massachusetts leaders in the eighteenth century, using its history with Native American neighbors as the foundation for both landed property and freedom from metropolitan interference. Dummer denied earlier English monarchs had the authority to grant North American lands, because the continent "was full of Inhabitants . . . and neither Queen Elizabeth by her Patents, or King James by his afterwards, could give any more than a bare Right of Preemption."[84] In fact, the only right to the land came from "what is derived from the native Lords of the Soil, and that is what the honest New England Planters rely on, having purchas'd it with their Money."[85] Unlike their Spanish rivals, New Englanders "sought to gain the Natives by strict Justice in their Dealings with them" and "assur'd the Americans, that they did not come among them as Invaders but Purchasers."[86] Despite the prevalence of "an unworthy Aspersion that has been cast on the first Settlers of New England, that they never treated the Savages well but encroach'd on their Land by Degrees, till they fraudulently and forcibly turn'd them out of all," Dummer insisted Massachusetts and neighboring colonies had purchased their lands "publickly and in open Market. If they did not pay a great Price for their Purchases yet they paid as much as they were worth." Once established, colonists "aply'd their Cares for the Benefit of the Indians," sparing "no Pains to bring them acquainted by the gospel."[87]

Although many New Englanders came to accept Native land rights for pragmatic or idealistic reasons, others continued to wage a rear guard action against them. Writing in 1725, the Connecticut Reverend John Bulkley grumbled that "our Bigots to Native Right" had embraced the "Extravagant Principle" that Indigenous societies had the sophistication and sovereign power to claim "all Lands in [their] Country, whether Cultivated by them or not."[88] Just as bad, he claimed, the "Native Right" zealots tried to frighten everyone into agreement by insisting "'tis the only Security of Our Interests against the Claim of One beyond the Seas."[89] Bulkley admitted his argument stood "contrary to Vulgar sentiments in the present day" but nevertheless insisted those who advocated for Native rights as "our only Valuable Title to Whatever Lands are in the Country" did so for "other Considerations" than honest conviction.[90]

Bulkley was correct to point out that defenders of Native rights benefited from that position, although he neglected to mention critics of Indian deeds likewise stood to gain from discrediting them. In the years following the cessation of the frontier wars in 1713, critics of Native land rights waged an uphill struggle against a growing consensus among Massachusetts elites in their favor. The legal chaos of the Andros years coupled with the near-total destruction of Maine frontier communities at Wabanaki hands persuaded postwar leaders in the Bay Colony to ground their system of property based on the reality of previous—and ongoing—Native landownership.

Order and Independence

Massachusetts colonists had risen up to oust the unpopular Governor Andros in 1689 upon receiving word that the Protestant William of Orange had assumed the English throne after driving King James from the country in a "Glorious Revolution."[91] After receiving a new charter from William in 1692, Bay Colony leaders set about ensuring that colonial land titles could never be questioned by a royal official like Andros again. They also sought to bring order to the confusing welter of overlapping titles on the frontier as well as in towns closer to Boston.

Massachusetts leaders proved unable to fully reconcile their twin goals of achieving an orderly system of title for the eastern frontier and preserving it from metropolitan interference. Instead, they created a vague arrangement in which, by law, Indian land purchases were valid only if obtained to corroborate titles from the Crown or colony, but in practice, remained an essential basis of landed property on the Maine frontier. The jury-rigged arrangement that emerged by 1713 gave an emerging network of large-scale land speculators the best available chance to make their claims a reality. It also sowed confusion among different groups of investors and among neighbors in communities from Casco Bay to the Penobscot River. The resulting disorder also amplified the importance of Wabanakis as the guarantors of property within Massachusetts.

Laws dealing with Indian lands betrayed the contradictions underlying attitudes about Native land rights among Massachusetts colonists. Displaying a mix of altruism and self-interest that would remain a fixture among Bay Colony elites until the mid-eighteenth century, the legislature made it illegal to buy land from the Indians without permission, citing both a desire to protect southern New England Indians from being "imposed on and abused" and prevent "disturbance" of "lands and inheritances lawfully acquired."[92] In other words, lawmakers—many of who themselves held extensive land claims from a variety of sources—feared new sales could jeopardize those titles. The same law nullified all Indian purchases made without the permission of colonial governments since 1633, though it carved out several exceptions, the most expansive dealing with Maine. East of the Piscatqua River, lawmakers clarified, Indian deeds were valid provided they were made "for further confirmation of other lawful titles and possessions," meaning town, colony, and royal grants.[93] This act—passed in 1701—appeared to confirm metropolitan views on Native land rights, only granting Indian land sales the status of "quieting" otherwise illegal occupants. However, the General Court had no choice when crafting the legislation, because the King's Privy Council would repeal any law that contradicted royal sovereignty, as it did in 1692, when the General Court passed "An Act for the Quieting of Possessions and Setling of Titles." The Privy Council repealed it, insisting Massachusetts insert a clause "for saving the rights of the Crown."[94]

The General Court's actions failed to permanently settle the status of Indian land deeds in Massachusetts. Nor could they, as long as the desires of Bay Colony elites so contradicted English law. The act of 1701 banning "Clandestine and Illegal Purchases" was a masterpiece of obfuscation, declining to specify which "other lawful titles and possessions" the Indian deeds in Maine had ostensibly confirmed. The act's inexact language allowed for a wide range of interpretation, of which proprietors and colonists alike took advantage in subsequent disputes. For most people, the principled reasons for using Indian—or any other—land deeds took a backseat to immediate concerns of proving ownership over a contested tract. An anonymous petition to the General Court urging that "Indian Grants in this province of Main[e] are not sufficient to Eject a present possessor" demonstrated how ordinary colonists opportunistically coped with the confusion. The petitioner, concerned with a grant on Munjoy neck in Falmouth, invoked the Gorges patent, Massachusetts acts to quiet possessions, and laws dictating how to register deeds to invalidate "Indian Grants." But the petitioner also argued "if Indian

Titles be of force," that the grant in question "Cannot bee good being nott obtained from the Right Saggamore."[95]

For their part, imperial officials interfered in colonial land disputes only on the rare occasions when a proprietor would send an agent to London to appeal a case. When Massachusetts proprietors invoked Indian deeds during correspondence with the Board of Trade, they referred to them as having force *in Massachusetts*. Arguing for the Muscongus Company, Adam Winthrop described their "Secure title . . . to the said Tract of Land both by grant from the Crown and purchase from the Indians, which is allways held inviolable in these parts."[96] Winthrop did not dwell on whether the Crown or Indian validation of the Muscongus title had more weight in Massachusetts, a question he—like many other land speculators—preferred to let the Bay Colony answer for itself in due course.

From his perch on the Governor's Council, Winthrop worked with his colleagues (many of whom held similar investments) to craft a colony-wide property system from Boston that would benefit men like them, with consequences that reverberated across the eastern frontier. By freezing new land purchases from the Indians, Winthrop and other Massachusetts leaders prevented ordinary colonists from securing legal title to Maine lands without going through the large-scale proprietors. No longer could men like John Parker—a fisherman hailing from the West Country in England—hope to amass private estates by negotiating directly with the Indians. At the same time, the legislature enshrined the legal authority of absentee proprietors to thwart resident nonproprietors' attempts to play an active role in the distribution of land in their communities. The General Court moved to distinguish, once and for all, the *proprietors* of town common lands from the *residents* who lived in town without holding such a claim. The Court passed a series of acts granting the proprietary bodies the power to divide land, sue for it in court, and admit new proprietors or "commoners," while stripping town bodies of those same powers.[97]

For numerous poor frontier residents who held no share in their town proprietorship, this law carried grave consequences. A 1687 petition from Scarborough explained to the governor that many residents lived in poverty "by Rason of severell persons that Layes Claimes to all the Lands or the Gratest parte of Both Land and medows in our Towne." Although "there are severell hundred Acors of Meddow that as never made Like to be," the residents lived crowded together "that wee Can Cale to one anothers howses" on six- or eight-acre plots apiece "and noe meddow . . . all though here is suffitiant [land] for the settlment of many of his Mejestes subjects more than all Redy settled [here.]"[98] Confronted by what they viewed as a rigid, inflexible legal system that did not respond to community needs, the Scarborough petitioners argued that the law should be modified in the interest of fairness. War intervened before the Scarborough petitioners could seek redress, but when they returned in the eighteenth century, residents resumed the struggle against local absentee landlords. The resulting clashes encouraged absentee proprietors to fear for their investments and to rely even more on their Indian deeds to preserve them from new threats.

The generation of violence that ended with the Treaty of Portsmouth in 1713 had a lasting effect on the networks of belonging on the Dawnland frontier. Amid the disruption of imperial conflicts and dynastic change, Massachusetts elites came to believe that a system of property rooted in acknowledged Native land deeds would best protect their claims to Maine. The wars also grew British influence in the maritime Northeast at the expense of France, forcing the Wabanakis to rely more on their own strength to manage relations with the British. The character of those relations came to turn ever more on how different parties understood landownership and how they interpreted the terms of agreements made long ago, yet newly relevant as Indians and colonists alike struggled to secure where they belonged.

3 /   Land Claims, 1713–1722

The Wabanakis sometimes called New England colonists *Bostoniak*—
literally "Boston people." The label referred to the well-known fact that
New Englanders originated in the village of Boston before spreading
out into the Dawnland.[1] Their appellation became even more accurate
after the Treaty of Portsmouth in 1713, when a wealthy group of Boston-
based land speculators rose to prominence on the Dawnland frontier.[2]
In the years surrounding the close of the Third Anglo-Wabanaki War,
groups of investors formed companies to buy up abandoned land claims
on the war-torn Maine frontier. Absentee land speculators played a role
in New England colonial schemes from the first days, but in the early
eighteenth century they reached a new level of influence. Companies like
the Pejepscot and Muscongus Proprietors boasted members sitting in
courts, the Massachusetts House, the Governor's Council, and even the
governor's chair itself. As a new century unfolded, these companies did
their best to ensure that the fate of the eastern frontier would be decided
not in distant Whitehall, or even in the Massachusetts legislature, but at
proprietors' meetings in Boston taverns like the Green Dragon and the
Orange Tree.

These *Bostoniak* hoped to usher in a new era of order and prosperity
in Maine. This prosperity would stem above all from a uniform system
of landed property acknowledged by Indians and colonists alike. Having
secured title to vast swathes of territory, the proprietors planned to invite
colonists to build new communities and make the land valuable. The

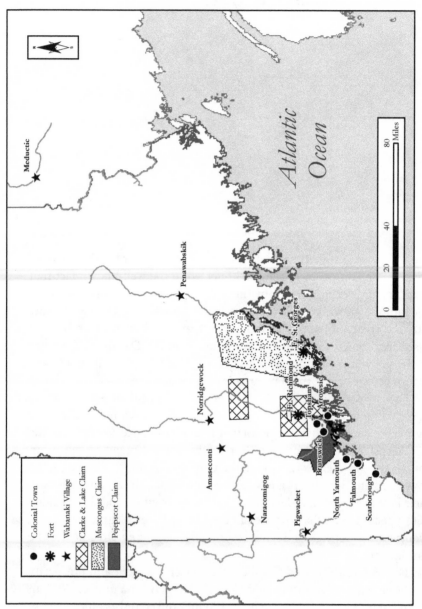

Legend:

● Colonial Town
✳ Fort
★ Wabanaki Village

▨ Clarke & Lake Claim
⠠ Muscongus Claim
▰ Pejepscot Claim

Meductic ★

Atlantic Ocean

Penawabskik ★

Norridgewock ★

Fr. St. Georges

Amasseconti ★

Ft. Richmond ✳
Topsham ●
Arrowsic
Brunswick ●

Naracomigog ★

Pigwacket ★

North Yarmouth ●
Falmouth ●
Scarborough ●

0   20   40   80
Miles

MAP 3.1 Maine frontier after 1713.

proprietors would provide the necessary direction. The Wabanakis would acquiesce to this vision because the British Empire had vanquished the French (who the British believed were behind most Wabanaki resistance to their plans) in the latest war, and because the speculators had secured lawful title to their land claims from the region's rightful Indigenous owners. All would benefit from this new order, especially the proprietors. They had, after all, risked considerable sums to acquire title to property that stood to become worthless if Britain lost the wars of 1688–1713 with the Franco-Wabanaki alliance.

Like the plans of so many other aspiring imperialists, the proprietors' grand schemes capsized on the unforgiving shoals of reality. The Wabanaki and Anglo residents of the Dawnland frontier seldom behaved as the proprietors wished. The colonists who could be persuaded to journey to a still-dangerous frontier did not intend to scratch out a subsistence living just so a clique of absentee investors could grow rich as the surrounding landscape became valuable. Instead, colonists appropriated vacant tracts surrounding their homes and harvested the timber to supplement their meager incomes, shrugging off the speculators' protests. But if colonists could complicate the proprietors' bid for control over the region, the Wabanakis retained the power to stop it cold. Renewed warfare could return the Maine frontier to a state of chaos and desolation.

The *Bostoniak* rose to power at a time when shifting imperial dynamics coincided with changing ideas about how to manage the Anglo-Wabanaki relationship on both sides of the frontier. After forty years of intermittent warfare, the Wabanakis, the British, and the French all reassessed their strategies for dealing with neighbors. The French cession of Acadia to the British at the Treaty of Utrecht, coupled with New France's ongoing shortage of supplies, colonists, and funding contributed to their waning influence in the Dawnland after 1713. At the same time, Britain's enlarged claims to political sovereignty in the American Northeast served to increase the importance of land disputes in the Anglo-Wabanaki relationship.

Wabanaki leaders also looked to new strategies to restore their vision of order to the Dawnland. The French had proven unsatisfactory allies during the imperial wars, and a generation of fighting had not restored the incorporative ideal of the Common Pot with the *Bostoniak*. If violence had failed, so had the seventeenth-century agreements, if only because the British newcomers consistently violated them. Most Wabanakis instead attempted to create a new relationship with the *Bostoniak*, with narrower goals than the seventeenth-century iteration. The villages stopped welcoming the British to partake any more in the Common Pot in a manner the colonists could interpret as inviting further colonization. Whereas most Wabanakis permitted the British to reoccupy their coastal enclaves and expressed a desire for trade and friendship, their diplomats emphasized colonists needed to remain in their former towns. Presenting a united front on the issue of new land sales was a vital component of this strategy. Madockawando and Egeremet's unauthorized 1694 cession remained both a potent negative reminder of the importance of unity, and proof that the Wabanakis' success on this front after 1713 was not preordained.

Both the Wabanaki and proprietary vision for the Dawnland frontier rested on shaping the interpretation of seventeenth-century land agreements to suit their contemporary needs. Each in its own way, both visions relied on selective framing of these often vague exchanges to suit a particular ideal of landownership and diplomacy. Disputes over trade, religion, and imperial sovereignty would continue to trouble the Dawnland in the decade following the Treaty of Portsmouth, but nothing else loomed so large as the contest to define the nature of landownership.

The rise of the Boston-based speculators affected the lives of all the residents of the Dawnland frontier after 1713 with mixed portents for the future. The proprietors' use of Indian deeds to justify their claims sowed the seeds for a more cooperative relationship between the speculator-dominated Bay Colony and the Wabanakis. However, the land companies' stubborn refusal to acknowledge any Native interpretation of their claims—abetted by Governor Samuel Shute and the Massachusetts General Court—pushed the region into yet another costly war.

Enterprising Gentlemen

Before they acquired a single acre, the land companies that dominated the eighteenth-century Maine frontier depended on Indians. In an ironic paradox, the speculators owed their post-1713 supremacy to the wartime chaos and devastation they hoped to tame. The military catastrophes of the 1690s had emptied the frontier of colonists east of Wells while creating a class of refugees with nearly worthless land titles. Betting that Massachusetts would win the war and eventually reclaim the frontier, wealthy speculators snapped up many of these titles. When the fighting ceased, these men were waiting in the wings to profit from attempts to recolonize Maine. In 1713 the Massachusetts legislature appointed a Committee of Eastern Claims, which invited everyone with Maine land titles to present their evidence in Boston.[3] The land speculators presented the largest claims, but they were far from alone.

Successive waves of fleeing and returning colonists had left a tangle of claims in Maine by 1713. The evidence presented to the committee was as diverse as the multitude who came forth to show it. Thomas Burroughs, a Boston pewterer, claimed a quarter-acre lot in Falmouth he had purchased in 1683. Jeremiah Dummer, agent for Connecticut and Massachusetts in Britain, filed a claim for 800 acres near Scarborough.[4] In all, the Committee of Eastern Claims received more than 350 separate claims from more than two hundred individuals and families.

The claims reflected the tangled legal landscape shaped by successive governments in Maine punctuated by wars. Around 10 percent of claims relied on oral testimony alone, either from witnesses or their own statements. In some cases this was because the deeds had been lost or destroyed in the war, in others because no deed had ever been written out. A smattering of other colonists filed claims based on town grants (29) or royal or provincial patents (29). Indian deeds comprised just under 13 percent of the total claims for which the committee recorded a source, but they made up over a quarter of the claims northeast of Casco Bay.

Of great significance for the future, Indian deeds tended to be larger than those stemming from other sources, and the largest deeds tended to be the least precise. Twenty-one Indian deeds were among the largest of all claims filed, seven others claimed entire islands, twelve were too vague to measure, and only three, containing 1,000 acres or less, were surveyed into acres.[5]

The men on the committee tasked with evaluating and reconciling these claims had a vested interest in the process. Many of the members of the Committee of Eastern Claims—or their relatives—already held significant investments in Maine property. Committeemen such as Captain Oliver Noyes and Colonel Adam Winthrop had the opportunity to evaluate claims on territory they, too, hoped to possess.[6] During the war years and immediately after the Treaty of Portsmouth, Noyes and Winthrop had been among the investors speculating in abandoned frontier properties.

Winthrop, Noyes, and other large-scale speculators comprised the economic and political elite of Massachusetts society. Most lived in Boston, and many had already amassed fortunes as merchants, mill owners, or land investors outside of Maine. Many sat in the Massachusetts House of Representatives, in the Governor's Council (together called the

General Court), or served as judges. Other proprietors did not themselves hold political office but were bound by blood or kinship to those
who did. Some speculators owned shares in multiple claims. For example, aside from helping found the Pejepscot Proprietors, Adam Winthrop
held shares in the Pemaquid Proprietors and Muscongus Company.[7]
These family and business connections helped bind the Boston speculators together, encouraging them to use their considerable political and
economic influence to advance proprietary interests as a whole in the
courts and legislature. In 1715, at least sixteen of the twenty-eight men
who served on the Governor's Council held land investments in Maine
or western Massachusetts, or had had relatives who did.[8]

Like their seventeenth-century predecessors, these speculators
formed land companies to colonize their claims. These companies took
the names of either the location of their patent, such as the Pejepscot
Proprietors, or of the original buyers, like the Clarke & Lake Proprietors.
Until these patents were surveyed and divided, proprietors owned shares
of unknown acreage. The shares could be divided for sale or doled out
to heirs, resulting in fractions of a fraction changing hands. Over the
years, the four original parts of the Plymouth Patent split into 192, with
8/192 counting as a full share.[9] In 1757, the Kennebeck Proprietors auc-
tioned off shares held by the heirs of an original proprietor amounting to
37/960.[10] Even a fraction of a valuable patent could turn a profit, however.
The four original Kennebeck Proprietors spent £400 in 1661 acquiring
the Plymouth Patent. William Brattle's 6/192 share sold for £149 in 1757.[11]
A 1/8 share in the Pejepscot Patent sold for £140 in 1714; thirteen years
later, it sold for £1000.[12]

However many people held shares in a patent, a small number of
major proprietors wielded decision-making power within the company.
At meeings, the proprietors weighted votes according to shares in the
patent. When the Pemaquid Proprietors met at Boston's Orange Tree
Tavern, Habijah Savage held thirty of the ninety total shares, giving him
one-third of all the votes in company affairs. In contrast, Thomas Ruck's
one share gave him one vote.[13] A Boston merchant named Samuel Waldo
amassed the majority of shares in the Muscongus Patent by the mid-
1730s, allowing him to run that company as he saw fit.[14] Although some
minor shareholders in the land companies hailed from more humble
backgrounds, most ordinary people in Massachusetts would have struggled to pay company fees for the lawsuits, meetinghouse construction,
and other expenses involved in planting towns on a company claim.[15]
The relatively small and egalitarian Wiscasset Company listed the

occupations of its thirty shareholders, which included two goldsmiths, a gunsmith, and a "Mathematicall Instrument maker," who all held a share each out of sixty-four. All members had paid £40 "towards building on and improving" company land by the time of an early resolution in 1733.[16]

Practical considerations further concentrated power within the land companies. Proprietors who lived outside of Boston often missed meetings. Although widows without children inherited their husband's shares, and "spinsters" inherited shares from their parents, and thus legal parity in the company, in practice the male speculators limited their influence. Female proprietors appear in the records only when the company required their signature on deeds or land divisions.[17] Rather than submit every decision to a vote at a general meeting, most companies delegated power to standing committees. Through these committees a handful of men directed the construction of company towns, prosecuted lawsuits against rival proprietors, and collected company dues levied on shares.

Few proprietors wanted to move to a remote and dangerous frontier, so they empowered individuals to serve as their agents on company land. Much like imperial officials in London, the *Bostoniak* struggled to control their far-flung representatives. The Pejepscot Proprietors spent years feuding with an agent in Brunswick who sold land to colonists at prices far lower than instructed.[18] The Kennebeck Proprietors, exasperated with Samuel Goodwin, their agent in Pownalborough, fired him for selling land without permission. However, Goodwin had moved his family into the local courthouse—built with company funds—and refused to leave. After several attempts to evict their truculent former employee, the Proprietors gave up, probably because they had a closet stuffed full of legal skeletons, and they knew Goodwin held the keys.[19]

Although they sometimes failed to control their employees, the proprietors excelled at influencing the men in charge of Massachusetts. Soon after the General Court established the Committee of Eastern Claims to direct the Maine reoccupation, it received a petition from the newly formed Pejepscot Proprietors. In exchange for confirmation of their grant, the company promised to build two towns of fifty families each. In justifying their claim, the proprietors drew upon several types of deeds. They explained the Pejepscot claim descended from "Indian Purchase long since, long possession and Improvement [by early colonists]," from the Ferdinando Gorges claim, and an "Antient Patent from the Councill of Plymouth."[20] The Pejepscot Proprietors also took the committee on a three-week trip to view the company claim. Although the frontier may have been rugged, the journey was not; the Proprietors spent £43 on food and liquor. Their total outlay for the tour—£109—equaled almost 10 percent of their expense buying the title to the patent the year before.[21] While the proprietors may have spared no expense winning their favor, several members of the committee needed no persuasion. Of the eight-man committee, two (Oliver Noyes and Adam Winthrop) were Pejepscot Proprietors, and a third (Edward Hutchinson) had a son in the company.[22] The proprietors succeeded in winning over the other five committeemen, who issued a report several weeks later endorsing the Pejepscot plan, while dismissing another proposal to reoccupy a claim above North Yarmouth, noting the petitioner had been unwilling to pay for a tour to visit the spot.[23]

The committee's report described several problems that would bedevil frontier towns for decades. The report noted, "In Many Places . . . a Regular Settlement is at present hindred, by reason of some persons claiming Large Quantities of Land, which they are not capable themselves to settle, as the Law directs." In others, "Claims may interfere, and so Persons may be fearful of taking up and clearing Land, lest they should be afterwards disturbed in their Possession."[24] The report proved prescient. The problem of so-called dormant claims meant that colonists taking up lots in Maine had to worry about being sued off of their land by distant proprietors wielding old deeds.

In its rigid commitment to absentee property rights, the committee reflected the values held by most members of the General Court. Representatives and members of the Governor's Council were among the wealthiest members of Massachusetts society, and most of those men either held or aspired to landed wealth. As a result, large-scale land speculators in and outside of the legislature ensured the Massachusetts imperial project in Maine unfolded in a manner that would benefit men of their class. The speculator-dominated legislature's unwillingness to extinguish any old or obscure claims protected possible future investments but contributed to an atmosphere of instability for colonists and proprietors alike. As late as 1749, William Douglass remarked in his *Summary, Historical and Political* of Britain's North American colonies, "Most of the Grants and Conveyances in [Maine], are not to be found upon Record, which occasions great Confusion in Claims."[25]

Southwest of the Pejepscot Patent, smaller-scale town proprietors managed the resettlement of the abandoned communities around Casco Bay. These town proprietors operated like miniature versions of the big companies, with the bounds of their claims encompassing a town, rather than tens of thousands of acres. The proprietors of communities like Scarborough, Falmouth, and North Yarmouth included a few large-scale speculators in their ranks, along with judges, military men, and wealthy Boston merchants.[26] All the absentee proprietors viewed their holdings, and the communities around them, as investments rather than homes.

Regardless of the size of their investments, all proprietors needed to build towns both to shore up and profit from their often-contested claims. For this task, they relied on the cooperation of frontier residents. Soon after arriving in Maine, they challenged the speculators for control over their communities. Clashing ideas about land use and ownership formed the heart of the struggle.

Frontier, Unsettled

Most Maine colonists did not seek adventure and danger; they wanted to live in stable, prosperous communities. Like their contemporaries in southern New England towns, prospective colonists sought to live with neighbors like themselves in homogeneous communities of like-minded people. The organ of civil government, the town meeting, reflected the New England desire for consensus. Massachusetts law granted the local franchise to any inhabitant with an estate of £20, allowing broad participation in government.[27] However, the goal of this participation was not open debate but the achievement of consensus for town decisions.[28] Town records reflected this pursuit of harmony by seldom recording the number of votes cast on a given issue and rarely noting dissent. New Englanders regarded the power to admit new members into the community as a vital tool for maintaining local cohesion.

Clashing goals put the proprietors at odds with residents of frontier towns. The proprietors administered company towns until they grew enough for incorporation, and even afterward controlled the undivided land surrounding them. In most cases they sold rights to lots of land—making the buyers inhabitants—rather than shares in the undivided land of prospective townships, which would confer proprietary rights as well. Absentee proprietors operating on a smaller scale than the Pejepscot and Muscongus companies exercised similar control over the resettlement of many abandoned towns like Scarborough, Falmouth, and North Yarmouth. In both cases, the absentee proprietors operated as investors, making decisions they thought increased the value of their landholdings. The proprietors aimed to give or sell away small portions of land at a low price, then allow the rest of their land to appreciate in value as a town grew up around it. If forced to choose between creating a stable community or a profitable one, they opted for the latter course. In contrast, colonists wanted better land or larger lots for themselves, and the power to grant the surrounding vacant land to willing settlers at their discretion.

Maine's reputation as a dangerous and difficult frontier aggravated this divide by deterring potential colonists, making stability or profit difficult to attain. Rather than hazard Maine's rocky soil, short growing season, and risk of Indian wars, most people cast about for better options. As a result, Maine colonists tended to be poor, temporary, or recent European immigrants—sometimes all three. Reverend Thomas Smith, a Harvard-educated preacher who visited Falmouth several times before settling permanently in 1726, described the community as containing "Fifty-six families, such as they were, most of them very poor," including some soldiers "that had found wives on the place."[29]

For their part, frontier colonists resented when absentee speculators foisted temporary tenants onto their communities. Inhabitants of Georgetown asked Colonel Edward Hutchinson to remove his tenant in 1719, noting "he will be a person that will not be very acceptable to the Town we being all very unwilling that he Should be an Inhabitant amongst us."[30] James Parker complained to a House committee created to oversee the resettlement of North Yarmouth that most of the dozen arrivals in 1727 "are Tennants Which we Did not Expect, and Humbly Desire that this may be prevented."[31] Of the newcomers who took up lots on their own behalf, Parker complained, most were "more Ready to sell and let Out than To Settle themselves."[32]

Despite carping by speculators and colonists about the suitability of landholders, a deficit of quantity, not quality, hamstrung efforts to rebuild Maine towns. In 1715, the Pejepscot Proprietors offered to give away 100-acre lots to the first fifty families who moved to the planned towns of Brunswick and Topsham. Subsequent residents could buy 100-acre lots for £5. These and subsequent enticements failed to attract many colonists. Lot number eight in Brunswick changed hands three times in two years as a succession of grantees failed to build anything on it.[33] The company shipped in 160 Irish Protestants in 1718 to make up the shortfall.[34] The Clarke & Lake Proprietors followed suit, contracting with Anglo-Irishman Robert Temple to bring over five shiploads of Irish colonists, although few stayed long, "for Fear of the Indians," Temple later recalled.[35]

As the colonists struggled to raise their crops of corn, barley, wheat, rye, beans, flax, and potatoes (introduced in the early eighteenth century), they sought other sources of subsistence and income.[36] Many grazed livestock on their own meadowland or town commons. Colonists kept gardens, some hunted, and others fished in nearby rivers.[37] In lean times some families turned to digging for clams.[38] Large numbers of fishermen plied the coasts in small shallops and ketches, some based in the farming communities, others in fishing villages scattered along the coast.[39]

Their quest to achieve economic competency in difficult circumstances soon brought resident colonists into conflict with the absentee proprietors. Casting about for ways to supplement their income, many residents engaged in the lumber trade, while others pushed the proprietors to expand land grants or tried to seize greater local control over the distribution of property. Maine was home to rich stands of timber. Agents of the Royal Navy marked the tallest white pine trees for the king's use, waging an uphill battle against illegal logging throughout the eighteenth century.[40] By law, all other trees belonged to whoever owned the land on which they stood. However, Maine's vast stands of trees on vacant, absentee-held tracts posed a tempting target for unscrupulous timber cutters. Frontier residents joined gangs of loggers operating from coastal vessels to supply growing numbers of sawmills in Maine to provide masts, spars, planks, and firewood to consumers throughout New England. Farmers could engage in logging during the winter, when logs were easier to transport, then sell them to ships on the coast or down-river in the spring in time for planting.[41] Loggers operating from ships cut indiscriminately and cared for little besides profit, drawing the ire of resident and absentee proprietors alike.[42] But some colonists logged on absentee claims in the teeth of resistance by the proprietors and their agents—an action with political significance, indicating a disregard for absentee land claims. The low number of colonists and sparse documentation for the 1710s obscure the extent of illegal frontier logging between 1713 and 1722, but after the conclusion of Dummer's War in 1727, frontier residents took it up with a vengeance, incurring a flurry of complaints and lawsuits by the proprietors.

Although timber thieves frustrated the absentee proprietors, residents who challenged their claim to unoccupied land posed a far greater threat to their title. In unincorporated Brunswick, inhabitants held meetings they proclaimed to be "Leagual," although the Pejepscot Proprietors' position on the matter remains unclear. In some towns during the 1710s and 1720s, clerks specified meetings with designations such as the "Legall Town Meetting of the proprietors free holders and other inhabitants" in Arundel, and the "Legal Town meeting of the freeholders etc. of said

Town" of Falmouth, both in 1719.[43] In Brunswick, selectman and clerk Joseph Heath simply recorded "Leagual" meetings, including a May 8, 1719, gathering that included a town vote granting Brunswick inhabitants the power to strip landownership from anyone who did not build or improve on it within "the Space of halfe a year."[44] By law, only the town proprietors—in this case the Pejepscot Company—had the power to grant or revoke land titles. Falmouth residents joined those of Brunswick in asserting municipal control over local land, voting to revoke any grant unsettled after six months.[45] But Falmouth voters went further, assuming authority to grant land "as persons shall come to receive them: such as the selectmen shall approve of."[46] Voters granted a number of three-acre house lots on the condition that grantees improve and reside on them without resale "for seven years next to come, unless driven off by a War."[47] By asserting the authority of municipal officials to distribute land to willing residents (and, by implication, not tenants), Falmouth residents challenged the untrammeled property rights of the absentee proprietors.

Returning refugees to neighboring Scarborough opted for a different strategy to obtain the legal authority to distribute town land, simply declaring themselves proprietors in 1720. Because Scarborough had been abandoned before the 1692 law mandating the creation of distinct town proprietors, no such body had yet existed. Although they held meetings under that name, the newly minted Scarborough Proprietors behaved like a town meeting, assigning votes per person rather than by share.[48] Their first act reserved the white pine timber in the commons for use of the town, rather than proprietors, forever.[49] The proprietors also banned any nonresident from calling a meeting and levied a £1 3s. 4d. fee on any absentee grants they confirmed.[50]

While challenging absentee dominance over local affairs, the Scarborough Proprietors also placed former tenants on equal footing with wealthy elites. John Libby III—lifelong Scarborough resident until its abandonment in 1690—had called the first meeting, even though he had held land as a tenant on the 1,170-acre estate of Captain Joshua Scottow. When Boston merchant Timothy Prout, Scottow's heir, presented deeds for a total of 2,750 acres and a further four square miles at a 1720 meeting, the proprietors—including some of Scottow's former tenants—refused to admit him as a member unless he allowed his vote to be weighed the same as every other man's. If Prout's votes had been weighed according to his share of Scarborough land, he would have been able to run future meetings as he saw fit, which was what the merchant had in mind. Asked to relinquish that power by an assembly of people he thought should be his tenants, Prout, who considered the proceedings illegal, refused.[51]

Colonists across the Maine frontier moved to assert municipal control over vacant lands to benefit local communities at the expense of absentee investor claims. In response, speculators rallied to defend their property.[52] The ensuing clashes added to the atmosphere of uncertainty on the frontier, one that was already high. As a result, towns and land companies alike had difficulties attracting new colonists to Maine.

Boston blacksmith Bartholomew Flagg spoke to a concern on everyone's mind in the years after 1713. Flagg agreed to take up a lot in North Yarmouth, intending to "Settle on it in person" with his family, but his wife balked after hearing about "the Danger of the Indians." Flagg informed the town proprietors he could "by no means Prevail with her to live there."[53]

At the same time that would-be colonists like Flagg fretted over the risk of war breaking out with the Wabanakis, the ambitions of the land companies made that prospect ever more likely. Even as they worked to ensure colonists acknowledged their title to frontier lands, the speculators lobbied to convince the Wabanakis to do the same. And just like the colonists, the Wabanakis had their own ideas about the nature of landownership that shaped their response.

Resettling the Dawnland

For the Wabanakis, the rise of the Boston-based land companies was a major—but far from the only—factor forcing them to rethink their stance toward New England. Wartime losses and the decline of French power raised the potential cost of further military confrontation with the British, which gave strength to leaders advocating a more conciliatory approach. A Penobscot sagamore named Querabannet told Massachusetts governor Joseph Dudley in 1714 his people wished to achieve friendship with the British "as [it] was in our Grand Fathers Days."[54] Even the most optimistic Wabanakis did not expect that friendship to be on the same terms, however. The British had proven unwilling to modify their land use practices, which the Indians learned were incompatible with their own. They made clear numerous times after 1713 that the presence of colonists ruined an area as a resource for hunting or fishing.[55]

The reduced numbers of Wabanakis rebuilding their communities bore testimony to the human cost of the war in the Dawnland. In all, perhaps 2,500 Wabanakis lived in five major villages for at least part of the year, with the Pigwackets, Amarascoggins, and small, unaffiliated family bands contributing several hundred people more to the total.[56] Some chose to remain in the two major mission villages of St. Francis (Odanak) and Becancour (Wowenock) near the St. Lawrence River, which between them contained about 900 people. Another 400 Wulstuk-wiuks lived in Meductic on the St. John River. Perhaps 750 Penobscots returned to Penawabskik on the Penobscot River, while 500 Kennebecs resettled Norridgewock along the Kennebec River. Smaller numbers of Amarascoggins lived in the villages of Amaseconti and Naracomigog on the upper Kennebec and Androscoggin Rivers, respectively. The Pig-wackets lived in a village by that name on the upper Saco.[57] The last two groups had been put under the most pressure from British incursions, and their populations declined accordingly as the eighteenth century wore on. Along with disease and wartime casualties, growing numbers of Pigwackets and Amarascoggins decided either to move to the rela-tive safety of the Canadian villages or to live in smaller family bands, in most cases in locations where they would be less likely to encounter colonists.[58]

As the Wabanakis rebuilt their communities in the Dawnland, they also had to reassess their relationship with the French. Wabanakis had entered a second imperial war (1703–13) in North America against the English more from a desire to preserve their alliance with the French than a new grievance with Massachusetts. The lackluster Franco-Wabanaki performance in that conflict—coupled with growing Gallic inability to keep their Native partners supplied—tested that relation-ship as never before. Worse, British negotiators at Portsmouth in 1713 informed the assembled Indians that the French had ceded much of the Acadian peninsula to them.[59] Outraged Wabanakis confronted their res-ident missionaries on the subject. The priests were only able to deflect the questions by (accurately) insisting that the treaty language was vague on the subject of boundaries, therefore (falsely) arguing the French had not, in fact, granted away Native land without permission.[60] The Wabanakis learned just what their previous help to the French had won them when tensions with Massachusetts mounted over the speculators' incursions after 1715. When a delegation of Kennebecs asked Governor Philippe de Rigaud de Vaudreuil if they could depend on his help in driving away the newcomers, he promised to send them arms and ammunition in secret. "Is this how a father helps his children?" asked the Kennebecs. Vaudreuil lamely promised he would "engage other Indian nations" to help but received mocking laughter in response. The Kennebecs informed their host that they would unite to drive out *all* foreigners if they so pleased. The Indians departed unconvinced by the governor's offer to lead them against the British in person, perhaps because he was in his seventies. According to one Jesuit's assessment, dissatisfaction with the French spread along with the news throughout Wabanaki villages.[61]

Rather than a dramatic new departure in the Franco-Wabanaki relationship, this disappointing episode marked a continuation of French overpromising and failing to deliver, which had been a feature of the alliance since the 1690s.[62] In truth, Vaudreuil and his colleagues could do little but fret over their situation. Although most of New France remained intact, a quarter century of warfare in Europe had taken a heavy toll on French power in ways especially devastating to its colonies. The war had ruined the kingdom's finances, requiring a period of fiscal retrenchment. The French navy dwindled, felled not by enemy cannons but by drastic budget cuts that left most ships decommissioned in port. The fleet did not recover for a half century. The network of Indian alliances that shielded New France against the British depended on gifts for Native American diplomacy and ships to bring them there. British naval superiority after 1713 meant that the Wabanakis could depend on neither as French allies during wartime.[63]

Preoccupied with their own difficulties after the Treaty of Utrecht, French officials in Quebec had little to say about Wabanaki land claims at all. They had no direct knowledge of the disputed lands in question, though Jesuits like Sebastian Rasles were happy to support Wabanaki interpretations of their post-1713 borders that were likely to provoke confrontation with Massachusetts.

Realizing that British behavior had made their seventeenth-century ideal of a close, reciprocal relationship unworkable and that the French were becoming less reliable as allies, the Wabanakis developed a new strategy of containment. From 1713 on, Wabanaki speakers invited the British to reoccupy their "antient Plantations," but nothing more.[64] They "desire a line might be run," Judge Samuel Sewall, a participant in numerous discussions on the issue, noted in 1717.[65] They differed on how to achieve that goal, however. Far from new, the divide between hard-liners and Wabanakis favoring negotiation with Massachusetts (which historian David Ghere first identified as the Confrontational and Conciliatory rather than pro-French or pro-British factions) had existed since the late seventeenth century.[66] A growing number of Wabanakis advocated a more conciliatory position toward the Bay Colony by 1713. Previous military successes enabled them to use the threat of violence

while attempting to negotiate for a clear boundary between the Dawnland and Massachusetts. They doubted continued military resistance—
with or without French help—would preserve the integrity of their land.
A minority faction of holdouts (concentrated in the Canadian villages,
although with some supporters closer to the frontier) refused to acknowledge the legitimacy of British towns almost anywhere in the Dawnland
and opposed any reoccupation of abandoned British communities, proposing the Saco River as an acceptable boundary between Maine and the
Common Pot.[67] Articulating their position in 1717, a Kennebec named
Wiwurna declared to Governor Shute: "We don't understand how our
land has been purchased. What has been allowed was by our gift."[68]
Bound up with that statement was the assumption that this "gift" could
be revoked, unlike a sale. The hard-liners were more likely to threaten (or
enact) violent reprisals against Massachusetts's attempts to expand, and
more likely to seek French help in doing so. The fluid nature of Wabanaki
band structure meant that individuals and families shifted support for
leaders representing different poles in the debate. The French and British
both tried to influence different sagamores by dispensing commissions,
gifts, and other rewards, but these diplomatic efforts mattered less than
whether or not Massachusetts respected the integrity of the Dawnland.[69]

Although they did not always agree on methods, the Wabanakis
expressed broad agreement on the meaning and significance of the 1713
Treaty of Portsmouth. They believed the agreement signaled a fresh start.
Massachusetts governor Joseph Dudley gave them cause to believe this
was so when he insisted during the ratification that the treaties all the way
back to the hated 1693/4 agreement between Madockawando and William Phips "must be forgotten and put away," a statement that garnered
immediate agreement from the Indians.[70] Querabannet, a Penobscot
who often spoke for the more accommodationist Wabanakis, claimed
with some hyperbole in 1714 that "we Jump for Joy" at the prospect of
future good relations.[71] Well he might have, if Querabannet believed the
Bostoniak wanted to sweep away the Madockawando cession.

The Wabanaki position began from the shared assumption that economic considerations (in this case, the old land deeds) could not be
divorced from political relationships. The relationships begun by those
deeds could, all Wabanakis believed, be subject to renegotiation when
the needs of the participants changed. In all subsequent negotiations
with Massachusetts the Wabanakis therefore sought to tie discussion
of land exchanges to larger discussions of political events. Wabanaki
speakers believed their destruction of most Maine towns between 1688

and 1713 and the subsequent peace treaty mattered more when determining the future Anglo-Wabanaki border than a bundle of old deeds. For the Wabanakis, the deeds of seventeenth-century negotiations for land beyond the coast represented outdated totems of a different set of circumstances. They argued—correctly in most cases—that agreements between various sagamores and seventeenth-century proprietors like Christopher Lawson and Thomas Lake had been intended to permit truck houses and surrounding residences, not towns like Brunswick or Georgetown. Wabanakis recognized different usufruct rights to land, so letting a proprietor construct a mill or truck house did not signify a carte blanche to build Falmouth-sized towns up the Kennebec River. In any case, the Wabanakis believed the 1688–1713 warfare, followed by the Treaty of Portsmouth, nullified those seventeenth-century agreements.

Wabanaki statements at a 1717 meeting of assembled Pigwackets, Amarascoggins, Kennebecs, and Penobscots with Massachusetts governor Samuel Shute and members of his council also revealed a broad consensus that the new Anglo-Wabanaki border should be drawn where the line of former British colonization ended. Wiwurna, a Kennebec leader whom the French considered their best hope to foment anti-British sentiment in Norridgewock, and as far removed from Querabannet on the Wabanaki political spectrum as possible, emphasized that colonists returning to former towns did so "at our request" and that they were welcome, but "We Desire there may be no further Settlements made."[72] Speaking the next day, Querabennet concurred. "In the [1713] Articles of Peace," he told Shute, "the English should Settle where their Predecessors had done: and we agree to those Articles . . . And Desire the English may Settle as Far as ever they have done."[73] Although Wiwurna's pointed refusal to let Shute interrupt or intimidate him contrasted with Querabannit's more reassuring style (and provoked Shute into threatening to leave the gathering in a huff), in substance there was little difference between their positions.[74]

The difference that *did* prove consequential was the one between the Wabanakis and the Bay Colony's understanding of what constituted former possession. When Indian speakers invited colonists back to their old towns, they meant the places Britons had built homes, mills, and farms on. For the land companies dominating Massachusetts government, former possession also encompassed places to which they had bought title but had not yet physically occupied. This view enabled Governor Shute to believe he spoke the truth when he assured the Wabanakis at Arrowsic in 1717 that "we will not take an Inch of their Land: nor will we part with an Inch of our own," even as the Pejepscot Proprietors constructed the new town of Brunswick.[75] Of the misunderstandings that plagued the Anglo-Wabanaki relationship during the eighteenth century, none proved quite so intractable as this one stemming from different concepts of ownership.

"Ideoms of Speech Necessary for the Understanding Thereof"

Even if the discussions between Wabanaki and Bay Colony leaders after 1713 had been defined by an overflow of goodwill and a desire for perfect understanding, linguistic and cultural differences would have made that goal elusive. The backgrounds and mandates of the handful of interpreters tasked with conveying ideas as complex as "sovereignty" and "property" made that outcome even less likely. The three men who served as interpreters for Massachusetts spent their boyhoods as captives (after seeing relatives killed) in Wabanaki villages during the 1688–1713 warfare. Samuel Jordan, Joseph Bean, and John Gyles all held commissions in the colony's militia, commanded troops, and were partisan supporters of the Massachusetts imperial project.[76] Gyles doubled as a spymaster for the Bay Colony, cultivating a network of paid informants who, he bragged to the lieutenant governor in 1727, kept him abreast "of any Councill or afear of moment Round the Continent."[77]

Part of the interpreters' service may have involved deliberately mistranslating treaties to the Wabanakis. Thomas Bannister, a Boston merchant hoping to secure royal permission for a new colony east of the Kennebec, informed the Board of Trade in London, "I have been present when an Article of the Peace has run in one sence in the English, and quite contrarie in the Indian, by the Governour's express order."[78] Several historians have used Bannister's accusation to undercut the credibility of Massachusetts translators.[79] However, Bannister's name does not appear on the long list of gentlemen attending the Treaty of Portsmouth or subsequent conferences, and his accusation, while plausible, does not mention specific cases.

French Jesuits living in Norridgewock and Penawabskik served as scribes and translators for Wabanaki parishioners while at the same time serving their royal masters with the same enthusiasm as their British counterparts. As they worked to foil the creation of a strong Anglo-Wabanaki relationship, Fathers Sebastian Rasles and Etienne Lauverjat both echoed Bannister's allegations of British duplicity during treaty negotiations.[80] Of the two, Rasles had the more forceful presence. The priest waded into the thick of Kennebec politics during his time in Nor-ridgewock, throwing his influence behind confrontational leaders in councils. In that role Rasles wrote letters to Massachusetts on behalf of the Kennebecs and other Wabanakis. He also wrote personally to Massa-chusetts officials, promising to eject any Kennebecs from his church who visited England, mocking Bay Colony interpreters ("they speak nothing but Gibberish"), and claiming to have a veto power over all debates in Norridgewock.[81] Next to the bombastic Rasles, Etienne Lauverjat cut a less impressive figure in Penawabskik. Soon after his arrival in the vil-lage in 1718, his parishioners bullied him into writing a letter smoothing over the murders of two Penobscots at the hands of British fishermen, much to the annoyance of Governor Vaudreuil.[82] In fairness to Lauver-jat, the Penobscots had a much stronger conciliatory faction than the Kennebecs during the 1710s (speculators claiming Penobscot land did not act until 1719), and the priest had to compete for influence with a pair of mixed Franco-Wabanaki traders boasting a pedigreed lineage. Descended from a minor French noble turned fur trader, Baron Jean-Vincent d'Abbadie de Saint-Castin, and Pidianske, daughter of Madock-awando, Joseph and Barenos continued their father's lucrative trading business.[83] "A confusing mixture of French and Savage," according to one governor in Quebec, they grew up among their mother's people, accepted officers' commissions from the French, and, according to Lau-verjat, flooded Penawabskik with alcohol as they undermined both his diplomatic and religious mission at every turn.[84] Unfortunately for Lau-verjat, everyone knew that priests were replaceable, but well-connected Franco-Wabanakis descended from a great sagamore's family were not. Lauverjat suffered on (though not silently, as his repeated complaints to his superiors attest) until the early 1730s, when French officials removed him out of fear he would alienate Joseph (who had by then inherited the Baronetcy of Saint-Castin) and his brother Barenos.[85]

Even if the cluster of dedicated partisans who translated the Anglo-Wabanaki conversations after 1713 did not wish to distort the meaning of previous deeds and treaties, the transfer from speaker to interpreter to recorder to (sometimes) printer complicates any attempt to locate inten-tional deception. Some records contain phrases that colonists clearly put in Indigenous mouths, including a 1740 conference where several sagamores, lacking money to pay damages for cattle their people killed, "pawned the honour of their Government," promising to pay next spring.[86] While it strains credulity for Wabanakis to make an offer to "pawn" any-thing, Samuel Denny, who attended the conference, promised to "pawn my honour for the truth" of a claim he made to Edward Hutchinson in a 1766 letter.[87] In this case, the sentiment, if not the phrase, was probably genuine. John Gyles swore an oath after a 1714 conference describing how he approached his job. "The aforegoing Questions and Answers are the Substance of the Conferences," he said, and were "Truly rendered as spoke on either side allowing only for Ideoms of Speech necessary for the understanding thereof."[88]

When Gyles and his colleagues merely employed idioms and when they deliberately manipulated the oral and written record remains a subject of debate, but in both cases, they played an outsize role in shaping the nature of negotiations.

Deception, Sovereignty, and Property

The decline of the Anglo-Wabanaki accord of 1713 presents a paradox: Bay Colony representatives' repeated lies about what treaties said regarding Native sovereignty proved far less of an obstacle to peace than much more genuine differences over property.

Massachusetts governors had been inserting clauses of Indigenous subjugation into written Anglo-Wabanaki agreements since 1693, always rooting the practice in the often repudiated Madockawando-Egeremet "submission" and cession to Governor William Phips. The brazenness of the practice in the face of periodic Wabanaki contradiction is, on its face, textbook imperial arrogance. Despite these written statements of Native subjection, no Massachusetts administrations attempted to make those claims a reality. Justices of the peace did not hear cases in Meductic, and the General Court did not levy taxes on Pigwacket.[89] Instead, the Bay Colony continued to negotiate with the Wabanakis like the sovereign power they were, while posturing for the benefit of imperial officials in London. Massachusetts claims of sovereignty over the Wabanakis was one of countless face-saving lies on both sides of the Atlantic that oiled the gears of empire. In a similar vein, in 1736 Governor Jonathan Belcher described £200 worth of diplomatic gifts to the Penobscots in 1736 as "about £35 sterling" to the Duke of Newcastle, thus allowing Belcher to portray the Penobscots as grateful subjects rather than powerful neighbors.[90]

Most governors knew not to press the issue over sovereignty during conferences with the Indians or had interpreters like Joseph Bean finesse the matter. When Samuel Shute made the mistake of contesting the point at Arrowsic with Wiwurna in 1717, he received a rude shock. "Other

Governours have said to us that we are under no other Government but our own," Wiwurna informed him. When Shute tried to interrupt him and insisted the Wabanakis "be Obedient to King George," Wiwurna replied they would, on the condition that "we are not Molested in the Improvement of our Lands," a proviso that violated any meaningful British definition of the term.[91] Most of the time, Massachusetts interpreters did not interpret the written treaty statements of Native subjugation to their Wabanaki audience.

The ongoing divide in how Wabanakis and Britons defined treaties also conversely helped reduce the potential for Massachusetts duplicity to cause problems. The Wabanakis continued to regard treaties—and deeds—as expressions of an ongoing relationship, to be renegotiated when needs of the parties changed. (This linking of economics with politics explains their argument that Wabanaki success in destroying some inland Maine outposts voided some old deeds.) Massachusetts leaders insisted on the permanency of written treaties and deeds. When Wiwurna spoke to Governor Shute at Arrowsic in 1717, he told the governor, "We have done with the Treaty at Piscataqua [meaning Portsmouth] and now proceed to a new one." Shute asked if the Wabanakis "Ratify and Confirm former Treaties," and Wiwurna replied they did.[92] To Shute, this meant the Wabanakis agreed that their "submission" to King George, and all other terms contained in previous documents, still applied. For the Wabanakis, acknowledging the previous treaties meant recognition of other gatherings to reconcile Massachusetts and the Wabanakis, which were subject to renegotiation when participants would "proceed to a new one." Since successive administrations made no efforts to enforce written (and usually untranslated) claims of sovereignty, the discrepancy did not torpedo the Anglo-Wabanaki relationship.

In contrast, Massachusetts speculators had every intention of making their land claims in the Dawnland a reality. The land companies' drive to build new towns after 1715 ruined any chance contradictory interpretations of the old agreements could coexist. Discussions in 1714—even before the first colonist arrived in the new town of Brunswick—boded ill for the new peace. At a meeting that year to confirm the Treaty of Portsmouth, various Wabanaki leaders engaged in what can only be called competitive hosting with Governor Joseph Dudley. A man the British recorded as John Dony rose to inform Dudley that "Cochecha [present-day New Hampshire] is his land, but the English are very welcome to live there." Ouinamus and Nimpcoot, the "right heires of [Saco] River" followed suit, inviting the colonists to return. Dudley responded by inviting

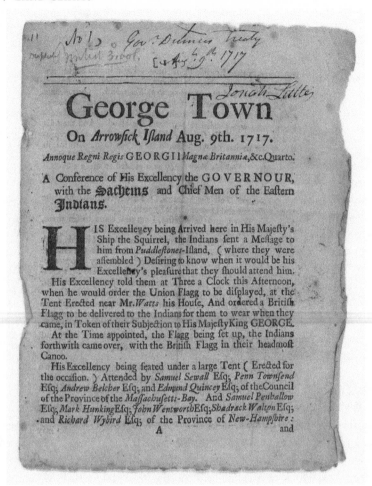

FIGURE 3.1. Published copy of the Treaty of Arrowsic later acquired by proprietor Josiah Little. Courtesy of the Maine Historical Society.

Dony's people to live on British land and insisted the Saco belonged to Massachusetts, emphasizing Wabanaki neighborliness there was not a goodwill gesture but an obligation. Both sides professed themselves pleased with the exchange.[93] By maintaining their status as the original grantors even of areas long occupied by colonists, the Wabanakis indicated they would not quietly submit to new British incursions.

The Wabanakis responded in a targeted manner to specific Massachusetts violations of their land rights. The Clarke & Lake claimants founded Georgetown on Arrowsic Island in 1715, and the Pejepscot Proprietors followed suit with Brunswick soon after.[94] The Kennebecs did not wait long to make known their displeasure with these new towns at the mouth of their river. Young men destroyed colonial property and tried to frighten the trespassers away.[95] In 1717 the Kennebecs emphasized their position by choosing prominent hard-liner Wiwurna to speak for them at a conference with Massachusetts governor Shute at Arrowsic. Wiwurna's staunch refusal to let Shute browbeat him into submission contributed to the governor threatening to sail home early. Enough of the other Wabanakis in attendance—especially the Penobscots, whose land remained unspoiled—prevailed in a subsequent council to replace Wiwurna with the milder-talking Penobscot Querabannet and continue the talks.[96]

Later that year the Massachusetts General Court published an official account of the Arrowsic talks, beginning a practice that lasted until the 1750s of publishing all major conferences with the Wabanakis. The Arrowsic document (described as a "Treaty") included descriptions of attendees, a transcript of talks, and a copy of articles supposedly agreed to.

The written version of the Treaty of Arrowsic, unlike the verbal exchange, was a product of the Massachusetts interpretation of events and served as a blueprint of the proprietary vision for Maine, in which Indians and colonists accepted the property rights and paternalistic guidance of the speculators, who had also introduced the Reverend Joseph Baxter to them at Arrowsic in the hope the Indians would welcome his missionary efforts. Massachusetts delegates inserted an article into the written treaty granting the British the right to "Improve all the Lands which they have formerly Possessed, *and all they have obtained a Right and Title unto*" (emphasis mine).[97] Even the conciliatory Wabanakis had never agreed to this.

However, if the treaty reflected elites' unbending commitment to the sanctity of land deeds, it did not envision complete Native dispossession. The sentence after "Right and Title" proclaimed "mutual and reciprocal Benefit and Advantage to them and us," and a desire to "Cohabit" in the Dawnland—albeit on British terms.[98] Massachusetts delegates also believed that colonial town growth would gradually frustrate Native strategies of resource use.[99] The 1715 report by the Committee of Eastern Claims, advocating the construction of a town in Merrymeeting Bay, noted "a Strong settlement there will greatly tend to dislodge the Indians from their principall Fishery, keep them from their chief carrying places, and be possibly a way of removing them further from us, if another war should happen."[100]

Of equal significance, the "Right and Title" that Shute and other Massachusetts representatives claimed they had to the Dawnland stemmed from Indian purchase, not royal grants. Although Bay Colony representatives inserted Native admissions of King George's political supremacy into the treaty, they did not attempt to attach ownership of landed property to this fact. This choice indicates Massachusetts leaders had a commitment to acknowledging Native ownership of unsold lands. The proprietors' acceptance of previous and current Native landownership was a necessary, if not sufficient, ingredient for a lasting peace on the frontier. However, the proprietors' stubborn refusal to budge from their strict defense of all old land claims made continued peace after 1717 increasingly unlikely.

That likelihood dropped close to zero in 1720. That year a new land company (the Muscongus Proprietors) tried to take advantage of the hated Madockawando land cession to build towns on Penobscot land.[101] Put another way, the Muscongus Proprietors tried to use the most controversial deed in existence to intrude on the largest tribe living near the Maine frontier. Until that point the Penobscots had played an important role in tempering the militancy of the rising hard-line faction among their Kennebec neighbors. Like the Kennebecs, the Penobscots permitted colonists to return to places they had occupied before 1688, which chiefly meant a scattering of fishing hamlets on the coast around Pemaquid. The arrival of the Muscongus agents soon soured the Penobscots' relationship with Boston.

The Muscongus Company's attempt to negotiate with the Penobscots (chronicled by the Reverend Thomas Fayerweather, one of the proprietors) reveals the extent to which concerns over property drove Anglo-Wabanaki relations. The proprietors conducted the negotiations independently of the formal organs of Massachusetts government, although they operated with its approval. Indeed, membership in the Muscongus Company and the General Court overlapped to such a degree that discussing them as two distinct entities risks obscuring their intimate ties. In May 1720, three agents deputed by the company sailed to the St. Georges River to show the Madockawando deed to the relevant Penobscots and offer them further payment if they would "confirm our former deed unto us."[102] At no point did the proprietors consider abandoning their plans if the Penobscots rejected the deed. When the agents presented the request through an interpreter to the local sagamore, a man named Nimquid, he did just that, denying that Madockawando "had any right to this place." Nimquid tried to delay the agents, telling them he could do nothing without consulting the other sagamores, although Fayerweather believed the Penobscots were willing to sell. But the proprietors missed the veiled threat behind Nimquid's polite warning that if they built a storehouse on his land before they received his answer "he did not know who might come here and do damage to Em," and instead prodded Nimquid about the Madockawando deed again—a foolish choice that wore out their welcome. Nimquid again refused to acknowledge the deed, proclaiming "he did not love abundance of talk" and urged the agents to "use discretion . . . and that he had said all he had to say relating to it."[103]

Fayerweather and his companions received news on their way home to Boston that should have given them further pause. Two sons of Wenangonet, the Penobscot sagamore, had hastened to Captain Samuel Moody at Georgetown to relay their concerns to Governor Shute. They told Moody that "We wonder that any sh[ould] go down to view our land in order to [make] a settlement without our knowledge or consent." Wenangonet's sons also indicated that the Penobscots believed the 1713 treaty had settled the issue of where the British could rebuild: where they had previously occupied, and no farther. Moody—himself a proprietor in Falmouth, and no stranger to these disputes—asked if the Muscongus agents showed the Indians a deed, prompting the by now standard disavowals of his authority to sell land without securing broad consent.[104] Ignoring all of these cues, the Muscongus proprietors planned to obtain a new deed from the Penobscots confirming their entire patent at a meeting in August.

The Muscongus Proprietors sent a larger delegation to Penobscot country for this second meeting, where they received an unusual (for Anglophone witnesses) front seat to Wabanaki decision-making. The Penobscots directed the proprietors to the village of Agemoggan, near where the Penobscot River met the Atlantic coast. Agemoggan contained thirty wigwams and a chapel, with approximately two hundred residents during ordinary times of peak seasonal residence. The community was therefore considerably smaller than the major Penobscot village of Penawabskik. More than one hundred Penobscot men (perhaps two-thirds of the adult male population) had assembled in a large house built in Agemoggan for the meeting. The Indians listened as interpreter Samuel Jordan relayed to them Governor Shute's letter in support of the Muscongus claim.[105] The Penobscots sent the proprietors away several times to hold private councils, from which they also excluded Father Etienne Lauverjat and Joseph Saint-Castin.[106] After extensive deliberations involving the assembled men (who had in all likelihood consulted with the rest of their families), the Penobscots told the Muscongus delegation they would allow a trading house on an island in the Muscongus River, but "their Lands belong to their young men and they could not dispose of them from 'Em." Alongside these considerations of property, the Penobscots "did not care to have the English settle among 'Em," being all too aware of the "difficulties and inconviency the tribe of Indians at Kennebeck" suffered, "which they did carefully avoid."[107]

Try as they might, the Muscongus Proprietors failed to crack the Penobscots' united front against any new incursions. Although the Fayerweather diary contains a rare detailed observation of the Penobscots working out this policy through the painstaking process of achieving group consensus, their methods did not differ from those employed by the Kennebecs or Pigwackets. Wabanaki villages across the Dawnland after 1713 devised and maintained their position on new British arrivals in their country through the same processes in councils seldom recorded by European observers, in discussions that involved the bulk of adult Wabanakis at some point.

At the same time the Muscongus delegation received its final rejection, the Pejepscot and Clarke & Lake Proprietors faced the same resistance from the Kennebecs. A fact-finding committee dispatched by the Massachusetts legislature to investigate the reasons for a rash of threats against new colonists—accompanied by livestock killings—received an unequivocal explanation from the Kennebecs.[108] Local Indians objected to the new incursions north of Merrymeeting Bay, singling out the new Scots-Irish community of Cork sponsored by Clarke & Lake's heirs, and the Pejepscot colonists on Swan Island in the Kennebec River, "all of which the Indians utterly deny to have disposed of." The Kennebecs complained that the signers of the Pejepscot Company's 1684 deed to Richard Wharton "were all [Amarascoggin] Indians (except one) and never had any Right thereto." In addition, the only previous colonists present had built "House of Trade and only so allowed or permitted by the Indians."[109] By the Kennebecs' reasoning, for the speculators to build a town on the site of a former trading post was a grotesque manipulation of an old agreement. Some Kennebecs raised these objections in person to Clarke & Lake colonists in person, threatening to destroy trespassers' buildings and livestock in the process.[110]

Collision

When faced with Kennebec and Penobscot refusal to accept the speculators' interpretations of their claims, Massachusetts leaders faced a
choice—they could urge the land companies to moderate their claims, or
they could back them and risk another costly war. Rather than face this
unpalatable truth, Governor Shute and many members of his council
and the Massachusetts House tried to have their cake and eat it too. They
blamed the French for stirring up the Wabanakis, Sebastian Rasles most
of all.[111] If only the papist firebrand could be removed, they reasoned, the
Wabanakis could be persuaded to accept the speculators' titles. In fairness to Massachusetts, Rasles did his best to give them the impression he
held unchallenged influence among his flock in Norridgewock. Rasles
penned a number of outspoken letters denouncing British perfidy and
trumpeting his own influence among the Kennebecs.[112] In reality, the
cleric wielded far less clout than the British feared or the French wished.
More conciliatory Kennebecs and the traditional shamans opposed his
interference in their affairs. Summing up reports from his network of
informants in 1727, interpreter John Gyles described some of the Kennebecs as theologically "a mixed Crew, many of them Don't Pray, and Sum
ar Wizards [shamans] a mong them."[113] At the same time, the priest's
potential as a conduit for French aid made him an attractive spokesman
for the confrontational faction in Norridgewock.[114] In private correspondence, Rasles admitted the very real limits on his influence, which were
on display for all to see in 1719, when Kennebecs rebuked him in front
of Massachusetts delegates to Norridgewock, insisting he "spooke his
mind, and not theirs."[115]

Governor Shute and the General Court threw their full support behind
the speculators' claims, moving to address the symptoms rather than
the cause of Wabanaki property violence. In a move that quickly back-
fired, Bay Colony delegates at a 1720 talk took four Kennebec sagamores
as hostages to secure a ransom for damaged property. The sagamores
who volunteered to travel to Boston had been outspoken voices for con-
ciliation, and their departure swelled the influence of the hard-liners in
Kennebec councils. Kennebec leaders like Wiwurna responded by inviting like-minded Wabanakis from all the villages to assemble in Norridgewock, finally swamping the conciliatory faction in council.[116] They
also invited French observers, hoping to thereby prompt more direct
French involvement in any resulting war. Perhaps 250 men—nearly half
the available manpower in the Dawnland—heeded the call, including

100 Penobscots spurred on by the recent Muscongus trespasses.[117] The assembled Wabanakis marched to the coast to confront the Massachusetts garrison of Arrowsic (and Shute, who decided to skip the meeting when informed of the Indian delegation's size) to demand the release of the captive sagamores and to assert their arguments for a fair boundary between Massachusetts and the Dawnland.

The assembled Indians read a letter to Captain John Penhallow and his officers that articulated the hard-line Wabanaki position on the question of disputed lands. God had placed them on that land, they said, and the British could claim the land neither by gift, purchase, or conquest. The letter explicitly denied the authority of any Indians who had invited the colonists to reoccupy former towns as influenced by drink and speaking only for themselves. The letter likewise disavowed the old deeds as products of the same colonial rum-pushing trickery. The Wabanakis had driven the unwanted colonists from the Dawnland before, which added rights by conquest to their own birthright. Claiming "all the nation" withdrew its permission for colonists to occupy the Dawnland, the letter asserted the new boundary as the Saco River.[118] Written by Fathers Pierre de La Chasse and Sebastian Rasles, the letter (translated into French, "Sauvage," and Latin) contained evidence of La Chasse's linguistic skills and Rasle's fire-breathing style.[119] It also reflected a desire to present a united front, breaking from the usual practice of individual sagamores signing the document. In place of signatures were totems representing nineteen villages and nations from the Pigwackets to the Algonquins. Claims to speak for groups like the distant Montagnais should probably be read not as the literal truth but as the desire to appear as a united front of numerous allies.[120]

Massachusetts leaders did not believe these claims of unity, but they took the threats of violence against trespassers seriously. The Massachusetts House voted to publish the "Impudent, Sawcy and Insolent Letter," in the belief that it provided a *casus belli* and dispatched additional soldiers to the Maine frontier.[121] The efforts of a handful of Penobscot and Wulstukwiuk sagamores to diffuse the situation did not deter Bay Colony leaders from more drastic actions.[122]

By late 1721, Massachusetts Indian diplomacy had degenerated into a series of kidnapping attempts, some more successful than others, in the forlorn hope that by seizing enough high-profile troublemakers, the province could ensure Wabanaki submission. A company of thirty men arrested Joseph d'Abbadie Saint-Castin for his ostensible role as a French agent among the Penobscots, a move that only served to further alienate his kinsmen from the British.[123] Under pressure from the House, Shute dispatched soldiers to seize Rasles and various Kennebecs whom witnesses had implicated in the ongoing property destruction.[124] In January 1722, Massachusetts militiamen narrowly missed capturing Rasles at Norridgewock when most of the villagers were dispersed for the winter hunting season.[125]

Even as Massachusetts leaders focused their attention on removing Rasles (while avoiding an international incident, as Britain and France were allied in Europe) and on stopping Wabanaki violence against property, proprietary concerns influenced their response.[126] The Governor's Council, which contained a far higher percentage of land speculators (nearly a quarter held shares in Maine land companies), consistently balked at the bellicose proposals emanating from the House, which contained a far smaller percentage of large-scale speculators.[127] A war therefore risked frontier investments without even guaranteeing what the speculators coveted most: Indian acceptance of their titles. When the council spoke of Massachusetts property at risk from the Indians, they made specific statements in defense of "English Claimers and Purchasers" as well as those actually living in Maine.[128] In contrast, the House issued statements in support of the "Just Right and Title of the English Subjects" and the "Honour" of the king but did not single out the speculators' unoccupied claims per se.[129] With less at stake, as well as less experience than the council (many of whom participated in negotiations with the Wabanakis) with actual Indians, the House clamored for action.[130] Incredibly, Shute and his council thought that kidnapping Rasles, Saint-Castin, and a few other hard-line leaders would embolden the conciliatory faction while appeasing the House.

Instead the response achieved what the hard-liners and their French backers could not secure on their own: Native unity. The Wabanakis repaid Massachusetts's kidnapping attempts with interest, plunging the Maine frontier into a bloodless quasi-war. After planting their spring crop, Indians from a number of villages captured sixty-five colonists on the Kennebec River. They released all but five in a final effort to initiate the release of the Kennebec hostages in Boston. Massachusetts leaders did not respond fast enough to prevent further escalations, however. Confrontational Wabanakis stepped up their campaign of property destruction, and in July 1722 they put Brunswick to the torch. Killings soon followed when a militia company led by Captain Johnson Harmon slew several of the sleeping raiders in a night assault.[131] For Wabanakis and colonists living on the frontier, Governor Shute's belated declaration of war on July 25 was merely a formal recognition of an obvious fact.[132]

The rise of the land companies after 1713 had the potential to enhance Wabanaki security. Most of the speculators were committed to a system of land titles rooted in the belief in the importance of Indian deeds. The turbulent nature of competing claims among colonists and speculators only amplified the importance of Native acknowledgment of titles. Against this backdrop, the Wabanaki strategy of establishing a clear boundary between the Dawnland and Massachusetts with the *Bostoniak* stood a plausible chance of success.

However, the resumption of warfare in 1722 proved that the land speculators' commitment to the notion of Native land rights in the abstract was not enough to produce their respect for flesh-and-blood Indians and their demands. The real Indians in the Dawnland maintained their own understandings of ownership and of the previous agreements forming the heart of the proprietors' claims. Enduring Native power meant that any lasting peace in the region would have to incorporate Wabanaki understandings of ownership and reciprocity.

4 /   Breaking—and Making—the Peace, 1722–1727

The flames rose higher, consuming the wood houses arranged in orderly rows. Most of the three hundred residents of Norridgewock had fled. Twenty-six remained, their corpses still on the ground, disturbed only when the victorious militiamen lifted the heads to cut the scalps off. Father Sebastian Rasles, who had lived among the Kennebecs for years, joined them in death. For the militia, each scalp was worth £60, making the lopsided victory all the more sweet. An unknown number of villagers were gunned down as they fled across the Kennebec or drowned attempting to make the crossing. Only three of Captain Johnson Harmon's men died, including a Mohawk warrior who had traveled with two companions to participate in the fighting.[1]

Harmon's attack on Norridgewock was both the province's biggest victory over the Wabanakis in a half century of fighting and a terrible display of Massachusetts vengeance. Judge Samuel Sewall witnessed "great Shouting and Trembling" when Harmon's men returned to Boston brandishing their scalps on August 22, 1724.[2] Boston printer James Franklin (elder brother to the famous Benjamin) published a ballad celebrating the victory, "The Rebels Reward," which included a verse describing the encounter between Harmon's men and the sagamore Mogg's wife and children in the village. "[Mogg's] wife and two young Children / were then dispatch'd with speed / Who sat in tears bewailing / and for their Lives did plead."[3]

Dramatic though it may have been, the Massachusetts victory at Norridgewock ended neither the war nor Wabanaki power. It did,

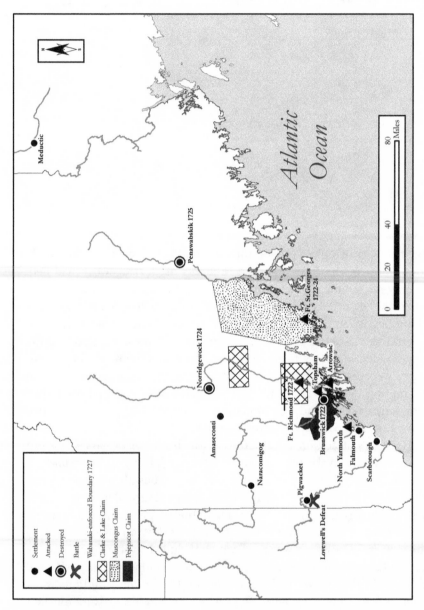

MAP 4.1. Maine frontier in the 1720s.

however, emphasize the major lesson of the Fourth Anglo-Wabanaki War: although their warriors retained the ability to harass the Maine frontier, making the cost of colonization prohibitive, the Indians lacked the strength to achieve a decisive victory without French help. The Wabanakis also learned that as long as the French and British kings remained at peace in Europe, King Louis's subjects in America would not join his Indian allies against New England. That realization—more than their losses at Norridgewock—forced the Wabanakis to reconsider their strategy. By depleting Kennebec numbers and dispersing them to seek refuge either in Canada or with the Penobscots, the battle's primary long-term significance can be found not in ending Indian power in the Dawnland but in shifting its center of gravity east from Norridgewock to the village of Penawabskik on the Penobscot River.

Between 1725 and 1727, the Penobscots succeeded in brokering the most successful Anglo-Wabanaki treaty ever signed in the Dawnland, in the process refashioning Wabanaki power to rest on their status as former proprietors of Maine lands. In a trio of conferences collectively known as Dummer's Treaty (for the prominent role played by Lieutenant Governor William Dummer), the Wabanakis and Massachusetts succeeded in bridging the divide between their different understandings of landownership, diplomacy, deeds, and treaties. Although marred by some of the same misunderstandings and deceptions that affected previous conferences, the strengths of Dummer's Treaty outweighed its weaknesses.

The product of two years of negotiations, Dummer's Treaty confused contemporaries as well as future generations of historians. By the time participants signed the final document in 1727, Massachusetts and Wabanaki diplomats had sailed, paddled, and walked from Casco Bay to Montreal to Boston to haggle over successive drafts. When it concluded, Indian and Massachusetts leaders and even French observers all issued statements attempting to affix their own interpretation onto the proceedings. The treaty represented both an agreement between the participants and a performance for the benefit of distant imperial officials. Paying attention to the role of the speculators—and their land deeds—in the negotiations, however, reveals the treaty's true significance.

Led by the Penobscots, the Wabanakis achieved a diplomatic coup. While compromising on certain land claims, the Wabanakis succeeded in attaching Indian expectations of reciprocity onto most of the old land sales, bridging the divide between different cultures of ownership. The proprietors still clung to their belief in the importance of permanent, exclusive individual ownership of land proved by paper deeds, while the Wabanakis continued to understand land transfers as part of an ongoing relationship. However, as long as they continued to recognize Dummer's Treaty, the Wabanakis would acknowledge the land cessions contained in the seventeenth-century deeds. But the Wabanakis tied recognition of the treaty to Massachusetts's fulfillment of its promises, making the practical validity of certain proprietary titles contingent on the province maintaining friendly diplomatic relations with the Indians.

This blending of property and diplomacy motivated Wabanaki and Massachusetts leaders to establish a working relationship based on Dummer's Treaty after 1727. Even though the two sides did not interpret the agreement in identical ways, and even though speculators sometimes proceeded from misguided conceptions of what took place, Wabanakis and the proprietors dominating Massachusetts benefited more from papering over ongoing differences than scrapping the treaty. As a result, proprietary and Indian notions of landownership helped facilitate cooperation rather than conflict for nearly two decades after 1727.

Contesting Ownership in the Fourth Anglo-Wabanaki War

The Fourth Anglo-Wabanaki War, waged between 1722 and 1727 (also variously named Dummer's War, Father Rasles' War, Lovewell's War, and Gray Lock's War, helped pave the way for a genuine peace because Wabanaki and Massachusetts leaders perceived its futile, indecisive character.[4] Although the wartime violence left a legacy of bitter memories between some colonists and Indians, its destructiveness vindicated moderate leaders on both sides. The Wabanakis held the initiative for the first two years, striking exposed towns and eluding colonial forces. But without French help the Wabanakis lacked the numbers and firepower to score victories like they had in the 1690s and 1703. For their part, Massachusetts forces struggled to bring the more mobile Indians to bay. The Indians abandoned their old villages before advancing militia, moving beyond their reach. Although New France would not send troops, it provided supplies to enable Indian warriors to keep fighting. Despite numerical inferiority, Wabanaki fighters outclassed Massachusetts militia in the first two years of skirmishes. "It is surprising that so small a number of Indians should be able to distress a Country so large and populous," marveled Samuel Penhallow, New Hampshire's treasurer.[5]

To break the stalemate, both sides attempted to widen the war. Massachusetts and the Wabanakis sent delegates to the powerful Iroquois

Confederacy, which decided to remain neutral.[6] The Wabanakis sought help from New France, but Governor Philippe de Rigaud de Vaudreuil would never oblige them while Britain and France remained (temporary) allies in Europe.[7] Massachusetts had no better luck persuading Connecticut, Rhode Island, or New York to join the fighting. The colonies of New Hampshire and Nova Scotia waged parallel struggles against Wabanakis on their borders, but only New Hampshire (a distinct colony that nevertheless shared a governor with Massachusetts until 1741) was able to support offensive efforts. Most European residents of Nova Scotia were French Acadians with little desire to help their Anglo conquerors, and colonial forces in the region were fully preoccupied with fending off Mi'kmaq and Wulstukwiuk attempts to destroy the new British outposts. For their part, the Wabanakis along the Maine frontier enjoyed the support of the rest of the confederacy but failed to secure any allies powerful enough to tip the balance of power on the frontier. Nova Scotia Mi'kmaqs and Sokokis and Cowasucks around Lake Champlain waged parallel wars against nearby British colonists, but only the Mi'kmaqs made any serious attempts to coordinate with the attacks on Maine towns.[8] The Wabanakis also (with covert diplomatic assistance from Vaudreuil) persuaded the Hurons of Lorette and some of the Iroquois living in Canada to join them in raiding the British.[9] However, the Wabanakis failed to win any allies powerful enough to achieve decisive results.

With little outside help, the Wabanakis nevertheless implemented a strategy aimed at clearing the disputed land of intruders. Although the Wabanakis did not fight under an overall commander, their attacks revealed clear objectives.[10] Between 1722 and 1724, warriors from multiple villages trained their guns on objectives with particular local significance. The Penobscots attacked Fort St. Georges four times; Wabanakis from Norridgewock and the Canadian villages focused on the Kennebec River area; while Pigwackets and Amarascoggins harried towns in western Maine and New Hampshire.[11] Raiders destroyed the town of Brunswick and drove away colonists from other new communities dotting the coast on Pejepscot, Clarke & Lake, and Muscongus Company claims. These forceful articulations of Wabanaki land claims got the point across. Some of the hardest-hit towns—like Cork, a community of recent Irish arrivals on Merrymeeting Bay east of the Kennebec—were never reoccupied.[12]

The Wabanakis were unable to translate these early successes into decisive victory, however. Although formidable in ambush, their warriors posed little threat to fortified garrisons. Because the basic Wabanaki economic unit was the extended family group, consisting of between twelve and twenty individuals, with each adult male playing a well-defined role as hunter, even modest combat losses could threaten families' ability to obtain enough food and supplies.[13] As a result, Indian forces were reluctant to storm prepared fortifications even when they enjoyed numerical superiority. The Penobscots showed resourcefulness in their repeated attacks on Fort St. Georges—trying to dig under the walls in 1722, turning two captured vessels into fire ships in 1724—but their unwillingness to suffer many casualties gave the defenders a crucial edge.[14] Wabanaki fighters also took to the sea, capturing a number of fishing vessels. By the summer of 1724, they had brought the northern New England fishery almost to a halt.[15] While these maritime attacks further added to the war's financial toll for Massachusetts, they did not bring the Bay Colony to its knees. Father Sebastian Rasles lamented the impasse to his superiors in a letter found by Massachusetts forces when they stormed Norridgewock. "The English still keep their forts and . . . unless the French Join with the Indians the Land is Lost. This is what now Discourages the Indians."[16] The losses suffered at Norridgewock only underlined that sentiment.

Staggering toward Peace

Although Bay Colony leaders tried to portray the destruction of Norridgewock as an epic triumph, the accumulating burdens of war gave a hollow ring to celebration over the two-dozen Wabanaki scalps brought back by the victors. Perhaps sensing this, or indicating how little many people in Massachusetts cared about Maine, the Boston newspapers reporting on the attack carried the news on page 2.[17] "Notwithstanding the advantages we have lately had over the enemy," Lieutenant Governor Dummer informed the Council of Trade and Plantations as 1725 began, "the expence of the war is so great and insupportable to this Province that unless it shall please God to put a speedy end to it, it will inevitably ruin us."[18] Soon after Norridgewock, New Hampshire's Lieutenant Governor Wentworth informed the Council, "This Indian War is greatly Impoverishing to New Hampshire in particular . . . we are wasteing boath in Numbers, and also the [sic] Impoverishing the pore inhabitance."[19] Samuel Penhallow, treasurer for New Hampshire, estimated the war's total cost at £240,000.[20] Nor had Wabanaki fighters lost their edge. In May 1725, Pigwackets ambushed a force of volunteer scalp hunters led by Captain John Lovewell looking for their village on the Saco River.

The Pigwackets slew Lovewell and a number of his men, sending the survivors fleeing for home.[21] Mutual war weariness rather than British triumph formed the backdrop of initial negotiations in 1725.

So, too, did divisions within the Wabanaki Confederacy. A Massachusetts commission in Canada to secure the release of British captives in early 1725 encountered both hard-liners as well as Indians seeking a truce when visiting St. Francis. For their part, the French continued to encourage military resistance.[22] Access to French supplies and proximity to British forces shaped the decisions of confederacy members. Shielded from likely British raids and enjoying regular material assistance from the French, the Indians living in the Canadian villages were more resistant to talk of peace. By 1725 this faction also included many refugee Kennebecs and at least some Amarascoggins and Pigwackets who had moved to Canada when the fighting began.[23] In contrast, the Wulstukwiuks and Penobscots remained in their respective homelands (although Bay Colony forces destroyed the empty Penobscot village of Penawabskik in the spring of 1725), where the opposite strategic situation prevailed. French observers were not surprised when the Penobscots took the lead in peacemaking.[24] No one recorded the Pigwacket and Amarascoggin positions at the time, but their small populations encouraged them to defer to stronger members of the confederacy after 1713.[25]

Tentative peace talks in Canada during the winter of 1725 revealed that the same differences that had led to war—clashing interpretations of seventeenth-century land deeds—formed the major obstacle to peace. As they had before 1722, disagreements over trade, war captives, religion, and the precise Wabanaki relationship with the French complicated peace talks, but none of these issues bedeviled the negotiations like the land deeds. A commission sent by Lieutenant Governor Dummer to demand the release of British captives held in Canada learned that fact during talks with Governor Vaudreuil and a number of Wabanaki leaders in Montreal. The Wabanakis in attendance represented St. Francis and Becancour—home to the Indians most suspicious of the Bay Colony land claims. As they had in 1721, the Canadian Indians insisted the British remain west of the Saco River, which, as the commissioners complained in a report, cut off "several towns and many hundred inhabitants . . . some of it possessed fourscore years." [26] According to a French report of the encounter, the Indians argued this was a compromise on their part, as their true claims extended to the Connecticut River.[27] When the commissioners displayed several deeds (which someone—probably Muscongus Proprietor Samuel Thaxter—had carried several hundred miles through the northern woods) to lands west of the Kennebec, the Wabanakis pointed out these did not cover lands occupied by the new, despised forts at St. Georges and Richmond. And besides, the Indians insisted, the deeds were forgeries.[28] The Indians insisted any peace terms had to include British surrender of the disputed land and indemnities for the destruction of Norridgewock.[29]

Penobscot statements several months later revealed that the Canadian Wabanaki articulation of the proper extent of the Dawnland was a maximalist position of one faction rather than a shared consensus. During the summer of 1725, the Penobscots sent out peace feelers to Boston via a pair of prisoners the British had paroled for the purpose.[30] Captain John Penhallow recorded the resulting meeting of a trio of British commissioners with an assembly of thirteen Penobscot leaders at Fort St. Georges. Through interpreter Joseph Beane, the Penobscots informed the commission that they fought "to defend their rights of Land w[h]ich was unjustly taken from 'em by the English who Came and built forts where they pleas'd and particularly at St. Georges which land they had never disposed of and that that [sic] Garrison was built before they knew of it." When the Boston commission replied the land "was formerly Bot, and the English had good deeds for it," the Penobscots "said they did not remember it, and if they had been made sensible of it [they] should have been easey." According to Penhallow, the Penobscots admitted that the land taken up by the fort was, by itself, "not worth while to Contend [over]," but the garrison's presence spoiled the hunting and fishing in the area.[31]

When the commissioners asked the Penobscots to outline the extent of their land claims, "Sepperate from Other Indians," the Indians deliberated overnight before delivering their answer. According to Penhallow, the Penobscots expressed their own boundaries in terms of waterways, running "up Sheepscot River . . . and so round arrowsic Island, but they had no claims to arrowsic and Parkers Island, and the other islands." When asked to define their rights along the Kennebec River, the Penobscots answered that they claimed fishing rights "along the Sea Shore" and bounded by "rivers [illegible] above."[32]

Penobscot peace overtures reached Massachusetts leaders at a time when they had begun to reflect on a half century of conduct toward the Wabanakis that had been stubborn at best, arrogant, duplicitous, and stupid at worst. As the war ground on, a swelling chorus of critics pointed out that the fighting was in fact the Bay Colony's fault. These voices included the governor of neighboring Connecticut, who informed

Dummer he had been credibly informed "the War was not just on the English side," because "the Indians had been wronged in their Lands."[33] Although the aging Samuel Sewall retired from public life in 1725, other members of his personal network continued to condemn the Bay Colony's Indian policy.[34] John Minot echoed some of Sewall's arguments in a 1725 letter to his father, Stephen, a founding Pejepscot Proprietor and well-connected Boston merchant. "We should Consider [the Wabanakis] have a Native right to all the Lands they have not Sould," he wrote. Like Sewall, Minot argued the Indians' fear of Massachusetts expansion aided the Jesuits in the struggle for Native souls, and blamed the latest war on Wabanaki desire to protect their lands. Minot urged "that some Considerable part of the Country should allways remaine to them," insisting if we put it to our selves and Examine by the golden rule of doing as we would be done by I think we should cheerfully come into it."[35] Other missionary advocates like Samuel Penhallow, who did not venture as far as John Minot, agreed that successful conversion of the Indians required a fairer treatment of them.[36]

Criticism of Massachusetts leaders was widespread enough that Samuel Penhallow could not ignore it in his generally laudatory 1726 account of their conduct, *History of the Wars of New England with the Eastern Indians*. Penhallow began his narrative by admitting he was not "unsensible that many have stigmiatiz'd the English as chiefly culpable in causing the first Breach between them and us; by invading their Properties, and defrauding them in their Dealings."[37]

Assertions that Massachusetts had defrauded Wabanakis in land exchanges hit a sore spot; fair treatment of the Wabanakis had long been a part of the Bay Colony's self-image. Jeremiah Dummer's *Defence of the New England Charters*, published just before the war, based its arguments in part on the assertion that New England, in contrast to the Spanish, had "sought to gain the Natives by strict justice in their dealings with them," and their conduct had disproven the "unworthy Aspersion that has been cast on the first Settlers of New England, that they never treated the Savages well, but encroach'd on their Land by Degrees, till they fraudulently and forcibly turn'd them out of all."[38] This foundation of just treatment underlay Dummer's claim that New England landowners' fair purchase "from the native lords of the soil . . . seems the only fair and just one," preempting any interference by a distant monarch.[39] If the critics were right, and Massachusetts had indeed caused the war by pilfering Indian lands, its charter could be as tattered as its reputation.

Although Massachusetts leaders could never be accused of excessive humility in their approach to Indian diplomacy, they nevertheless softened their approach to dealing with the Wabanaki land question. Massachusetts delegates asked the Penobscots to define their western borders because they were interested in finding the *true* Indian claimants to the disputed Arrowsic and Parker's Islands. British diplomats journeyed hundreds of miles to show bundles of deeds not to just any Indian but to the aggrieved parties who claimed the deeds were invalid. It is possible to interpret the Bay Colonists' belief that showing their deeds to the proper Indians would solve the current crisis as a stubborn inability or refusal to accommodate Wabanaki ideas about land use and exchange. And to a great extent it was. But it also represented a genuine desire on the part of Massachusetts leaders to take Indian arguments about the disputed claims seriously and ensure that documentary claims matched the realities on the ground.

The land companies played a central role throughout the entire process. As they had before the war, most commissions who met with the Wabanakis included speculators. Muscongus Proprietor Samuel Thaxter had been one of the delegates who traveled to Canada during the winter of 1725. The Stoddard family also held interest in the Muscongus Patent, and John Stoddard was one of three commissioners to meet the Penobscots outside of St. Georges in July 1725. Later, Penobscot emissaries to Boston met with Dummer and his entire council, which included numerous investors in the Clarke & Lake, Pejepscot, and Muscongus Patents.[40] Securing a lasting peace on the frontier and clear Wabanaki recognition of seventeenth-century land deeds was the surest way to protect company investments. Despite the speculators' desire for peace, reconciling company and Wabanaki land claims remained the greatest—but far from only—obstacle to that goal.

That fact became evident when two Penobscot leaders accompanied the British to Boston at the end of July 1725. The Penobscots tried to emphasize room for agreement, stressing that the land taken up by the Muscongus incursion around St. Georges was small and "not worth contending for." Dummer disagreed.[41] The Penobscots told Dummer they had no authority to sign a peace treaty at the moment but suggested Massachusetts withdraw southwest of Casco Bay (naming the point at Cape Elizabeth, in the southern portion of Falmouth) as a starting point for negotiations, and invited Dummer to give them the Bay Colony's terms to take home. They also promised if Massachusetts could "shew fair purchases of Land," they would reconsider the Casco Bay boundary. Dummer promised them that Massachusetts would make no new demands.[42] The Penobscots traveled north carrying the Bay Colony's written account of what had transpired, Dummer's warning that any French interpretation of the document different from his own was lies, and the threat that Massachusetts militia no longer got lost in the forest and could "reduce the Indians to utmost Extremity" should the war continue.[43] The French did read Dummer's written terms (demanding a status quo ante bellum based on the Bay Colony's self-serving reading of previous treaties), and the Wabanakis in Canada refused them, along with wampum belts the Penobscots sent to entice their confederates to enter peace talks.[44]

Loron's Treaty

Up to this point, all of the players had acted according to a familiar script. Massachusetts arrogance served as a perfect foil for the French to amplify to the Canadian Wabanakis, who in any case needed little persuasion to mistrust the British, and frustrating the attempts of more conciliatory Wabanakis to bridge the gap between them. The Penobscots who remained in their lands near the Maine frontier had the most to lose from the deadlock continuing, so they decided to try something new. Unable to convince the other Wabanakis to participate in negotiations, and knowing that they stood little chance of extracting favorable concessions from Massachusetts on their own, the Penobscots sent four emissaries to Boston anyway, putting on a show of unity for the *Bostoniak*. The delegation claimed the authority to speak for the Wabanakis "so far as Cape Sables [the Mi'kmaqs] . . . in a Treaty of Peace."[45] In reality, this statement glossed over the significant divisions among the Wabanakis about what terms they would accept. But if Massachusetts thought the Penobscots spoke for a unified Wabanaki Confederacy, the delegation had a better chance to secure terms that *would* be acceptable to the hard-liners.

The Penobscot responsible for executing this diplomatic tightrope walk was a rising speaker named Saugaaram.[46] His name, which Europeans seemed to invent new spellings for each time they met him, meant "One who speaks with intent to injure," suggesting spiritual power.[47] Massachusetts records usually referred to him by his "alias," Loron, which was an Anglicization of his French baptismal name, Laurent.[48] The name appears to be the one the Penobscot speaker used for himself most often in the company of the British. As with most Native people, the historical record remains frustratingly silent about most of

Loron's life. Although his age is unknown, in 1726 Loron had a son old enough to serve as one of two messengers to Canada.[49] No Europeans recorded whether Loron had distinguished himself as a hunter, warrior, or through spiritual prowess before the mid-1720s, but after surfacing in Massachusetts records in 1720, Loron spoke for the Penobscots in nearly every major conference until 1751.[50] The name "Saguaaram," if meant to denote powerful oratorical skill, was appropriate. Even through the filter of translators and scribes, Loron's statements in treaty records over the years are replete with metaphors beyond what other Wabanaki and Massachusetts diplomats used. Loron wanted troublesome Massachusetts demands "put under the Table."[51] Tensions threatened "like Gunpowder," but even though peace had been "blasted . . . when the Ground is manured it will not be so apt to blast again."[52]

Loron's oratorical skills (which would have included ritual knowledge) and diplomatic acumen gave him considerable influence among his people, even though he never became head chief.[53] Wenemouet, the Penobscot leader until his death in 1730, was ill in 1726, and poor health may have encouraged him to delegate more responsibilities to Loron during negotiations.[54] Wenemouet and other Penobscot leaders also chose Loron over Espegnet, described in Massachusetts records as the "Second chief" of the Penobscots.[55] In 1725, the province secretary recorded Loron as a "Captain," meaning he probably led a lineage of several family bands.[56] Whatever his formal office, Loron's influence among the Penobscots—the most powerful Wabanaki tribe after 1725—made him an important player in frontier politics for the next quarter century. For most of his career, Loron occupied a middle position between the confrontational and conciliatory factions within Penawabskik. Loron cultivated ties with Massachusetts leaders, both on the frontier and in Boston, unlike the minority hard-liners who generally avoided attending conferences with them. However, he struck a more independent tone toward successive colonial governors than prominent postwar accommodationists like Arexis. Never wavering in his defense of Penobscot territorial or political sovereignty, Loron challenged Massachusetts leaders whenever they attempted to win by gifts or deceit what they had not achieved in war. But that lay in the future. In 1725, Loron had to play a difficult game—claiming authority to negotiate for all Wabanakis in order to secure a peace favorable enough for hard-liners in Canada to accept, bolstering Penobscot influence in the process.

Massachusetts leaders prepared for the next round of negotiations in a different manner, assembling the support not of people but of documents.

As Loron returned to Boston at the head of a Penobscot delegation, Adam Winthrop submitted a report on behalf of the Committee of Eastern Claims. Winthrop had a considerable stake in determining the Anglo-Wabanaki boundary, holding shares in the Pejepscot and Muscongus Proprietors.[57] His report (of which the Pejepscot Proprietors kept a copy) took pains to highlight the strength of those company claims that caused the recent war.[58] Winthrop traced the history of supposed Wabanaki submissions beginning in 1693, followed by the lines in the 1713 and 1717 treaties permitting Massachusetts reoccupation of all lands "which they have obtained a Right and Title unto."[59] The committee listed all the areas along the coast previously occupied by colonists, and made more expansive claims for the province based on various seventeenth-century agreements between various colonists and the Indians along the Kennebec River for permission to erect truck houses (a contemporary term for trading posts). Based on the provincial courts holding jurisdiction over the handful of English colonists there, Winthrop and his colleagues argued this proved royal sovereignty on land that had been devoid of colonists since the 1670s.[60] The report concluded by suggesting if the "Great number of Deeds . . . were all inspected would together . . . probably comprehend the Greatest part of the Lands" extending to Penobscot Bay, thirty miles up the Androscoggin River, seventy miles up the Kennebec, and two miles up the Muscongus, "which the Indians by all the Treatys hitherto made have Consented to quit and disclaim, and may well be Insisted on by the Government in the next Treaty."[61] Winthrop and his committee (which included other absentee landowners like William Dudley, who, with his brother Paul, owned most of the town of Dudley, Massachusetts) also took the lead in the next round of talks with the Penobscots.

The bulk of these negotiations turned on the perennial issue of defining what acts counted as demonstrating British "possession" of land.[62] When the commission attempted to replicate a version of the 1713 and 1717 treaties, the Penobscots asked them to clarify "what is meant by the Words former Settlements whether the English design to build Houses further than there are any Houses now built or Settlements made."[63] The committee answered, "When We come to Settle the Bounds We shall neither build or settle any where but within our own Bounds so settled without your Consent."[64] This answer left room open for different interpretations, as Massachusetts leaders could interpret "our own Bounds" to include all areas contained in deeds, rather than previously built on, but the Penobscots appear to have construed it more narrowly, as they expressed satisfaction, saying: "We understand it well now. It is best to understand what is said."[65] Their statement also reflected the Penobscots' conviction that misunderstandings and ambiguity had defeated previous attempts at peacemaking.

Following that ambiguous promise, the commission proposed the Wabanakis agree to a method for judging British and Native claims. They suggested "a Committee of able faithfull and disinterested Persons" would "receive and adjust [British] Claims of Lands in the Parts Eastward" and then take those claims they judged valid "down into those parts of the Province" and "with a Number of the Indian Chiefs appointed for that purpose shall show forth and ascertain the Bounds of such claims and challenges accordingly." In the meantime, no new towns would be built in the disputed area.[66] After some consideration, the Penobscots suggested that "it would be better to come wholly upon a new Footing, for all those former Treaties have been broke because they were not upon a good Footing."[67] For the Penobscots, the treaties of 1713 and 1717 were conflated with the disputed deeds and incorrectly indicated Wabanaki acceptance of them. Because the Indians viewed the land use agreements as moves in a reciprocal relationship, they believed they could be renegotiated as the nature of that relationship changed. The changing needs of the parties, they believed, justified adjusting the distribution of land, much as sagamores did among their own people. As a gesture of good faith, the Penobscots asked that Massachusetts abandon the forts at St. Georges and Richmond (instead of everywhere in the Dawnland north of Cape Elizabeth, as they had requested earlier). Acknowledging they believed the commission had been "reasonable" and amenable to compromise, they said "it seems reasonable that We should insist upon those two Places only," but they insisted on that point "that there may be no Misunderstanding when the Peace is concluded, by the English settling to[o] nigh us." The Penobscots claimed "all the Tribes" had agreed on this point.[68]

After consulting with Dummer, the commissioners responded to the Penobscot request for land cessions by defending their possession with deeds. They insisted "we have good deeds" for the lands on which the forts stood.[69] Assuring the Penobscots that Forts Richmond and St. Georges would be used as trading posts rather than for offensive purposes, the commission displayed a number of deeds, reading aloud "Indians Names who signed those Deeds," whom the Penobscots "acknowledged that they had heard of . . . and that there was some of them now alive."[70] The commission also told the Penobscots "how long agoe those deeds were made," believing that the venerability of the documents gave them added weight. As subsequent negotiations would make clear, the Indians disputed this analysis.

Loron and his companions did not lodge further protest and instead shifted their focus from securing better terms to gathering accurate information for their leaders. The clerk recorded them replying, "We are well pleased to see the old Deeds for the Lands," before declining to endorse them. "If we should proceed further as to the Boundaries of Lands we should goe beyond our Instructions," they explained.[71] Like all Wabanaki diplomats, the Penobscot delegation were not permitted to make their own policy before consulting with the communities from whose consent they derived their authority. Loron's party did ask the commissioners to clarify if Massachusetts planned to build towns near Fort St. Georges. In addition, they wanted to know if they would be paid for unsold lands "in Spaces between what has been purchased . . . when the English come to settle," a question based on the reality that European land use practices would eventually ruin them for hunting and fishing.[72] Penobscot spokesmen admitted as much in July 1725, when they complained the fortifications and scattering of houses on the Muscongus Patent "Spoiled their Hunting etc."[73] The Penobscots also asked, as a clerk recorded, "whether We shall not have a further Gratuity or Acknowledgement made to us for what has been purchased of our Forefathers."[74] Loron and his companions were probably not, as the commission (and Dummer) believed, asking for the equivalent of a second payment for a permanent transaction. Instead, the request likely signified a desire to obtain Massachusetts's "acknowledgement"—through gift giving—of the Wabanakis' legitimate claim on the disputed areas, like the 1678 Treaty of Casco Bay, which had contained annual payments by Maine colonists.

The next day the commissioners delivered Dummer's response, which reiterated his rigid defense of private property rights, coupled with vague promises of future fair treatment. The lands around St. Georges "are the Property of particular Persons who have the Indian Right by fair Purchase," he answered, "and you cannot reasonably expect that the said Proprietors should be hindred [sic] of making Improvement of what is their own."[75] By the same token, Dummer rejected the thought of future payments (by his understanding) for the St. Georges, because "there is no reason to expect the Lands should be paid for over again."[76] However, Dummer promised "no Encroachment shall be made on you" and future proprietors and their colonists would "treat you as Friends and good

Neighbours," reiterating the Indians would have free use to hunt and fish wherever British land was unenclosed.[77]

Loron's delegation departed Boston with very different ideas of what had occurred than Massachusetts leaders did. Loron and his companions signed a preliminary treaty on December 15, differing in tone and substance from the draft they had been presented in November. The draft treaty promised the Indians would retain all their unsold lands, and the British would produce proof to verify their claims to the disputed areas at the treaty ratification.[78] The December version still promised the Indians their unsold lands, but Dummer's verbal promise about the joint committee to evaluate land claims was not included. In its place, the December treaty declared "His Majesties Subjects the English shall . . . Enjoy All and Singular their rights of Land and Settlements . . . within the Eastern Parts . . . without any Molestation or claims by us, or any other Indians."[79] The December treaty also included a preamble blaming the Wabanakis for the war and making "our Submission" to the king.[80] In it, Loron and the three other delegates were "Impowered to Act" on behalf of all Wabanakis and pledged the Penobscots in particular would "Joyn their Young men" with Massachusetts against any Indians who continued fighting in "reducing them to reason."[81]

When Loron learned about the discrepancy, he disavowed the treaty, explaining what the Penobscots believed had taken place. Etienne Lauverjat, missionary to the Penobscots, had read the treaty copy that Loron's delegation brought home, and Loron dictated a response through him. After Lauverjat read the treaty aloud, Loron replied through the Jesuit, "I have found the articles entirely deffering from what we have said in presence of one another, 'tis therefore to disown them that I write this letter unto you." Loron denied ever offering his submission to King George, or that his ancestors had. Instead, "I did not understand to acknowledge Him for my king butt only that I owned that He was king in His kingdom as the king of France is king in His." Nor did Loron accept blame for starting the war. Instead, he came to Boston "att your invitation of my Nation . . . that they accept of the cession of Arms which you have offered them." Loron also denied "many other Articles whereof I make no mention here" and declared "the disagreement I find between your writings and that I spoke to you viva voce stops me and makes me suspend my negotiation till I have received your answer," which he wanted in French, "so that more people can understand it."[82]

A combination of deception and genuine misunderstanding contributed to the clashing interpretations of the 1725 agreement. Some

Penobscot actions encouraged Massachusetts leaders to believe all Wabanakis would soon accept provincial terms. Throughout the talks, the Penobscots made repeated assertions that they spoke on behalf of all Wabanakis, omitting (for good reason) the fact that the confederacy did not yet agree on peace terms.[83] This maneuver encouraged the already prominent British habit of assuming Indian leaders held greater authority over their followers than they actually did.

Massachusetts leaders also erroneously interpreted Penobscot tact as a willingness to concede the disputed lands. Loron and his companions adhered to a diplomatic protocol that emphasized seeking areas of mutual agreement. Conferences were not debates but instead opportunities to deliver prepared statements and build consensus.[84] After the delegates asked that Massachusetts abandon Forts Richmond and St. Georges, they responded to provincial follow-up questions by emphasizing "the two small articles [forts] which have been mentioned it is no great Matter the giving up them [sic] two only and We hope will not hinder our Proceeding in the present Treaty."[85] In reality, Loron and his associates believed they had secured a cease-fire and a pledge to further negotiate about the forts. They did not renew their objections because they wanted to give both sides more time to consider what had been said and did not wish to derail the turn toward peace.

Massachusetts compounded these genuine misunderstandings with willful deception. The draft treaty and the comments by Dummer's commissioners did not emphasize Penobscot submission to King George, and Loron's insistence that he only acknowledged King George's sovereignty over Great Britain echoed Wiwurna's 1717 declarations of independence. Interpreters Samuel Jordan, John Gyles, and Joseph Bean could have translated the terms to Loron in a way that obscured their real intent.[86] The belated insertion of the clause blaming the Wabanakis for the war also suggests a deliberate effort to trick the Indians. Most significant for securing the peace, the December draft of the treaty omitted any explicit reference to a committee evaluating the justice of British claims to Native land.

Other evidence complicates this picture of Machiavellian deception by Massachusetts. The province had included pro forma declarations of sovereignty over the Wabanakis in every treaty since 1693 without attempting to enforce them. By themselves these declarations amounted to little more than Massachusetts leaders performing claims of supremacy over the Indians for the benefit of imperial officials in London.

Manipulation of land claims posed a more serious threat to peace, but the actions of the General Court suggest its members did not plan to defraud the Wabanakis—for the present, at least. On December 22, they formed a committee to gather all "Claims or Titles . . . to the Lands of the Eastern Parts of the Province" for presentation at the planned 1726 ratification, "and take care as far as possible to make out the same to the Satisfaction of the Indians, and to distinguish and ascertain what Lands belong to the English, in order to [sic] the Effectual Prevention of any Contention or Misunderstanding on that Head for the future."[87] The House also voted to ban the establishment of any unauthorized new towns northeast of North Yarmouth.[88] If Massachusetts leaders hoped to set the rules by which landownership would be decided, they still intended to remain faithful to them.

As Penobscot and Massachusetts leaders attempted to communicate, Etienne Lauverjat, missionary at Penawabskik, did his best to undermine the peace party there. Lauverjat had written Loron's complaint after reading him the treaty. Although he claimed to act merely as a translator and scribe, Lauverjat engaged in an interpreters' duel with John Gyles, Joseph Bean, and Samuel Jordan. At the behest of his superiors in Quebec and Paris, Lauverjat had used his influence in Penawabskik to bolster the confrontational faction for years, and his role as translator allowed him great power.[89]

Whatever Lauverjat told the Penobscots, Joseph Bean was nearby to contradict him. According to a report dispatched to Dummer in February 1726, "by Preswasion of the Jesuit," the Penobscots "disapprove of some Artickles in their Submission; but Capt Beane being present found that he misinterpreted them," and after he told them "the true meaning there of," most of the Indians were satisfied.[90] By this point Penobscot leaders had developed a well-founded mistrust of British and French interpreters, especially on paper. Little wonder Wenemouet later dictated a message to Dummer through John Gyles, with a disclaimer that "I don't understand writing Letters and if any thing [is] a mis and nott a Greable to you in the Letter . . . I desiar you to mention to me for I know not the contents of it."[91]

Whatever their misgivings, the Penobscots met Dummer for a second conference on July 30, 1726, although their actions soon dashed the governor's hopes that they would submit either to Massachusetts's authority or interpretation of the old land sales.[92] Instead, Penobscot behavior indicated they viewed 1725 as the opening round of negotiations, and they continued jockeying for diplomatic advantage before the second meeting. Wenemouet wanted the conference at Pemaquid, at the edge of Penobscot territory, although Dummer refused. Speaking for the Penobscots (perhaps in part because Wenemouet was ill), Loron blamed the British for the absence of the Canadian Wabanaki. He delivered wampum belts from the absent tribes and said that after they had previously insisted the talks should be held in Montreal, the Penobscots had expected to continue serving as messengers and mediators between the two sides. But instead, Dummer had invited the Penobscots to Falmouth, and they could not persuade the other Wabanakis to join them.[93]

Dummer did his best to secure the speedy Penobscot ratification of the 1725 articles, but Loron transformed the encounter into a negotiation, as the Indians had wanted. Although the governor's rhetoric sometimes took the style of demands, the text of the 1726 treaty, as recorded by Clerk of the Council John Wainwright, reveals a series of proposals and counterproposals between equals. Even when Dummer informed Loron on Saturday evening that the British would not be meeting "on the Lord's Day," the Catholic Loron informed Dummer that "We also keep the Day."[94] While the two sides dickered over the Kennebecs' absence, the exchange of captives, and Canadian Indians' proposals for locating the conference in Montreal, the contested lands remained the major source of contention.

As before, divergent ideas about the nature of landownership shaped the debates over how the seventeenth-century land deeds should be judged. Loron invoked Dummer's previous promise that "he would Settle no Lands, but what good Rights and Titles might be set forth to," and then elaborated what he thought constituted "good Rights."[95] If the disputed land had been sold during the seventeenth century, Loron said, "we have a Number of Young People growing up who never were Acquainted of the Land being Sold." In addition, Massachusetts was "a Great and Rich Government . . . and it would be but a small matter for the Government to make Allowance for them, and give them up."[96] When Dummer asked what sort of "Allowance" the Indians had in mind, Loron repeated their request that "no Houses or Settlements be made to the Eastward of Pemmaquid or above Arrowsick," and said the Penobscots in particular "don't know that they ever Sold any Lands."[97] From the Indian perspective, the deed's age reduced its relevance in current negotiations. Whatever the buyers had given for the disputed land was "small," and forgotten, making the exchange useless in maintaining a reciprocal relationship. Since the Penobscots believed they needed the land more, Massachusetts, as a "Great and Rich Government," should cede it to the Indians.

Dummer, like the proprietors whose claims he supported, rejected the Wabanaki interpretation of the old agreements. He believed the commissioners who brought a bundle of deeds with them to Falmouth were his trump card. Dummer mentioned the "fair deeds. . . . as well as divers Treaties Wherein" the Indians had supposedly acknowledged the validity of Massachusetts claims they brought. The commissioners spoke with the Penobscots apart from Dummer, who noted the disputed lands "being for a long time since Purchased by his Majesty's Subjects, and the Property Vested in them, the Government" lacked the authority to annul the agreements.[98] Dummer's statements revealed two key elements of colonial elites' worldview that played a powerful role in shaping frontier diplomacy. He regarded deeds and treaties as having equal legal standing and took care to emphasize that the government did not have the power to interfere with the proprietors' landed property without cause. Both the deeds and treaties, once properly signed and ratified, represented binding contracts with an abstract authority of their own rather than serving as mere totems of an ongoing relationship, as the Wabanakis believed.

Faced with this intransigence, Loron challenged the fairness of the deeds in a manner he hoped would resonate with Dummer, while also striving, in the Wabanaki diplomatic practice, to find points of reconciliation. After the Penobscots conferred awhile, Loron insisted, "We can't find any Record in our Memory, nor in the Memory of Our Grand Fathers that the Penobscutt Tribe have Sold any Land." The 1694 deed signed by Madockawando and Egeremet was invalid because neither sagamore had been a Penobscot, Loron insisted. He referred to "Machias Medockewondo," signifying the famed leader's origins to the eastward, among the Wulstukwiuks, and declared Egeremet had "belonged . . . towards Boston."[99] Loron was correct that, from the Penobscot perspective, the Madockawando sale had not been valid, because the sagamore had never received permission from the people living on the land in question before signing the deed. By drawing attention to Madockawando's "Machias" affiliation, Loron hoped to obscure his real authority among the Penobscots—at least before word of his unauthorized land cession leaked. (Egeremet, who witnessed the transaction, was a Kennebec leader.)[100] In any case, Loron maintained, "We do not remember any Settlements at St. George's," which, he reminded Dummer, was "a small Tract of Land, which is but a Trifle, and all is now finished excepting that, which is a Trifle."[101]

Dummer did not take Loron's hint. Instead, the governor interpreted Penobscot flexibility as his cue to turn over negotiations to the House committee bearing the assembled deeds. The Penobscots eventually agreed to let the committee show Wenemouet and the other leading Indians deeds from a bundle of twenty-nine, most of which, according to the clerk, were "opened and shown," while the interpreters translated their terms and told the Penobscots the commissioners were "disinterested persons" empowered to prove the documents' validity.[102] The committee took great pains to show the relevant deeds for the disputed lands, a tedious process the Penobscots found excruciating. The Indians finally stopped the process, saying "they supposed when they should meet [Dummer] again that matters would be adjusted."[103] The deeds had little meaning for them, serving as nothing but a symbol of older agreements, some of which had lost their usefulness. Declining to speak for the Kennebecs about their disputed lands, the Penobscots suggested that tribe be shown the relevant deeds.[104]

For the Penobscots, the mountain of documentary evidence of Massachusetts claims mattered less than repeated verbal promises of justice and equal treatment in any future disputes. Dummer vowed the Indians "shall always have equal Justice with His Majesty's English subjects in all Points, when ever any Difficulty shall arise concerning the Property of Lands or any other Matters."[105] This declaration convinced the Penobscots to compromise yet again. Speaking for the assembled Indians, Loron admitted they gave up hoping Dummer could "bring to pass what we have been proposing concerning giving way [on the disputed land]." However, in recognition of what they viewed as Dummer's efforts to bring "a good Settlement among us" with his promises of justice, they agreed to compromise, allowing the "House at St. George's which lies at our Door" to remain, provided "it shall be a Truck House, and that no other Houses be built there or thereabouts." Loron also emphasized that the Penobscots and "The Neighbouring Tribes" wanted "an Understanding together that there be no other Houses Built there, unless it be by purchase or Agreement," and settle a mutually understood boundary. The Indians worried "That if a Line should happen to be Run, the English may hereafter be apt to step over it."[106] Dummer made no explicit concessions about forts, but he answered them by promising only "Lawful Authority" would decide the justice of future proprietary land claims, "wherein the Indians shall have the Benefit of the Law, equal with any Englishman whatsoever . . . for we don't expect a peace to last on any footing than that of justice."[107] The Penobscots were "well pleased" with Dummer's answer, responding, "For want of that [justice] there has been Misunderstandings."[108]

After this agreement, the rest of the conference proceeded smoothly. Dummer and the Penobscots—with a representative from the Province of Nova Scotia—discussed prisoner exchange, the price of trade goods, and how to respond to the Canadian Wabanakis.[109] Wenemouet signed the treaty on behalf of all Penobscots.

Convinced they had secured acceptable terms, the Penobscots spent the following year persuading the other Wabanakis to accept them, in the process augmenting their own influence among the tribes. Penobscot speakers journeyed to the Canadian villages, and although a group of hard-liners remained in St. Francis, most of the villagers wanted peace.[110] John Gyles's network of informers kept him abreast of events, and he sometimes provided them with counterarguments against the militant holdouts.[111] The Penobscots worked to thwart both the hard-liners and any Wabanakis who would conclude a separate peace with Massachusetts that would, as Loron told Dummer, "Lessen the Penobscots formar Proceedings as they acted for the whole."[112]

Despite efforts of a confrontational faction encouraged by French officials (though not the Saint-Castins)[113] to frustrate a widespread ratification of the 1726 treaty, the greatest obstacle to peace emerged from ongoing discrepancies between the written 1725 treaty and its verbal translation to the Indians.[114] At Falmouth in 1726, Samuel Jordan interpreted the articles to the Penobscots, although the Massachusetts record of the exchange does not detail what he told them.[115] Loron asked to exchange the Penobscot copy of the terms of 1725 for "those they . . . left in the Hands of the Government [in Boston], in order to . . . confute" suspicions of mistranslation.[116] The Indians brought this copy home with them, and when Father Lauverjat translated the document, it once again diverged from the version read by Jordan, although French records do not specify what he told them.[117]

Determined to get to the heart of the matter, Wenemouet (who had adopted the new name of Wenengonet), Loron, and fifty Penobscots, Wulstukwiuks, and Canadian Wabanakis confronted Gyles about the discrepancy.[118] The Indians brought along Lauverjat and Joseph Saint-Castin. Loron asked Gyles to help resolve disputes between the Penobscots, the French, and other Wabanakis surrounding "the Interpretations of the articols Drawn at Boston" in 1725 by translating the document in front of everyone. When Lauverjat prepared to write down Gyles's translation, the interpreter protested, worrying Lauverjat and Saint-Castin served as "Spies . . . to take advantig of my Interpretation and Insult me," as Gyles later recorded the exchange.[119] After Lauverjat put aside his pen, and Loron said the Indians had invited the Jesuit, Gyles agreed to read the articles. When he finished, Loron said the Indians understood, "but you Do not Reed them as the Jesuitt Red em to us who is hear now Present, but we believe them to be as you Reed them."[120] The Penobscots' trust of Gyles over their longtime missionary revealed the decline in French influence in the Dawnland. Tepid French support during the war, coupled with Vaudreuil and his subordinates' cynical encouragement of Wabanaki resistance long past any reasonable hope of victory, had eroded their credibility in Wabanaki villages.[121] No European writers, the Penobscots learned, could be trusted. When the Penobscots dispatched three delegates to Boston after speaking with Gyles, Loron told him, "We Do not rite a Letter now for our Messengars Cary our Erand in their brest."[122]

A final grand conference at Falmouth in July 1727 included all Wabanakis in the ambiguous Anglo-Penobscot peace. Dummer never mentioned the deeds for the Kennebec River lands above Fort Richmond to Auyaumowett of St. Francis, speaker for the assembled Kennebecs, St. Francis, and Becancour Wabanakis, as well as the Androscoggins and Pigwackets.[123] Instead, Massachusetts interpreters read the 1725 and 1726 articles to the assembled Indians, which the published provincial record included in full. Whatever the interpreters told Auyaumowett, the written statement awarded "their Rights of Land and former Settlements" to Massachusetts, while reserving unsold lands to the Wabanakis, as well as "the Priviledge of Fishing, Hunting, and fowling as formerly."[124] Auyaumowett, who had only heard the treaty read by Lauverjat, said his people "never heard them read so fully to us, and are very glad we have now heard of them," indicating the likelihood of British manipulation.[125] Dummer also insisted the Indians hear his signed December 15, 1725, proclamation, promising, "care be taken as far as possible to . . . Ascertain what Lands belong to the English, in order to [sic] the Effectual Prevention of any Contention or Misunderstanding on that Head for the future," which prompted Auyaumowett to declare that "Every thing that lay in the way" of peace had been "cleared away."[126] On that note, the remaining talks, centering on returning captives and prices of trade goods, assumed a more amicable tone.

Wabanaki complaints of traders' malfeasance gave Dummer the opportunity to show the Indians a foretaste of promised impartial justice. The governor received Wabanaki testimony that Captain William Woodside, officer in command of Fort Brunswick, had overcharged several Indians more than £10 since the cease-fire. Dummer sided with the Indians after receiving an itemized list of the overpriced goods and forced Woodside to offer promissory notes to his cheated customers in a "piece of publick Justice . . . to the great Satisfaction of the several Tribes of the Indians."[127]

The treaty ended on an auspicious note, but its success depended on what each party believed they had agreed to and whether they kept their respective promises. Reflecting on its significance during the 1760s, Lieutenant Governor Thomas Hutchinson argued the treaty's success could not "be attributed to any peculiar excellency in this treaty, there being no articles in it of any importance, differing from former treaties. It was owing to the subsequent acts of government in conformity to the treaty."[128] Hutchinson was correct in assessing the importance of Massachusetts's fidelity to the agreement but failed to recognize how subtle— and novel—combinations of the Indian and European understandings of the treaty encouraged many speculators to advocate for later "acts of government" that helped preserve the peace.[129]

The Significance of Dummer's Treaty

Dummer's Treaty succeeded because it fused Native traditions of diplomatic reciprocity with the British fixation on written contracts and property law, convincing both Wabanakis and most of the land speculators that the agreement protected their land rights. That shared belief proved more important than the ongoing ambiguity and deception that marked the proceedings and their aftermath. Massachusetts's rigid interpretation of disputed seventeenth-century deeds had been the chief obstacle to peace. Dummer's Treaty tempered that threat by tying Wabanaki acknowledgment of most seventeenth-century deeds to Massachusetts promises to submit all contested claims to a fair hearing. Dummer's pledge, though a subtle change from earlier blanket assurances of Native rights to unsold land, marked an important development. Even though Dummer and his council envisioned that the "Lawful Authority" that would evaluate future claims would be European, not Indigenous, the move nevertheless gave the Wabanakis increased leverage to challenge bad deeds. The treaty made distinctions between acknowledged and unacknowledged deeds—above all the 1694 Madockawando cession—matters of public record. The way the Wabanakis acknowledged many deeds in 1726 tied that recognition to the treaty itself, encouraging many proprietors to support Massachusetts upholding its end of the agreement, and in the process making Dummer's Treaty the beginning of a more genuinely reciprocal relationship, which the Wabanakis still desired. Although the Massachusetts architects of Dummer's Treaty had not intended to couple the ratification of old land deeds to diplomatic obligations, this accidental pairing was the principal reason for the agreement's success.

The greatest long-term weakness of the treaty stemmed from the ambiguity clouding the Kennebec River claims. Dummer and his council had ignored the Penobscots' suggestion in 1726 that they show relevant deeds to the then-absent Kennebecs. As a result, the Kennebecs signing the treaty in 1727 had no idea that future Massachusetts land speculators might claim ownership of tribal lands above Richmond based on the seventeenth-century agreements to erect truck houses. Their later statements indicate they believed Native eviction of all colonists from the upper Kennebec River during the late seventeenth century had erased those claims, and they thought subsequent treaties had recognized their forcible readjustment of the border.[130] The Kennebecs had no reason to believe Massachusetts would not understand; European laws of war acknowledged transfer of territory by conquest.[131]

For their part, the two major companies holding Indian deeds to the Kennebec River region do not appear to have put much stock in them. After the Wabanakis dispersed the new Scots-Irish towns on company claims beyond the coast in 1722, the Clarke & Lake heirs confined their efforts to populating the uncontested portion of their claim in the vicinity of Arrowsic. The purchasers of the old Plymouth claims along the Kennebec had so little confidence their Indian deeds would withstand scrutiny that they eventually turned their energy toward challenging the validity of any stand-alone Indian deed. But that lay in the future.

In 1727, like the Penobscots, the Kennebecs were encouraged by Dummer's proclamation that future speculators had to prove their claims before "impartial judges" to do "equal justice." However, the proclamation that had so impressed the Indians was not mentioned in the articles of peace, which were still carried over from the original 1725 Boston draft, involving Wabanaki "submission" to King George, and willingness to be "Governed by His Majesty's Laws."[132] Etienne Lauverjat, the Penobscots' frustrated missionary, grasped this difference, noting Wabanaki statements that peace was conditional on British respect for Wabanaki land rights "are merely verbal, and have not been inserted into the Treaty."[133]

Lauverjat was correct that the difference between written and verbal versions of Indian treaties provided essential fodder for deception, but not in the straightforward manner some scholars have alleged.[134] Leaders in Massachusetts and New France both manipulated the record of events in the Dawnland to assure their superiors in London and Paris that they controlled the Wabanakis. Dummer and successive governors of Massachusetts never tried to enforce their claims of political and legal sovereignty over the Wabanakis. The residents of Penawabskik and Meductic never paid taxes, nor did the sheriffs of York County enforce Massachusetts law among them.[135] Instead, Massachusetts leaders staged these claims of sovereignty over the Indians for the benefit of imperial officials in London, in much the same way that seventeenth-century English buyers sometimes framed their Indian land purchases to Whitehall as "quieting." In a similar vein, Governor Jonathan Belcher described £200 worth of diplomatic gifts to the Penobscots in 1736 as "about £35 sterling" to the Duke of Newcastle.[136] This face-saving lie allowed Belcher to portray the Penobscots to Newcastle as grateful subjects rather than powerful neighbors.

French officials engaged in posturing of their own in correspondence to Versailles. Lauverjat and other Frenchmen needed to show their superiors the Wabanakis remained good Catholics and faithful allies. To that end, Etienne Lauverjat and the Saint-Castin brothers issued their own statement complaining of British deception at Falmouth. Claiming to speak for the Penobscots, they denied both Native wrongdoing in the war and submission to King George and his laws, insisting the printed treaty was different from their interpretation. All that had transpired, they said, was a cession of arms and a treaty of peace between the two nations.[137] Although Lauverjat had tried to prolong the war, the Saint-Castins signed his letter merely to stay in the good graces of the French. Lauverjat later complained to his superior in 1728 that the brothers had worked to prevent war in the early 1720s, tried to remain neutral so they could keep trading furs with all comers, and continued to press the Indians to listen to British peace overtures.[138] Unlike other Wabanaki statements, Lauverjat and the Saint-Castins' letter contained no totems of either individual sagamores or entire villages, as Rasles's 1721 Arrowsic letter had.

Loron joined various European leaders in attempting to clarify the significance of Dummer's Treaty. Either on his own initiative or at Lauverjat's suggestion, the missionary recorded Loron's version of events "in my [Loron's] own tongue." This claim, like so many others, was not true, since Lauverjat translated and recorded Loron's speech in French. The statement noted "the diversity and contrariety of the interpretations I receive of the English writing. . . . These writings appear to contain things that are not." Loron repeated his denial that in 1725 Dummer had ever proposed he give his loyalty or his lands to King George, nor had he admitted the validity of Massachusetts land claims. He had agreed to the principle of presenting grievances before an impartial judge, but "I did not understand that he alone be judge." Nothing new had been decided at the 1726 and 1727 conference, except to allow a truck house on the St. Georges, but not a fort, "and I did not give him the land." The statement closed with a warning that revealed an acquired mistrust of written documents. If "any one should produce any writing that makes me speak otherwise, pay no attention to it, for I know not what I am made to say in another language, but I know well what I say in my own."[139]

However eloquent, this letter should not be taken as "the Penobscot" position on Dummer's Treaty.[140] No other leaders signed it, and Loron made no reference to representing the consensus in Penawabskik. Wenongonet (formerly Wenemouet) still led the Penobscots, with Espegnet still his "second chief."[141] If Loron had been delegated to speak for the Penobscots, he would have said so. The letter's preoccupation with Penobscot independence from King George also hints at a perennial French concern. Although the Wabanakis insisted on their independence, as Wiwurna had at Arrowsic in 1717, most of the disputes at Dummer's Treaty had concerned land claims, which the letter scarcely mentions.[142] This foreshadowed 1736, when the Penobscots faced a crisis over renewed British encroachments on their land, but French reports fixated on a handful of sagamores that had accepted commissions from the governor of Massachusetts.[143] Nor was the letter sent to Boston. Instead, Lauverjat sent it to his superiors, who dispatched it to France alongside other colonial correspondence.[144] Scholars have correctly pointed out that John Gyles engaged in deception in the service of king and country, but few have acknowledged that Lauverjat had similar motives to use his power as translator to manipulate the written record.[145] However strong the bonds between the priest and his flock, Etienne Lauverjat, like Gyles, labored first and foremost in the service of his European masters. Based on Loron's career, the letter probably represented his sentiments, but if leading Penobscots and other Wabanakis shared his reservations, they did not convey them to Dummer in a subsequent conference in December 1727.[146]

Given the Bay Colony's checkered history, French—to say nothing of Wabanaki—suspicion of Massachusetts makes sense. But critics of Dummer's Treaty then and now fail to account for how the speculators and the printing business combined to minimize the discrepancies between the written and verbal treaties that so worried Lauverjat. Continuing a practice established in 1717, the printer for the Massachusetts

House published detailed accounts of the 1726 and 1727 conferences. If Dummer and other provincial leaders hoped to keep the governor's proclamation promising equal justice and a rigorous review of any British land claims separate from the treaty articles proper, they blundered by allowing the legislature to include them, verbatim, in its published account. Anyone who picked up *Conference with the Eastern Indians, at the Ratification of the Peace, held at Falmouth in Casco-Bay* for the years 1726 or 1727 could read Dummer's promises that "if the English cannot make out and prove their Titles to the Lands Controverted, they shall disclaim them."[147] Further blending oral and written pledges, Dummer and Wenemouet/Wenongonet signed the entire thirty-five-page transcript of the 1726 conference after the interpreters read it aloud to the Indians.[148]

Widely available published accounts of Dummer's Treaty meant that the governor's promises became a matter of written record, giving any supporters of Native land rights evidence to back their position. A market for printed Indian treaties had existed in Massachusetts since the governor and General Court decided the 1717 Treaty of Arrowsic be "made publick."[149] Printers produced copies for ordinary readers as well as politicians. Besides the copies made available to every legislator, Benjamin Eliot sold them "at his shop below the town house" in Boston.[150] Readers of the 1726 conference at Falmouth learned it was "Printed for Benj. Eliot, at his shop in King-Street, where may also be had the former printed conference with the Eastern Indians."[151]

Land companies and their agents became avid collectors of Indian treaties in Massachusetts. Belcher Noyes, clerk of the Pejepscot Proprietors after 1739, acquired a copy of the 1726 treaty, perhaps from his predecessor, Adam Winthrop.[152] Another Pejepscot Proprietor, Henry Gibbs, owned a copy of the 1727 treaty.[153] Other proprietors collected copies of later treaties.[154] Agents for the land companies consulted numerous treaties. Nathan Dane, for example, an attorney for both the Kennebeck and Waldo (Muscongus) Proprietors at the turn of the nineteenth century, compiled an extensive notation of treaty statements confirming company claims.[155]

The nature of the proceedings at Dummer's Treaty led the speculators to treat the entire record of the conferences as a form of deed. Wabanaki leaders had not ratified particular deeds. Instead, they assented to most of the deeds presented to them while continuing to deny the validity of the Madockawando cession of 1694. Companies like the Clarke & Lake and Pejepscot Proprietors, whose claims had not been explicitly denied,

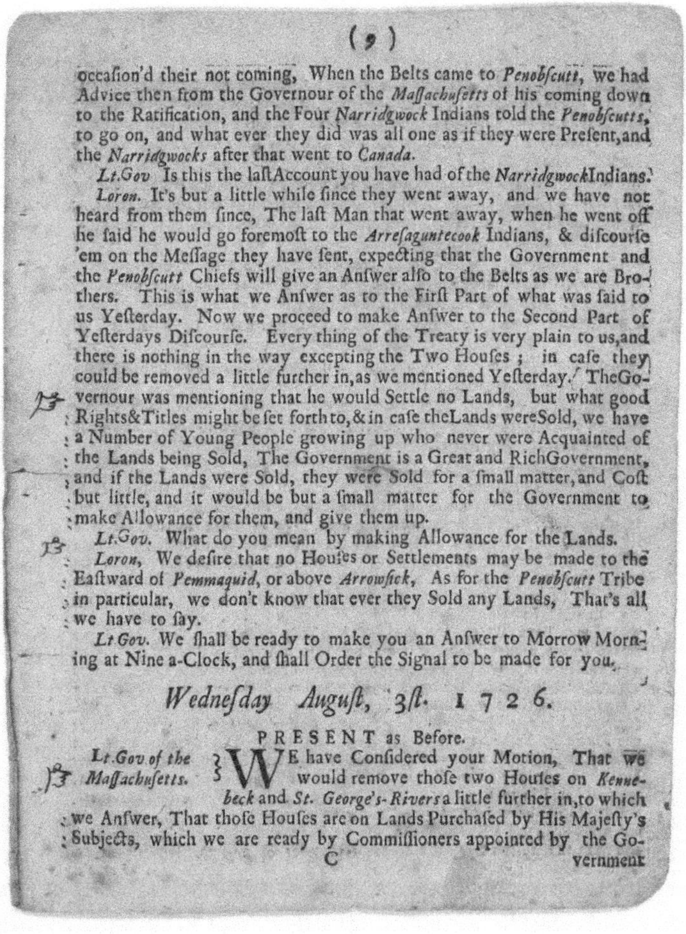

(9)

occafion'd their not coming, When the Belts came to *Penobfcutt*, we had Advice then from the Governour of the *Maffachufetts* of his coming down to the Ratification, and the Four *Narridgwock* Indians told the *Penobfcutts*, to go on, and what ever they did was all one as if they were Prefent, and the *Narridgwocks* after that went to *Canada*.

Lt.Gov. Is this the laft Account you have had of the *Narridgwock* Indians.

Loron. It's but a little while fince they went away, and we have not heard from them fince, The laft Man that went away, when he went off he faid he would go foremoft to the *Arrefaguntecook* Indians, & difcourfe 'em on the Meffage they have fent, expecting that the Government and the *Penobfcutt* Chiefs will give an Anfwer alfo to the Belts as we are Brothers. This is what we Anfwer as to the Firft Part of what was faid to us Yefterday. Now we proceed to make Anfwer to the Second Part of Yefterdays Difcourfe. Every thing of the Treaty is very plain to us, and there is nothing in the way excepting the Two Houfes ; in cafe they could be removed a little further in, as we mentioned Yefterday. The Governour was mentioning that he would Settle no Lands, but what good Rights & Titles might be fet forth to, & in cafe theLands wereSold, we have a Number of Young People growing up who never were Acquainted of the Lands being Sold, The Government is a Great and RichGovernment, and if the Lands were Sold, they were Sold for a fmall matter, and Coft but little, and it would be but a fmall matter for the Government to make Allowance for them, and give them up.

Lt.Gov. What do you mean by making Allowance for the Lands.

Loron. We defire that no Houfes or Settlements may be made to the Eaftward of *Pemmaquid*, or above *Arrowfick*, As for the *Penobfcutt* Tribe in particular, we don't know that ever they Sold any Lands, That's all we have to fay.

Lt Gov. We fhall be ready to make you an Anfwer to Morrow Morning at Nine a-Clock, and fhall Order the Signal to be made for you.

Wednefday Auguft, 3ft. 1 7 2 6.

PRESENT as Before.

Lt.Gov of the } W E have Confidered your Motion, That we *Maffachufetts.* } would remove thofe two Houfes on *Kennebeck* and *St. George's-Rivers* a little further in, to which we Anfwer, That thofe Houfes are on Lands Purchafed by His Majefty's Subjects, which we are ready by Commiffioners appointed by the Government

C

FIGURE 4.1. Published copy of the 1726 talks owned by Belcher Noyes, clerk of the Pejepscot Proprietors. Courtesy of the Maine Historical Society.

cited the treaty as confirmation their titles derived from fair, acknowledged purchases. So long as Dummer's Treaty remained in force, the proprietors could point to it as solid evidence the Wabanakis had accepted company claims, whatever may have occurred during the last war.

The proprietors often invoked Native recognition of their land claims in subsequent disputes with the royal agents, frontier colonists, and rival land companies. In a typical deposition for the Pejepscot Proprietors in

1753, John Gyles attested that "altho' (at Several Publick Treaties since that time) the Indians have from time to time disputed the English Claim to some of the Eastern Lands, yet they always Confessed that the Indian Deed made to Mr. Richard Wharton . . . dated July Seventh 1684 was a good and Lawfull Deed of sale of all the lands therein."[156] The practice, which increased after Dummer's Treaty, continued throughout the eighteenth century. The Draper heirs, who lacked more direct evidence of Native acknowledgment of their title in the Sheepscot River region during a 1795 dispute, secured the testimony of seventy-year-old Mary Varney, who told of witnessing "some Indian men (who I understood to be some of their Great men) who acknowledged [Draper] . . . as the owner of the lands."[157]

For the most successful land company in 1727, Dummer's Treaty assumed an outsized importance in subsequent legal clashes. Belcher Noyes, explaining the basis of the Pejepscot title to another proprietor in 1763, noted the company's 1684 Indian deed had been "produced at all the Treaties with the Indians for above forty years past, more especially . . . at Gov. Dummer's Treaty which is now allowed to be the Basis on which all the Subsequent Treaties are grounded."[158] The company copy of the 1684 deed contained the notation: "This instrument was shown to Winemuett chief Sachem of Penobscott and his tribe at a ratification of the Peace. . . . This was done by a Committee of the general court appointed for that purpose."[159] So long as the treaty remained in force, proprietors like Adam Winthrop could hold it up, as he did in a 1741 dispute with the town of North Yarmouth, as evidence that his company "have been from time to time treated with and acknowledged as Owners of sd Lands" by the Indians.[160] The Pejepscot Proprietors, along with other companies like them, had a vested interest in upholding the treaty, because Wabanaki repudiation would undermine its usefulness.

The importance of Indian treaties for speculators' investments therefore led to even greater proprietary involvement in the Bay Colony's Indian diplomacy in ways that redounded to the Wabanakis' benefit. The Pejepscot Proprietors took a particular interest in the province fulfilling its treaty obligations. Copies of the 1726 and 1727 meetings owned by Belcher Noyes and Henry Gibbs contain highlighting and drawn hands pointing to portions of the text. Although Noyes highlighted every mention of the Pejepscot claim by the Penobscots or the Massachusetts governor, he also underlined sections where Governor Dummer emphasized that Indians would "always have equal justice with his Majesty's English subjects on all Points, when ever any Difficulty shall arise concerning the

Property of Lands or any other Matters."[161] Gibbs marked his copy of the 1727 conference in a similar fashion, drawing small, pointing hands next to passages specifying both proprietary and Native land rights.[162] The company was still busy monitoring subsequent Anglo-Indian treaties for commitment to this policy in 1754.[163]

Dummer's Treaty, despite its flaws, provided a real foundation for making a durable peace on the Dawnland frontier. By tying English property law to Native practices of reciprocity, the treaty gave elite land speculators a financial stake in seeing its terms enforced. From their positions of power within the Massachusetts government, the speculators could serve as a brake on the desire of frontier colonists for either vengeance or unsanctioned territorial expansion. The speculators knew that Dummer's Treaty protected their property both from rival claimants and from wartime destruction. The results of the recent fighting— despite its framing in the Bay Colony as a great victory—showed how Native military power remained a threat to company investments. Aside from the casualty list—130 dead colonists and another 70 captured—the war exacted a heavy financial cost.[164] Raiders destroyed most of the new homes on the proprietors' claims, along with livestock and mills. The war further drained provincial coffers at a time when Massachusetts still staggered under the financial burdens accrued during the last half century of fighting.[165] If Dummer's Treaty prevented the renewal of warfare, then it would shield company property (and Bay Colony finances) from further destruction.

Parallel negotiations to end the fighting around Nova Scotia highlight the degree of influence the Boston-based speculators had in shaping Dummer's Treaty. The Mi'kmaqs and Wulstukwiuks had waged their own campaign against the emerging British colony of Nova Scotia since 1722, and unlike the St. Lawrence villages, appear to have deputed the Penobscots to negotiate on their behalf in Boston in 1725 with little pushback. Some histories of the Wabanaki Confederacy indicate the easterners occupied a ritual position as "last born" members, with the Penobscots ritually serving as "elder brothers."[166] Loron and his three associates signed a separate agreement with Paul Mascarene, representing Nova Scotia in Boston in December 1725.

In June 1726, Mi'qmaks, Wulstukwiuks, and several Penobscot representatives gathered at Annapolis Royall in Nova Scotia to ratify a version of the 1725 Boston Treaty. Penobscot messengers had notified Mi'kmaq and Wulstukwiuk villages of the activities of Loron's delegation. One of them, a man named Francois Xavier, arrived to take place in the

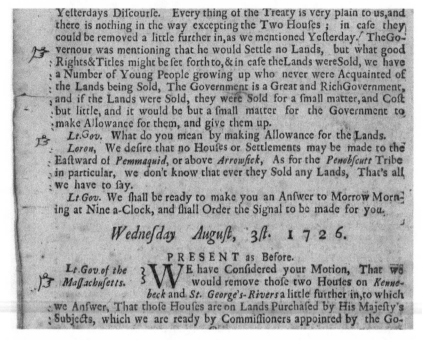

Yelterdays Difcourfe. Every thing of the Treaty is very plain to us,and
there is nothing in the way excepting the Two Houfes ; in cafe they
could be removed a little further in,as we mentioned Yeflerday.' TheGo-
vernour was mentioning that he would Settle no Lands, but what good
Rights&Titles might be fet forth to,& in cafe theLands wereSold, we have
a Number of Young People growing up who never were Acquainted of
the Lands being Sold, The Government is a Great and RichGovernment,
and if the Lands were Sold, they were Sold for a fmall matter,and Coft
but little, and it would be but a fmall matter for the Government to
make Allowance for them, and give them up.

    Lt.Gov. What do you mean by making Allowance for the Lands.

    Loron, We defire that no Houfes or Settlements may be made to the
Eaftward of *Pemmaquid,* or above *Arrowfick,* As for the *Penobfcutt* Tribe
in particular, we don't know that ever they Sold any Lands, That's all
we have to fay.

    Lt.Gov. We fhall be ready to make you an Anfwer to Morrow Morn-
ing at Nine a-Clock, and fhall Order the Signal to be made for you.

Wednefday Auguft, 3*ft.* 1 7 2 6.

    PRESENT as Before.

Lt.Gov.of the
Maffachufetts. } WE have Confidered your Motion, That we
would remove thofe two Houfes on *Kenne-*
beck and *St. George's-Rivers* a little further in,to which
we Anfwer, That thofe Houfes are on Lands Purchafed by His Majefty's
Subjects, which we are ready by Commiffioners appointed by the Go-

FIGURE 4.2. Noyes's marginalia inside the published 1726 treaty. Courtesy of
the Maine Historical Society.

Annapolis Royall ratification. Only four hundred British colonists lived
in Nova Scotia in 1726, for the most part clustered around Annapolis
Royall, so land claims did not take center stage as they did in the Casco
Bay negotiations. Captain John Doucett, the delegate on behalf of British
Nova Scotia, issued a set of reciprocal promises along with the treaty,
much as Dummer did. For the Mi'kmaqs and Wulstukwiuks, the 1726
treaty laid the foundation of formal diplomatic relations between them
and Nova Scotia on the footing of equals, transferring their relationship
with the French king to the British sovereign.[167]

    Dummer's Treaty completed an evolution in Wabanaki strategy that
began during the imperial wars of the 1690s and 1700s. For the Indians,
the results of the 1722–27 fighting showed the limits of what could be
achieved through force alone. The extent of Wabanaki casualties remains
unknown, but continued population decline at a time of Massachusetts
growth, coupled with France's failure to join the war, had eroded Native
power.[168] The Indians had failed to inflict damage to colonial people

and property on the scale of the previous three wars. They retained the ability to harass colonial forces and extract a high cost if Massachusetts resorted to force, but most Wabanakis realized the dwindling chances of successful military resistance. But if the recent war revealed the limits of Wabanaki military power, Dummer's Treaty showed the potential for a new form of power based on the Indians' status as the source of colonial landed property. As long as the Wabanakis remained united in choosing which seventeenth-century land agreements to acknowledge, they retained the ability to influence factious Bay Colonists.

For many influential players, then, Dummer's Treaty promised to be the basis for mutual peace and prosperity. The factors shaping the treaty's importance loomed ever-larger following 1727. In 1729, the pro-treaty speculators and the Wabanakis gained a powerful new ally in Jonathan Belcher, the new governor of Massachusetts. Under his administration, Massachusetts and Wabanaki leaders forged a working relationship that succeeded in overcoming challenges to the peace during the 1730s. This proved possible in large part due to Dummer's Treaty but also to a series of challenges to the speculators' claims from royal agents and frontier colonists. Under assault from rival claimants, the speculators clung tighter to their Indian deeds as the best source of landownership. In doing so they revealed the central role Indigenous presence on the land played in shaping ongoing struggles to define the nature of landed property on the frontier.

5 / In Defiance of the Proprietors, 1727–1735

It was not supposed to turn out this way. The ink was drying on Dummer's Treaty when Falmouth residents invited the Reverend Thomas Smith to become the first established minister in Maine east of Wells in 1727. The well-connected Smith appreciated the region's fraught history of Anglo-Wabanaki land conflict better than most—his father Thomas served as truckmaster and Indian agent at nearby Saco. After wartime visits to Falmouth, Smith noted how fighting kept the occupants "very poor, by reason of the Indians that keep the people from their farms . . . and confined them to garrisons."[1] But by the time Smith *fils* took up his new position, the fighting had ceased.

What Smith did not know was that the end of frontier fighting triggered a renewal of another related struggle over the future of Falmouth. Rival factions called the Old Proprietors and New Proprietors advanced clashing visions of community, law, and empire. As a brother to a large stakeholder in a venerable title and the assignee of another himself, Smith's sympathies lay with the circle of well-heeled Old Proprietors who claimed much of the land around town, whether they lived there or not.[2] Smith thought less of the ordinary colonists who had clung to their holdings in Falmouth during the war. Smith recorded in his diary at the end of 1726 that these colonists had "engaged to come to them" a set of newcomers "as bad as themselves, having a design of building up the town with any that came and offered," but the onset of war had foiled this scheme and made room for "some very good" replacements.[3] Smith believed the town showed "wisdom" in admitting "a number of gentlemen" as inhabitants, including Pejepscot Proprietor Job Lewis and Colonel Thomas Westbrook.[4] Falmouth's pastor believed these gentlemen of property should control the pace and nature of the development of the vacant lands surrounding the scattered houses hugging Casco Bay. Their deeds gave them legal title to it, and their status qualified them to lead. Many of the colonists living in Falmouth had other ideas.

Soon after Smith took up his post, a "caballing party carried all before them" in the annual election for town officers.[5] Voters replaced several Old Proprietors with new men bent on attracting more people to Falmouth by distributing vacant lands around town. The Old Proprietors claimed much of the empty land the new leaders hoped to distribute. Smith fretted in his diary as various factions struggled for control of town meetings, "as near fighting as possible."[6] Under the leadership of this "caballing party," the town of Falmouth assumed the power to distribute the commons, decide who participated in that process, and levy taxes to defend their power to do so in court. By assuming that power, the town body behaved like a proprietary company while still preserving the democratic style of voting of a town meeting. The resident faction in town later formed their own self-proclaimed proprietary company, and for several years rival sets of town proprietors claimed legitimacy. War may have ended in 1727, but chaos reigned in Falmouth until 1732.

Events in Falmouth formed part of a wider pattern of conflict on the eastern frontier over the nature and purpose of the British Empire in the region. Absentee speculators hoped to orchestrate an ordered occupation of their property with the arrival of peace, at long last making good on their investments. The latest war may have interrupted their plans, but Dummer's Treaty provided the foundation for a lasting peace while clarifying titles. Or so they had hoped. Many colonists rejected the notion that the speculators had a mandate to distribute municipal resources as they saw fit. Instead, they argued that residents of frontier communities should have a greater say in the distribution of land and timber rights. Although each community operated independently, colonists shared the same broad concerns. Absentee proprietors, complained a group of North Yarmouth residents in 1731, "are not to be a rule for us who are on the spot—the Circumstances are Vastly Different."[7] North Yarmouth residents echoed the complaints of inhabitants not only in neighboring Falmouth but also in Scarborough, where a similar local insurgency swept into power during the annual elections of 1730, inaugurating its own campaign of land distribution.[8] Inhabitants of Brunswick did not bother to record their specific grievances with the Pejepscot Proprietors in the town book when they illegally laid out 100 acres of land to Sepren Cornish provided he "make improvements on Said Land in Defiance of the proprietors."[9]

The speculators defended their titles against these challenges, invoking their property rights as British subjects while at the same time insisting those rights came from fair purchase of the land's Indigenous owners. This landed property, protected by the British constitution, yet originating from non-Britons, could not, they insisted, be taken by municipal decrees or royal fiat. Seizure of their property by colonists or anyone else, they argued, was a dangerous subversion of law and order.

In a series of confrontations in courtrooms, town meetings, and even in farmers' fields, antagonists struggled over the true nature of land-ownership. Did their venerable deeds provide the proprietors with an ironclad title to their vacant claims? Were the speculators vital agents of empire, or a hindrance on expansion into the Dawnland? Whom was the empire meant to benefit?

These conflicts occurred at the same time that the Boston speculators faced the renewed possibility of British interference with their claims to the eastern frontier. Just as clashes with Governor Andros and his backers in the 1680s had done, looming threats from imperial and colonial challengers to the speculators' claims elevated the importance of Native land deeds. Under heightened pressure from rival claimants, the Boston grandees could ill afford Wabanaki repudiation of their deeds. Property disputes in Maine after 1727 therefore underlined the importance of Dummer's Treaty, which continued to serve as a form of oversize land deed for companies like the Pejepscot Proprietors. As they rallied to defend their titles, the speculators depended on their Indian deeds—and continued Wabanaki recognition—as never before.

They did so even as Wabanaki presence in the Dawnland and the accompanying threat they posed to squatters tamped down enthusiasm among New Englanders to move east. The Pejepscot, Clarke & Lake, and Muscongus Proprietors all proceeded to reoccupy coastal towns on their claims at a slow pace. The major Pejepscot town of Brunswick finally incorporated in 1737. Although the fragmentary state of their records makes retracing Clarke & Lake business in the eighteenth century difficult, it appears they gave up attempting to put colonists on their (dubious) claims north of Fort Richmond on the Kennebec River, confining their postwar efforts to attracting occupants to the acknowledged company lands around Georgetown.[10]

Several smaller companies also began to stir after 1727. Heirs to the Draper claim along the Sheepscot River (the "Sheepscot Proprietors") began dispatching agents to the region in the early 1730s and finally assembled at the Sun Tavern in Boston to divide their 10,000-acre claim in 1738.[11] Their colonists alternately cooperated and feuded with Scots-Irish residents of the abandoned Clarke & Lake town of Cork, and the abortive Dunbar townships (discussed below).[12] Boston investors styling themselves the Wiscasset Proprietors bought up John Davie's old Indian purchase around Wiscasset Bay and began soliciting for colonists at this time as well.[13] Nearby, Christopher Tappan and Obediah Gove, having obtained Indian deeds to land around the Damariscotta, began issuing 200-acre lots in 1735, and by the early 1740s, the Pemaquid Proprietors finally assembled to make their claim on that peninsula a reality.[14]

Many of these claims overlapped, and the rival companies (often meeting in coffeehouses and taverns just down the street from one another in Boston) spent years engaged in furious litigation. Almost all of their titles descended from Indian deeds, albeit several dubious in origin. In 1729, however, a new arrival jolted all of these speculators into concerted action.

Dogs in the Manger: Dunbar and the Proprietors

That year, a reduced army colonel named David Dunbar sailed to New England with an appointment as surveyor of the King's Woods and orders to preserve 300,000 acres of the best pine and oak forest for the king's navy. Lumbermen had illegally cut down the largest trees west of the Kennebec River, so Dunbar set his sights on the underpopulated territory between the Kennebec and Nova Scotia. Rather than contend with the tangle of claims various Boston-based land companies had on the region, Dunbar planned to invite Irish and German Protestant colonists to build towns under Nova Scotian jurisdiction, sidestepping Bay Colony interference altogether.[15]

Arriving in Sagadahoc during the spring of 1729, Dunbar laid out the area between the Sheepscot and Muscongus Rivers into three townships: Townsend (modern Boothbay), Harrington (modern Bristol), and Walpole (modern Nobleborough and the northern part of Bristol). He also resurrected the ruins of old Fort Pemaquid, renaming it Fort Frederick, after the new Prince of Wales. Dunbar gave the arriving colonists assurance of title as leaseholders under the king, charging either the symbolic rent of one peppercorn or small amounts of money. Many of the colonists who took Dunbar's offer were hardy Scots Irish, like David Cargill, who secured a perpetual deed to 86 acres in 1732, paying one penny per acre to the king annually.[16] Under these terms, colonists began to take up lots in the new towns. Dunbar also took care to notify the local Penobscots of his plans. The Indians responded through interpreter John Gyles that as long as Dunbar's colonists remained within the bounds of earlier seventeenth-century towns, "we Consent to it," though they remained wary.[17]

Unfortunately for Dunbar, his relationships with Anglo New England residents began badly and grew worse. Massachusetts leaders protested as soon as they got wind of the scheme, and Dunbar's answers only aggravated their fears. Dunbar responded with two interlocking arguments. The Massachusetts charter did not, in fact, extend east of the Kennebec. Even if it did, the province's neglect in rebuilding the fort at Pemaquid and developing the land proved that the Bay Colony had proved incapable of managing it anyway. It was, he informed Lieutenant Governor William Dummer, "like the dog in the Manger (I beg pardon for the Comparison) that would not let the Horse eat hay or eat it himself."[18] As for the tangle of speculators' claims to the region, which seemed to grow "dayly," Dunbar believed the king should ignore them, "since there are so many of them that if they are allowed . . . the Country as hitherto may lye for Ever a Wilderness."[19] Dunbar's arguments were not new; assorted schemers had been offering proposals to seize the land east of the Kennebec River for decades.[20] Most of them, like Dunbar, pinned the blame for years of bad relations with the Indians on the Bay Colonists—an argument guaranteed to find a favorable hearing in Whitehall. Unlike his predecessors, however, Dunbar had authority.

What authority he had remained a matter of dispute for several years. As surveyor of the King's Woods, Dunbar did not have the power to commission militia officers, appoint judges, or perform other official administrative duties. For a time, Dunbar was able to secure the cooperation of the governor of Nova Scotia, Richard Philipps, but he was only able to stretch his commission as surveyor so far. To complicate matters further, Dunbar soon found Bay Colony leaders were far more invested in resisting his efforts than Phillips was in supporting them.

A new Massachusetts governor arrived in 1730 to take charge of the anti-Dunbar movement. The son of a prominent Boston merchant, an ally for the proprietors, and a staunch advocate for the Bay Colony, Jonathan Belcher wasted little time in joining forces with Dunbar's growing list of enemies. He took a personal dislike to the ambitious royal official, which only grew when Dunbar secured an appointment to serve as Belcher's lieutenant governor in New Hampshire.[21] (The colonies of

Massachusetts and New Hampshire shared an executive until 1741.) Throughout his career, Belcher displayed an intense dislike of both the Irish and anyone whom he suspected of challenging his prerogative, two descriptions that perfectly described Dunbar.[22] He took to criticizing his new lieutenant governor, "a vile fellow," in colorful terms, calling him "the Tent pitcher" and "Teague."[23] Although Belcher hesitated to press his superiors to replace his unwanted subordinate, the speculators had no such concerns.

Unfortunately for Dunbar, his new colony sat upon the claims of several Boston-based land companies. Dunbar's activities triggered howls of protest from the Pemaquid, Sheepscot, and Muscongus Proprietors, who complained to the Massachusetts General Court that Dunbar had intruded on their land—however empty it may have been.[24] Only a direct order from the King in Council prevented the Massachusetts legislature from sending militia to seize Dunbar's rebuilt Fort Pemaquid.[25] The Muscongus Proprietors stood to lose the most from Dunbar's activities. The surveyor was delighted to hear the Penobscots criticize the company's ill-gotten Madockawando deed during a visit to his fort and dismissed their "pretence to Indian purchases" in a letter to his superiors.[26] In response, the proprietors dispatched a young merchant named Samuel Waldo to London to argue for Dunbar's removal, his efforts cheered by other companies.[27]

Indians—as enemies, potential allies, and a source of land title—played an important, if indirect, role in the ensuing collision. Proprietors like Adam Winthrop knew their Indian titles alone would not withstand metropolitan scrutiny. Instead, Winthrop hedged his bets when writing on behalf of the Pemaquid Proprietors, claiming his associates held "a Secure title" to land Dunbar claimed "both by grant from the Crown and a purchase from the Indians," which, the speculator emphasized, "is allways held inviolable *in these parts*" (emphasis mine).[28] The attorney and solicitor general decided whether the Bay Colony held a legitimate claim to the disputed territory, framing the issue as whether Massachusetts, and by extension the speculators, had "by their neglect and even refusal to defend, take care of and improve [Maine], forfeited their said Right to the Government" of the region.[29] Dunbar assembled a bevy of statements claiming that a "base and fraudulent" Massachusetts government swindled the Indians and bungled the settlement of Maine, while affidavits provided by Waldo's side claimed that, "wholly owing" to Indian wars, "the Eastern parts of said province of Massachusetts Bay are not now in an improved setled condition."[30] The attorney and solicitor general found in favor of Massachusetts. They went further, adding that in America, "the same regularity and exactness is not to be expected as in private suits concerning Titles to Lands in England, but that in these cases the principal Regard ought to be had to the Possession and the Expenses the partys have been at in endeavouring to Settle and Cultivate such Lands."[31] In other words, provided the speculators planted at least a small settlement marking possession of a tract of land and demonstrated that enough money had been invested, the land belonged to them, even at the expense of a more direct supply of mast timber for the Royal Navy. This 1731 ruling gave full governmental backing to the Boston land companies' method of colonizing the Maine frontier while at the same time avoided wading into any provincial disputes over land titles.

Not for the last time, the triumph of the speculators came at the expense of local colonists. The predominantly Scots-Irish families who had moved to the now defunct Province of Sagadahoc were left to shift for themselves. Unsure of their titles, and with troops withdrawing from the coastal forts, the inhabitants scattered. One resident, John Campbell, later testified about the effects of "Dunbar's Removall by His Majestys order obtained by Col. Waldo who with others claimed the Lands." Of the sixty families living on the Damariscotta River in 1732, "a great part of the said Sixty Familys quitted thee Settlements, some of whom went to New Settlements on the St Georges River, and others to Boston and parts Adjascent" while others remained and set about "Farming and Lumbering."[32] Many of Dunbar's former colonists, including Campbell, took up under Samuel Waldo, where they had to contend with yet another set of original claimers; the Penobscots.[33]

Even as the proprietors celebrated their victory, Dunbar could take solace in their inability to enjoy its fruits in peace. "There are many people tearing one Another to pieces upon disputes of Lands in the Province of Maine," he wrote, "many familys at Casco who have Setled and improved thereabouts for several years are now to be turned out by old Claimants to the same Lands who have layn dormant."[34]

"The Irregular Proceedings of the Town"

Although staged over different territory than the Sagadahoc, a series of clashes to the southwest in the communities hugging Casco Bay also centered on rival sources of land title. In the towns of Scarborough, Falmouth, and North Yarmouth, residents confronted absentee landowners claiming vast tracts of vacant land in their communities. Dummer's War exacerbated the divide between absentees and residents as the wartime destruction fed colonists' conviction that safety lay in numbers. Eager to attract new neighbors, inhabitants sought to offer them vacant land on the condition they live in town for a minimum number of years or forfeit the grants.[35] However, enough proprietors—both absentee and resident—opposed measures distributing portions of the commons that inhabitants had little hope of achieving their aims in proprietors' meetings.

In response, residents moved to circumvent the proprietors' power. For residents frustrated by the actions of absentee proprietors, town meetings served as the most effective venue for the exercise of local power. In most New England towns, everyone who had been granted the status of "Inhabitant" by the town body was entitled to vote in town meetings, and the votes had equal weight.[36] Resident factions in town meetings could therefore bolster their support by granting inhabitant status to more people. In contrast, proprietors' meetings were open only to those who held shares in the town commons, and votes were weighted according to shares held. As a result, even a handful of proprietors with enough shares could dominate the decisions of that body.

The rising resident faction in Falmouth's town meetings that frightened Reverend Thomas Smith had counterparts in neighboring Scarborough and North Yarmouth. Scarborough inhabitants had begun organizing in 1720, although Dummer's War interrupted their efforts. A reinvigorated resident faction swept into power during the 1730 annual selection of town officers. Under their leadership, Scarborough residents voted to confirm earlier grants contested by "Old Claimers"—many of them absentee—including Boston merchants Timothy Prout and Samuel Waldo. Nor did Scarborough residents stop there. They also voted to pay for an agent to represent them in court against the Old Claimers.[37] Depopulated North Yarmouth did not incorporate until 1733, but its residents began to hold gatherings that functioned like town meetings, and even began recording their decisions in an unofficial town book.[38]

Activities in town meetings provoked a furious response from absentee proprietors and their allies, who pointed out that dividing the commons and distributing it to newcomers lay outside of the legal power of the township according to a provincial law passed in 1692.[39] The Old Proprietors of Falmouth protested that the "the Inhabitants shall have Town meetings and act as a Town And the Proprietors Shall have their meetings." However, "the Inhabitants thinking or Desireing to think this Power was all given to them, have at their Town meetings taken all the

Lands into their Own hands gone on admitting Inhabitants and making them Proprietors," thus breaking the law.[40] Eyeing the turmoil in Falmouth, two absentee proprietors of North Yarmouth fretted "With out doubt the [residents] would be very Glad it might be So that thay might devide the [absentee claims] amongst them and run all things into Confusion as is the unhappy Case and State of Falmouth in Cascobay there Neibouring Town."[41]

Residents in several towns tried to circumvent this legal obstacle to municipal control of lands by forming their *own* network of proprietors. After the Old Proprietors succeeded in demolishing the town's legal basis for granting lands (addressed below), Falmouth inhabitants sidestepped the issue by forming their own group of resident "New Proprietors," which functioned much like the Falmouth town meetings by another name. Two days before the first New Proprietors meeting, Falmouth inhabitants voted to grant commons rights to ninety-one men, the bulk of whom became the New Proprietors. Their subsequent behavior reflected the same priorities as the town meetings, such as a vote in November 1731 to require all newly admitted proprietors to build a house and "bring in a settlement in their own persons"—with no typical proprietary allowance for furnishing of agents or tenants—on their land grants.[42] Attendees who recorded their dissent at the May 11 town meeting that birthed the New Proprietors formed the Old Proprietors, along with other nonresident landowners.[43] The Old Proprietors afterward held separate meetings to plan legal challenges to "the irregular proceedings of the Town of Falmouth."[44] Between 1730 and 1732, Falmouth housed dueling groups of proprietors. There was some overlapping attendance between them, as members of opposing groups attended competing meetings to lodge protests.[45]

Scarborough residents pursued a similar strategy to their Falmouth neighbors, although the sequence of events occurred in reverse, with residents first attempting to act through the proprietors before moving the locus of their activity to the town meetings, then back to the proprietors again. From 1727 until the mid-1740s, the goal of Scarborough residents remained unchanged. As one call to a proprietors' meeting in 1739 put it, they believed the "Large tracts of land in [Scarborough] Claimed by virtue of antient grants . . . the bounds whereof are not Known" had "hindred" the "settlement and growth of the town."[46]

The resident faction in Scarborough managed to exert a greater influence in the proprietors' meetings than in Falmouth, demonstrated by the conduct of their meetings as early as 1720, when they voted—counter to

Massachusetts law—to weigh votes equally, like a town meeting, instead of by shares.[47] Ignoring the protests of large landholders like Timothy Prout, the Scarborough Proprietors continued to conduct themselves like a town meeting for the next several decades. They decided that only resident proprietors could call a meeting in the future. The proprietors also voted to levy a tax of £1 3s. on twelve newly admitted proprietors who did not live in Scarborough, and later passed stringent residency requirements for new grantees.[48]

Lacking a local body with any semblance of legitimacy for them to take over, North Yarmouth residents decided to create their own. Their predicament stemmed from a combination of Wabanaki and absentee proprietary power. The Wabanakis drove colonists out of North Yarmouth in 1676 and again little more than a decade later. During Dummer's War the town was almost abandoned for the third time in fifty years, but some of the townspeople held out in several blockhouses.[49] Just before the fighting started in 1722 a number of proprietors had successfully petitioned the legislature to empower a committee "dwelling in or near to Boston . . . to Regulate the Settlement."[50] The appended signatures included Jacob Royall, descended from one of the original four trustees of the town, and the wealthy landholders (and Boston residents) John Smith and John Powell. Anyone wishing to prove their claims to the proprietors after Dummer's War had to bring claims to the proprietor's clerk in Boston, where the meetings were held.[51]

When the decisions of the Boston committee proved too slow and inefficient for the colonists who joined the wartime holdouts in North Yarmouth, they started assuming the title of proprietors for themselves. A gathering of self-styled "proprietors and settlers" that included tenants complained the committee "put [them] off with fair promises and nothing more" while "the greatest part of the lots remain unsettled."[52] When the committee subsequently laid out land for a road, residents held what they called "a meeting of the proprietors residing" to consider the decision and agreed the road's placement was "incommodious for the Settlement of the Town." The Boston committee, themselves proprietors, was not convinced by this creative relabeling and "Disallowed" both its request and existence.[53] Despite the frigid reception they received from the committee, resident proprietors in North Yarmouth continued to hold illegal meetings.[54]

The resident factions of the Casco Bay towns justified their extralegal actions by arguing that fairness and reason should trump the law. When Falmouth appointed agents to justify municipal seizure of vacant land, they described town proceedings as "fairly and honestly acted." Because Falmouth had behaved reasonably, they argued, the Old Proprietors had no grounds to move for the overturning of the authority exercised by Falmouth for the past twelve years. If the actions of the town appeared extraordinary, they justified these measures by reminding the General Court that "during the last Indian War . . . they were much Exposed and during which time they have received no help" from the absentee proprietors "but their pretences." Instead, the absentees "Slept till the war and all danger was over and when the Inhabitants stood the brunt of it, and supported their Settlement and so made the Lands Valuable, then some of these pretended ancient proprietors started their dormant claims."[55] Writing on behalf of North Yarmouth in a dispute with the neighboring Pejepscot Proprietors, Ammi Ruhama Cutter mocked the company's "vast and exorbitant Claim." If the Pejepscot Proprietors received the contested lands between them and North Yarmouth, the decision would "hurt the Interests of the Province either by leaving the Land unsettled," or introducing inhabitants loyal not to Massachusetts, but to a land company. In addition, North Yarmouth residents had "their Blood Spilt upon the Land in defending their just Possessions."[56]

According to frontier colonists, venerable deeds and invocation of privilege could be fig leaves used to dispossess those who had occupied and improved land, and therefore had a stronger claim to it. Boston merchant Timothy Prout complained to fellow speculators that he had witnessed a group of Scarborough residents "going over some Pattent Land granted by Sir Ferdinando Gorge[s], Stamping upon it and Crying out, we have got Firdinando Gorge and all his Pattents underfoot long ago."[57] A millwright in York echoed their sentiments in an early eighteenth-century case. Facing eviction from a family claiming title to his land by virtue of a 1638 grant, Samuel Webber insisted that title by possession "goes beyond all."[58] North Yarmouth's self-styled resident proprietors pointed out that absentee proprietors could afford to let their tenants struggle to cultivate "the Bad land as well as the good" while allowing other potentially valuable land to appreciate in value, but "we residents here say we must have the Best and most Comodius Land first to Enable us to get our Bread . . . And not tamely Submit to those delusions which may make us Miserable."[59]

For the absentee speculators and their allies, events in the Casco Bay towns represented not local efforts to bolster exposed frontier communities, but an assault on law, property, and hierarchy. In a series of protests lodged in town and proprietors' records, along with petitions to the governor and General Court, the speculators articulated their own vision of what the empire should look like.

Defenders of Law and Property

The absentee proprietors invoked Massachusetts law to defend their prerogatives. The "Ancient Proprietors" of Falmouth noted (accurately) that according to law, "the Inhabitants shall have Town meetings and act as a Town And the Proprietors Shall have their meetings." However, "the Inhabitants thinking or Desireing to think this Power was all given to them, have at their Town meetings taken all the Lands into their Own hands gone on admitting Inhabitants and making them Proprietors," thus breaking the law.[60] The resident allies of the absentee Falmouth proprietors agreed, deploring the "irregular proceeding of our select men and committees . . . contrary to the act of the General Court."[61] In Scarborough, the absentees protested the resident proprietors' method of voting like a town meeting to grant away absentee claims, "Contrary to Law or Common Reason," and assailed the "Illegull manner" of the meeting.[62] The absentee faction entered their protests into the town book, "as for a proprietors Book we don't Suppose their to be any their never being any Transaction of that nature according to law or justice."[63] Like their Falmouth counterparts, the absentee Scarborough proprietors had the letter of the law on their side.[64] The absentee proprietors insisted the undermining of their maintenance of claims and authority would harm not only their interest but also the public good. Timothy Prout warned the General Court in 1752 that if Scarborough's appropriations of his land continued unchecked, "this Town, if not the whole Country, will be kept in very Distressing Circumstances."[65] In 1750, Prout assailed the proceedings of the Scarborough resident proprietors as "Contrary to the good and wholesome Laws of the Government of the Massachusetts."[66]

While all colonists shared in the belief that the British Empire functioned in part to protect the property of its subjects, the absentee proprietors believed that some subjects should benefit more than others.[67] Christopher Toppan, a proprietor living in Newbury, Massachusetts, wrote the governor in 1727 after hearing that "Severall persons" had been cutting down trees on his property in Damariscotta. He asked the governor to instruct the local garrison commander to send a few soldiers "across the woods" a dozen miles away to identify the perpetrators.[68] According to the absentee proprietors of Falmouth, the town's decision to grant away their "Proper Estates" revealed "they are resolved Whether the Indians or English have the land the right owners shall be no better for it."[69]

According to the absentees and their allies, the actions of resident factions in the Casco Bay towns also brought undesirable elements of society into the political process. The Libby family in Scarborough, who took the lead in rejecting Timothy Prout's membership as a proprietor, personified those fears; they had been seventeenth-century tenants on the estate Prout claimed.[70] Reverend Thomas Smith of Falmouth was not alone in disdaining many of the humbler frontier residents, fearing their attempts at "building up the town with any who came and offered."[71] Falmouth's absentee faction urged the General Court to overturn the town's decision to admit so many new inhabitants, suggesting that "if there are still vacancies," the proprietors and a committee sent by the court could together admit "the best of those persons that have been irregularly introduced into the town."[72] The absentee proprietors of North Yarmouth complained the resident proprietors "often meet and alow those that are not Proprietors nor Quallifyed to vote among them."[73] When absentee proprietors in Maine asked for the General Court to step in and overturn municipal decisions, they sought extraordinary measures to correct what they believed was a proportionally extraordinary disruption.

Order in the Courts

Court cases played a major role in deciding clashes over land and authority in Maine. They also reveal the two competing cultures of ownership at work within colonial society. The absentee speculators relied on chains of paper deeds—often stretching back a century—to prove ownership of land. Residents relied heavily on eyewitness testimony and town grants.

What juries thought of particular evidence remains unclear in many cases. Court records seldom included reasons why juries reached the verdict they did. Nor did they mention what the presiding justices told them about a particular case (and they sometimes instructed juries at length). In addition, case files containing evidence presented at trial are often incomplete, so we cannot even be certain what juries heard or saw. Cases often ricocheted back and forth up the three-tiered court system, with verdicts being reversed on appeal, then reversed again with no obvious explanation.[74]

One alleged miscarriage of justice reveals how the courts functioned and how juries sometimes reasoned. Moses Pearson of Falmouth lost a suit of ejectment against John Thomes in the York County Court of Common Pleas in June 1751, then brought forward an appeal for the June 1752 session of the Superior Court of Judicature. According to Pearson, his evidence was so strong that the justices "Sum'd up the cause to the Jury in favour" of his case. He lost, and later he learned that Samuel Small, one of the jurors, had a case against Timothy Prout in Scarborough that same session, and "the foundation" of Small's claim "was the same" as Pearson's adversary. Small managed to persuade the others—at least one of whom also owned land abutting Prout—to side against Pearson to help set a precedent "in Support of the Action wherin he was interested."[75] An earlier complaint in 1722 described similar reasoning in a York County jury, which delivered a verdict in favor of smallholders against a wealthy Boston absentee claimant.[76]

The small population of York County often made the legal process a personal affair. Timothy Prout leveled repeated charges of jury bias in York County to the General Court, protesting that networks of friends in eastern towns made finding an impartial jury there impossible.[77] Scarborough residents responded to Prout's allegations not by denying jurors knew each other but by pointing out that the proprietor himself "carefully Examins and knows every man on the Jury in every Cause he is concern'd in and whence he came."[78] Prout also rendered colorful— though unverifiable—descriptions of these networks colluding against powerful outiders. "I have seen a man Red hot going into Court, to be Sworn upon the Jury Solemly Protest that they would not allow any man to Posess above One hundred Acres of Land in thare County," he complained to fellow absentee proprietors in 1754.[79] Prout lamented that "it is a common practice to Try Causes in the Taverns in the County," and in Scarborough there was "a Company of Crafty fellows" who met in the local tavern to "Consider how they shall disappoint any Person who Claims any Large Tracts of Land in the County."[80] The mixed record of York County verdicts contradicts Prout's vivid descriptions of an organized cabal of economic levelers, however.

Instead, the evidence from Falmouth and Scarborough cases suggests that residents challenging absentee claims required at least the appearance of proprietary authority—even in the form of upstart, self-appointed town proprietors. The biggest case in Falmouth illustrated this point. The dispute centered on the 310-acre Munjoy claim on the eastern side of Falmouth Neck (the peninsula jutting eastward into Casco Bay, on which most of the town then sat). Falmouth had been granting land on the Munjoy claim, and the case decided whether those actions would hold up in a court of law. The Munjoy heirs, a network of gentle-men, merchants, and physicians led by Joseph and Samuel Moody, sued Joseph Bayley and Phillip Hodgkins, a shipwright and cordwainer who had been living on the disputed property. In the October 1729 trial, the Munjoy heirs presented an unbroken series of deeds beginning with a grant from Sir Ferdinando Gorges to George Cleeve and Richard Tucker in 1636.[81] Bayley and Hodgkins traced their rights to a purchase from Robert Lawrence, a widower and second husband of Mary Munjoy. Their case hinged on a series of witnesses who testified to Lawrence's occupancy and improvement of the property until his death.[82] The jury backed the Munjoy title over mere occupancy, and a series of appeals ultimately proved fruitless.[83] The decision prompted Falmouth residents to form their own rival group of proprietors, who enjoyed greater suc-cess. In January 1732, the absentee proprietors sued John East, a leader of the resident faction in town, for trespass when he built a house on their land claim, granted to him by the town-created New Proprietors. The history of Falmouth's dueling proprietary bodies was entered into evidence, and the jury found in favor of East, referring to the absentee faction as "Mr. Edmund Mountfort and others who call themselves Pro-prietors of the Common and Undivided Lands."[84]

The Scarborough cases unfolded in a similar pattern, with York County juries upholding individual claims in the face of town or squat-ter possession, but viewing the ad hoc resident proprietary bodies more favorably, even when absentee proprietors challenged their proceedings. Although Timothy Prout complained on multiple occasions that he was unable to get a fair hearing by a York County jury, he won several trials validating his Scottow claim in 1728.[85] Prout lost only when he tried to eject neighbors living on lands granted by the Scarborough Proprietors in a series of cases from 1735 onward.[86] The Millikens—Prout's allies in his struggle against the resident faction in Scarborough—based their claim on a 1651 Indian land sale and initially fared the same as Prout, losing a series of trials in front of York County juries against neighbors who held lands granted by the resident Scarborough Proprietors.[87] However, when the Millikens appealed their cases to the Suffolk County–based Superior Court (which included the absentees' hometown of Boston), they man-aged to reverse most verdicts.[88]

In both Falmouth and Scarborough cases, frontier juries were more inclined to find in favor of resident claimers against the absentee factions. Residents lost this advantage when cases moved to the distant Superior Court on appeal. Over time, this meant that the absentees gained the upper hand in many disputes—at least in court. But achieving comity in frontier towns took more than a few verdicts, requiring the reconciliation of absentee and residents' land use goals.

"Agreeable to Town and Propriety": Qualified Resolution

The fitful process of reconciling absentee and resident factions was a multistage process. Court decisions often formed the catalyst for resolving conflict by closing off one side's legal options. But court decisions alone could not restore order and cooperation in frontier communities. That step required further local action in town and proprietary meetings, and usually involved more compromise than the outcome of particular court cases might dictate.

Practical and ideological factors contributed to both sides' willingness to compromise. The absentee landowners depended on frontier residents to respect court decisions. If they did not, then the absentees would face an unpalatable choice: allow locals to squat or strip valuable timber off of the absentee lands unhindered, or pay agents to bring costly and time-consuming lawsuits against the offenders. For their part, residents preferred wealthy allies to enemies in Boston. In addition, they had no more willingness—and less money—to pay for lawsuits when it was possible to negotiate a compromise. Both sides also shared a political culture that prized cooperation and consensus at the municipal level.[89]

Despite the worries of the absentees, the colonists' conservative goals also aided reconciliation. Frontier residents were not social levelers. They objected not to the proprietors' wealth but to how their pursuit of it hampered the struggle for both security and prosperity by frontier residents. The frontier quest for stable community involved the "warning out" of poor people alongside moves to seize vacant claims. As North Yarmouth inhabitants decided how to best challenge the absentee claim hindering town growth in 1739, they ordered eight men (and their families) too poor to pay taxes out of town.[90]

Colonists also believed—like their contemporaries in the rest of Massachusetts—that stable communities needed the leadership of wealthy, prominent citizens.[91] Nascent Maine towns sought to attract them when possible. Falmouth's Reverend Thomas Smith, ally of the absentee faction, noted with approval in 1727 that the new grantees included "a number of gentlemen that stand their friends."[92] Falmouth's resident proprietors even admitted Jeremiah Moulton, a war hero and justice of the peace, "notwithstanding his not complying with the condition of the rights being granted to him."[93] Wealthy residents provided necessary funds for sawmills, bridges, and other beneficial works, and towns granted them land or other benefits to do so. The North Yarmouth town body—still mixing proprietary and municipal functions in 1735—voted to tax each proprietary right fifteen shillings and give the money to John Powell "for Building and maintaining a good Suffiicient Bridg . . . provided the Non Resident proprieters will pay their parts . . . [and] Powel[l] maintain the Said Bridg for Ever."[94]

As a result, colonists sought to incorporate the absentee landowners into their communities by defining their estates and curbing their excesses, not by excluding them. At the height of the conflict between the Old and New Proprietors in Falmouth, the New Proprietors admitted absentees Thomas Westbrook and Samuel Waldo after those men signed an agreement turning over several acres of their claim in the heart of town in exchange for 100 unclaimed acres outside of it.[95] Dominicus Jordan, a resident Old Proprietor in Falmouth, agreed to quitclaim the rest of his family's vast, vague claims in exchange for the town acknowledging his right to a specific 1,200-acre tract. After the town voted 50 to 1 in favor of acceptance, Jordan switched allegiance and became a powerful advocate for the resident interest.[96] The resident-dominated Scarborough Proprietors even admitted the troublesome Timothy Prout in 1737, despite his ongoing complaints and lawsuits against his neighbors.[97]

Falmouth's resident and absentee factions reached a grand settlement in 1732, prompting Reverend Thomas Smith to exclaim "Thanks to God" in his journal.[98] Resolving "there hath been meetings in said town by diferent partys to the great detriment of the publick good of the town," they agreed to "combine and incorporate into one body." The New Proprietors incorporated the Old, who acknowledged the admission of all of the proprietors admitted since May 13, 1730. The New Proprietors who had taken up lots on the previously disputed "ancient" claims would remain proprietors but would move to new unclaimed land. The remainder of the common lands would "be divided between the Antient Proprietors and the New Proprietors according to their several interests agreeable to town and propriety votes."[99] While the Falmouth Proprietors continued to admit new members who could prove descent from seventeenth-century "setlers under President Danforth," they never again admitted large numbers of new colonists without such titles.[100] The New Proprietors had succeeded in growing the town, however, and the Old Proprietors had managed to restore—in their view—respect for law and order. Reverend Smith claimed, with good reason, the agreement was "entirely to the satisfaction of everybody."[101]

In all the Casco Bay towns, population growth helped to reduce points of conflict between resident and absentee factions. Town bodies surrendered control over common lands to the proprietors by 1750, coinciding with the waning need to attract new residents.

Turmoil in Casco Bay communities highlights the crucial—if indirect—role that the Wabanakis played in the contest over property in Maine towns. The Alger and Gedney claims that caused so much rancor and confusion in Scarborough and North Yarmouth, respectively, were descended from seventeenth-century Indian land sales. As military foes, the Wabanakis also forced the abandonment of all three towns, which contributed both to the confusion of overlapping and abandoned claims and the rise in land speculation. Recognition of enduring Native power provided a major incentive for colonists to consider drastic action to attract more residents and form defensible communities. North Yarmouth residents made this point explicitly when they petitioned their Boston committee for resettlement in 1729, insisting the small population "tends very much to the discoragement of such setlers as are upon the spot and is great encourage ment to the Indians in case they are designing for mischief and wil certainly prove the utter ruin and over throw of the settle ment without a speedy remedy."[102]

The turmoil in Casco Bay communities conversely helped to stabilize Anglo-Wabanaki relations along the Dawnland frontier. The well-connected proprietors in both regions continued to base their claims in large part on Indian land deeds, and challenges from frontier colonists reinforced the importance of those agreements. Members of the large land companies were well aware of clashes in Casco Bay towns; some of them even owned land there. Samuel Waldo, majority shareholder of the Muscongus Proprietors, held extensive acreage in both Scarborough and Falmouth.[103] For many of the great land companies, Dummer's Treaty still functioned as a gigantic deed, and the proprietors could not afford to weaken a key foundation of their titles.

Motivated in part by this realization, Governor Jonathan Belcher and most speculators cooperated with the Wabanakis to defend Native land rights in the years following Dummer's Treaty, a time when the interests of Massachusetts and Wabanaki leaders converged.

Samuel Waldo rarely lost property disputes. He never lost them gracefully. (He seldom *won* them gracefully either, as his many rivals could
attest.) In July 1736, however, Waldo could at least be forgiven his surprise at being informed that the Massachusetts General Court sided with
the Penobscots against him, finding that much of his Muscongus Patent
was based on an unacknowledged Indian land deed and therefore void.
Waldo spoke on his own behalf on July 3, but to no avail. After hearing
of the General Court's decision, Waldo fired off a series of petitions for
appeal. What his arguments lacked in quality they more than made up
in quantity: he sent petitions on July 5, 6, 26, and 27 and published a
lengthy justification of his claims for the public.[1] But the General Court
and Governor Jonathan Belcher rejected them all.

If the General Court's decision was an unpleasant surprise for Waldo,
its results proved far worse for his Scots-Irish colonists. Soon after their
leaders returned from Boston that summer, groups of Penobscots confronted colonists like Thomas Gregg, who held 100 acres from Waldo.
Gregg received a visit from "A Considerable Number of Indians" who
"sett up a Mark a Little Below My house and threatened Either to pull
Down or Burn the said House if I did not within one Month Remove,"
informing him of the decision in Boston. At the end of the month,
reported Gregg, "two Indians were sent by the tribe to see If I, and the
others who ware at the Same time warn'd of[f], ware removed, and
the Houses Down, which finding they went away without Doing Any

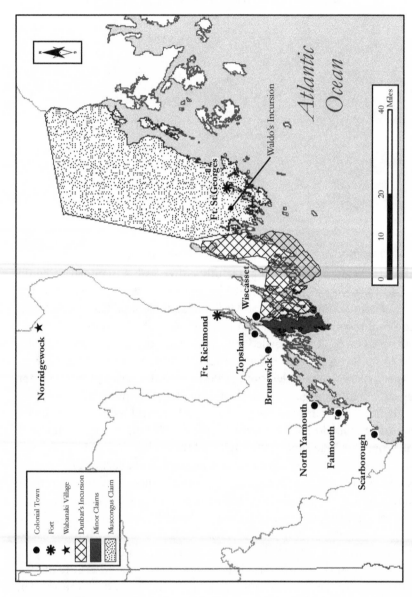

MAP 6.1. Changes to the frontier, 1727–49.

Mischiefe." Gregg's neighbors described similar experiences.[2] Colonists like Samuel Boggs who remained in their homes upriver from the "Mark [the Penobscots] had set up" faced additional pressure. A Penobscot named Sabbis "called at My house," Boggs later recalled, "and Left a gun flint with My wife . . . which Much Intimidated me and my Neighbors."[3] Boggs dismantled his house and moved his family to safety. The Penobscots carried out this eviction with the full knowledge of the nearby garrison of Fort St. Georges. Boggs and his neighbors did not have to resort to their guns, and the entire operation concluded without bloodshed.

Upsetting to Waldo and frightening for his luckless colonists, the events surrounding the dispute over the St. Georges River were a vindication of Wabanaki strategy. At Dummer's Treaty they had grafted the Wabanaki desire for a relationship with reciprocal obligations onto the speculators' prized land deeds. With the treaty serving as a form of enormous deed for the land companies, they proved open to Wabanaki complaints when Waldo attempted to revive the never-ratified Madockawando cession of 1694.

Wabanakis and speculators alike realized it was within their best interest that, as Governor Jonathan Belcher intoned in 1736, "the Articles of Peace . . . Shall be Strictly Performed."[4] Those articles of peace allowed the land speculators to justify their continued authority over the colonization of the Dawnland frontier. The same treaty that preserved the peace and promised an orderly transfer of previously sold Wabanaki land to the speculators served as a bulwark against outsiders hoping to stake their own claims—be they royal agents like Dunbar or frontier squatters acting independently. For their part, so long as they remained united and made no new land sales, the Wabanakis could invoke Dummer's Treaty to obtain Bay Colony cooperation in policing the new boundary.

The eviction of Waldo's colonists in 1736 marked the peak of cooperation between Massachusetts and Wabanaki leaders following Dummer's Treaty. Occurring without military action or French involvement, the episode has received scant attention from scholars.[5] Exploring the reasons why the Penobscots triumphed over Samuel Waldo in 1736 reveals the multiple actors who had a vested interest in the Dummer's Treaty settlement, while at the same time exposes its underlying weakness. The cultural divide over landownership continued to drive both conflict and cooperation throughout Waldo's bid to colonize the St. Georges River region on the west side of Penobscot Bay. Waldo and the Penobscots repeatedly clashed over the meaning of different rituals of ownership in multiple encounters. Most other speculators in the General Court backed the Penobscots not because they endorsed the Wabanaki culture of ownership but because Waldo's claim proved to be shaky even by the standards of absentee proprietors. The coalition that resisted Waldo in 1736 represented a convergence of interest, not understanding.

The Governor and the Speculator

The episode on the St. Georges showed that two essential components for Massachusetts adhering to Dummer's Treaty were the influence of the speculators who relied on the agreement to secure their land titles and the cooperation of the provincial governor. It was no accident that the longest peaceful interlude during the era of frontier warfare in Maine coincided so closely with Jonathan Belcher's eleven-year tenure as governor. Son of Boston merchant Andrew Belcher, Jonathan was tied to the city's commercial elites by family and business.[6] A devout Congregationalist in the old Puritan mold, Belcher joined the Company for the Propagation of the Gospel in New England, a London-based society dedicated to converting the Indians to Christianity. Throughout his years as governor, Belcher pursued this elusive goal, though he received little support for his project.[7] Before his appointment, Belcher had engaged in land speculation in Maine and elsewhere with his father. After 1729, the only project in which he retained a share was an investment in a mining enterprise in Simsbury, Connecticut.[8] Belcher remained a supporter of frontier speculative enterprises, however.[9] After his first official trip to Maine in 1732, he gushed over "the fine harbours and rivers full of fish, and border'd with champion lands.... I think that Country well deserves the particular Care Protection and Encouragment [sic] of this Government."[10]

More than most land speculators, Belcher hoped to combine fairness toward the Indians with a profitable, orderly expansion of the British Empire into the Dawnland. At a time when many New Englanders displayed a growing racism toward Indians, Belcher displayed a principled, even antiquated goodwill toward them.[11] Although Massachusetts law tried to keep Indians physically separate from white colonists, Belcher wanted to combine a program of intensive missionary efforts with marriages between whites and Indians.[12] Belcher also supported the integration of Indian volunteers with white troops on a military expedition to the West Indies in 1740, arguing, "They are the King's natural born subjects, bred up after the English manner . . . and their having black hair and tawny faces don't at all disable them from being good souldiers." He insisted their white fellow soldiers "should not insult or use them ill."[13]

In the early 1730s, Belcher launched a campaign to win Wabanaki friendship for Massachusetts. He clamped down on abusive private traders who cheated their Native customers.[14] On several occasions the governor received complaints from groups of Indians about colonial dams disrupting their fishing. Belcher intervened on their behalf, as in 1739, when he wrote a letter to one dam owner, asking him to "treat the Indians kindly" and keep a sluice open for the fish to pass through, emphasizing its importance for the Indians.[15]

Belcher also demonstrated skill at the personal aspects of successful Native diplomacy. When his wife died in October 1736, Belcher sent six pairs of gloves for Fort St. Georges commander and interpreter John Gyles to distribute "As a token of my Respect . . . tell 'em it's english [sic] Fashion to give Gloves at Funerals," asking "they (my Brethren) will mourn with me." [16] This incorporation of gift giving and familiar metaphors fit well with the Wabanaki practice of diplomacy.[17] Belcher also awarded commissions to friendly Wabanaki sagamores, investing them with authority to lead their warriors on behalf of Massachusetts, should the need arise. Alongside the authority, the commissions came with annual payments to the recipients.[18] The symbolic importance attached to the commissions was not lost on the Wabanakis. Those leaders who wished to emphasize their independence turned them down, so Belcher's venture met with only limited success. Leaders among the weaker tribes were the most receptive.[19]

In 1735, however, Samuel Waldo's actions threatened to upset Belcher's charm offensive. Unlike most of the other major speculators or the Wabanakis, Waldo had no stake in Dummer's Treaty. His company, the Muscongus Proprietors (named for the land tract they claimed), had not benefited from an Indian guarantee of their title. Unlike their rivals, they did not base their title on a sale acknowledged by the Wabanakis. Instead, the Muscongus Patent rested on an inherited share of the vast, vague Plymouth Grant of 1629, and from the disputed Madockawando land cession.[20] Compared to its rivals, the company had done a lackluster job of establishing viable towns on the claim before 1722.[21] In 1734 Samuel Waldo agreed to take over the job himself in exchange for 100,000 acres, or one-quarter of the entire patent. With the addition of other inheritances and purchases, Waldo had by then become the dominant shareholder in the company.[22]

A hard-driving businessman, Waldo's bare-knuckle tactics helped enshrine the image of large land speculators as grasping and corrupt. Waldo and his business partner Thomas Westbrook conspired to have a man named Richard Fry arrested and thrown in jail to win a lawsuit over Fry's paper mill.[23] Waldo also sued Westbrook for a debt of more than £7,500, arranging to meet with his partner in Falmouth to resolve the dispute before it went to trial in Boston. Waldo kept delaying the meeting with Westbrook, meanwhile sending his attorney to Boston to present a writ against Waldo's now unrepresented partner.[24] The harried Westbrook died bankrupt several years later. Fearing Waldo would seize the body of his business partner to extract repayment, Westbrook's family hid his remains.[25] In 1734, Waldo turned his formidable energies to settling two towns on the Muscongus Patent.

Speculator Diplomacy

Waldo's entire scheme highlighted the power of the wealthy land speculators within Massachusetts. Acting without any explicit approval or support from the government, Waldo organized the establishment of new towns in the Dawnland, conducting himself like a representative of the Crown. While requesting and even expecting provincial support in the form of military protection and the services of the interpreter at Fort St. Georges, Waldo proceeded without bothering to ask Governor Belcher or anyone else about how his plans influenced Massachusetts Indian policy. Waldo held two conferences with the Penobscots and even gave them gifts at the conclusion of the second one, much as a governor would.[26]

Waldo's diplomatic overtures emerged from the Penobscots' ongoing refusal to acknowledge the legitimacy of the Madockawando cession that encompassed much of the Muscongus Patent. This had not stopped Waldo from shipping in colonists (many of them Protestants from Ulster, and eventually Germany and Scotland, with Waldo hoping Europeans would be more amenable to living as his tenants, unlike most New Englanders, who preferred freeholds),[27] and advertising that his "title is indisputable."[28] The Penobscots were quite ready to dispute the title, however, and in April 1735, a month after the first colonists arrived on the west side of the St. Georges River, Waldo sailed to the area to meet with the Indians.

Even though Waldo and the Muscongus Proprietors created the only records of the speculator's foray into Indian diplomacy, the rosy company perspective could not conceal the Penobscots' deep unease with the process. Waldo published his account of the April 1735 meeting— which doubled as an advertisement for more colonists—in part as a transcript of the conference. In it, Waldo claimed the Indians had "freely consented" to his proposals to build two towns on their land (unlikely) after he invoked his private property rights as a British subject, informing them that "the English constitution was different from the Indians[']," and "English Men had a right to settle their own lands as they pleas'd."[29] Although the publication claimed that prominent Penobscot leaders were present and expressed satisfaction with Waldo's promises, the speculator himself admitted a year later that at this meeting "their Young Men were surpriz'd into a Consent without Consideration."[30] (Published reports of treaties referred to important sagamores as "Old Men," as Waldo knew.) Probably the Penobscots confronted by Waldo's bluster lacked the authority to give him a definite answer and had stalled for time. Whomever Waldo spoke to, all participants agreed to reconvene that autumn.

Unused to taking no for an answer, Samuel Waldo ignored warning signs that his venture threatened to demolish the Anglo-Wabanaki peace on the frontier. Besides the Penobscots' well-documented refusal to acknowledge the Madockawando cession, one of the Muscongus Proprietors privately acknowledged that some people in Massachusetts opposed the venture.[31] Waldo approached his meetings with the Penobscots as necessary formalities to convince them of the validity of the Muscongus Patent rather than as actual negotiations. Before his second conference with them in November 1735, Waldo bound himself to provide land in St. Georges to forty-one Irish Protestant families, pledging £10,000 if he failed to do so.[32]

Throughout 1735, Governor Belcher was little more than a spectator to the unfolding crisis. Although Belcher supported the expansion of Massachusetts through purchase of Indian lands, he was suspicious of the speculator's scheme. In fact, Belcher disliked both Waldo and the Irish colonists he imported, mocking the efforts of the "Eastern Trampoorer" to bring more colonists from "Bogland" in private correspondence.[33] When interpreter John Gyles reported that the Penobscots opposed Waldo's plans, Belcher directed him to repeat the Bay Colony's pledge to abide by Dummer's Treaty. When Waldo requested the use of the province sloop to transport his colonists to St. Georges, Belcher, with the advice of his council, refused. But for the time being, he did nothing to stop the plan beyond notifying the king's council of events that soon threatened to spin out of control.[34]

The second conference between Waldo and the Penobscots in November 1735 did not resolve the underlying disagreements surrounding the

Muscongus Claim. The participants clashed over the question of which Indians had authority to alienate land and even negotiate for their communities. Both surviving accounts produced by the Muscongus Proprietors agreed that Loron spoke not only for the assembled Penobscots (more than sixty adult men, accompanied by "a Considerable Number of Squaws and Children") but also for the entire tribe of around eight hundred people.[35] In that capacity, Loron denied the Indians who had previously met with Waldo had any authority to speak for their people. Loron also disavowed the Madockawando deed, as he had a decade ago, insisting Madockawando had no right to sell the St. Georges region to anyone.[36] Waldo brushed these protests aside, along with the Penobscots' insistence that the falls of the St. Georges River marked a boundary between their land and his. Instead, the speculator proceeded to inform the Penobscots that because all sources with which he was familiar referred to Madockawando as great leader, it followed he must have had the authority to sell the St. Georges. Waldo displayed his deed to the Indians and announced his intention to push forward with his plans.[37] Furthermore, Waldo blustered, "Should any one endeavour to amuse them with false Notions of his having no Right to those Lands . . . they should find themselves very much deceived therein."[38] After withdrawing to discuss their response, the Penobscots agreed to permit continued occupation of the west side of the St. Georges River (which flowed from northwest to southeast, emptying into Penobscot Bay), even above the falls, to preserve the peace.[39]

This concession, difficult enough for even conciliatory leaders like Espequent, who had taken commissions from Belcher, was too much for most Penobscots.[40] During the winter they grappled over how to best respond, and those opposing Waldo's encroachments carried the argument. In April 1736, they dictated a letter to Belcher through interpreter John Gyles. Despite "misconstructions of what we have said . . . as though some French-men or others had filled our Heads with what we should deliver," the Penobscots insisted they had decided on their own to bring their complaints to the governor. They repeated their disavowal of the basis for Waldo's claim, but "through extream fondness for Peace, we assented to his Settling the Lots and finishing the Houses which he had begun upon the River," but "upon long and serious consideration of its Attendants and Consequences we now repent of, and desire you to prevent. We expect you have power to do so."[41] Since Belcher had written to the Penobscots in the winter of 1735, reminding them of his authority to survey and to "plant English Houses and build Forts upon King Georges

Lands where I think proper," the Penobscots thus made it more difficult for Belcher to claim he had no power to intervene in land disputes involving deeds, as other governors had insisted.[42] As for the consequences the Indians foresaw, they did not elaborate in the letter, but they made frequent contemporaneous complaints, like when "Thorma an Indian man of the Tribe of Penobscutt" told Jane and Ann Woodside of Pemaquid that once colonists moved to an area, "it Spoild their hunting."[43]

The letter also indicated a rise of the Penobscot hard-liners over the winter. If Waldo's colonists remained, the ten signers warned, "it will cause the breach of peace."[44] The leaders included names not found on other treaties or conference records, indicating the participation of various lineage leaders.[45] Loron signed, but not Espequent or Arexis, two leaders who had been most willing to compromise.[46] As usual, unanimity had not been achieved, and the writers also asked Belcher to "take no notice" if "one or two of our Tribe should write" unless they spoke for "a General Council."[47]

The Penobscot letter also provides a window into their ideas about land transfers, which recognized the legality of wartime conquest as opposed to squatting. "When Lands are taken from us in time of War," they said, "we are content, but if in time of peace we cann't [sic] rest satisfied."[48] In this, the Indians shared European ideas about the legality of conquest through war. While they did not like to lose a war any more than Europeans, in the years following 1713, the Wabanakis acknowledged the reality of Massachusetts gains, regarding peace treaties as a form of deed. The Penobscots objected here not to conquest, but trespass. "If persons would settle Lands not their own," they said, "we choose that they would tell us plainly, and not wind themselves in, and encroach upon us subtlety [sic], for then we should immediately come to some resolution."[49] Belcher and his council agreed to host Penobscot delegates to Boston in June for a hearing.[50] The meeting was probably the last chance to avoid a renewal of violence on the frontier.

The Penobscots chose the pro-accommodation Arexis and Espequent instead of Loron to speak for them in Boston, the only time between 1727 and 1742 the nation selected someone besides that gifted speaker. Possibly the Indians thought the conciliatory speakers would make the most persuasive case, or that Espequent's commission from Belcher would carry extra weight with the *Bostoniak*. (Loron had refused a commission.)[51] Or perhaps Loron had become exasperated by British duplicity about the St. Georges region and refused to attend. Whatever the reason for the choice, the meeting was probably the last chance to avoid a renewal of violence in the Dawnland.

Decision in Boston

In June 1736, Governor Belcher and the entire General Court listened as Arexis and Espequent described a situation that made a mockery of the General Court's claims to authority over the residents of the St. Georges region.[52] The Penobscots said Waldo's colonists "croud nearer to us than what was agreed by us and Mr. Waldo, at which we are very uneasy," warning it would bring "Blood and War."[53] Only through great effort, they said, did "our Old Men at Several Meetings in Council . . . at last prevail on the younger Sort to agree to a Settlement of the English on the Main River as high as the Falls."[54] Belcher asked the Penobscots, since they "had no Order from me, or Agreement for the Settlement; what private Agreement had you?"[55] The Penobscots answered by describing their meetings with Waldo, who had "said he had no regard to English or Indians, he had purchased the Lands, and would settle them."[56]

When Belcher asked if Waldo showed them any deeds, the Penobscots revealed their interpretation of "deeds." The delegation answered that Waldo "did not read any Deed, but shewed us a Paper with a large seal to it, and said that was his Title."[57] Waldo "shewed us a great many Papers, one he said came from England, another he said was from Medakawando," whose "Right or Title" the Penobscots again denied.[58] The Penobscots, through years of dealing with the British, had become familiar with deeds of sale from Indians to Europeans.[59] But they did not accept the idea of a patent originating with the king. For example, in one recorded 1724 exchange, a lieutenant informed some Wabanakis that the land around Fort St. George belonged to the king. The Indians responded by asking why King George's men did not "go to King George to get any of his Land."[60] Even if Madockawando did have a right to sell, the Penobscots said, someone would have received money for the land, which the tribe would have known about. This, they insisted, had never happened."[61] By the Penobscots' reasoning, if a deed was an exchange of payment for land between the party who resided there and the purchaser, then Waldo had no deed for the St. Georges. This reasoning would have appealed to numerous colonists faced with intrusions by patent-waving speculators, but peace depended on whether that logic convinced Belcher and the General Court. Belcher asked a seven-member joint committee from his own council and the House of Representatives to consider the evidence presented by Waldo and the Penobscots, then make a report.[62]

On July 2, 1736, the committee read its report, containing as full-throated an endorsement of Native land rights as Massachusetts legislators ever uttered. They declared: "From time to time the Right of the Indian Natives to the Lands in this Country has been acknowledged, and in several late Treaties with them the Government has not only given them Assurances of their Justice with respect to their Lands but promised them to disclaim such Controverted Lands, the Title or Right to which cannot be made out or proved." The committee went further, agreeing the Penobscots had never acknowledged the Madockawando purchase, and even denied that the 1629 Plymouth Grant met the standards of the 1727 treaty, insisting Native lands be "fairly purchased." They asserted that previous royal guarantees of British subjects' private property in Maine against the Crown were not issued "in opposition to the Indian Right." Therefore they advised Belcher "to assure the Penobscott Tribe that this Government will not Encourage, nor Countenance Mr. Waldo or any others in Settling or Improving any Lands on George's River above the Falls or flowing of the Water, until this Government shall be satisfy'd that those Lands have been fairly purchased of such Indians, as were the rightful owners thereof."[63]

The committee's report soon became policy. After listening to the first of many complaints lodged by Samuel Waldo, the House voted to support the findings of the committee.[64] On July 6, Belcher and the General Court met with the Penobscot delegation again, and Belcher announced the verdict to the Indians, promising they "may entirely depend on the observation of all the Articles of Peace, they shall be strictly performed."[65]

"The Government Are Obliged": The Anatomy of Success

Massachusetts leaders went to war against the Indians in the 1720s rather than compromise on land companies' titles. Yet in 1736, the General Court sided with the Penobscots against Samuel Waldo and the Muscongus Company. This shift in behavior represented less of a departure from the speculator-dominated government's eagerness to defend private property of British subjects than might be guessed. The logic of events on the eastern frontier by 1736 meant that most speculators' property stood to gain from protecting Indian land rights.

As always, other motivations besides questions of landownership influenced events. Some members of the General Court sincerely believed, as Governor Belcher later wrote to relatives in England, "the government are obliged by one treaty after another not to abuse [the Indians] in" their "claim and right to those lands" not previously sold.[66] Others hearkened back to an earlier generation of Massachusetts leaders, including Samuel Sewell and prominent speculator Adam Winthrop, who emphasized the

importance of fair dealings with the Indians for the mission of converting them to Protestant Christianity. The sentiment was popular enough
around Boston that the 1732 election-day sermon for the Boston Artil-
lery Company emphasized the "more excellent Way . . . to overcome and
win over to us the Indian Tribes [is] by observing strict Justice in our
Commerce with them."[67] Others disagreed but voted to back the Penobscots anyway. John Stoddard served on the committee that advised the
General Court to side with the Indians, and also advocated the use of
dogs against Indians in wartime with two different administrations.[68]

Various considerations of state worked in the Indians' favor in 1736.
Massachusetts had already expended much blood and treasure fighting
the Wabanakis. The province had emerged victorious from Dummer's
War, but at a heavy cost. During the 1730s, the Massachusetts legislature
wanted to cut military spending, and in 1737 members forced Belcher to
halve the garrisons stationed in Maine.[69] Backing Waldo virtually guaranteed a renewal of frontier warfare, which would require raising taxes
while also endangering new towns on the Pejepscot Patent and elsewhere
in Maine. Siding with the Penobscots also enabled the Governor and
General Court to reassert their authority over the Maine frontier. Waldo
had charged ahead with his plans without consulting leaders in Boston,
endangering stability in the region. In contrast, the Penobscots sent letters and delegates asking Governor Belcher to resolve the dispute. Even if
the Indians viewed the exchange as asking Belcher to rein in a disobedi-
ent subject to prevent a war, Belcher and the General Court believed they
were acting as arbitrators between two subjects under their authority.
Although the Penobscots did not see themselves as dependents of Massachusetts, resolving the dispute in their favor allowed Belcher and the
General Court to perform that role.

Equally important, a new war threatened many proprietary titles.
Massachusetts had waged war in the 1720s to secure Wabanaki recognition of certain proprietary claims to the Maine frontier, above all the
Pejepscot Patent. Adam Winthrop and the other Pejepscot Proprietors
had played a major role in negotiating the treaty, which had included
Wabanaki acceptance of their title. All the eastern land companies
viewed Indian land deeds as an important mark of ownership, and for
the Pejepscot Proprietors, Dummer's Treaty had been a singular triumph.
With this recognition now secure, the influential Pejepscot Proprietors
had a vested interest in avoiding future conflicts. If the Penobscots
became disillusioned and disavowed Dummer's Treaty, their influence
among the other Wabanakis would lessen its usefulness for the Pejepscot

Proprietors, who would be more vulnerable to rival claims from neighboring companies and squatters.

The Penobscot arguments proved effective because they appealed to these concerns while striking the ideal combination of firmness and flexibility to influence the General Court. The Penobscots' April 1736 letter, by acknowledging the legality of conquests "in time of War," further confirmed that the Penobscots would recognize Dummer's Treaty, including Massachusetts expansion between 1713 and 1727.[70] Although the Penobscots denied the legitimacy of the Madockawando deed, they did not explicitly protest further Massachusetts expansion based upon other sales. The Penobscots even granted Waldo permission to place colonists on the western side of the St. Georges River out of a desire to keep the peace. Only the minority of colonists who had moved across the river would have to be evicted to satisfy the Penobscots. If so inclined, the General Court could therefore side with the Indians while still reserving the right to embark on further wars of conquest or (more likely) to insist other, still undisclosed deeds to Wabanaki land be enforced.

The only parties to the 1736 controversy who stood to lose from the legislature's decision were the Muscongus Proprietors and their colonists unlucky enough to have moved to the wrong side of the St. Georges River. Unfortunately for Samuel Waldo, his success in acquiring so much of the Muscongus Company reduced the pool of potential supporters in the legislature with enough shares at stake to risk a war. Elisha Cooke, one of the few members who still held a major stake in the company, used his influence in the House to move they reconsider the vote to accept the Council report in favor of the Indians. He waged a lonely struggle, however, and the revote produced the same result.[71] Three Muscongus Proprietors sat on the Governor's Council, but there is no evidence they could sway the other twenty-five members from recommending that Belcher back the Penobscots.[72] As for the Scots-Irish colonists already on the land, the legislature paid no more attention to their misfortunes than it had to their predecessors in the abandoned town of Cork in 1722 and those enticed to Dunbar's planned towns in the late 1720s.

Triumph and Its Aftermath

For all these reasons, the Penobscot delegates returned home after the meeting in triumph, bearing £200 worth of gifts including feathered hats meant "to distinguish" the sagamores who had accepted commissions from the governor.[73] Carrying these emblems of power, the Penobscots intended to use the weight of imperial authority to enforce their own sovereignty. Even though Belcher intended for his gifts to emphasis the Indians' subject status, they did not carry that connotation for the Penobscots, who lost no time ordering the colonists living east of the St. Georges River—or above the fall line—to leave, threatening to burn down any structure that remained in a month. Penobscot actions frightened the colonists on the receiving end of this performance, but the Indians executed an organized, restrained eviction. An ensign stationed at a blockhouse on the St. Georges who was "well acquainted with moste of the Penobscot Indens" reported that Arexis, the conciliatory leader fresh from his visit to Boston, led the operation in his vicinity.[74]

The expulsion succeeded without bloodshed, placated most of the Penobscot hard-liners, and did not provoke any retaliatory violence. The delegates to Boston had been aware of the delicate situation, asking Belcher on July 6 "if anything should happen by our young men, we pray there may be a hearing and inquiry into the matter first."[75] Arexis's personal involvement in delivering the message to the blockhouse near the falls directing Henry Alexander to leave could have been an attempt to preempt hotheaded "young men." In 1737, the Penobscots grew impatient with some of the colonists who disregarded their instructions. Holdouts like Samuel Boggs received more threatening visits (including by the Penobscot who left "a gun flint" with Mrs. Boggs, suggesting the family would soon have need of it if they remained) that achieved the desired result without violence.[76] The Penobscots also left Captain John Gyles and his garrison at Fort St. Georges alone, which the hard-liners would not have abided had Belcher and the legislature not enforced Dummer's Treaty.[77]

Waldo's response to his defeat highlighted not only how Dummer's Treaty had successfully interwoven concerns of Anglo-Wabanaki diplomacy with the speculators' land titles but also how remote from that process the French had become by the 1730s. Besides bombarding Belcher and the legislature with petitions (mentioned at the beginning of this chapter), Waldo published a lengthy justification of his claims complete with excerpts of various conferences and depositions.[78] He also visited the Penobscots again in 1736 in a futile attempt to reconcile them to his title.[79] More fantastically, Waldo concocted a claim that the Penobscots only resisted his plans at the behest of Belcher and his allies, who wanted to undermine the Muscongus Company out of spite. Waldo gathered statements in support of a conspiracy theory that implicated actors from the governor to interpreter John Gyles. Aside from the likelihood that

Waldo bribed the colonists who made statements on his behalf, Waldo's theory relied on the participation of John Gyles—a former Indian captive, master of a network of paid Penobscot informants, partisan of the Massachusetts imperial project, and someone who probably mistranslated statements and documents at conferences on behalf of the Bay Colony.[80] Indeed, when Belcher asked the Penobscots about the allegations against Gyles, they were as surprised as anyone else, replying, "We generally look upon it that Capn. Gyles takes Mr. Waldo's part."[81]

In a bizarre turn of events, Waldo's scheme also involved a Jesuit temporarily ministering to the Penobscots in 1736 and 1737.[82] Several of the witnesses rounded up by the enterprising speculator claimed that Father Jacques Syresme told them that John Gyles had encouraged the Penobscots to resist Waldo, and (just as implausibly) that the Penobscots who had accepted commissions from Belcher (the more conciliatory leaders) "were the greatest Enemys to the settlement."[83] The allegations stirred Belcher to ask a doctor on the frontier, Captain Ammi Ruhama Cutter, who had treated Syresme for rheumatism in 1737, to shed light on the matter.[84] Their conversation (conducted in Latin) did not clarify matters, as Syresme, according to Cutter, alluded to various Britons at Fort St. Georges putting the Penobscots up to resisting Waldo, but he did not name anyone specifically.[85] Perhaps Syresme was deliberately stirring up trouble for Massachusetts, or possibly Cutter misunderstood him. The most striking aspect of Syresme's involvement in Waldo's campaign against the Belcher administration is that it appears to have begun at the speculator's behest, not in response to any direction from the Jesuit's superiors.

Nothing is more evocative of French remoteness from the discussions over landownership on the Maine frontier ten years after Dummer's Treaty than the fact that Syresme's minor role in the affair was the extent of their participation. The administration of the Marquis de Beauharnois, governor of New France, spent the years of crisis on the St. Georges preoccupied with convincing the handful of Penobscots who had accepted commissions from Belcher to get rid of them. Although Beauharnois received periodic reports from the Franco-Penobscot trader Joseph d'Abbadie de Saint-Castin throughout the 1730s about that situation, Saint-Castin had little or nothing to say (at least that Beauharnois thought worth reporting to his superiors) about Waldo's dispute with the Penobscots.[86] Even though the brief Anglo-French alliance in Europe (1716–31) was reverting to a more familiar posture of rivalry, the Penobscots did not invoke the specter of a Franco-Wabanaki alliance when threatening Massachusetts over the St. Georges dispute, or it seems, even bother informing their erstwhile allies of their troubles. The French would remain both a necessary diplomatic counterweight and source of arms to prop up Wabanaki power well beyond 1737, but the events on the St. Georges revealed their declining importance in the Indigenous strategy of containment following Dummer's Treaty.

Both Penobscot and Massachusetts leaders held firm in the face of Waldo's best efforts, much to the dismay of the proprietor and his colonists. Governor Belcher remained steadfast in enforcing the terms of their agreement, assuring the Penobscots of his ongoing support.[87] Waldo's Scots-Irish colonists did not fare so well. They had arrived expecting to prosper on the "rich and valuable soil" of the Muscongus Patent, but instead, they complained to Waldo in 1738, they were "confined" to a six-square-mile strip, "and that of the Meanest of your Lands," while subject to "Insults of the Indians."[88]

Samuel Waldo did not accept defeat. Instead, he sailed for England once again, this time to work for Jonathan Belcher's replacement by a candidate more congenial to his interests. Waldo would get his wish in 1741, inaugurating a new administration that would show, however inadvertently, how influential Belcher's good-faith diplomacy had been in shaping Massachusetts policy toward the Wabanakis, and how the influence of the speculators, though it could work to benefit Indian land rights, did so only under the right circumstances.

Those circumstances had all been present on the St. Georges in the 1730s, and an essential component involved an active Wabanaki presence on the land in defense of their rights. Although the Penobscots prevailed in the greatest test of Dummer's Treaty during those years, other Wabanaki groups performed the essential work of containment in their portions of the Dawnland. A band of Pigwackets remained on the Presumpscot River near Falmouth, continuing to fish in the area. Their sagamore, Polin, lodged complaints with Governor Belcher about Thomas Westbrook (before the latter was harried into an early grave by Samuel Waldo's lawsuits) damming the waterway and ruining their fishing, which prompted the governor to intervene on their behalf. Westbrook continued his activities in violation of several colonial laws that addressed the damming of fisheries until his death in 1744. Polin's band continued to resist the intrusions, destroying a number of mills and dams in the 1740s.[89] Unidentified Indians also halted construction of a meetinghouse in New Marblehead, just outside of Falmouth, forcing the town proprietors to form a committee to "know their Demands" and bring about "a Speedy end or Settlement." (The written record is unfortunately silent on what occurred afterward.)[90] Along portions of the Dawnland frontier where dwindling numbers of Pigwackets and Amarascoggins did not demonstrate the same level of active presence on their lands, Massachusetts authorized several new towns, including future Buxton.[91]

Residents of Brunswick provided the most eloquent descriptions of the Amarascoggin and Kennebec Indians' active policing of the Common Pot. Fearing that the Bay Colony legislature was going to abandon neighboring Fort George, Brunswick inhabitants sent a petition to the governor and legislature. "Brunswick time without mind has been the place of the annual Randevouze of all the Tribes," they reported. The Indians "look upon us as unjust usurpers and intruders upon their rights and priviledges, and as spoilers of their idle way of living. They claim not only the wild beasts of the forest, and fowls of the air, but also fishes of the sea and rivers." The Brunswick petitioners claimed that even with the fort, some residents suffered "houses rifled, and peace purchased by gratifications pleasing to them [the Indians.]"[92] According to the Wharton deed covering the Pejepscot Patent (which included Brunswick), the Indians retained all of those rights, as they well knew.[93] What Brunswick residents experienced as slights and intimidations was the Wabanakis' way of ensuring that colonists remained aware that this was still Native land. They knew that, without proper precautions, as Loron had said at Dummer's Treaty, "if a Line should happen to be Run, the English may hereafter be apt to step over it."[94] This policy did not preclude trade with Brunswick colonists (as locals fined for selling rum to neighboring Indians in those years could attest) but did involve reminding them to stay on their side of the line.[95]

But it was the Penobscots who had successfully dealt with the most substantial stepping over the line during the 1730s. Their experience on the St. Georges points to the ways that concepts of property influenced diplomacy on the Maine frontier and worked together to reinforce the Anglo-Wabanaki relationship. Although different visions of landowner- ship continued to foster misunderstandings and conflict between Mas- sachusetts and the Wabanakis, most of the land speculators active in the region adhered to a system of property law that required they respect Native rights to unsold territory—or they would jeopardize their exist- ing titles in Maine. The speculators believed Dummer's Treaty protected their titles and that potential Wabanaki disavowal of the agreement could jeopardize them. For their part, the Wabanakis did not need to subscribe to English property law in order to wield it to their advantage,

however unknowingly in many cases. Differing notions of landownership therefore presented obstacles as well as opportunities for cross-cul-
tural cooperation in Maine. The interactions on the St. Georges reveal
both the possibilities and limits of Anglo-Wabanaki collaboration. That
mutual self-interest, not understanding, drove the relationship would
become all too clear in the 1740s.

7 /   Troubled Times, 1741–1752

Beginning in 1741, the dynamics encouraging influential Maine land speculators to view their own investments as tied to Indian land rights began to shift. Multiple factors accounted for this turn of events, but the most important was the arrival of William Shirley to replace Jonathan Belcher as governor of Massachusetts. A member of the Muscongus Company, an associate of Samuel Waldo, and a strident Francophobe, Shirley devoted his fifteen years (1741–56) in the governor's chair to gaining wealth through land speculation and prestige by fighting the French. Previous Bay Colony governors had engaged in frontier land speculation, but never before had Massachusetts Indian policy been helmed by a man so personally invested in overriding Wabanaki land claims. The Muscongus Proprietors had already led the way among land companies in conducting their own diplomatic initiatives in 1720 and in 1735, provoking crises each time. With a Muscongus Proprietor now responsible for conducting Bay Colony relations with the Wabanakis, the land companies' already strong influence over Massachusetts's Indian policy rose to new heights. Unlike during the years immediately following Dummer's Treaty, this influence would now more often work against Wabanaki land rights and the frontier détente in general.

As it had before 1741, the contest over landed property operated alongside ongoing negotiations over trade, religion, and occasional acts of violence between Wabanakis and colonists—usually involving livestock killings. Growing numbers of colonists in Maine (totaling perhaps twelve thousand) led to an uptick in those events.[1] The machinations of imperial powers on both sides of the Atlantic also sent shockwaves across the region. The renewal of war between the British and French empires in North America temporarily brought violence back to the frontier, while hardening many colonists' attitudes toward both Indians and absentee land speculators. Despite the turmoil, Wabanaki and Massachusetts leaders (Shirley notwithstanding) achieved notable success in resolving their differences unrelated to the question of landownership. Dummer's Treaty still held significant weight as a foundation on which the two sides could negotiate. Not least, many speculators' ongoing reliance on Indian land rights—at least in the abstract—and desire to avoid investment-destroying wars meant that the treaty still helped to bind Massachusetts to a reciprocal relationship with the Wabanakis, however troubled.

"A Proper Reprimand to the Country"

In an unfortunate turn of events for anyone hoping to avoid a return to war, William Shirley's road to becoming governor of Massachusetts led him into a close relationship with Samuel Waldo. A younger son of an old gentry family, Shirley followed the path of many other well-connected Englishmen who had spent away their inheritance, seeking a job in the colonies. He eventually secured appointment to the admiralty court in Boston thanks to the Duke of Newcastle, who controlled appointments for Britain's American colonies at the time. In that capacity Shirley became involved in the enforcement of the law against New Englanders illegally cutting lumber reserved for the king's navy. Governor Jonathan Belcher, himself born and raised in Massachusetts, shared in the widespread disdain for the law. Shirley's activities had earned him much favor with Belcher's growing ranks of enemies, who included Samuel Waldo. Besides land speculation, Waldo was also a subcontractor responsible for supplying the Royal Navy. Belcher's barely clandestine aid to colonial lumber thieves caused Waldo almost as much distress as his opposition to the Muscongus Patent, and Shirley was the barrister Waldo turned to for help.[2] From then on Shirley became a confidant of Waldo and Elisha Cooke—another major Muscongus Proprietor and influential member of the Massachusetts House—who decided that Shirley would make a splendid replacement for the hated Belcher. Before departing for England to lobby in that cause, Waldo took care to pay Shirley for his legal services in Muscongus Company shares. When finally measured out, these amounted to more than 15,500 acres on both sides of the Penobscot

River.[3] Planting towns on the Muscongus Patent would greatly increase its value. For comparison, in 1737 the Pejepscot Proprietors charged £25 for 100 acres in Topsham, their still-unincorporated town on the Androscoggin River.[4]

Along with company shares, Shirley also acquired Waldo's crude habit of interpreting Wabanaki actions not as the product of independent actors but as extensions of factional politics within Massachusetts. Shirley came to believe Waldo's assessment that the Penobscots who opposed the Muscongus expansion on the St. Georges had been acting at the behest of a vindictive Governor Belcher. In 1739, Shirley wrote to Waldo predicting that once "the grand Enemy [Belcher] is removed . . . the Indians will be complying enough." In addition, expanding the Muscongus holdings would serve as a "proper reprimand" to the company's political foes for unjustly siding with the Penobscots against them.[5]

On his own, Waldo lacked the clout to secure Jonathan Belcher's replacement. But William Shirley displayed the same talent for making friends that Belcher seemed to have for making enemies. Unfortunately for Belcher, his success at Indian diplomacy did not translate to his other endeavors, and when the Duke of Newcastle decided that the prickly Belcher had become a liability in 1741, Shirley's network of allies (coordinated in England by his wife, Frances, who journeyed there in 1736 to lobby on his behalf) convinced the duke to give the post to Shirley.[6] In doing so, Newcastle unwittingly granted enhanced influence to the Muscongus Company.

Muscongus Diplomacy

Shirley's inaugural conference with the Wabanakis provided a study in contrast between the new governor and his predecessor. Although Jonathan Belcher identified with—and supported—the major land speculators, he was also a devout Congregationalist who viewed the Indians as potential converts and insisted they be dealt with fairly. Perhaps Belcher's closest tie to the land companies was through his nephew and namesake, Belcher Noyes, heir to one of the original Pejepscot Proprietors, who were among the strongest advocates for (and beneficiaries of) using Indian land deeds to prove land title. Other major Pejepscot families, including the Minots and Winthrops, also shared Belcher's commitment to proselytizing among the Indians. Belcher spent part of his first major conference with the Wabanakis in 1732 trying—with little success—to get them to accept a Protestant missionary. A decade later,

William Shirley, who had little interest in evangelizing, instead tried to get them to accept a fraudulent land deed.

In 1742 the Wabanakis were eager to meet the new governor, hoping to continue the relatively good relations of the Belcher years (1729–41): as many as six hundred of them may have attended, including thirty-five sagamores and leading men present from every major tribe.[7] Both sides also wished to resolve Wabanaki and colonists' complaints over prices of trade goods and Indian poaching of farmers' livestock, respectively. They succeeded in this without undue difficulty, as they had in 1740.[8] But when Loron, speaking on behalf of all the assembled Indians, pressed for the renewal of promises made in Dummer's Treaty to keep the British to the coast, Shirley pushed back. Loron recalled that "the English then told us, they would not step a Foot over that Line [of the saltwater in the rivers]." (He could have been referring either to promises made in 1727, 1736, or both.) However, Loron noted, alluding to Waldo's incursions, "It is a very long foot that reaches from that Line to the Place from whence we came [meaning, where the Penobscots lived in 1742]."[9] Loron was hoping Shirley would reaffirm the promises Massachusetts made in 1736 that Waldo's colonists would spread no farther. He was to be disappointed.

Shirley responded to Loron's invocation of Dummer's Treaty by bringing up the Madockawando deed. Referring to the Penobscots' ongoing denial of the chief's authority to cede their land, Shirley declared, "We find about Fifty four Years ago in our History and Records that He was your Sachem."[10] The tone of the conference abruptly shifted. Three centuries later, Loron's answers fairly crackle on the page. Loron responded to this diplomatic brick through his window by repeating his people's denial that Madockawando "was a Proprietor of Land here"—the interpreters' word choice indicating Loron denied the chief's right to sell rather than his authority—and concluding: "We have heard so often about him. We don't desire to hear any more."[11] Shirley pressed on in language he hoped would sway the Indians, claiming, "One of our Old Men" present in 1694 was at the conference and could remember seeing Madockawando with "a Hundred Indians" receive "a Hatt-full of Pieces of Eight, and sundry Blankets."[12] Loron replied his people "have heard of that very often, and if we should hear of it again, it would signify nothing." In any agreement, he said, "we desire all those Things may be put under the Table."[13]

For the time being, Shirley had intended only to gain acknowledgment of the Madockawando deed, not to push for further expansion. He assured Loron, with revealing language, that the "the English are not about to settle any other Lands than what you have at two several Times agreed to in Conferences with some of the Proprietors in 1735."[14] Significantly, Shirley invoked Waldo's private meetings with the Penobscots rather than the official 1736 conference between the Penobscots, Governor Belcher, and the General Court. Shirley's choice made little sense for him to make in his capacity as governor, for the 1736 conference in Boston had been called because the Penobscots had rejected Waldo's 1735 talks with them. The 1736 agreement—including the ruling by the General Court—had superseded the 1735 talks.

Loron either missed or did not care about the distinction, and his answer echoed Shirley's reassurance, saying he only wished "to put you in mind of your Agreements not to go a Foot over the Line agreed to." For his part, Shirley—again speaking as a Muscongus Proprietor—repeated his promise that "the Proprietors of that Land granted by Medockawando [sic]" would not cross the St. Georges River.[15] Again, Loron either missed the significance of—or chose to ignore—Shirley's repeated insistence that the Madockawando sale had any legitimacy. (The Penobscot speaker was sick at the time and claimed he was "scarce able to attend," but such were his powers that the Wabanakis selected him to be their voice anyway.)[16] Loron emphasized his people were always willing to let the British move to the Dawnland, provided "they should settle so as not to croud us in our Settlements," and said the Penobscots adopted the same position toward the French. "We are more tender of the English, than any People . . . but would not be crowded nor croud them."[17] Shirley repeated his ambiguous promise that Massachusetts would not "take an inch" of Wabanaki land but would support all "Settlement of Lands to which [colonists] have a just Right and Pretension," to which the Indians professed themselves satisfied, easing the tension.[18]

The 1742 conference also highlighted the ongoing importance of Dummer's Treaty even as Massachusetts and Wabanaki delegates attached different meanings to it. Perhaps because Shirley was a new face in an old diplomatic process, Loron gave an opening speech elaborating on the importance and uses of Dummer's Treaty in Wabanakia. The speaker called it "really the first Treaty," emphasizing "those that were at the Treaty then," and their descendants "are obliged to observe it. This is what we depend upon . . . and both Sides [will] be judged by it." The Wabanakis had brought their copy, which "we have safe by us here, and though we don't understand Writing, the Treaty will speak for itself."[19] Although the Wabanakis could not read the words on the paper, they remembered and retold its contents to each other. As Shirley learned, the written and spoken treaties did not always match. Loron claimed

Dummer had promised the Wabanakis annual gifts of powder and shot, "Which present we never have had."[20] When Shirley told him the written treaty made no mention of annual gifts, Loron responded, "It may not be wrote; but it was told us so then."[21] For the Wabanakis, the written treaty served as much as a totem of an agreement that had occurred, which they wanted Shirley to renew in 1742. For Shirley and the rest of his delegation, the writing *was* the treaty. "As the Treaty is in Writing," Shirley told Loron, "we must resort to that for the Truth of Things."[22] Despite Shirley's provocations, the assembled Wabanakis joined him in renewing Dummer's Treaty.

Shirley's ongoing advocacy for the Muscongus Proprietors and the discredited Madockawando deed boded ill for the future. So did Shirley's continued belief that the Indians operated as tools of his enemies. The governor believed he had acquitted himself brilliantly, which "disappointed the Expectations of two or three persons, who had endeavourd to make vile impressions upon the Indians in order to prepare em to be Insolent, unreasonable in their Demands and Rude at the Interview, which they were so sure of effecting that they reported it a done thing," even though the Indians had shown Shirley more respect, he said, "than they had done to any of my Predecessors."[23] (Shirley probably meant, at least in part, that no Indians in attendance in 1742 had made any pro-French gestures, which said more about waning French influence in the Dawnland and the positive results of Belcher's diplomacy than anything else.)[24]

William Shirley was far from the first Massachusetts leader influenced by his connections to the speculators. The significance of those ties lay in the fact that the governor and his partners had an interest in overturning, first, Dummer's Treaty, and then—in the 1750s—the use of Indian deeds as a valid way of proving land title. And while it is true that Shirley's conduct toward the Indians cannot be explained *only* by his financial ties— he shared many New Englanders' enthusiasm for war with France, and he often viewed Native American actions through that lens as well—his language and actions in 1742 made sense only for someone with an interest in the Muscongus Company. Only Waldo and his associates tried to claim that Madockawando received a hatful of silver in payment for the St. Georges region. Only that company believed Belcher was behind the Penobscots' 1736 protests of the patent. And only Samuel Waldo and his backers claimed that his 1735 talks with the Penobscots had any lasting significance. The General Court never revoked its 1736 decision in favor of the Penobscots, and most land speculators continued to depend on

Dummer's Treaty to validate their titles. Nevertheless, Shirley's brazen advocacy on behalf of the Muscongus Company—and himself—at the 1742 conference did not destroy the peace established in 1727.

Samuel Waldo, delighted with the new governor, seemed to be doing his best to accomplish that task, however.[25] The speculator immediately began advertising for more colonists to move to his disputed patent. The bulk of the newcomers were German Protestants from the Palatinate, lured by unmet promises of bountiful provisions. They complained of conditions so terrible that they sparked an investigation by the Massachusetts House, although Shirley and his council displayed no interest.[26] By 1744, forty to fifty new families joined Waldo's mostly Irish tenants, establishing a second town.[27] Although the colonists remained on the western, and therefore approved, side of the St. Georges River, their presence worried the local Penobscots, some of whom engaged in livestock theft and acts of intimidation.[28]

"They Are Not to Be Trusted": Imperial Interlude

A different imperial clash occurred in 1744 before Waldo's latest colonists had much chance to disrupt the St. Georges. The spread of a European war to the Maine frontier showed the ongoing importance— and limits—of imperial power politics in shaping the Anglo-Wabanaki relationship following Dummer's Treaty. When news arrived that the British and French empires were once again at war (this time as part of yet another European dynastic dispute, called the War of Austrian Succession), the French and British hoped and feared, respectively, that the Wabanakis would once again take up arms against New England.

As was often the case, the complex motivations of Indian actors proved beyond the ability or willingness of colonial administrators to grasp. Although the largely Catholic Wabanakis shared a bond with their French coreligionists, the Wabanakis had learned the hard way that joining a French war (as they had in 1703–13) did not lead to reciprocal assistance, as Dummer's War (1722–27) showed. Swelling numbers of colonists also lengthened the odds of military success for the Wabanakis, whose population remained relatively stable at between 2,500 and 3,000 people.[29] (The demographic center of gravity had, however, continued to drift north to Canada and east to Penawabskik and beyond, away from the pressures of Maine towns.) As they had since 1713, most Wabanakis sorted their political differences by voting with their feet. Most of the French partisans in the Dawnland had already moved to the Canadian villages of St. Francis and Becancour, whose inhabitants wasted little time launching raids against the British.[30] The minority of Penobscots and Kennebecs eager to join them pointed their canoes northward at the outbreak of hostilities.[31] But most Wabanakis who wanted to live in the part of the Dawnland near British towns (most Kennebecs, Penobscots, and some Wulstukwiuks) tried to remain neutral. For them, it was enough to use the threat of violence—which, to have credence, required the French supply of arms, and potentially more direct support—in their strategy of containment to achieve their aims, as events since 1727 appeared to show. Only the much-diminished band of Pigwackets still living on the Saco River, sensing they could not survive the brewing storm alone, threw in their lot with the British, with warriors providing military service in exchange for a refuge for their families.[32] The Amarascoggins employed a different strategy for survival; they dissolved as a political unit. Families no longer met annually at Amaseconti or Naracomigog. Some scattered up their river valleys farther from the frontier, while others joined existing Wabanaki villages elsewhere.[33]

Unfortunately for the Indians who hoped to stay clear of the fighting, Governor Shirley interpreted their rejections of his invitation to take up arms for King George as a sign of latent hostility.[34] Garrison commanders and even many colonists shared his suspicion. The new commander of Fort St. Georges, Captain Jabez Bradbury, offered a representative assessment in his report that the local Penobscots "present all the appearance of friendship towards us, both in word and behavior that can be, But they are not to be trusted, and it's my opinion that the French will once more Set them against us notwithstanding all that the Government can or will do."[35] Shirley's offer of bounties for Mi'kmaq and Wulstukwiuk scalps—including £50 for those of women and children "killed in fight"—did the Bay Colony no favors in Wabanaki villages, but most Kennebecs and Penobscots remained stubbornly neutral until the summer of 1745.[36] When their leaders refused to hand over several men who joined raiders from Canada in attacking Pemaquid, Shirley declared war on both nations.[37]

The fighting that took place on the Maine frontier achieved little of wider military significance, but it injected an enduring bitterness between Indians and colonists with lasting consequences. Wabanaki raiders struck towns as far south as Casco Bay. As before, they avoided direct assaults on fortified garrisons as they killed livestock, torched buildings, and picked off isolated colonists like Seth Hinkley of Brunswick, whose brother reported the Wabanakis had "kild him . . . and scalped him and stript all his cloes."[38] The Wabanakis' own casualties encouraged, according to a French report, their "more zealous" prosecution of the war.[39] Warriors struck the newest towns—especially on the Muscongus patent—particularly hard, forcing their near abandonment by 1748.[40] Many Penobscots, Kennebecs, and Wulstukwiuks had already moved to safety near Quebec.[41]

Decisions by provincial leaders worsened the plight of frontier colonists. At the outset of war, Maine residents volunteered in droves for service against the French, helping to conquer the great Cape Breton Island fortress of Louisbourg in 1745. Maine's largest landowner, William Pepperrell, led the expedition, with Samuel Waldo in command of a brigade.[42] Massachusetts leaders remained preoccupied with fighting the French in Acadia, in the process stripping the Maine garrisons almost bare over the protests of hard-pressed locals. Beleaguered garrison commanders echoed Samuel Denny, who wrote from "naked and defenceless" Georgetown in 1748 to warn that Wabanakis had already killed a messenger carrying his earlier letters describing his vulnerable situation.[43]

Colonists focused their anger not only on the Indians but also on distant elites who either would not or could not provide protection. During 1749, two Pejepscot Proprietors touring company lands learned this firsthand. Residents of both communities had been poor even before the war.[44] In 1739, cash-strapped residents of recently incorporated Brunswick received permission to pay for their (often £5) lots in lumber.[45] In 1740, visiting proprietors learned that some residents were simply squatters.[46] When Belcher Noyes and William Skinner ventured from their Boston homes on behalf of the proprietors to size up affairs in the company towns of Brunswick and Topsham, they discovered how badly the war had loosened the company's grip on them. They reported farming at a standstill, "by reason of the Warr."[47] Upon their arrival in Brunswick, they had difficulty convincing Captain Benjamin Larrabee, the company agent (and longtime frontier resident), to turn over the papers they had sent empowering him to grant land, but "after some persuasion Madm Larrabee delivered to us, and to our Surprize found they were not duly recorded" in court. They also discovered "many of the Setlers have neglected to record their Deeds," although their report did not include speculation as to whether scorn for the company, fear of being killed by Indians on the way to York, or both, accounted for this neglect.[48]

In unincorporated Topsham, which had suffered even more than Brunswick, Noyes and Skinner reported outright hostility. Topsham had suffered "about 25 inhabitants killed" and had only "38 Setlers" (probably heads of household) left. At a conference with Noyes and Skinner, "No one offered to pay, or seemed willing to comply" with company demands for payment.[49] Instead, Topsham residents responded by asking for more land on their existing lots.[50] Noyes and Skinner observed "the unhappy disposition of these People," who had been "addicted . . . to pillaging and destroying the Lumber . . . and they seemed to make their Boast of so doing because the Proprietors had never yet made Examples of any of them."[51] Concluding his account of their tour, Noyes reported, "we could not but observe in the People a Disposition to lay hold of every Objection to our Title and improve the same to our Disadvantage."[52]

Far from emptying the frontier, however, wartime raids—and the failure of Massachusetts leaders to stop them—contributed to colonists' growing sense of alienation from both Indians and provincial elites. The population of colonists in Maine (a 1749 tally of 2,485 "fencible" militia, assuming an average family size of five, computes to just under 12,500 people) had grown large enough to pose a formidable challenge to either Wabanaki or metropolitan attempts to control them.[53] The troubled coda to the War of Austrian Succession in Maine revealed that even as most Massachusetts and Wabanaki leaders desired peace, frontier colonists had the will—and ability—to upset those plans.

Murder and Diplomacy

With no land claims at stake, Wabanaki leaders met with Governor Shirley in the autumn of 1749 to sign a peace treaty with little dispute. Throughout the talks both sides invoked Dummer's Treaty, and the 1749 peace accord was little more than a renewal of that agreement.[54]

Lingering wartime hatreds threatened the peace on two occasions in 1749. The first occurred before Wabanaki and colonial leaders could gather to renew Dummer's Treaty, when Loron led a vocal minority of Penobscots in a bid to stop peace talks.

The war had been hard on the respected orator: in 1745, Loron had barely escaped a Massachusetts scouting party with his life while returning from a goodwill mission.[55] Then, in 1747, he lost a son in battle.[56] Loron's efforts caused evident consternation among the delegates representing the majority of the Penobscots' "Captains and young men" at the peace talks, who disavowed Loron's party.[57] This minority of holdouts afterward relayed a terse missive to Shirley accepting the decision, but according to Egeremet, a leading accomodationist speaking for the Penobscot delegates attending the conference, Loron planned for a renewal of hostilities "when there is [another] French War."[58]

A sensational murder in the immediate aftermath of the conference threatened to grant Loron his wish. A group of six sailors attacked a camp of Kennebec and St. Francis Indians at Wiscasset on the night of December 2, killing Saccary Harry, "alias Hegen," a Kennebec chief, and wounding another minor Kennebec leader and a St. Francis Indian.[59] The victims had been returning home from the peace talks. The assault sent shock waves rippling across the region as Massachusetts leaders scrambled to contain the fallout. Wabanakis in villages across the Dawnland sent notice to Boston that they expected justice.[60]

The ensuing crisis took three years to resolve, largely because colonists tended to sympathize with the sailors instead of their Wabanaki victims.[61] Frontier residents gave shelter and aid to the fugitives, and on several occasions mobs tried to free suspects from custody. Justice of the Peace Jabez Fox, the man directing the hunt for the accused, marveled at the "spirit almost universally prevailing amongst those that live the most Exposed to the Indian Enemy in Warr time" in favor of concealing "murderers from the hands of Justice."[62] He failed to grasp that many colonists, embittered by years of brutal warfare and governmental indifference, no longer trusted Indians or provincial elites. The fugitives shared this ethic. A York County justice reported one suspect's father "was killed by the Indians" during the last war, which [Samuel] Ball and one of his accomplices had served in.[63] Lieutenant Governor Spencer Phips (Shirley had departed for England) and the General Court feared a renewal of war, and events in the York County courts did not comfort them. In a process that dragged on until June 1751 (in part due to the General Court's fear of Indian-hating Maine jurors), juries acquitted the ringleader, sentenced one man to twenty lashes for wounding "Captain Job and Andrew," and a third suspect escaped jail. No one else faced charges.[64]

As they waited, many Wabanakis concluded the wheels of British justice turned slowly (and inefficiently) indeed. A mixed force of warriors from several villages struck Fort Richmond and the surrounding communities, including Wiscasset, in September 1750. They killed livestock, destroyed homes, and took twenty prisoners. In the spring and summer of 1751, Kennebec warriors joined men from St Francis and Becancour in further raids, taking nine more captives and killing two men.[65] The Indians made clear this was a targeted reprisal, keeping the attacks west of Damariscotta (near the scene of the murder) and focused their efforts on destroying property and taking prisoners, all but two of whom they kept alive.[66]

Frontier colonists called for help—and for vengeance—from Lieutenant Governor Spencer Phips. St. Georges residents asked for provisions. Cooped up in blockhouses and unable to tend to crops, they had to survive on clams.[67] Residents of Sheepscot, North Yarmouth, and Georgetown also wrote for help.[68] Enoch Freeman, a militia officer and Falmouth attorney, demanded retaliation in a blistering note to Phips after raiders killed "an honest blacksmith" near his home, insisting, "If the Government don't take some speedy Measures to help us, we are ruin'd, and I must leave it to their Superior Wisdom to project some Efectual way to live, or rather have a being on the Frontiers."[69] A Sheepscot militia captain named Alexander Nichols took a more direct approach, asking Capt. Jabez Bradbury, the commander (and interpreter) at Fort St. Georges, to inform "those Indians that is our Supposed friends have warning to keep out of our way," because he and his garrison planned to "go out upon the back Sid[e] of our Settlement to see if we Can meet them [the raiders] in the woods give them a little of their own play until we have aid from the province."[70]

Lieutenant Governor Spencer Phips managed the Wiscasset crisis with a deft touch. When Bradbury notified Phips of Nichols's plans to fill the woods with trigger-happy militiamen, Phips ordered Nichols to stand down. "I cannot approve of sending out Men to give the Indians their own Play as you expressed it," he wrote, "for you cannot distinguish between Friends and Enemys and by this means may involve the government in a War which otherwise might have been avoided."[71] For their part, the majority of Wabanakis also wished to avoid a war. They worked to dissuade raiders from attacking and, when that failed, warned the British.[72] Phips took conciliatory Wabanakis at their word, instructing commanders like Nichols to avoid attacking peaceful Indians.[73]

Phips's very presence in the Bay Colony's top job highlighted the tangled network of speculators active in Massachusetts politics in 1750. Phips himself was the adopted son of William Phips, the governor responsible for the controversial Madockawando purchase of 1694. Spencer Phips sold most of his rights to the claim (which became the Muscongus Patent) in 1719, though he retained a minority share.[74] Phips's sterling biographical credentials landed him the position of lieutenant governor in several administrations, including Shirley's. Then in 1749, Governor Shirley left Phips in charge so he could travel to England and defend his conduct against accusations leveled by the man who had by then acquired a majority stake in the Muscongus Patent—Samuel Waldo. The dispute began after the Louisbourg campaign, when word leaked that Waldo was selling the muskets and keeping the pay of his dead soldiers. Shirley eventually won a civil suit against Waldo in 1749, prompting the notoriously litigious speculator to try to bury his former ally in lawsuits. After Shirley made his case to the Board of Trade in London, he served on a Franco-British commission formed to try to draw clear boundaries between the empires in North America and did not return to Massachusetts until the summer of 1753.[75] In an ironic twist, by (indirectly) removing the jingoistic Shirley from North America, Samuel Waldo helped bring peace to the Dawnland frontier.

For the last time, unencumbered by major land disputes (and with Shirley safely an ocean away), Massachusetts and Wabanaki leaders managed to renew Dummer's Treaty.[76] They did so even despite French offers of encouragement and supplies for further Wabanaki raids.[77] The Penobscots complained about trespassers on Matinicus Island (a valuable location for catching fish and seals), hunters encroaching in their woods, and new buildings above Fort Richmond. They invoked Dummer's Treaty and reasserted their boundaries, and commissioners dispatched by Phips promised to investigate and that "Justice will be done you."[78] Phips had instructed the commission to "avoid as much as may be all Controversies respecting any Land claimed or settled by us" which they adhered to.[79] In comparison, the negotiations over releasing captured colonists proved straightforward. Loron, once again representing the Penobscots, assured the commission that "there was some Difference between us, but not much, if it had been it would have been like Gun-powder."[80]

Loron's return to his role as a principal Penobscot spokesman during 1751 was an important factor in renewing the peace. The old diplomat had been the first Penobscot to complain about the Matinicus Island squatters, but he also promised to use his influence to retrieve British prisoners and bring in recalcitrant Kennebec and Canadian Indians to peace talks. It was Loron's words that convinced Massachusetts commissioners that the Indians were "hearty in the good work of peace."[81]

That work became far more difficult as leadership changed after 1752. Loron made his last appearance speaking at a treaty in 1751, and his departure was a heavy blow for the Wabanakis, especially his own Penobscots. Although never the highest-ranking sagamore himself, Loron had been a forceful speaker on behalf of the Penobscots since 1725, carrying great influence in that role.[82] Treading a middle path between the hardliners and those eager to accommodate the British, Loron had faced off against three Massachusetts governors. Pressure from Loron encouraged Dummer, Belcher, and Shirley to clarify Massachusetts obligations to the Indians in a manner that entered the written record. As the principal Native speaker at Dummer's Treaty, Loron had helped craft it and could lay better claim to remembering it than any other Wabanaki by 1750. In a culture that relied on oral history, this gave him great power. In 1742, he invoked his role there to Shirley, saying, "As I was the Chief in that Day [not technically true] and was the Cause of our Tribes complying with that Treaty," the assembled Wabanakis "desire me now to strengthen myself and have it confirmed."[83] Loron again invoked his authority as a peacemaker in 1751 when Massachusetts commissioners questioned his ability to persuade other Indians to negotiate. "I have been the Man that has been the first in all Treatys," he chided them, "but you think I am not capable to manage for the other Tribes. I have been the Man that has quelled all the rest."[84]

As much as anyone, Loron had come to embody Dummer's Treaty, and his diplomatic career coincided almost exactly with its vitality. Loron vanished from all treaty records after 1751, and a statement by Governor Shirley in 1754 referred to his death.[85] That statement occurred at the twilight of the relationship that the deceased Penobscot orator had played such an important role in preserving.

For the Penobscots and other Wabanakis, Loron could not have passed from the scene at a worse time. Even as Loron and other leaders had worked to hold together their strategy of containment that had preserved the Dawnland since 1727, a new force arrived to transform the debate about the nature of property on the Maine frontier. At the 1752 renewal of Dummer's Treaty, the Kennebecs had been eager to tell Massachusetts commissioners that "above Richmond there are some Things doing, which we believe you know nothing of." The commission in fact knew all about it. "What is doing there," they answered, "is by private Persons who imagine they have an Undoubted Right to those Lands," and said the government would "examine into their Title."[86] Those "private Persons" were a new company known as the Kennebeck Proprietors, and one of their members—Jacob Wendell—stood in front of the Wabanakis as a commissioner that day.[87] As Wendell's presence indicated, the company wielded considerable public influence. By 1753, their activities threatened to destroy the consensus that had bound Wabanaki and Massachusetts leaders together since 1727.

That consensus, which had minimized the spread of imperial violence on the Maine frontier after 1744, depended on the speculators' reliance on Dummer's Treaty to protect their titles. That reliance was in turn rooted in the Bay Colony's commitment to Indian deeds as the best way to prove landownership. The arrival of the Kennebeck Proprietors posed a challenge to the foundations of the Massachusetts system of landownership, which had formed the heart of the Anglo-Wabanaki relationship.

8 /   Contrary to Their Own Laws, 1749–1755

Hardscrabble Maine colonists and their Wabanaki neighbors disagreed on a great deal, but they both shared a fear that, as one York resident put it in 1716, a stranger from Massachusetts might appear with documents claiming *he* had a right to their land, even though these "Deeds & Conveyances . . . may be made under a hedge."[1] The piece of paper that changed the Dawnland frontier forever was not created in the bushes, but as far as the residents of Norridgewock or Wiscasset were concerned, it might as well have been. In reality, a minor shareholder named Samuel Goodwin found the original Plymouth Company Patent in a Rhode Island house in 1744.[2]

The most active members of the land company that arose to make the vast, three-million-acre claim a reality brooked no opposition to their designs from rival companies or from the Wabanakis and colonists already living on the land. The Plymouth Company (more popularly known as the Kennebeck Proprietors) soon realized much of that opposition was rooted in claims based on Indigenous land rights. They therefore resolved to attack the validity of Indian land deeds—and Wabanaki land rights in general—in the process, sparking a renewed contest over the nature of landownership. Ordinary colonists living on disputed land could not escape the clash: rival companies feared direct legal confrontation and instead targeted small farmers holding title under their competitors for lawsuits. Growing in numbers and assertiveness, colonists played a greater role in the unfolding struggle than before.

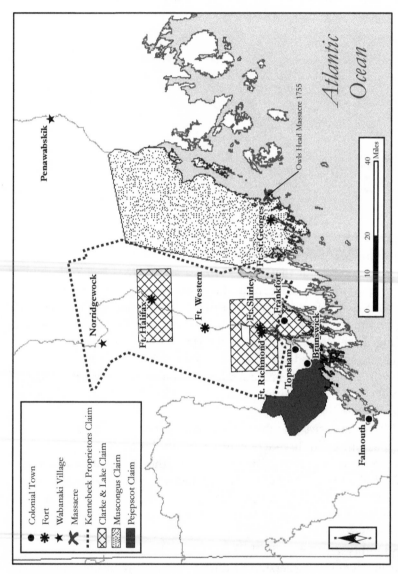

MAP 8.1. Frontier post-1749 Kennebeck arrival.

The Wabanakis faced the most severe threat of all from the new land company. The Kennebeck Proprietors' arrival threatened to ruin the Wabanaki strategy of containment based on Dummer's Treaty at the very time that the Indians were most dependent on it. Waning Native military power relative to Massachusetts (a situation linked to a simultaneous decline in the French Empire's ability to supply—let alone protect—its colonists and allies against their British rivals in wartime) made the Wabanakis increasingly reliant on the influence of land companies basing their titles on recognized Indian deeds.

Wabanakis, rival land companies, and frontier colonists scrambled to respond to the Kennebeck Proprietors' challenge in an environment of heightened conflict between the British and French Empires. Without a doubt, brewing tensions and the subsequent global clash of empires known as the Seven Years' War shaped the protagonists' decisions. But it would be a mistake to allow the drama of the Seven Years' War to obscure the importance of the Kennebeck Proprietors' arrival as a decisive turning point in the long-running contest to define the nature of landownership in the region. In fact, the chaos sown by the Kennebeck Proprietors—aided and abetted by the shareholding Governor William Shirley—more than the efforts of more distant imperial actors ensured that the violence of the Seven Years' War would spread to the Maine frontier. Unlike previous clashes that had restored some form of balance to the region, the Seven Years' War resulted in the permanent destruction of the prewar order, with catastrophic consequences for the Wabanakis.

The Kennebeck Company Arrives

To validate their claims, the Kennebeck Proprietors relied on a document hearkening back to another era of royal and council grants. Written in 1630, the patent expanded an original 1629 grant by the Council of New England to the Plymouth Colony. The vast, vague grant contained at least three million acres, stretching for fifteen miles on each side of the Kennebec River. The residents of Plymouth Colony had engaged in fur trade with the local Indians until selling the claim (the value of which had been declining as a source of furs) to four Boston merchants in 1661. The outbreak of war in 1675 halted the fur trade there, and it did not recover. The four original proprietors traded and divided their shares to various investors during the subsequent imperial wars while waiting for a more favorable time to make good on their claim.[3] That time arrived during the 1740s, when Samuel Goodwin located the original title, which had gone missing. (The most careful scholar of the company suggests a rival in Rhode Island deliberately hid the patent.)[4] The relatively mild damage to Maine towns during King George's War encouraged the proprietors, who, according to a company account, had "been much Incommoded by the Incursions of these Indians which Renders their Interest a meer Dead stock."[5] Reduced Wabanaki strength would matter to the shareholders because they did not intend on claiming their title from an Indian sale. In 1749, the major shareholders assembled in Boston for the first legal meeting of the Kennebeck Proprietors.

Although they relied on an old patent, the leading members of the company were rising members of what one historian called the "middling gentility on both sides of the Atlantic," families with business and social networks on multiple continents.[6] Company members included some of the richest families in Massachusetts, such as Edward Winslow, William Brattle, and William and James Bowdoin. Even minor shareholders like David Jeffries boasted connections to ruling families such as the Belchers and Wentworths.[7] The most energetic member by far was a Boston physician and drug importer named Silvester Gardiner, a businessman in the pugilistic mold of Samuel Waldo. In cooperation with James Bowdoin, Gardiner drove the company's aggressive strategy from his perch on the standing committee, which conducted most company business without calling shareholder meetings.[8]

Under their leadership, the Kennebeck Proprietors posed a far greater threat to the post-1727 status quo on the Maine frontier than Waldo ever had. The Muscongus Proprietor had spent the past two decades attempting to resuscitate the discredited Madockawando cession that underlay his claim. Despite his mounting frustrations over periodic setbacks, Waldo did not question the prevailing orthodoxy in Massachusetts regarding the validity of Indian deeds. Instead, Waldo accepted their inclusion in the convoluted constellation of possible sources of title and embarked on a twenty-year effort to convince the General Court, the public, and the Board of Trade that his claim passed the test. In a 1736 defense of his title, Waldo boasted that his right was based on a "Grant from the Crown" (a portion of the very same Plymouth Patent the Kennebeck Proprietors located) *and* "Purchase from the Indians" *and* "Improvement of the Lands in time of Peace, and Defence of 'em in time of War," *and* his two meetings with the Penobscots he called "treaties."[9] In contrast to Waldo's Sisyphean struggle for acceptance, the Kennebeck Proprietors were willing to dynamite the very foundations of their opponents' titles.

In a 1752 letter to their attorney in London, Silvester Gardiner and two associates admitted that they even though they as yet lacked a documentary base to seize the lands of colonists living on the company claim (and for which their agent had already been coercing residents into paying the proprietors), they planned to "Plead the Illegality" of Indian deeds.[10] (In that same letter, the proprietors suggested they planned to make the cynical argument that the Wabanaki land sales were invalid because "if Subjeckt to any Prince," the Indians were subjects of "France, and not of England," ironically using the reality of Wabanaki sovereignty to undermine Indigenous property. They evidently backed down from contradicting the Bay Colony's interpretation of every Indian treaty since 1693, however.) The leading proprietors came to the conclusion that the quickest way to negate the claims of their major adversaries was to challenge the validity of stand-alone Indian deeds. The strategy had the advantage that, as London-based shareholder Florentius Vassal explained, if the company had no right to a disputed tract, "no one else has," and the title would revert to "the Crown and Govermt of the Massachusetts."[11] Not least, by (accurately) pointing out how many proprietors' use of Indian deeds was, as Vassal put it, "Contrary to their own laws" (the Act of 1701 had effectively reverted Indian land sales to the early seventeenth-century status of "quieting," as discussed in chapter 2), the Kennebeck Proprietors compensated for the vague nature of their own claim.[12] In the same 1752 letter to their London attorney, the proprietors admitted they had no idea what the bounds of the Plymouth Patent actually were and asked him to find additional documentation.[13]

The Kennebeck Proprietors decided to attack the system of land title based on the reality of Indigenous property rights for the same reason their rivals had constructed it, and the same reason Silvester Gardiner gave for why the company secretly granted shares to Governor William Shirley: "The Company thou't it for their Interest."[14] In pursuit of that interest, the Kennebeck Proprietors granted shares in the company to two consecutive Bay Colony governors (Shirley and his successor), pushed for the creation of a new county in Maine when York County juries refused to acknowledge company title, and then offered to build a new courthouse in this proposed county, to better influence cases tried in it.[15] But the most lasting legacy of the company's bid for mastery of the Kennebec River region was the final destruction of the Anglo-Wabanaki détente based on a mutual recognition of Indigenous property rights, fortified by mutual self-interest and expressed in Dummer's Treaty.

"Pacific Measures"

As the Kennebeck Proprietors began to assert their claim in 1750, hundreds of Maine colonists experienced what had become a familiar process for their Wabanaki neighbors: strangers from Boston arrived at the door to inform the inhabitants that they lived on land belonging to someone else who had never set foot there. Samuel Goodwin—now an agent and company clerk—did most of the legwork, giving colonists the choice of either admitting "they were on the said proprietors lands and requesting grants" from the company, or risking a lawsuit.[16] Goodwin provided applicants with preprinted forms to speed up the process. By early May, 1751, the company received applications from 329 individuals living in nineteen separate towns and hamlets, extending along the coast from Pemaquid to Damariscotta and Sheepscot, up the Kennebec River to Richmond, and southwest through Topsham, Brunswick, and North Yarmouth. The proprietors demanded payment from many (though not all) residents for company grants, depending on location, collecting a total of £6119, 16s, and 8d. Some colonists had lived on the land for decades, like Georgetown farmer Charles Snipe, who petitioned the company for 98 acres, on which he had built a house and lived for the past seventeen years.[17]

The Kennebeck Proprietors also confronted entire communities. In May 1750 they directed the standing committee to "write to several Towns" on the company patent demanding they "Call ameaditely a town meeting and vote to hold under the Propritee" in exchange for a quitclaim from the company and the promise of "what Land more the Commite [sic] may think Proper to Grant them."[18] The town of Newcastle on the Sheepscot River received one of those letters. In it, the standing committee explained the sources of the company title and assured Newcastle residents they would "leave the Settlers undisturbed . . . and ratify to them their Improvements." In exchange, they asked "that you would make some Enquiry into the Titles among your Neighbours, how they derive their Right and come by their Posessions, what ancient Deeds they have . . . and after this Enquiry if you please to communicate the particulars thereof." The committee informed Newcastle it expected many residents did not hold deeds but that the Proprietors would "Cheerfully . . . Secure them a good Title to their Lands." Because this would provide "Encouragement of the Settlements and promoting of Justice," they expected cooperation in these "pacific measures."[19]

Led by the aggressive Gardiner, the Kennebeck Proprietors took measures that few frontier residents found "pacific." To protect company interests and intimidate opponents, the Kennebeck Proprietors issued certificates of "impowerment" to certain frontier residents, deputizing them to "hinder" anyone from "improving" on the company claim, while charging them with informing on their neighbors who might need to be "prosecuted according to law."[20] Although other companies had similarly deputized colonists to act on their behalf, the Kennebeck Proprietors added an aggressive new twist on this practice by authorizing so many people to serve as agents in other people's communities. The proprietors also began, unasked, to assume responsibility for governing certain communities on the patent, issuing directives for some to lay out acreage for meetinghouses and cemeteries.[21] Some of these places, like Brunswick, already had a meetinghouse and had been running their own affairs for years.

The Kennebeck Proprietors' arrival triggered a range of responses from residents. Some frontier colonists tried to use the ensuing confusion to their advantage. Samuel Denny (the justice of the peace initially involved in arresting the Wiscasset killers) petitioned the Kennebeck Proprietors to grant him his 150 acres at Arrowsic and an additional 324 acres of ungranted land. Denny had hosted an unsanctioned proprietors meeting at his home in 1737 to divide some land in the area claimed by the Pejepscot Proprietors. Taking up under the Kennebeck Proprietors may have given him a chance to enlarge his estate at the expense of a company he disliked.[22] Jonathan Williamson, an agent holding under the neighboring Wiscasset Proprietors, sent a letter in February 1751 informing them that "the whole place Except my Self and one or two more" had taken up titles under the Kennebeck Proprietors. Williamson claimed that even though "they have Promised to give me a Warrente" to protect his land from lawsuits, he had resisted, though he took the opportunity to add that the neighboring Pejepscot Proprietors had also promised to defend those on their patent. Had the Wiscasset Proprietors done the same, "it might have put a stop to their [the Kennebeck Proprietors'] Proseding in the manner they have."[23] Williamson suggested the proprietors take action as soon as possible and left little doubt that action should involve warranting his deed. Many other colonists just wanted to stay out of trouble. Intimidated by the Kennebeck Proprietors' formidable resources, they chose to repurchase their own lands rather than face an expensive legal battle. However, anyone taking up under the aggressive new company risked lawsuits from rival proprietors fighting to preserve their own claims. Colonists living in disputed zones were caught up in the contest whether they wanted to be or not.

Some smaller land companies took their cue from the colonists and hesitated to resist the Kennebeck onslaught. The Pemaquid Proprietors adjourned a meeting in late 1749, unable to agree on any course of action, and did not reassemble until January 1762.[24] The Wiscasset Proprietors (despite Jonathan Williamson's urgings) also hunkered down to wait out the storm.[25] Others resisted. The largest of them, the Pejepscot Proprietors, rallied to mount a vigorous defense not only of their patent but of Indian land deeds in a contest waged before the public.

"Too Firm to Be Shaken": The Pejepscot Proprietors Respond

The Pepepscot Proprietors were both beneficiaries from and embodiments of the post–Dummer's Treaty order on the Maine frontier. The Pejepscot Patent enjoyed recognition in that treaty, and the company's ranks included over the years a number of noted advocates of just treatment for the Wabanakis (often for religious reasons) including Adam Winthrop, Thomas Hutchinson, and John Minot.[26] Belcher Noyes, who guided company strategy as clerk during its confrontation with the Kennebeck Proprietors, grew up in the care of his uncle (and namesake) Jonathan Belcher, the Bay Colony governor who most shared the views of Winthrop and his associates.[27]

Although Belcher Noyes did not take the same public interest in Indian conversion as either his uncle Jonathan Belcher or as his predecessor as company clerk, Adam Winthrop, his papers indicate that Noyes took the notion of Wabanaki rights to land and equal justice seriously, above all as a way to secure firm foundations for the Pejepscot title. Noyes's copy of Dummer's Treaty highlighted a number of portions dealing not just with the Pejepscot title but also with Native claims to unsold land and a statement by Dummer promising the Indians "equal justice with his Majesty's English Subjects in all points, when ever any Difficulty shall arise concerning the Property of Lands or any other matters."[28] In his own records, Noyes traced the chain of the company claim back to Richard Wharton's 1684 purchase from Warumbee and other sagamores around Merrymeeting Bay, followed by their repeated acknowledgments. "A title so well supported," he noted, "one would think needed no other Evidence to prove its Authenticity." Citing Jeremiah Dummer's *Defence of the New England Charters*, Noyes concluded "the *Native Right*, as Superior to any other Title whatsoever."[29] In correspondence with fellow proprietor Enoch Freeman, Noyes singled out "Dummer's Treaty" as the most important subsequent

Wabanaki acknowledgment, because it "is now allowed to be the Basis on which all the Subsquent Treaties are grounded."[30]

The Pejepscot Proprietors realized they would have to rely even more on "the Native right" after Noyes returned from a fact-finding mission to company lands in 1749 (discussed in chapter 7). Noyes and another visiting proprietor received a cool response from the residents of Brunswick and Topsham. Many of them had yet to pay the company for their lots, and few of those who did had bothered to record their deeds. Together this meant the presence of the colonists on the land would not by itself provide legal evidence of company title. In 1751 Noyes summoned all of the shareholders—including New Hampshire governor Benning Wentworth—for a rare meeting of "the whole interest" to raise funds for the impending confrontation with the Kennebeck Company.[31] Although the company put on a public display of bravado in an advertisement posted in the Brunswick meetinghouse, privately the proprietors tried to hedge their losses.[32] Noyes entered into a scheme with prominent Tophsam resident Adam Hunter to sell the entire Pejepscot interest in town to the inhabitants for £6,000. The plan collapsed, with Noyes accusing Hunter of stalling on purpose to "have another Winters run in Cutting and destroying the Lumber before you conclude this Bargain."[33] The proprietors also granted 1,200 acres of land bordering the Kennebeck encroachments to members Henry Gibbs and William Skinner on the condition they shoulder the legal costs for defending it.[34] Rather than hazard their patent in an uncertain lawsuit, the Pejepscot Proprietors instead took their case before the public, engaging in a pamphlet war with the Kennebeck Proprietors over the validity of that company's claim.

A Clash of Visions

The stakes in the struggle between the Pejepscot and Kennebeck Proprietors transcended which company could claim the lands along the Kennebec River. The rivals advanced not only opposing titles but also different interpretations of the validity of Indian deeds as a basis for landownership within Massachusetts. At times the exchange descended into excruciating detail (at one point the Pejepscot Proprietors apologized for engaging in "such Peurilities" as quibbling over the word "which") but nevertheless carried far-reaching implications for the future of the frontier.[35] If Indian deeds had no legal weight, many current landholders in Maine, large and small, risked losing their property. That change would

also undercut the function of Dummer's Treaty in linking colonial property to Indian land rights.

The Pejepscot Proprietors knew many Maine landholders based their
titles on Native land rights and accordingly built their arguments on a
robust defense of them as the source of all property. The Pejepscot pamphlets, probably written by Belcher Noyes, never even acknowledged the
validity of the original Plymouth Colony Patent per se, instead arguing
that an Indian deed from 1665 conformed those bounds—which were
located far north of the Pejepscot Patent (see map, figure 8.1).[36] The proprietors published a number of extracts of relevant deeds to back up their
case, along with a map based on several surveys of the Kennebec River
region.

The Pejepscot map depicted the Kennebec River region's Wabanaki
origins. Engraved by Thomas Johnston at the direction of Pejepscot Proprietor Henry Gibbs, the map detailed various land grants touching the
Kennebec River, all except one from the Indians. A corner of one rectan-
gular grant contained the note "Patent to Colony of Plymouth, January
26, 1629," but left the extent of that patent unclear, as every rectangle
on the map corresponded with a named and dated Indian land sale. An
elaborate seal on the bottom-right corner further drove the point home
about where land rights originated. The seal depicted two Indian men
dressed in contemporary trade hunting shirts. One carried a flintlock
musket, and the other wielded a knotted war club. The man on the left
proclaimed, "God hath Planted Us Here." His companion gestured to the
map above them, saying "God Decreed this Land to Us."[37]

The map also depicted several communities in Maine, including
North Yarmouth, the company town of Brunswick, and the Kennebecs'
own "Norridgewock Town," outside of any of the patent boundaries.
British towns appeared on the map as meetinghouses, while Norridgewock appeared as a cluster of small houses around a central taller building, which anyone who traveled to the village knew was the chapel. If
the Indians were no longer central to the future of the empire laid out in
the various deeds, the Pejepscot map depicted the reality of an enduring Native presence in the region. In a more fanciful turn, the map also
contained several truck houses on possible sites where the Clarke & Lake
Proprietors had erected them before 1675. (Viewing the relatively slug-
gish Clarke & Lake heirs as far more preferable neighbors to the aggressive Kennebeck Proprietors, the Pejepscot Proprietors endorsed the
long-dormant Clarke & Lake claim to the upper Kennebec to preempt
Gardiner and his associates' designs on it.)

FIGURE 8.1. Published copy of the Thomas Johnston map in support of Pejepscot and Clarke & Lake Claims. Courtesy of the Maine Historical Society.

The Pejepscot pamphlets backed the imagery on the Johnston map with more detailed arguments attempting to undermine the idea of any titles descending from non-Native sources. They accused the Kennebeck Proprietors of decrying Indian deeds only because of "the Insufficiency of their own."[38] But the Pejepscot Proprietors argued that the Plymouth Colony, which was the source of the Kennebeck claim, "call[ed] these Indians Proprietors of the Lands."[39] In fact, the original owners of the

FIGURE 8.2. Detail of the Johnston Map. Courtesy of the Maine Historical Society.

Plymouth Patent had a "Design . . . from the beginning to corroborate with Title to said Tract with the Right of the Natives, tho' they have but ill executed it."[40] They took time to emphasize this point, noted the writers, because their rivals claimed "Indians can no more have Property in Lands, than Wolves, Foxes, or other wild Beasts."[41] Although the Pejepscot writers did not invoke Jeremiah Dummer's *Defence of the New England Charter*, they noted that Psalms 115, verse 16 proved the Earth was "given to the Children of Men," which included the Indians.[42]

For the Pejepscot Proprietors, Native sovereignty—mediated through English legal practices—provided the essential legal basis for landownership. Indian land needed to be conveyed by a proper deed, with witnesses, and executed as such in a county court. Criticizing several of the documents presented by the Kennebeck Proprietors, the Pejepscot Company asked "whether a Paper containing the Consent of any Number of Indians, without any Date, be of any Force against a Deed of a certain Date, executed properly."[43] Along with English law, a good deed required Native consent, and the Pejepscot Proprietors took pains to prove their own 1684 deed met that standard. They secured the testimony of witnesses like interpreter John Gyles, who claimed that although the Wabanakis "from time to time disputed the English Claim to some of the Eastern Lands . . . they always Confessed that the . . . [Pejepscot] deed was a good and Lawfull Deed of sale of all the lands therein."[44]

The Kennebeck Proprietors did their best to downplay the implications of their assault on Indian land deeds but made clear in imagery and textual arguments they sought a different source of validation. For them, the combination of Indian consent and English law held no weight. Landownership could descend only from royal or provincial grants, and the only valid Indian deeds were those that confirmed provincial grants—as they argued the Indian deeds to Plymouth had. Like the Pejepscot Proprietors, the Kennebeck Company produced revealing imagery to justify their land claims. In stark contrast to their rivals, the Kennebeck map ignored the Native past—and present—in its desire to highlight the plans and accomplishments of the proprietors. The map, engraved by the same Thomas Johnston who made the Pejepscot map, contained no imagery of Indians in its seal, which instead featured a dedication to Governor William Shirley. In another revealing bit of symbolism, the Kennebeck Proprietors also hired Thomas Johnston to engrave the company seal, which contained the motto "Nec Frustra, Dedit Rex" (The King Never Gave in Vain) emblazoned over an anchor with a codfish over it.[45] On the map, a bold line marked the company claim, engulfing Brunswick, Topsham, and the village of Norridgewock. All three communities appeared only as names, unlike distant North Yarmouth, depicted as a chapel, or Frankfort and other tracts laid out by the company, set in large rectangles. A small inset map of the northern borderlands included a physical representation of Norridgewock, but viewers would have had to squint to see it. For all practical purposes, the company had erased the Wabanakis from the landscape.

Like many imperial powers, the Kennebeck Proprietors indulged in cartographic megalomania to justify their claims. Visually the map did not distinguish between developed and undeveloped tracts on the patent, blurring the distinction between plans and achievements. Nor did it bother to define the full extent of the company claim; the lines tapered off against the dense text informing the reader of the chain of ownership from 1629 to 1754. The text contained no visual corroboration, encouraging the reader to accept the company claim as proof, much like a modern warranty agreement. The map also lavished great detail on enlarged depictions of Forts Frankfort, Western, and Halifax (all built on the

Kennebeck Patent during 1754), which loomed over the landscape. In reality, all three forts were wooden stockades encircling a few log block-houses, built (like most frontier forts) to house garrisons of only a few dozen soldiers for any length of time.

The Kennebeck Proprietors also challenged the validity of Native land deeds in writing, although, perhaps aware of the potential for incurring a backlash, they attempted to conceal the scope of their intentions. "As to Indian Deeds, we never did decry them in the Gross," they insisted in a lengthy printed rebuttal to the Pejepscot Proprietors. (In private, the proprietors did just that.)[46] Instead, they merely challenged the Pejepscot deeds "and deeds such as theirs."[47] However, anyone who followed the Kennebeck arguments another forty-four pages past this second-page statement would read that "deeds such as theirs" meant virtually every deed issued for land in Maine. The Kennebeck Company claimed that the Massachusetts law passed in 1701 nullifying Indian land sales after 1633 west of the Piscataqua River applied in Maine, as well. The only exceptions, they insisted in enlarged print, involved "Confirmation Of Their Other Lawful Titles And Possessions" such as their own.[48] For emphasis, the company repeated this statement three more times on the following page.[49]

The Kennebeck interpretation of the act of 1701 was a radical departure from how almost everyone else in Massachusetts had viewed it. That included current Kennebeck Proprietor Robert Temple, who had been involved in a plan with the Clarke & Lake Proprietors before Dummer's War to plant several hundred Irish colonists on their claim, which he knew was based on an Indian deed. Aware of this inconsistency, Temple helpfully furnished the company a letter for publication in which he explained that during the 1740s, after reading the Plymouth Colony charter and other Kennebeck papers, these "open'd my eyes as to the Prejudices I lay under respecting Indian Titles" and "till of late Years I tho't those Indian Deeds might be of some Consequence, not having seen the particular law against purchasing from the Natives, nor the Plymouth Patent."[50] In Temple's haste to educate the public, he neglected to mention his current interest in the Plymouth Patent.[51]

With the stakes so high and neither company certain of victory, both sides waged a proxy war while avoiding major lawsuits. The Pejepscot Proprietors took that strategy to the greatest extreme: much of their writing defended not just their own deeds but the seventeenth-century Indian purchases of the Major Thomas Clarke and Captain Thomas Lake in the region. (The less-organized Clarke & Lake heirs appear to have let

Belcher Noyes and the Pejepscot Proprietors take the lead in the pamphlet war.) As they jockeyed for position, both sides restricted their lawsuits to desultory harassment of frontier colonists unfortunate enough pick the wrong patrons. Compounding the plight of colonists caught in the crossfire, the companies rarely warranted their deeds, meaning they assumed no responsibility for defending their land grants if a colonist was sued. The ensuing legal skirmishes (which extended to opposing gangs of men destroying buildings, fences, and other evidence of physical possession by their rivals) achieved little beyond making life worse for small landholders.[52]

Those clashes, disruptive as they were, became a part of a wider confrontation sparked by the Kennebeck Proprietors' attempt to build new towns in the heart of Kennebec Indian country.

Colonizing the Kennebec

The Kennebeck Proprietors knew that planting colonists would solidify their claims and increase land values. "Unless the Lands is inhabited," they wrote to an agent in London during 1752, "it [sic] is not Worth anything."[53] The Pejepscot Proprietors flaunted their own accomplishments on this score by publishing pamphlets under the name of the Brunswick Proprietors, after the incorporated town on their patent. Like their predecessors, the Kennebeck Proprietors turned to Europe for a supply of pliable colonists, recruiting a group of German and French Protestants to found the town of Frankfort in the spring of 1752. News of shoddy company treatment of the arrivals (the proprietors levied a series of demands on residents resembling feudal dues and denied the community a participatory government, among other complaints) traveled back to Europe in time to force the company to abandon plans for three new towns in 1753.[54]

The company activities, coupled with rumors of a planned town even farther north on the Cobbosseecontee River, triggered a strenuous protest from the Kennebecs, who viewed these encroachments as a breach of Dummer's Treaty. Indians in the path of the planned towns dictated a complaint to the governor through William Lithgow, commander at Fort Richmond, warning the British to remain south of the fort.[55] At the same time, Penobscots complained about hunters and squatters on their land. Frontier post commanders relayed the chorus of complaints with their endorsements. "The People here abouts are Afraid these things will breed a Disturbance," wrote one.[56]

Massachusetts leaders had anticipated these complaints after listening to Wabanaki protests during the last conference about resolving the Wiscasset killings in 1752, so the General Court had formed a committee in December of that year to decide on its answer to the Indians in 1753. Although the House *Journal* did not record the vote as such, the legislature was in reality deliberating whether to endorse the Kennebeck Proprietors' use of unacknowledged Indian deeds to make an end run around Native land rights, or to engage in a good-faith honoring of Dummer's Treaty. The House printed notices in the Boston newspapers "that all Persons claiming any Right there [on the Kennebec River], under Indian titles, may bring in the Evidence." It later broadened the call to include not just titles from deeds, but "any Cession made by the Indians, by Treaty or otherwise," out of concern that "doubt may arise," since treaties had long mingled with deeds on the frontier.[57] Sensitive to the political ramifications of the committee's deliberations, the House appointed as its members two of the commissioners present in 1752— Speaker of the House Thomas Hubbard and Judge Chambers Russell. The House also forwarded ongoing reports of the situation on the frontier to the committee.[58]

In an April 1753 report soon endorsed by the governor and General Court, the committee sided with the Kennebeck Proprietors, justifying their claims on the vague 1648 and 1653 Indian deeds to Plymouth Colony representatives, and the 1693, 1713, and 1717 treaties where the Indians had agreed to a status quo ante bellum. Anticipating the Wabanaki reaction, the report recommended that frontier garrison commanders "keep the Indians quiet" until commissioners could meet with them.[59] In actions that repeated previous patterns of behavior, Massachusetts leaders then made efforts to address other Wabanaki complaints that did not interfere with the speculators' agenda. The day after the committee's report, Lieutenant Governor Phips restricted colonial beaver hunting east of the Saco River and soon afterward authorized the removal of squatters on Penobscot-held Matinicus Island.[60] A subsequent committee convened in response to the ongoing Kennebec complaints recommended the Kennebeck Proprietors find a way to give "satisfaction" to the Indians to avoid trouble.[61] Having received Bay Colony backing for their venture, the Kennebeck Proprietors agreed to cooperate, although in reality nothing short of respecting earlier treaties would give "satisfaction" to the Indians.

Dummer's Treaty Undone

Since 1727, different Wabanaki and Massachusetts interpretations of the terms of Dummer's Treaty had coexisted. Colonial pretensions of Indigenous subjugation to King George could serve as suitable posturing for an overseas audience, while ignored in actual Anglo-Wabanaki dealings. The publication of Dummer's oral proclamation to the Wabanakis promising reciprocity as part of the official treaty had fused Native and European diplomatic traditions, while Wabanaki diplomatic acumen (above all by Loron) backed by enduring Native power steered Massachusetts into converting Indian land deeds they intended on the English model into totems of an ongoing negotiation on the Wabanaki model, thus accommodating the speculators' and the Wabanakis' traditions of property, as well.

The true source of weakness in the treaty for the Wabanakis and any Britons hoping it would be a lasting foundation to resolve disparate land claims lay in a key bundle of seventeenth-century deeds to territory along the Kennebec River. Massachusetts commissioners in 1726—themselves invested in many of the deeds—showed them to the Penobscots, who urged the *Bostoniak* to show the deeds to the then-absent Kennebecs who actually lived on the land.[62] When the Kennebecs arrived for the 1727 talks along with other Wabanakis, no commission repeated the procedure. Massachusetts representatives considered 1727 a mere ratification, and the Wabanakis had no reason to ask to see any deeds. As a result, the final version of Dummer's Treaty never directly addressed these dormant (and shaky) British claims to the Kennebec River. Some of these deeds secured part of the Kennebeck Proprietors' claim, while others formed the basis of the Clarke & Lake heirs' claims. The latter proprietors had, after the Wabanakis drove off offending colonists edging up the Kennebec in 1722, devoted their efforts to luring new residents to coastal portions of their claim. Although the Clarke & Lake heirs never formally renounced their deeds to the land, they also never tried to make these claims a reality. Instead, it was the Kennebeck Proprietors, who were simultaneously at work undermining the acceptance of Indian deeds' validity, who prodded Massachusetts leaders into reopening the issue.

The committee dispatched to meet with the Kennebecs embodied how interwoven the land companies had become in the process of Indian diplomacy. Its five members who journeyed east in September 1753 included two current Kennebeck Proprietors (James Bowdoin and

Jacob Wendell), a man who accepted grants from the company in April 1754, and two shareholders in the neighboring Wiscasset Company.[63] Like Samuel Waldo in 1735, the committee did not intend to negotiate with the Kennebecs so much as to present them with proof of company ownership of Indian land. This time, however, the proprietors had the full backing of the Governor William Shirley (just returned from England) and the General Court.

At the conference, the commissioners listened as the Kennebecs complained about the recent construction of a new garrison above the unauthorized town of Frankfort.[64] Speaking for the Kennebecs, a sagamore named Quenois invoked Dummer's Treaty, which he understood to mean "no settlement should be made above Richmond Fort."[65] To their dismay, the Kennebecs listened as interpreter Walter McFarland told them that at Dummer's Treaty, they had ratified seventeenth-century deeds selling portions of their land to Christopher Lawson, Robert Spencer, and Thomas Lake in the 1640s and 1650s.[66] The commissioners then informed the Kennebecs through McFarland that the land in question was British by virtue of "ancient trading Houses up this River, by ancient Settlements, and by ancient Deeds now produced," which they showed the assembled Kennebecs. According to the treaty minutes, the Kennebecs recognized the names of the signers of the committee's seventeenth-century deeds. None of the family bands directly in the path of the sales were present in 1753, indicated by the Indian delegates' promise to inform "the Relations and Friends to the Owners of these Lands what has been said."[67] The meeting broke up for the night on that note.

On the second and final day of proceedings, Quenois explained (through McFarland) the Kennebecs' understanding of the history of their land cessions to Massachusetts since the Treaty of Portsmouth in 1713, in the process providing a rare extended insight into the Wabanaki version of past treaties. At Portsmouth, "the Indians desired the English might not settle further Eastward than Brunswick, which was then settled. We were then bid, that if any Englishmen should settle further Eastward . . . to inform the Governor of it, and they should pay dear for it." After discussing with the Penboscots and "Arrasagonticocks [sic]" (British sources sometimes used this term to embrace all the Wabanakis living in Canada, including temporary residents like the Amarascoggins and Pigwackets), the Indians had consented when Governor Dudley had said, "It would not hurt us if the English settled . . . Brunswick, North Yarmouth, Casco-Bay [Falmouth and Scarborough] and Saco." Then Quenois recalled the 1717 Treaty of Arrowsic, when the Kennebecs, at the urging of Governor Shute, had allowed the British to "go as far up the River as Richmond."[68]

Other unidentified Indians made statements appealing to Governor Shirley—through his representatives—to carry out his proper role in their diplomatic relationship. They praised Shirley and all previous Massachusetts governors, and insisted, "We have never heard that any of the Governors desired the English might settle higher up than Richmond; although we have heard it from other people." The Kennebecs reminded the commission how important the issue was to them and that this meeting was their third complaint on the matter. They conceded the land up to Frankfort but drew a firm line there. The Kennebecs then invoked the relative wealth of Massachusetts and the Kennebecs: "You have Land enough below [Frankfort]. . . . [W]e have but a little Space; we desire to live as Brothers."[69] When the commissioners promised the Indians that they would be permitted to keep hunting and fishing rights, the Kennebecs gave an answer both sides knew to be true: "If the English should settle . . . it would drive away our Game, which has been the Case with Respect to the Lands between Richmond and the Sea."[70]

The commissioners ignored the Kennebec appeals to necessity, fixating on the legality of the purchase. The land, they declared, had been "fairly purchased" and registered with acknowledged deeds, and to deny it was to "disturb" *their* rights. The Kennebecs tried another approach, suggesting the English had gotten the signers drunk, and asked why the payment was not recorded. But the commissioners brushed Native protests aside, insisting if the deeds were fraudulent, the Indians would have challenged the English who "settled" there. The Kennebecs (correctly) recalled little more than a truck house up the river. For the Indians, allowing a truck house did not mean the same thing as a town. The Kennebecs produced an old man who testified that he "never heard any of them say these lands were sold." The commissioners remained unmoved. Without any other Wabanaki tribes present to support them, the Kennebecs had no choice but to back down. They agreed to further "enquire of our old Men . . . respecting the Lands," and ratified the 1749 and 1752 treaties.[71]

After the conference, both the Indians and the proprietors dug in their heels over the land controversy. The Kennebeck Proprietors had never put much faith in their existing Indian deeds, so in November 1753 they authorized their agent Samuel Goodwin to obtain a quitclaim from the Kennebecs for the entire patent, provided he not spend more than the relative pittance of £50.[72] The proprietors also warned against

Goodwin being "too generous," believing, perversely, it would encourage the Indians to violence.[73] By 1754, growing numbers of Kennebecs did contemplate violence, though not because of an excess of generosity from the company. As they had in the past, when threatened by British expansion, the Kennebecs sought French aid. With Anglo-French tensions on the rise, Governor Ange Duquesne de Menneville was eager to recruit Indian allies. He promised to provide forts and troops to protect the Kennebecs. Although Duquesne never delivered on his promise to build forts, the Wabanakis decided the threat of one might serve the same purpose, so in January 1754 they began spreading rumors about a new French fort at the head of the Kennebec River.[74] These rumors worsened the growing climate of mistrust and panic on the frontier fed by clashes along the Connecticut River between Wabanakis from villages along Lake Champlain and the St. Lawrence and Bay Colonists trespassing upriver. The resumption of a Jesuit presence in Penawabskik and Norridgewock further worried Massachusetts leaders.[75]

Governor William Shirley never needed much persuasion to fight the French, so the Kennebecs' bluff about new French forts had the opposite effect than intended. It was high time, he urged the Massachusetts legislature, to end the practice of buying Indian land: "Whilst we have been suing in vain to a few Indians for their Permission to settle Lands within the undoubted Limits of this Province . . . and have in effect promis'd them a yearly Tribute," the French were expanding across the continent.[76] The time had come for a final confrontation. In correspondence with officials in Whitehall, Shirley shared an expansive vision of British imperial claims, advocating for construction of forts far up the Kennebec, Penobscot, and St. Johns Rivers. Force, not treaties, would succeed in "keeping Canada in a proper respect."[77] Shirley's bellicosity outpaced that of the Massachusetts General Court, which nevertheless agreed with him that the French posed a mortal threat to the king's North American domains. Enough legislators still clung to the hope that diplomacy and gifts might preserve peace with the Wabanakis that they volunteered additional funds for the purpose without prompting.[78]

Shirley's interest in defending the British claim to the Kennebec River did not arise from patriotism alone. The Kennebeck Proprietors offered to fund a government fort at Cushnoc (future Fort Western, in present-day Augusta) if Massachusetts built one farther upriver at Teconnett Falls (present-day Waterville), a proposal the House accepted.[79] One month after Shirley authorized a military expedition up the Kennebec, his daughter Harriet married the son of wealthy Kennebeck Proprietor

Robert Temple. In December 1754, the company secretly gave Shirley a share of Silvester Gardiner's portion of the company, although they never entered the transaction into county records. The company clerk recorded the transaction in a discreet fashion, tucking the share belonging to "His Excellency William Shirley Esq" on the bottom half of a page containing William Brattle's accounts.[80] Gardiner himself wrote later that "the Company thou't it for their Interest, that Governour Shirley should be interested in their patent."[81] Soon after becoming a secret proprietor, Shirley wrote to the Board of Trade to suggest the king issue a new, expanded charter to the Kennebeck Proprietors and that their title appeared sounder to him than any their rivals "pretend to set up to them."[82] He neglected to mention his new affiliation with the company—a potential scandal even in an age when people viewed political office as a form of personal property. True to form, the Kennebeck Proprietors covertly copied the letter without his knowledge for use in England.[83]

Shirley repaid the Kennebeck Proprietors' investment full during 1754. He arrived in Falmouth in June with eight hundred militiamen at his back to cow the Wabanakis into submission before proceeding up the Kennebec River to deal with the French and build a fort. To prevent the Indians from acting in concert, Shirley met first with the Kennebecs and sent them home before the Penobscot delegates arrived.[84] The Indians were already badly divided as they struggled to agree on the best course of action to cope with growing numbers of trespassing colonists who now far outnumbered them. Although the combined population of the Canadian villages and Wabanaki communities closer to the New England frontier had probably grown since 1727 to more than three thousand people (with more than six hundred warriors), Maine towns tallied about three thousand fighting-age men alone, to say nothing of the many thousands more available in Massachusetts.[85]

The outnumbered Kennebec delegates (twenty-seven men accompanied by fifteen family members) could do little but listen as Shirley invoked Dummer's Treaty to justify the Kennebeck Proprietors' incursions and the new forts. He also offered a novel interpretation of the political history of the region, arguing that the 1724 destruction of Norridgewock meant that all lands south of that village belonged to Massachusetts "by Right of Conduct in War," and "it was interely owing to [British] Kindness" that the Kennebecs were allowed "your present possessions."[86] After sharing his contrived version of events, Shirley pointed to the marks of Wenemouet, Egeremet, and Loron on the treaty, insisting that "their Marks must now speak for them," by which he meant on his behalf. In a cynical turn of events, the governor seized on the deceased Loron's absence to push a novel interpretation of Dummer's Treaty, using the only writing the Penobscots' greatest orator had left on the agreement in a bid to undo the version of it he had worked in life to preserve.

At this point the Kennebecs pointed out that none of their sagamores had signed the document he had brought. (He had been brandishing the 1726 version, which contained only Penobscot signatures, rather than the final 1727 treaty.) Whether this was due to Shirley's ignorance or a monomaniacal fixation on the Kennebec River deeds discussed only in the 1726 treaty is unclear. In any case, Shirley plowed onward, informing the Indians they had repeatedly endorsed the treaty "and submit[ted] to it's [sic] Rules."[87] In response to Kennebec protests over the forts, Shirley responded, "I did not ask your consent."[88]

In previous Anglo-Wabanaki conferences, Loron had been present to refute egregious distortions of what had occurred in the making of Dummer's Treaty. No one of his stature remained in 1754 to confront Shirley. The record of the proceedings published in Boston later that year depicted the Kennebecs as divided and uncertain—a plausible scenario, given that absence, coupled with the presence of eight hundred soldiers.[89] To make matters worse for the Kennebecs, their Jesuit missionary had left Norridgewock for Canada, and the British had intercepted his correspondence, hamstringing any efforts to coordinate resistance.[90] The Kennebecs had no choice but to let Shirley build a fort wherever he liked.

When the thirteen Penobscot delegates arrived at Falmouth, Shirley informed them the Kennebecs had already agreed to his demands. Since the land in question had never belonged to them, Shirley insisted, the issue did not concern them. The surprised Penobscots denied any knowledge of French forts or planned attacks, and after Shirley displayed the intercepted Jesuit letter, they disavowed that, too. They agreed, as the Kennebecs had, to work to prevent any raids by Canadian Wabanakis, and to re-sign the 1749 peace treaty.[91]

The Kennebecs and Penobscots may have signed a piece of paper saying otherwise, but for them, Dummer's Treaty was dead. Shirley's novel argument about Kennebec lands belonging to the Bay Colony by right of conquest (which he later repeated in a letter to a superior in Whitehall) and his decoupling of active Wabanaki acknowledgment of deeds for them to be valid forever destroyed the treaty's usefulness as a shield for Native land rights. Nor would the Wabanaki strategy of appealing to the Massachusetts governor for protection against trespassers work: Shirley would use his power to support even the flimsiest of proprietary claims.

The Slide to War

Shirley's subsequent march up the Kennebec River accelerated the unraveling of the Dawnland status quo. Massachusetts forces failed to locate the imaginary French forts that had justified the expedition but succeeded in erecting Fort Halifax at Teconnett. The outnumbered Kennebecs could not hope to tackle the large Bay Colony force on their own and offered no resistance. The Kennebecs scattered, never to reassemble as a cohesive political unit again. Some remained near the fort, asking to live in peace, while others joined their Penobscot neighbors at Penawabskik or traveled to the Canadian villages, joining militants from other villages who had already moved there.[92] As the British and French faced off for what proved to be their final contest for mastery in North America, the French encouraged the Wabanakis to take part in the fighting. From Lake Champlain to Nova Scotia many did, but the Penobscots and Kennebecs remaining near the Maine frontier tried to remain neutral.

The Kennebeck Proprietors and William Shirley had pushed some of the Kennebecs to war in 1754, but the following year, the rising tide of colonial hostility to all outsiders—especially Indians—helped end the last vestiges of the old Anglo-Wabanaki relationship. When Massachusetts declared war on all Indians east of the Piscataqua River except the Penobscots, Governor Shirley followed in the footsteps of earlier administrations and offered bounties on scalps of Wabanaki men, women, and children. The House also declared that the latest peace treaties bound the Penobscots to directly aid them in fighting other Wabanakis. Massachusetts would provide shelter for warriors' families "if they come among us."[93] The homicidal proclivities of frontier colonists since 1749 no doubt reduced the appeal of the offer for the Penobscots who gathered at Fort St. Georges to hear interpreter Jabez Bradbury convey it, especially once a cluster of them burst into the meeting.

Frustrated by what they perceived as government softness toward Indians, the local men who made up most of the garrison at Fort St. Georges took matters into their own hands. By 1755, their communities had been enduring near-annual Indian raids for the past decade, and nothing their leaders had done seemed to offer relief. A group of twenty men Bradbury described as "being greatly inrag'd" burst into the conference to demand the Indians agree to whatever the governor demanded.[94] The Penobscots agreed to all terms save moving their families closer to British towns before departing.[95] The Penobscots did not travel far before a company of scalp hunters led by James Cargill surprised them at a place called Owls Head Bay, killing a dozen of them. Cargill and his men never bothered to identify their victims.[96]

The massacre embarrassed Massachusetts leaders, who rescinded their demand for Penobscot auxiliaries, but at least some Maine colonists reacted to Owls Head Bay in a different manner. An officer stationed in North Yarmouth asked his superior for permission to form a scouting party two weeks after the killings. "Notwithstanding I hear that Captn Cargill meets with Trouble about his killing Indians I have a mind to try what I can Do," wrote Benjamin Moggaridge. "Who knows but that wee may find Some Cripled Indian that want[s] to Die or be Brot in among the English and if we can find one we will help him a Long Either Dead or a Live."[97] Uncertain both of Penobscot loyalty and the government's ability to protect them from future James Cargills, acting governor Spencer Phips (Shirley was directing military operations against the French) and the General Court demanded the Penobscots move closer to Fort St. Georges, where they could be protected and watched. Phips explained, "Our people cannot distinguish between your tribe and [Indians at war with New England]." Phips warned if they refused, the Penobscots would probably "be destroyed," insisting that if that occurred, "the blame will ly upon you."[98]

The Penobscots did not find this logic persuasive. On November 1, the Massachusetts House declared war on them, and soon after, Phips extended the offer of bounties on Wabanaki scalps to include the Penobscots, too.[99]

The global scope of the conflict known as the Seven Years' War between Britain and France (and other powers) has had the effect of overshadowing local factors influencing the conflict's spread to the Maine frontier while giving the process an aura of inevitability. But many Wabanakis who made their homes in communities like Norridgewock and Penawabskik had resisted French invitations to join the fighting in 1754 and even most of 1755. Shirley's decision to build two forts on the Kennebeck claim was crucial in driving events.

Some contemporaries noted the importance of the Kennebeck Proprietors—and their member serving as governor—in shaping his decision. After all, Massachusetts had previously constructed fortifications to protect locations where towns *already existed*. Writing in 1767, an anonymous author with knowledge of Shirley's relationship with the company (almost certainly James Flagg, son of one of the proprietors) criticized the governor for building the forts "under a hypocritical, plausible Pretence of serving the public Good." Unfortunately, that placed them in "a howling Wildernes," in a location where they left actual towns "expos'd to the Indian Enemy."[100] Thomas Hutchinson (who had served on the Governor's Council) later observed that the expedition to build the forts "was, in every part of it, the project of the governor," although because it had "the appearance of originating in the assembly, there was no room for complaint." Hutchinson believed "the Expence was to no beneficial purpose," as the Franco-Wabanaki threat to the frontier was exaggerated.[101]

The Kennebeck Proprietors did not, of course, cause the spread of the Seven Years' War into Maine on their own. However, that conflict would accomplish the company's goal of destroying the post–Dummer's Treaty status quo on the frontier, in which land speculators and Wabanakis shared an interest in Native land rights. This change boded ill for the Wabanakis: an imperial project in the region bent on erasing its Native past had no use for them in its present or future, either.

Conclusion. Treaties Buried and Lost: Indigenous Rights and Colonial Property since 1755

In the spring of 1759, the son and namesake of the great deceased Penobscot speaker Loron met the new governor of Massachusetts, Thomas Pownall, face-to-face at Fort St. Georges. Pownall was in Penobscot country on a military expedition to build a fort on that nation's river to, as he put it, "make the land English." As for the Penobscots themselves, Pownall announced, "I seek not their Favour nor fear them, for they can do me neither good nor harm."[1] Loron was at the fort "as a hostage," and two other Penobscots and a Wulstukwiuk man "had come to the fort to negotiate with Pownall."[2] The governor's haughty conduct toward the Wabanakis reflected how rapidly the balance of power had shifted since 1755. Pownall informed the Indians their conversation was an "Examination" rather than a "Conference or Treaty," and then demanded to know why the Wabanakis had violated the oaths of loyalty they had ostensibly given in several treaties, "especially Governour Dummers."[3] Loron the Younger left no record of his own of this exchange, but as he waited for interpreter Walter McFarland to relate the substance of Pownall's pointed inquiries, perhaps his mind turned to how much had changed for his people in such a short time since this latest war began. And although Loron did not—and could not—know all of this at the time, the war had unleashed dramatic changes for everyone in the Dawnland and in the place the *Bostoniak* called Maine.

The Great War for Empire and Its Consequences

Unlike the outcome of previous imperial conflicts, Britain's victory in the Seven Years' War (the Eurocentrically titled conflict between the British and French Empires and their allies in the Americas, Europe, and Asia between 1754 and 1763, which raged for seven of those years in Europe) was decisive. The British Empire committed unprecedented military and financial resources to fighting the French in North America, and by 1760 had crushed the French navy and conquered Canada. In 1763, France ceded all of its North American colonies to Britain in the Treaty of Paris.

For the Wabanakis the war was a catastrophe. Warriors serving as auxiliaries with French armies contracted smallpox and brought the contagion home to their villages. Badly outnumbered Wabankis abandoned their communities near the Maine frontier, but colonial forces followed them even to Canada, destroying the village of St. Francis in 1759, although all but thirty inhabitants escaped with their lives.[4] The Pigwackets, Amarascoggins, and Kennebecs never reformed as political units, and colonists moved onto their lands with impunity.[5] Even with French backing, the Wabanakis' ability to hold back the tide of colonists in Maine—twenty-three thousand people by 1763, up from twelve thousand twenty years earlier—had been dwindling.[6] Wabanaki power had long depended in part on the credible threat of force rather than direct military action to deter squatters and encourage speculator cooperation. After 1763, with the prospect of French supplies of arms and ammunition—let alone direct military aid—gone, the Wabanaki strategy of containment collapsed.

In its place, Dawnland communities adjusted to their reduced power as best they could. Many Pigwackets, Amarascoggins, and Kennebecs remained in Maine west of the Penobscot River. Instead of gathering in large villages as in earlier times, these Wabanakis lived in smaller family bands. The Kennebeck Proprietors' missionary in Pownalborough observed in 1766 that "a great number of Indians frequent this neighborhood. They are the remnants of the ancient [Kennebec] Tribe and lead a rambling life. They . . . are very savage in their Dress and Manners." In addition, he noted, "they have a great Aversion to the English Nation," which he characteristically blamed on the Catholics.[7] Mobile family groups of Wabanakis could better maintain their independence, although that did not mean avoiding the colonists altogether. Wabanakis frequently camped near towns like Freyburg, built next to the old village of Pigwacket, to fish, hunt, and trade.[8]

All Wabanaki communities had to make adjustments to deal with the unprecedented numbers of colonists entering the Dawnland after 1763. By 1775, forty-seven thousand colonists lived in 120 townships in Maine, up from only 21 (15 of those incorporated) in 1750.[9] Another eight thousand New England colonists emigrated to Nova Scotia and New Brunswick by 1768.[10] Veterans of the Seven Years' War joined thousands of other newcomers to assert their own claims on the land. Departing overcrowded communities in southern New England, new arrivals often endured grinding poverty as they tried to scratch a living from the soil. The Kennebeck Company missionary described the residents of Wiscasset in 1760 as barefoot families living in "miserable huts" and living on "scarce anything" but potatoes.[11]

From Topsham to Thomaston, colonists employed the arguments their predecessors had made in the coastal towns, that local needs and common fairness should trump the claims of a distant, uncaring elite. Rejecting the protests of the absentee proprietors that their patents constituted a more significant investment than labor and danger on a rough frontier, the colonists moved to make their own vision of landownership a reality. Their rhetoric reveals how their experiences informed their beliefs.

To their dismay, the land speculators could not control the newcomers any more than the Wabanakis could. Although the speculators celebrated the British triumph in the Seven Years' War with everyone else in the colonies, perhaps some of them privately reflected that the decline in Native power did not make their task of profiting from their investments any easier.

Emboldened by their role in the victory over the Indians, colonists had no intention of allowing the absentee speculators to reap the fruits of others' labor. Edward Hutchinson, an absentee proprietor (and Clarke & Lake proprietor) near Wiscasset, received a panicked letter from his agent on the ground bearing grim news: "People here . . . Signifie that they have a just Right to the Land . . . Because Som of them Lived heare in Wartime; and Others Because they were Souldiers in the War. They Say the proprietors Bought it for a few ponkins and that your title is not so good as theirs who have Defended it." Lest Hutchinson think this was an isolated case, "You may Depend this is the temper of the people here in general."[12]

Belcher Noyes, the harried clerk of the Pejepscot Proprietors, had to contend with similar declarations from residents of the company towns of Brunswick and Topsham. He noted that a Brunswick resident charged with trespassing "talkt very insulting to me and told me they had as good aright to the land as we."[13] In Topsham, a resident named Thomas Wilson led a movement against company attempts to collect inflated payments for local lots. Residents complained about company agents who "pretended great things" while "Jamming themselves into peoples' Possession."[14] A number of residents wrote to Noyes, informing him: "If you do not consider us in this thing, we shall be obliged to revolt, as we are Stiled Rebellious. We have the possession and have it fenced and are resolved to defend it against all Opposition."[15] Wilson's faction cut timber and hay on vacant company land, provoking years of lawsuits.[16] In 1771, Wilson unsuccessfully petitioned the General Court, explaining he thought that the Pejepscot claim, based on an Indian deed, "was contrary to Law," and argued the "Government" still owned the land, asking that the province "provide such remedy for him Thomas Wilson that he may hold his Land that he bought and paid for by some Lawful Right."[17]

One speculator who did not have to take part in these clashes (the perpetually self-pitying Belcher Noyes might have called him lucky for it) was Samuel Waldo. He had spent the past quarter century striving to make his Muscongus claim a reality, shoring up his title at the expense of the Wabanakis, the peace on the frontier, and the luckless families he lured across the Atlantic with inflated promises of the good life in Maine. At the pinnacle of triumph, the speculator accompanied Pownall's 1759 expedition up the Penobscot River to survey his property. As he stood on the land he hoped would make him a fortune, Waldo dropped dead of a stroke.[18]

The American Revolution temporarily halted disputes over landownership in Maine, but struggles over the nature and purpose of landed property returned with renewed intensity. Maine residents styling themselves "Liberty Men" resisted the efforts of the so-called "Great Proprietors" to revive their old claims. The Liberty Men insisted the Revolution had been about securing not only political liberty but also sufficient land to enable a republic of smallholding citizens. When they felt the law denied them justice, the Liberty Men donned mock "Indian" garb to carry out extralegal acts of vandalism against proprietors and their agents. In a symbolic twist rich in irony, these "White Indians" invoked the land's original owners to defend what they viewed as their rightful claims.[19] In doing so, the Liberty Men in Maine joined ordinary smallholders from the Carolinas to Vermont in a series of contests to decide the relationship between the distribution of property and citizenship.[20] Although the local conflicts fizzled in the early nineteenth century, their larger questions remain alive today.

Indigenous Rights in a New World

An important shift in how colonizers viewed Indian people and their ownership of land also began in 1763. That year, hoping to prevent expensive wars and rein in unruly frontier colonists, King George III issued the Proclamation of 1763, which prohibited (among other things) private purchase of Indian land. After the proclamation, Anglo-Americans seeking Indian land had to obtain it through colonial governments, who would henceforth sign treaties with Indian nations to obtain land. Since that change meant colonists obtained their land from a colonial grant, it eased the way toward an intellectual climate in which land title did not originate from the Indians at all, and these treaties were not purchases so much as gifts to pacify savage occupants rather than legitimate owners. In addition, within a few decades, most landholders in what became the United States no longer traced their title to Indian purchase at all.[21]

This logic combined with the frontier colonists' culture of ownership by 1800, with catastrophic implications for Native Americans. The writings of James Sullivan, a native of Berwick, Maine, who rose to become attorney general and then governor of Massachusetts, demonstrate this intellectual shift. Born in 1744, Sullivan spent his first thirty-four years in Maine and practiced law in York County. He wrote the first history of Maine, and another legal text detailing the "principles [for determining land title], which had been in use here before the Revolution" to aid the state in the new century.[22]

In both texts, Sullivan cited John Locke and embraced his argument that labor created property.[23] Echoing earlier frontier colonists, Sullivan argued, "The idea of obtaining vacant lands to sell again, is clearly wrong, unless the purchase is made, to promote the settlement of a number [of people], in similar circumstances of want and distress."[24] Indian deeds and royal grants, he argued, originated from people who had no rights as owners of the land they sold, but they served a convenient legal fiction in their time, enabling settlers to assume the right of the first possessor who annexed his labour to it."[25]

Sullivan dismissed Indian land rights using an old argument, though he claimed to be "expressing a new opinion." He even suspected he "may perhaps draw the attention of those, who feel from habit, or education, the strong force of an old and very different one." Sullivan dispelled this "old and very different" argument that Indians did, in fact, own their land, by using the same argument John Winthrop did two hundred years ago.[26] Since the Indians "did not claim a permanent, exclusive right in a particular place," they therefore held no title.[27] Or, as Winthrop had put it, that "which is common to all is proper to none."[28]

Unlike Winthrop, Sullivan had no plans to coexist with or even convert the Indians. In fact, Sullivan had no plans regarding the Indians at all. In this his writing reflected the rising ideals of Jeffersonian America, which celebrated the white independent farmer. God had intended to place America in the hands of Europeans, "as should be honourable and useful to his rational offspring, and for the glory of his own mighty name."[29] If the Indians failed to become "like the emigrants" who presumably assimilated into Anglo-American society, they would cease to exist as a nation. Rather than offer any solutions for the Indians' predicament, Sullivan concluded that "a writer is not obliged to hold himself accountable for the consequences of any of the established principles, upon which the world is projected."[30]

Sullivan led the way in expressing a view that rapidly gained currency among white American politicians and jurists: that Indians had right of occupancy, not ownership. Ignorance (sometimes willful) of past and ongoing Indigenous agriculture enabled most nineteenth-century Americans to brush aside the realities of Indian land use and ownership and replace it with stereotypes of nomadic hunters. The Supreme Court enshrined this reading of history and of Indigenous property rights in *Johnson v. M'Intosh* in 1823.[31] By then, the Court was merely putting a constitutional imprimatur on what had become state and federal policy toward American Indian nations, most of whom faced forced relocation or annihilation at the hands of an emerging and self-declared Empire of Liberty.[32]

Bringing Treaties to Life

As had always been the case, where different Wabanakis lived shaped their experiences during the American Revolution and afterward. The Penobscots threw in their lot with the new United States against the British during the war, inspired in part by Massachusetts reversing Pownall's diktat of conquest from the end of the Seven Years' War. The new state forbade trespassers on Penobscot lands and promised to establish more respectful trade relations.[33] Other Wabanakis from Odanak and

Wowenock on the St. Lawrence to Meductec on the St. John were more ambivalent, and most did their best to stay out of the fighting, although some Wulstukwiuk and Passamaquoddy sagamores chose sides, with most aligning with the Americans against the British in Nova Scotia.[34]

On the American side of the new international border, the Wabanaki experience differed from most other Indigenous nations within the United States in that their questions of territory until recently have involved the Commonwealth of Massachusetts and State of Maine rather than the federal government. By conducting treaties and purchasing land from the Wabanakis on its own, Massachusetts (and later Maine) violated the 1790 Nonintercourse Act, which reserved such powers to the United States government. The Bay State ignored this, continuing to march to its own drumbeat in these matters as it always had. Eventually this policy had lasting consequences.

In the short and medium term, however, it did not, and the *Bostoniak* continued their quest to acquire more of the Dawnland. The Penobscots (who absorbed many Kennebecs, Amarascoggins, Pigwackets, and other Wabanakis from the west) did not sign a treaty with Massachusetts officially ceding any land until 1796.[35] The agreement began a Penobscot strategy of focusing their efforts on attaching their rights to the Penobscot River (and all the islands within it from Old Town northward), which was the spiritual and subsistence center of their homeland. Well into the nineteenth century, however, Penobscots and Wulstukwiuks continued to hunt and fish beyond their state-allotted territories. The Penobscots also strategically leased timber rights on some river islands and attempted to reconcile their fishing needs with the practices of incoming whites. In 1820, the vastly outnumbered Penobscots leveraged the new State of Maine's desire for them to extinguish any Massachusetts claim to their lands to gain recognition of some limited repurchases of waterfront land near Brewer, Maine.[36] Nevertheless, the state chipped away at Penobscot territory in the years after statehood, along with the neighboring Passamaquoddies living on the border of Maine and New Brunswick. Wabanakis living north of the international border after the Revolutionary era faced similar challenges.[37]

Wabanaki communities persisted in the Dawnland, but beginning in the 1960s they began to—as Mi'kmaq educator and activist Marie Battiste put it—bring the treaties back to life on both sides of the international border by fleshing out the context of the old agreements, using oral and written history to dispel self-serving imperial fictions used to dispossess their ancestors.[38]

This process began in the early 1960s with a discovery at Pleasant Point, a Passamaquoddy reservation in eastern Maine. There, tribal elder Louise Sockabasin discovered a copy of the 1794 Massachusetts treaty with the Passamaquoddies, along with official letters from General George Washington to the tribe. The documents had been in a shoebox under a bed in her home.[39] Almost two centuries before, Samuel Goodwin's discovery of the missing Plymouth Patent had provided the catalyst for the reunion of the Kennebeck Proprietors, who had done so much to demolish the Bay Colony's respect for Dummer's Treaty and Wabanaki land rights. Now another discovery prompted a countervailing series of events.

The Penobscots joined the Passamaquoddies in successfully arguing that Massachusetts and Maine land acquisitions from the Wabanakis following the 1790 Nonintercourse Act were illegal. Almost two-thirds of the state rightfully belonged to the Wabanakis. The resulting Maine Indian Claims Settlement Act of 1980 delivered an $81.5 million settlement in what became a landmark legal victory for American Indians, particularly in the eastern United States.[40]

In Atlantic Canada, the 1982 Constitution Act enshrined recognition of First Nations treaty rights into the Canadian constitution. That act and a spate of subsequent legal battles brought renewed attention to the early Anglo-Wabanaki treaties, beginning with the Mi'kmaq and Wulstukwiuk corollary to Dummer's Treaty in 1726.[41] Mi'kmaqs and other Wabanakis in Canada have articulated their ongoing understanding of the "living" nature of the treaties and brought substantial evidence to bear for such an expanded vision of Nova Scotian obligations in them.[42] In Canada, as in the United States, the contest to define the old treaties continues.

The latest episode in Maine hearkens back to a long history of colonial governments engaging in willful misreading of written treaties. The State of Maine argues that the 1980 Settlement Act grants the Penobscots title to Indian Island and the islands northward in the Penobscot River but does not extend into the river itself, ignoring both centuries of Penobscot affiliation with the river and that tribe's long-established strategy of focusing its territorial claims on that river. In the summer of 2017, the First Circuit Court of Appeals—based in Boston—ruled against the Penobscot.[43] The Penobscots plan to fight on. The contest continues.

This book has examined an earlier stage in that contest to define the meanings and obligations of property and diplomacy. Each in their own fashion, Wabanakis, colonists, and absentee speculators tried to bring order to a turbulent world and to articulate their own understandings of the ongoing series of encounters between cultures. The results were often confused and contradictory. The process, however, was indeed a conversation, carried out by numberless ordinary people in village councils, town meetings, Boston taverns, and formal treaties. It was also a conversation frequently marked by misunderstanding, deception, and even violence.

What *Properties of Empire* has tried to show is that understandings of property and diplomacy in this corner of early America were formed in a dynamic environment, with Wabanakis and different factions of colonists reacting to one another. The reality of Wabanaki power and presence on the land forced would-be colonizers to craft a new system of property—however haphazard—to acknowledge that reality. In turn the Wabanakis adjusted their own approach to allowing the newcomers to partake in the Common Pot. Wabanaki unity in the face of colonial divisions enabled them to devise a workable strategy of containment that preserved the integrity of the Dawnland while creating a powerful constituency in Massachusetts with a vested interest in Native land rights. That interest proved vulnerable to undermining from within, in the form of the Kennebeck Proprietors' assault on the validity of Indian title itself. Once they had enlisted the jingoistic Governor William Shirley in their efforts, the Kennebeck Proprietors succeeded in using the looming imperial conflict with France to destroy the existing Anglo-Wabanaki relationship based on a mutual—though often confused and imperfect—adherence to Dummer's Treaty.

In May 1759, as Loron and his three associates faced Governor Thomas Pownall, that relationship and the treaty that had enabled it were finished. Loron the Younger's own father had played a vital role in shaping that agreement, in keeping its memory alive, and in ensuring that Massachusetts would be reminded of its obligations. But as the son of that accomplished orator listened through an interpreter to Governor Thomas Pownall, he heard the governor tell him that in that treaty, the Penobscots had "acknowledged themselves Subjects of King George." Pownall also indicated that Samuel Waldo (then only days from death) and several other gentlemen present at this interrogation "had been Witness" to several treaties indicating as much. Loron and the other Wabanakis had already told Pownall that they had acknowledged themselves "as Brethren," but not as subjects of the King.[44]

So it was likely with a tone of defiance, but possibly mixed with a note of sorrow, that the Wabanakis replied to Pownall's invocation of "Old times" that "their Old men were Dead, and the Treaties buried and lost, and that they were young men and knew nothing of it."

ACKNOWLEDGMENTS

Good editing makes most projects shorter, but not so with acknowledgments. The more careful I am with naming the people who have helped along the way, the longer the list grows. I'd better get on with it, then.

This project began as a response to a question in one of the first classes I took as a graduate student with my advisor, Tim Breen. His irreplaceable guidance throughout the process has kept me from losing sight of my portable arguments in the Maine woods. Perhaps just as important, he gambled that a history master's student who wrote a thesis about early modern English Christmas would make a passable early Americanist. Also at Northwestern, Gerry Cadava, Melissa Macauley, Ed Muir, Susan Pearson, and Mike Sherry provided much-appreciated support. Caitlin Fitz and Scott Sowerby read every word of the dissertation stage of this book, and their insights infinitely improved it. Writing would have been a far lonelier process without graduate student friends and colleagues. My entire first-year cohort—especially Andy Baer, Ashley Johnson Bavery, Alex Hobson, Valeria Jiménez, Charlie Keenan, Matt Khan, Nate Matthews, Adam Plaiss, and Wen-Qing Ngoei—provided insightful critiques at countless writing group sessions and workshops. So, too, did Kevin Baker, Kyle Burke, Ryan Burns, Neal Dugre, Emma Goldsmith, Beth Healey, Mariah Hepworth, Matt June, Amanda Kleintop, Michael Martoccio, Laura McCoy, Jesse Nasta, Aram Sarkasian, Leigh Soares, Amanda Kleintop, Mariah Hepworth, Emilie Takayama, Marlous van Waijenberg, and Ariel Schwartz. Sam Kling commented on drafts and listened to extended rambles about Indian deeds on runs. Alexandra Lindgren-Gibson not only read drafts but shared in the experience of learning French via *Harry Potter et la Coupe feu*. Jamie Lynn Holeman and Jonathyne Briggs helped a novice decipher some tangled French prose on multiple occasions. Don Johnson, my fellow early Americanist in our cohort, brought formidable knowledge and home-brewing skills to bear on many a problem.

I was fortunate to begin my research at the Maine Historical Society (MeHS), which became an academic home away from home for long stretches of time. Nick Noyes, Jamie Rice, Bill Barry, and the rest of the staff proved expert guides into regional history, and Jamie Cantoni became a dear friend as well as a welcoming host. The MeHS continued to be an irreplaceable resource throughout the writing of this book. At the Maine State Archives, Anne Small and Anthony Douin went above and beyond the call of duty in helping a new researcher out. Martha Cook, Jennifer Fauxsmith, Rachel MacAskill, and Elizabeth Bouvier likewise helped me find my feet while navigating court files at the Massachusetts State Archives. Peter Drummey at the Massachusetts Historical Society generously shared his voluminous expertise, as well as an extra copy of a map that changed my thinking. James Francis Sr., the Penobscot Nation's Tribal Historian, shared his expertise as well as lunch during my visit to Indian Island. Chief Kirk Francis also took time out of a busy schedule to see me. Both shared stories and further reminders of the ongoing relevance of the events in these pages to Indigenous people in particular today.

During revisions, other members of the hardy band of Wabanaki/northeastern colonial scholars were generous in sharing their insights, and I thank Zachary Bennett, Lisa Brooks, Jim Leamon, Daniel Mandell, Alexandra Montgomery, Alvin Morrison, Micah Powling, Darren Ranco, Ashley Elizabeth Smith, and Alan Taylor in particular. Tad Baker gave invaluable guidance on thorny seventeenth-century questions. Working at Bates gave me access to the formidable minds and unfailing generosity of Bruce Bourque and Joe Hall. Both read manuscript drafts, although their contributions went above and beyond that. I'm certain this book (and my academic career) would have been poorer for it had I not met them. Farther afield, conversations with Harvey Amani Whitfield, Patrick Griffin, Ted Andrews, Timothy Shannon, and Stephen Foster all enriched my thinking and this project. Jim Merrell deserves at least two votes of thanks here for giving the manuscript one of his trademark careful readings and most of all for his teaching and mentoring during my undergraduate years at Vassar. If he's not a scholar, colleague, and teacher worth emulating, then I haven't met any.

The brilliant minds at the Early Atlanticists' Writing Group provided needed perspective during early stages of revision, especially Robert Bucholtz, Seth Cotlar, Nicole Dressler, Peter Kotowski, and Jim Sack. When I was researching and writing in Portland, I was lucky Kelly Brennan Arehart and Nicholas Gliserman were, too. Nick was generous with his cartographical knowledge and thousands of images he'd gathered. Kelly provided the undertaker industry's perspective when I needed it most. Both made the Slug House the most happening place in town. I was fortunate to work with phenomenally supportive colleagues at Bates College, St. Mary's College of Maryland, and Alfred University while teaching, applying for still other jobs, and attempting to write something insightful. Dennis Grafflin, Karen Melvin, Adriana Brodsky, and Emrys Westacott were all the sort of department heads everyone hopes to have.

This book was written in coffee shops, most of all at Arabica and in the Hay Building in Portland, and Terra Cotta in Alfred. I would be remiss if I didn't thank all of the baristas for making my offices of choice so pleasant.

At NYU Press, Clara Platter, Amy Klopfenstein, and Isla Ng provided the ideal mix of guidance and encouragement to a first-time author. Two anonymous readers for NYU Press provided valuable feedback. During the editorial process, Tim Roberts and Susan Murray saved me from more than a few unforced errors. William Keegan of Heritage Consultants created superb original maps for this book. Sofia Yalouris of the MeHS coordinated the processing of the in-text images, and I'm grateful to the Society for their use.

Institutional grants provided welcome support during the years of work on this project. Grants from Northwestern University, Bates College, and the Society of Colonial Wars in the State of Maryland assisted the research process. A fellowship from the Newberry Library provided the ideal environment for the revision process. Faculty support from Bridgewater State University helped cover the cost of preparing the index.

With all of this help, any remaining errors in fact or judgment are entirely my own.

Whatever is best in this work began long ago. Without my parents raising me to treasure history and the written word, while taking me to countless museums and historic sites (as well as helping an early career academic move across the country and back again), this book would never have been written. And without my sister Meghan putting up with the endless parade of historical detours on family vacations with such good humor, the journey wouldn't have been nearly as fun as it turned out to be or have included so many trips to the pool. This book is dedicated to them.

Abbreviations

AAS	American Antiquarian Society. Worcester, Massachusetts.
BL	Jonathan Belcher Letterbooks. Microfilm. MHS.
CMeHS	*Collections and Proceedings of the Maine Historical Society.*
CMHS	*Collections and Proceedings of the Massachusetts Historical Society.*
CMNF	*Collection de manuscrits contenant lettres, memoires et autres documents relatifs a la Nouvelle France.* 4 vols. Quebec, 1883–85.
CSP	*Calendar of State Papers Colonial, America and West Indies, 1574–1739.* 44 vols. 1860–1994. British History Online.
DCB	*Dictionary of Canadian Biography.* www.biographi.ca.
DHSM	James Baxter, ed. *Documentary History of the State of Maine.* 24 vols. Portland: Maine Historical Society, 1869–1916.
DL	Cotton Mather. *Decennium Luctuosum.* Boston, 1699.
HJ	*Journal of the House of Representatives of Massachusetts, 1715–1779.* 55 vols. Boston: Massachusetts Historical Society, 1902–90.

HKM   Microfilms of the Henry Knox Papers. Owned by the New England Historic Genealogical Society and deposited in the Massachusetts Historical Society Boston, 1960. 55 reels. Copies accessed in MeHS.

JAH   *Journal of American History.*

JR   Rueben Gold Thwaites, ed. *The Jesuit Relations and Allied Documents: Travels and Explorations of the Jesuit Missionaries in New France, 1610–1791.* 73 vols. Cleveland: Burrows Brothers Company, 1896–1901.

KPP   Kennebec Proprietors Papers/Plymouth Company Records. MeHS.

LAC   Library and Archives of Canada, Ottawa.

MAC   Massachusetts Archives Collection. In MSA, Boston.

MeHS   Maine Historical Society, Portland.

MeSA   Maine State Archives, Augusta.

MeSL   Maine State Library, Augusta.

MHS   Massachusetts Historical Society, Boston.

MSA   Massachusetts State Archives, Boston.

MSM   Maine State Museum, Augusta.

NEHGR   *New England Historical and Genealogical Register.* Boston: Published by the Society, 1847–.

NET   Daniel Mandell, ed. *New England Treaties, North and West.* Vol. 20 in *Early American Indian Documents: Treaties and Laws, 1607–1789,* edited by Alden Vaughan. Washington, DC: University Publications of America, 2003.

NEQ   *New England Quarterly.*

NYCD   E. B. O'Callaghan, ed. *Documents Relative to the Colonial History of the State of New York; Procured in Holland, England and France/* 15 vols. Albany: Weed, Parsons and Company, 1856–87.

NYMP   North Yarmouth, Maine Papers. 5 vols. David Shepley Collection, MeHS.

NYPL   New York Public Library.

PEM	Phillips Library of the Peabody Essex Museum, Salem, MA.
PPP-MeHS	Pejepscot Proprietors Papers, MeHS.
PPP-PEM	Pejepscot Proprietors Papers, PEM.
SCJ	Superior Court of Judicature–Suffolk Files, MSA.
SCJRB	Superior Court of Judicature Record Book, MSA.
SHG	John Langdon Sibley and Clifford K. Shipton. *Sibley's Harvard Graduates: Biographical Sketches of Those Who Attended Harvard College.* 17 vols. Cambridge: Harvard University Press, 1873–1975.
SP	Samuel Penhallow, *The History of the Wars of New England with the Eastern Indians.* Corner House, Williamstown, MA: 1973. Boston, 1726. Reprint, Edward Wheelock Williamstown, MA: Corner House, 1924, 1973.
WL	William Blake Trask, ed. *Letters of Colonel Thomas Westbrook and Others Relative to Indian Affairs in Maine, 1722–1726.* Boston: George E. Littlefield, 1901.
WMQ	*William and Mary Quarterly Journal.*
YCCPCF	York County Court of Common Pleas, Case Files, MeSA.
YCCPRB	York County Court of Common Pleas, Record Book, MeSA

Notes

Introduction: Power and Property

1. Affidavit of Nicholas Byram, August 24, 1736, HKM, vol. 40, item 15; Affidavits of Thomas Gregg, Samuel Boggs, Andrew Momford, Henry Alexander, and Thomas Kilpatrick, May 13, 1738, in the "St. Georges Affidavit," HKM, vol. 40, item 11.

2. Waldo, *Samuel Waldo of Boston, Merchant, Intending with All Possible Expedition.* . . .

3. Adelman and Aron, "From Borderlands to Borders." See Hinderaker, *Elusive Empires*, for a sequential look at empire in the Ohio Valley.

4. Smith, *Smith Journals*, ed. Willis, 49.

5. Chemelowski, *Spice of Popery*; Christopher Bilodeau, "Understanding Ritual in Colonial Wabanakia"; Morrision, *Embattled Northeast.*

6. Nash, "Abiding Frontier"; Little, *Abraham in Arms*; Bilodeau, "Economy of War." For blended families in early colonial New England, see Plane, *Colonial Intimacies.*

7. Plank, *Unsettled Conquest*; Lennox, *Homelands and Empires*; Greer, *The People of New France*; Prins, *The Mi'kmaq.*

8. Preston, *Texture of Contact.*

9. M. Begon to Count de Mourepas, April 21, 1725, in *NYCD*, 9:944.

10. Baker, "Scratch with a Bear's Paw"; Leavenworth, "The Best Title That Indians Can Claime"; Siminoff, *Crossing the Sound*; Little, "Three Kinds of Indian Deeds at Nantucket"; Ray, "Maine Indians' Concept of Land"; Dunn, *The Mohicans and Their Land.*

11. Preston, "Squatters, Indians, Proprietary Government," uncovered a different variation of this tripartite dynamic in the eighteenth-century Susquehanna Valley.

12. For sovereignty, see Belmessous, ed., *Native Claims.* For a sweeping comparative analysis that does distinguish between the two, see Greer, *Property and Dispossession.*

13. Wilson, *Chaos of Empire*; Hodson, "Rethinking Failure."

14. Pagden, *Lords of All the World*; Macmillian; *Sovereignty and Possession*; Seed, *Ceremonies of Possession*.

15. Hardesty, *Unfreedom*, 8.

16. For a work applying this theme to U.S. history, see Hixon, *American Settler Colonialism*.

17. Greer, *Property and Dispossession*, 425.

18. Attwood, "Law, History, and Power," passim (quotation on 188). See also McHugh, "A Pretty Government," in *Legal Pluralism*, ed. Benton and Ross, 21–42.

19. Robinson, *The White Possessive*; Horsman, *Race and Manifest Destiny*; Vaughan, "From White Man to Redskin."

1 / Networks of Property and Belonging

1. Snow, "Ethnographic Baseline of the Eastern Abenaki," 303. Wabanaki numbers hovered between 2,500 and 3,000 from 1713 until 1755 (Ghere, "Myths and Methods," 527). The colonial population grew at an anemic pace until 1725 and reached about 9,000 by 1735 (Williamson, *History of the State of Maine*, 2:126).

2. Smith, *Smith Journals*, ed. Willis, 137n2 for population; 85, 86, 96, 151, and 196 for shortages and supply ships.

3. Moody, *The Debtors Monitor*, ii.

4. See, for example, "Accompt of What Skins Peltry and Castorium I have Seized . . . ," June 24, 1700, Cyprian Southack Letters, MHS.

5. Thayer, "Fort Richmond, Maine," 142. See also Baxter, ed., *Christopher Levett of York*, 123.

6. Account of Expenses Submitted to the Council by Daniel Farnum, January 24, 1751, MAC, 32:88.

7. Among other Eastern Algonquian–speaking groups, Wabanaki is a general term referring to people of the east, or people of the Dawnland, with variations applied to the Wampanoags and Wappingers in what is now southern New England (Lisa T. Brooks and Cassandra M. Brooks, "Reciprocity Principle," 27n1; Nash, "The Abiding Frontier," 1, 50) . Other scholars write the Wabanaki pronunciation of their endonym as "Wabanakiak" (Prins, "Children of Gluskap," 95).

8. See, for example, Loron's 1726 statement, "This Country is the place where we belong to," in *Conference* [1726], 15; and Polin's 1739 explanation in Conference with Polin and Indians of Presumpscot, August 10 and 13, 1739, in *DHSM*, 23:259.

9. For example, see An Act for Regulating of Townships, Choice of Town Officers, and Setting Forth Their Power, November 16, 1692, in *Acts and Resolves*, 1:68, ordering that any wandering poor warned out of a town would be "conveyed from constable to constable unto the town where he properly *belongs* or had his last residence."

10. Samuel Johnson listed seven different meanings of "belong" in Johnson, *A Dictionary of the English Language*, s.v. "belong." These included "to be the property of" or "to be the province or business of" or "to adhere, or be appendent to" or "To have relation to" as in, "to whom belongest thou? Whence art thou?"

11. Brooks, *Common Pot*, 3. For a comparative look at landscape and language, see Basso, *Wisdom Sits in Places*.

12. MacDougall, *Penobscot Dance*, 45; Nash, "Abiding Frontier," 69–71, 73.

13. Nash, "Abiding Frontier," 68–69.

14. MacDougall, *Penobscot Dance,* 36–37; Nash, "Abiding Frontier," 74–75. Stories collected from twentieth-century Western Abenakis mention Tabaldak, the Owner, and Odziozo, the Transformer, rather than Gluskap (Day, "The Western Abenaki Transformer," 75).

15. Brooks, *Common Pot,* 6. For a colonial parallel, see Moody, *Debtors Monitor,* 89–90.

16. Baker, "Finding the Almouchiquois," 81–82; Cronon, *Changes in the Land,* 38–39. For soil, see Gary W. Crawford, "Northeast Plants" in *Handbook of North American Indians* (Washington, DC.: Smithsonian Institution, 2006), vol. 3, 408. For maize agriculture along the St. John River, see Gyles, *Memoirs of Odd Adventures,* 103.

17. Demeritt, "Agriculture, Climate, and Cultural Adaptation," 183–202.

18. Ghere, "Abenaki Factionalism, 44–45; Prins, "Children of Gluskap," 98–99; Josselyn, *An Account of Two Voyages,* 127.

19. Hoffman, "Ancient Tribes Revisited," 20–21; Josselyn, *An Account of Two Voyages,* 55–56; Prins, "Children of Gluskap," 102–5.

20. Ghere, "Abenaki Factionalism," 38–49. The Wabanakis were not organized into formal clans (Speck, "Abenaki Clans-Never!," 528–30).

21. Morrison, "Dawnland Decisions," 24–65.

22. Baxter, ed., *Christopher Levett of York,* 117–18.

23. Father Joseph Aubery to Father Joseph Jouvency, October 10, 1710, in *JR,* 66:177.

24. For quotation and dress, see Josselyn, *Account of Two Voyages,* 143. For sagamores refusing to speak to commoners, see Levett, *Voyage into New England,* 117.

25. Nash, "Abiding Frontier," 151–53.

26. Nash, "Abiding Frontier, 159, 174–80; Baker, "Finding the Almouchiquois," 81–82; Morrison, "Dawnland Decisions," 29–30.

27. For a rare description of a Penobscot wife accompanying her husband to deliver a warning—then berating him for revealing too much information to the intended target—see Deposition of Jane and Ann Woodside, May 14, 1738, HKM, item 31.

28. Morrison, "Dawnland Decisions," 47–48, 54–55.

29. Waldo, *A Defence of the Title,* 12. For ratio of population at one warrior to five people, see Ghere, "Myths and Methods," 516, and 527–28 for Penobscot population estimates. For another example of such a large gathering in action, see Cyprian Southack to Gov. Joseph Dudley, November 30, 1702, Cyprian Southack Letters, MHS.

30. Alan Greer, "Commons and Enclosure," 372; Bishop, "Territoriality among Northeastern Algonquians," 37–63; Cronon, *Changes in the Land,* 58–67.

31. St. Georges Conference and Related Documents, September 20–29, 1753, in *NET,* 718.

32. For agreements where Wabanakis retained hunting or fishing rights, see, for example, Hull, ed., *York Deeds,* 1:6; 2:13; and Richard Wharton Deed, 1684, MeHS, misc. box 61/6, MS00277.

33. Petition of the Inhabitants of Brunswick to Maintain Fort George, April 25, 1737, PPP, MeHS, vol. 10, box 6, folder 2, pp. 50–51.

34. May 5, 1720, Thomas Fayerweather Diary, Bangor (ME) Public Library.

35. May 5, 1720, Fayerweather Diary.

36. May 11, 1720, Fayerweather Diary.

37. July 29–August 13, 1720, Fayerweather Diary, quotation on August 13.

38. Capt. Moody record of May 16, 1720, Georgetown Conference, copied in Fayerweather Diary, on May 29, 1720.

39. Nash, "Abiding Frontier," 196–97;

40. Cooper emphasized that, for interrelated family bands, politics and family were intertwined (Cooper, "Algonquian Family Hunting Ground System," 71). A. Irving Hallowell noted that Wabanakis adjusted the boundaries of land use according to ecological, as well as political, considerations (Hallowell, "The Size of Algonkian Hunting Territories," 35–45).

41. Lt. Governor Dunbar to Mr. [William] Popple, November 17, 1730, in CSP, vol. 37, doc. 533.

42. Simonoff, Crossing the Sound, 21–23.

43. Speck, "The Family Hunting Band," 289–305. The argument's latter-day proponent is Dean Snow (see his "Wabanaki 'Family Hunting Territories,'" 1143–51; and "The Ethnographic Baseline of the Eastern Abenaki," 291–306).

44. Raudot, Relation par lettres de l'Amérique Septentrionale, 198. Citation from Cooper, "Algonquian Family Hunting Ground System," 73–74.

45. DCB, vol. 2, s.v. "Raudot, Antoine-Denis," by Donald J. Horton.

46. Chadwick, "An Account of a Journey from Fort Pownal," 143.

47. Chadwick, "An Account of a Journey from Fort Pownal," 143.

48. See Cooper, "Algonquian Family Hunting Ground System," 73; Snow, "Wabanaki 'Family Hunting Territories,'" 1149. Cronon cites this account as evidence for "the eighteenth century," in Changes in the Land, 105.

49. Speck, "Family Hunting Band," 289–305; for Speck's motives, see Bourque, "Ethnicity on the Maritime Peninsula," 275.

50. Indian Letter to Gov. William Shirley, November 17, 1749, in DHSM, 23:322.

51. Petition of the Inhabitants of Brunswick to Maintain Fort George, April 25, 1737, PPP, MeHS, vol. 10, box 6, folder 2, p. 50.

52. Douglass, A Summary, 1:151.

53. See, for example, Josselyn, An Account of Two Voyages, 130; Gyles, Memoirs of Odd Adventures, 101–3; and Cronon, Changes in the Land, 40–41.

54. Cronon, Changes in the Land, 78–81.

55. Vickers, "Competency and Competition," 3–29; Vickers, Farmers and Fishermen; Innes, Creating the Commonwealth, 15.

56. MacFarlane, Origins of English Individualism.

57. Seed, Ceremonies of Possession, 18–19, 23–24.

58. Coke, First Part of the Institutes, 4a.

59. Chmielewski, Spice of Popery, 29–33, 181; Innes, Creating the Commonwealth, passim.

60. Moody, The Debtors Monitor, 12–13.

61. William Lithgow to Unidentified [Josiah Crump], July 6, 1747, box 1, folder 9, Doggett Family Collection, MeHS.

62. Samuel Sewall to Dear Brother, February 25, 1686/7, box 1, folder 9, Curwen Papers, AAS.

63. Russell, A Long, Deep Furrow, 25–27.

64. Keayne, "The Apologia of Robert Keayne," ed. Bailyn; Bailyn, New England Merchants in the Seventeenth Century, 41–44.

65. Green, Pursuits of Happiness, chaps. 3 and 8 passim.

66. Akagi, Town Proprietors of the New England Colonies, 176; Bushman, From Puritan to Yankee, 98–103; Breen, The Character of the Good Ruler, 153–67.

67. For the best history of changing consumer behavior in the Atlantic world, see Vries, *The Industrious Revolution*.

68. For these changes in Boston, see Nash, *The Urban Crucible*.

69. Nobles, *Divisions throughout the Whole*. 18–20.

70. Martin, *Profits in the Wilderness*, 110–18.

71. Martin, *Profits in the Wilderness*, 149–96, 219–35.

72. Martin, *Profits in the Wilderness*, 229–34; An Act for Regulating of Townships, Choice of Town Officers, and Setting Forth Their Power, November 16, 1692, in *Acts and Resolves*, 1:67.

73. An Act for Regulating of Townships, Choice of Town Officers, and Setting Forth Their Power, November 16, 1692, in *Acts and Resolves*, 1:65. See also An Act Directing the Admission of Town Inhabitants, March 12, 1700/1, in *Acts and Resolves* 1:451–53.

2 / Dawnland Encounters, 1600–1713

1. Scholars have hotly contested precise ethnographic terms and boundaries of the contact-era New England coast, but the above description rests on the consensus of the majority of current research. This paragraph sides with the arguments advanced in Hoffman, "Souriquois, and Etechemin and Kwedech," 65–87; Bourque, "Ethnicity on the Maritime Peninsula," 257–84; Bourque, *Twelve Thousand Years*, 105–7; Baker, "Finding the Almouchiquois," 73–100; and Prins, "Children of Gluskap," 98. For a dissenting view, that the original inhabitants of the Maine coast were all "Eastern Abenakis," see Snow, "Ethnographic Baseline of the Eastern Abenaki," 291–306. Snow discounts French sources and argues the Etechemin-Abenaki distinction is an "unnecessary complication" (305).

2. Baker, "Trouble to the Eastward," 59–62; Baker, "Finding the Almouchiqouis," 80–81; Snow and Lanphear, "European Contact and Indian Depopulation," 21–23.

3. Snow and Lanphear, "European Contact and Indian Depopulation," 23.

4. Baker, "Finding the Almouchiquois," 81; Bourque, *Twelve Thousand Years*, 119–20; Snow and Lanphear, "European Contact and Depopulation," 24.

5. Day, *Identity of the St. Francis Indians*.

6. Baker, "Trouble to the Eastward," 55–57.

7. Wiseman, *Voice of the Dawn*, 69–70.

8. Baker, "Trouble to the Eastward," 130–31.

9. Bourque, *Twelve Thousand Years*, 118–19.

10. Baxter, ed., *Christopher Levett of York*, 92.

11. Baxter, ed., *Christopher Levett of York*, 104–5.

12. Bourque, *Twelve Thousand Years*, 120–26.

13. Baker, "Portland as a Contested Frontier," 8–9; Baker, "Formerly Machegonne," 5–6; Pulsipher, *Subjects unto the Same King*, 252–56.

14. Jasper Maudit, agent of Massachusetts in London, in Yirush, *Settlers, Liberty, and Empire*, 3.

15. Arneil, *John Locke and America*; Yirush, *Settlers, Liberty, and Empire*, 12.

16. Winthrop, "General Considerations for the Plantations in New England," in *Winthrop Papers*, 2:120.

17. Winthrop, "General Considerations for the Plantations in New England," in *Winthrop Papers*, 2:120.

18. For New Hampshire, see Peter S. Leavenworth, "The Best Title That Indians Can Claime," 275-300; for Maine, see Baker, "Scratch with a Bear's Paw," 235-56; Baker, "Trouble to the Eastward," 148-77; and Nash, "Abiding Frontier," 151-53, 174-79. For a dissenting view, see Prins, "Chief Rawandagon, Alias Robin Hood," in *Northeastern Indian Lives,* ed. Grumet, 104-6. For the earlier argument that the English tricked the Indians, see Jennings, *The Invasion of America,* chap. 8.

19. Nanuddemaure Deed to John Parker, June 14, 1659, copy in proprietors' book, entered by Belcher Noyes, PPP, MeHS, vol. 1, box 1, pp. 25-26. Parker's occupation in Richard Wharton Deed to John Parker, July 15, 1684, copy in proprietors' book, PPP, MeHS, vol. 1, box 1, p. 26.

20. Nash, "Abiding Frontier," 151, 198-99; Baker, "Scratch with a Bear's Paw," 239-40; Prins, "Chief Rawandagon, Alias Robin Hood," in *Northeastern Indian Lives,* ed. Grumet, 93-115.

21. Baker, "Finding the Almouchiquois," 76-77.

22. Nanuddemaure Deed to John Parker, June 14, 1659, copy in proprietors' book, entered by Belcher Noyes, PPP, MeHS, vol. 1, box 1, pp. 25-26.

23. Mr. Roles to Humphrey Chadbourne, May 10, 1643, in *York Deeds,* ed. Hull, 1:6.

24. Bilodeau, "The Economy of War," 280-91; Lord, Sexton, and Harrington, *History of the Archdiocese of Boston,* 1:54-55; Morrison, "Dawnland Decisions," 89-91.

25. Bourque, *Twelve Thousand Years,* 121, 130; Baker, *Clarke & Lake Company,* 3-4.

26. Baker, *Clarke & Lake Company,* 7-9.

27. Baker, *Clarke & Lake Company,* 81-82 nn21 and 29.

28. Recorded copies of deeds in Lincoln County Deeds, vol. 1, Lincoln County Courthouse, 1-21. Most Merrimack Valley deeds in neighboring New Hampshire likewise referred to rivers and geographic features rather than acres (Leavenworth, "The Best Title that Indians Can Claime," 286).

29. Abecaduset to Lawson, Lincoln County Deeds, vol. 1, 12-13.

30. See *Conference Held at St. George's* [1753], 18-23.

31. For a view of the postwar treaties and boundaries, see the statement by Quenois in *Conference* [1753], 20; for the Wabanaki view—shared by Europeans—of the legality of conquest (or reconquest), see Penobscot statements in Waldo, *A Defence of the Title,* 12.

32. See, for example, July 15, 1725, John Penhallow Diary, MHS; and *Conference* [1753], 21.

33. Bourque *Twelve Thousand Years,* 138-42; Day, "The Ouragie War," in *Extending the Rafters,* ed. Foster, Campisi, and Mithun, 35-50.

34. Qtd. in Nash, "Abiding Frontier," 188-89.

35. Morrison, *Embattled Northeast,* 28-32; Calloway, *Pen and Ink Witchcraft,* 19-22; Nash, "Abiding Frontier," 151-53.

36. Certified extract of "Sir Ferdinando Gorges Instructions to his Agents Thomas Purchas and Others 21 June 1664," in PPP, PEM, box 1, folder 1.

37. For literacy, see Baker, "Scratch with a Bear's Paw," 244; for life in the early towns in mid-Maine, see Baker, "Trouble to the Eastward," 72-93.

38. Baker, "Scratch with a Bear's Paw," 236. See Leavenworth "The Best Title that Indians Can Claime," 291-92, for a similar situation in New Hampshire.

39. Konig, *Law and Society in Puritan Massachusetts,* chap. 6.

40. See, for example, An Account of the Proceedings of Mssrs Noyes and Skinner in Their Late Voyage to the Eastward, March 28, 1750, PPP, MeHS, vol. 7, box 4, folder 11, p. 431; Job Averell to Samuel Whittemore, August 11 1731 [date is incorrect, most likely 1751], Sheepscot Manuscripts, 1:17c, MeSL.

41. Hull, ed., *York Deeds*, 2:13, copy in PPP, MeHS, vol. 1, box 1, pp. 25–26. For Christmas as a time of social inversion and charity, see Hutton, *Stations of the Sun*, 9–10, 104–9.

42. See, for example, Derumkin, Daniel, and Robin, Indian Sagamores, to James Thomas and Samuel York, July 20, 1670, copy in PPP, MeHS, vol. 4, box 2, folder 3, p. 1. Parker, York, and Thomas may have also chosen Christmas because it was a convenient day to remember. Other deeds stipulated payment on March 25, the start of the New Year (Bourque, *Twelve Thousand Years*, 141). Bourque notes that dating payments on major holidays followed English legal forms.

43. Certified extract of "Sir Ferdinando Gorges Instructions to His Agents Thomas Purchas and Others 21 June 1664," PPP, PEM, box 1, folder 1.

44. Baker, "Trouble to the Eastward," 94–147. Stories of antebellum coexistence survived in local lore as well (Southgate, *History of Scarborough*, 100–102; Emery, *Ancient City of Gorgeana*, 64–65).

45. Mather, *Decennium Luctuosum*, 13.

46. Josselyn, *Account of Two Voyages*, 193–94.

47. "Complaint of Henry and Samuel Lane, July 27, 1688, in *DHSM*, 6:413–14.

48. Baker, "Trouble to the Eastward," 183–86.

49. Baker, "Trouble to the Eastward," 192–93.

50. Morrison, *Embattled Northeast*, 108.

51. Bilodeau, "Creating an Indian Enemy," 11–42; Baker, "Trouble to the Eastward," 202–13; Pulsipher, *Subjects unto the Same King*, chap. 9; Morrison, *Embattled Northeast*, 108–11.

52. Quotation from Pulsipher, "'Dark Cloud Rising from the East,'" 594–95. Preliminary negotiations described in Joshua Scottow, "Narrative of Ye Voyage to Pemmaquid," Fogg Collection, 420, box 8, fol. 57, MeHS.

53. Cotton Mather referenced these complaints in *Decennium Luctuosum*, 15; see also Edward Tyng to Gov. Andros, August 18, 1688, in *DHSM*, 6: 419; Pulsipher, "Dark Cloud Rising," 598–600, 605–6.

54. *JR*, 31:183–207, 36:83–111; 37:241–61.

55. The best study of the ethnicity of these migrants is Day, *Identity of the St. Francis Indians*.

56. Lord, Sexton, and Harrington, *History of the Archdiocese of Boston*, 1:20–21, 41–42, 56–57, 67; Bilodeau, "Understanding Ritual," 3.

57. Mather, *Decennium Luctuosum*, 155; Relation of Grace Higiman, May 31, 1695, MAC, 8:38; John Gyles, *Memoirs of Odd Adventures*, in *Held Captive by Indians*, ed. Vanderbeets, 112; Morrison, *Embattled Northeast*, 124–49; Bourque, *Twelve Thousand Years*, 159–69.

58. Morrison, *Embattled Northeast*, 159–63; Bourque, *Twelve Thousand Years*, 175–12.

59. Speck, "Eastern Algonkian Wabanaki Confederacy," 492–508; Walker, Buesing, and Conkling, "Account of the Wabanaki Confederacy," in *Political Organization of*

Native North Americans, ed. Schusky, 41–84; Nicolar, *Life and Traditions of the Red Man*, 137–39.

60. For treaty, see *DHSM*, 10:7–11; for notes and preliminary negotiations, see *DHSM*, 23:4–8.

61. Governor William Phips to Captain John Alden, August 8, 1694, in *DHSM*, 23:10. Lord, Sexton, and Harrington pointed this out in *History of the Archdiocese of Boston*, 1:54–55. For "trade and amity," see "Journal of Events in Acadia from September 15, 1693 to September 2, 1694," in *Acadia at the End of the Seventeenth Century*, ed. Webster, 53; Baker and Reid, *New England Knight*, 167–70.

62. Webster, ed., *Acadia at the End of the Seventeenth Century*, 62. Egeremet cosigned a second deed with Madockawando to Silvanus Davis, a member of Phips's council, the following day. However, there are no records of the Kennebecs complaining about Egeremet's behavior, perhaps because they were no longer using the coastal strip of their land west of the Muscongus contained in the cession (see Madockawando and Egeremet to Capt. Silvanus Davis, May 10, 1694 in *York Deeds*, ed. Hull, 10:257–58). For the Madockawando cession to Phips, see Hull, ed., *York Deeds*, 10:237–38; see also below.

63. Blackstone, *Commentaries on the Laws of England*, 2:296–97.

64. Convenant of Lands With Sir William Phips, by Madockawando, Sagamore of Penobscot, May 9, 1694, in *DHSM*, 8:12–15, quotations on 13, 12; Baker and Reid, *New England Knight*, 170–72.

65. However, one of the two interpreters was an Indian the colonists called "Sheepscot John," whose presence may have complicated such a deception. His Wabanaki name was "Ragatawawongan," and he was among the individuals left as hostages in the 1693 agreement (*DHSM*, 8:14 and 10:10).

66. Account of a Journey Made by M. De Villieu," in *Acadia at the End of the Seventeenth Century*, ed. Webster, 60–63.

67. R. P. Thury to Monseiur Le Comte de Frontenac, September 11, 1694, in *CMNF*, 2:161.

68. "Account of a Journey Made by M. De Villieu," in *Acadia at the End of the Seventeenth Century*, ed. Webster, 62.

69. "Account of a Journey Made by M. De Villieu," in *Acadia at the End of the Seventeenth Century*, ed. Webster, 62–63; "Journal of Events in Acadia from September 15, 1693 to September 2, 1694," in *Acadia at the End of the Seventeenth Century*, ed. Webster, 55.

70. Webster, ed., *Acadia at the End of the Seventeenth Century*, 77.

71. Baker and Reid, *New England Knight*, 173–77, chap. 11 passim.

72. Memorial of Sagamores, delivered in Boston, September 8, 1699, in *DHSM*, 23:27.

73. Memorial of Sagamores, delivered in Boston, September 8, 1699, in *DHSM*, 23:27. The best treatment of this phenomenon is Pulsipher, *Subjects unto the Same King*.

74. Casco Conference with Wabanaki Sagamores to Ratify Treaty, July 21, 1713, in *NET*, 142.

75. Ghere and Morrison, "Searching for Justice on the Maine Frontier," 381–82.

76. For origins of the Muscongus Patent, including the Madockawando sale, see Lincolnshire Company Records, pp. 1–24, MHS.

77. Pulsipher, *Subjects unto the Same King*, 250–53.

78. Palmer, *Present State of New England*, 9–10.

79. Rawson, *Revolution in New England Justified*, 13.

80. Rawson, *Revolution in New England Justified*, 14.

81. Rawson, *Revolution in New England Justified*, 15–16.

82. *An Appeal to the Men of New England*, 9.

83. For background, see Yirush, *Settlers, Liberty, and Empire*, 98.

84. Dummer, *Defence of the New England Charters*, 9.

85. Dummer, *Defence of the New England Charters*, 9.

86. Dummer, *Defence of the New England Charters*, 12.

87. Dummer, *Defence of the New England Charters*, 12, 13.

88. Bulkley, "Right of the Aboriginal Natives to the Lands," xxxv, xix, xvii. Bulkley was a reverend in New London, Connecticut, who wrote in response to local disputes surrounding Mohegan lands. For Bulkley's biography, see *SHG*, 4:450–53; for the Mohegan controversy, see Yirush, *Settlers, Liberty, and Empire*, 118–38.

89. Bulkley, "Right of the Aboriginal Natives to the Lands," lv–lvi.

90. Bulkley, "Right of the Aboriginal Natives to the Lands," xvi.

91. Lovejoy, *Glorious Revolution in America*; Stanwood, *Empire Reformed*.

92. *Acts and Resolves*, 1:471.

93. *Acts and Resolves*, 1:471–72.

94. *Acts and Resolves*, 1:41–42.

95. "Considerations Concerning Indian Grants," in *DHSM*, 6: 362.

96. Copy of Adam Winthrop Petition, "To the Right Honorable the Lords Commissioners for Trade and Plantations," PPP, PEM, series I, box 1, folder 2.

97. *Acts and Resolves*, 1:64–68, 182–83, 704. John Frederick Martin argues that these changes merely formalized existing practices in *Profits in the Wilderness*, 257–59.

98. Petition of Inhabitants of Scarborough, November 9, 1687, in *DHSM*, 6:290–91.

3 / Land Claims, 1713–1722

1. Brooks, *Common Pot*, 251. Penobscots pronounced this as *Pastoniak*.

2. See Campbell, *Speculators in Empire*; and Taylor, *Liberty Men and Great Proprietors*, for treatments of the speculator phenomenon later in the century.

3. The committee was first appointed in 1700, but the renewal of fighting in 1703 rendered it irrelevant for another decade.

4. *MHGR*, 5:156, 210.

5. Full data set in Saxine, "Properties of Empire," 421–23.

6. See, for example, the list of claims in the papers of the Pejepscot Proprietors, of which Winthrop and Noyes were members (Claims Presented for Adjustment, December 29, 1714, PPP, MeHS, vol. 7, box 5, folder 7, p. 372b).

7. Meeting of Pemaquid Proprietors on August 31, 1743, Pemaquid Proprietors Book of Records, 1:1, AAS; Lincolnshire Company Records, bound volume, pp. 14–20, MHS.

8. Six current or future frontier speculators served that year: Elisha Cooke, Samuel Brown, Elisha Hutchinson, John Clark, Isaac Winslow, and Thomas Hutchinson. For Cooke, see John Leverett deed to Elisha Cook, August 14, 1719, Lincolnshire Company Records, bound volume, pp. 8–13, MHS; for Brown and Clark, see Indenture to

the 20 Associates, March 17, 1719/20, Lincolnshire Company Records, bound volume, pp. 14–24, MHS; for Elisha Hutchinson, see "The Ancestry of Katherine Hamby, Wife of Captain Edward Hutchinson of Boston, Massachusetts," in *NEHGR*,145: 99–121; for Winslow, see "General Statement of the Title and Possession of the Kennebec Proprietors of the Kennebec Purchase, from the late Colony of New Plymouth," Nathan Dane Papers, box 16, folder 4, p. 4, MHS. For Hutchinson, see Proprietors Proposalls to the Committee appointed by the General Court, February 18, 1714/15, PPP, MeHS, vol. 1, box 1, p. 37. Edward Bromfield and John Higginson filed claims with the Committee of Eastern Claims. John Pynchon's family dominated the towns in western Massachusetts (Nobles, *Divisions throughout the Whole*, 20–23).

Samuel Sewall owned various land tracts in New England. For some of the land he gave away, see *SHG*, 2:351. Wait Winthrop and John Appleton had family members with land claims on the frontier. Winthrop claimed descent from Governor John Winthrop and was related to Pejepscot Proprietor Adam Winthrop. A Joseph Appleton held shares in the Muscongus Company (see Indenture to the 20 Associates, March 17, 1719/20, Lincolnshire Company Records, bound volume, pp. 14–20, MHS).

9. Kershaw, *Kennebeck Proprietors*, 31.

10. November 9, 1757, KPP, vol. 6, bound records, p. 137.

11. Kershaw, *Kennebeck Proprietors*, 12; November 9, 1757, KPP, vol. 6, bound records, p. 137.

12. Ephraim Savage Indenture to the Pejepscot Proprietors, November 5, 1714, PPP, MeHS, vol. 7, box 5, folder 7, pp. 351–60; John Ruck sale of Proprietary Share to Benning Wentworth, October 8, 1727, PPP, MeHS, vol. 7, box 5, folder 9, p. 395b.

13. Pemaquid Proprietors Book of Records, Pemaquid Proprietors Papers, 1:2, AAS.

14. For manuscript records of Waldo's acquisitions, see "The Plymouth Company Lands at Muscongus in Which Samuel Waldo Was a Great Proprietor," vol. 26, Lincoln Family Papers, AAS.

15. Large numbers of New Englanders invested in small shares of merchant vessels in the early eighteenth century as well (Innes, *Creating the Commonwealth*, 293).

16. "Obligation of the Proprietors of the Proprietors Lands at Wiscasset etc. etc. between Each Other to Pay the Charges of the Settlement 1733," Wiscasset Company Papers in Doggett Family Papers, box 3, folder 4, MeHS.

17. For example, see Sarah Noyes, "spinster," holding 1/5 of 1/8, and Hannah Fairweather, "widow," holding 1/5, both of the Pejepscot Patent, in Pejepscot Proprietors Quitclaim Deed to William Vaughan, April 6, 1724, PPP, MeHS, vol. 7, box 5, folder 9, p. 397.

18. Proprietors to Thomas Westbrook, May 1, 1731, PPP vol. 4, box 2, folder 4, pp. 31–33; Proprietors to Thomas Westbrook, February 11, 1738/9, PPP, vol. 5, box 3, folder 7, pp. 151–52; Thomas Westbrook to Proprietors, March 3, 1738/9, PPP, vol. 5, box 3, folder 7, p. 155; Adam Winthrop to Thomas Westbrook, July 3, 1739, PPP, vol. 5, box 3, folder 7, p. 165; Thomas Westbrook to Adam Winthrop, December 26, 1739, PPP, vol. 5, box 3, folder 7, p. 171. All in PPP, MeHS.

19. Kershaw, *Kennebeck Proprietors*, 53.

20. Proprietors Proposalls to the Committee appointed by the General Court, February 18, 1714/15, PPP, MeHS, vol. 1, box 1, pp. 34–37, quotation on 35.

21. Pejepscot accompt No 2 for the Charge of a Voyage made thither from 13 April to 4 May 1715, PPP, MeHS, vol. 1, box 1, pp. 31–33. The £43 did not include a 12-shilling

"Cheshire cheese" supplied by John Watts. Robert Moody noted that the committee was "royally entertained" (Moody, "The Maine Frontier," 358).

22. Moody, "The Maine Frontier," 357–58.

23. May 28, 1715, HJ, 1: 5; full text in The Committee's Report, May 27,1715, PPP, MeHS, vol. 1, box 1, pp. 37–40. (The sources each claim a different day for the report.)

24. The Committee's Report, May 27, 1715, PPP, MeHS, vol. 1, box 1, p. 39.

25. Douglass, A Summary, 1:386.

26. Pejepscot Proprietor John Wentworth was involved in the early organization of Scarborough (see March 30, 1720, Scarborough Town Records 1:41, MeHS). Elisha Cooke of the Muscongus Proprietors became a North Yarmouth Proprietor after serving on a committee to organize its resettlement (see entries for June 28, 1722, and January 20, 1733/4, Record Book of the Proprietors of the Town of North Yarmouth, mss copy by Augustus Corliss, 1879, 1:20–21, 144–46, MeHS). Samuel Waldo and Thomas Westbrook, both Muscongus Proprietors, owned land in Falmouth; for Waldo, see November 5 and 18, 1729, Falmouth Town Records, 1:344–46, MeSA; for Westbrook, see August 17, 1727, November 5 and 28, 1729, Falmouth Town Records, 1:120, 344–46, MeSA.

27. McKinley, The Suffrage Franchise, 363.

28. Zuckerman, Peaceable Kingdoms.

29. Smith, Smith Journals, ed. Willis, 49.

30. Some Georgetown Inhabitants to Col. Edward Hutchinson, April, 10 1719, folder 1, Hutchinson Family Papers, MHS.

31. James Parker to the Committee for Resettlement of North Yarmouth, January 22, 1727/8, NYMP, 1:62.

32. James Parker to the Committee for Resettlement of North Yarmouth, January 22, 1727/8, NYMP, 1:62.

33. Bound volume of Proprietors' Records and Brunswick Town Book, entries for August 15, 1717; 1718 [no more specific date]; and July 30, 1719, in PPP, MeHS, vol. 3, box 2, pp. 6, 8, 11.

34. Wheeler and Wheeler, History of Brunswick, Topsham, and Harpswell, 823–24; Samuel Shute to the King in Council, endorsement of The Humble Memorial and Petition of James Woodside late Minister of the Gospel at Brunswick, in New England, June 25, 1723, in DHSM, 10:163–65.

35. A Defence of the Remarks of the Plymouth Company, [1753], 20–21, Thayer, "Transient Town of Cork," 240–65; O'Brien, "The Lost Town of Cork, Maine," 175–84.

36. Wheeler, "Brunswick at the Time of Incorporation," 34; Day, History of Maine Agriculture, 35–36. Descriptions of early crop choices in Deposition of Tobias Oakman, June 12,1741, Lewis Family Papers, box 2, folder 1, MeHS; Affidavit of Tobais Oakman, March 31, 1742/3, Samuel Waldo Papers, box 1, folder 6, MeHS.

37. See above note. For fishing, see also March 13, 1731/2, Biddeford Town Records, 1:319, MeSA; December 14, 1738, Falmouth Town Records, 2:128–29, MeSA; Dom Rex v. Hugh Mitchel et al., Illegal Fish Netting, July, 1729, York County Court of Sessions Case Files, box 35, file 30, vol. 8, p. 34, MeSA.

38. Smith, Smith Journal, ed. Willis, 96.

39. "Sundry English fishing places" listed in 1701 in Report of the Committee of Council, November 17, 1725, PPP, MeHS, vol. 4, box 2, folder 16, p. 325.

40. Malone, Pine Trees and Politics; Albion, Forests and Sea Power, 241–62.

41. Wheeler, "Brunswick at the Time of Its Incorporation," 33-34; Dole, *Windham in the Past*, 225.

42. The town and proprietary records for numerous Maine communities contain references to illegal logging and efforts to prosecute the offenders throughout the eighteenth century. In towns where the municipal body retained greater power, the town meetings mentioned dealing with timber thieves (see, for example, February 11, 1723/4, Falmouth Town Records, MeSA, 1: 67); for examples among proprietors, see February 16, 1742/3, Gorham Proprietors Records, 17, MeHS; Job Averell to John Burt and Samuel Whittemore, June 11, 1741 [in Sheepscot], Sheepscot Manuscripts, vol. 1, p. 16a, MeSL; October 21, 1726, North Yarmouth Proprietors Records, pp. 29-30, MeHS; April 12, 1736, Scarborough Proprietors Records, pp. 22-23, MeHS.

43. November 18, 1719, Arundel Town Records, p. 14, MeSA; May 7, 1719, Falmouth Town Records, 1:8, MeSA.

44. May 8, 1719, bound volume, PPP, MeHS, vol. 3, box 2, p. 9.

45. May 7, 1719, Falmouth Town Records, 1:8, MeSA.

46. September 28, 1719, Falmouth Town Records, 1:10-11, MeSA; see also March 21, 1720, Andrew Hawes Papers, box 2, folder 10, MeHS.

47. May 4, 1720, Falmouth Town Records, 1:17, MeSA.

48. The Scarborough Proprietors, aware of the dubious legality of their meetings, did not keep complete records of early 1720s proceedings. However, Boston merchant Timothy Prout provided a detailed, if hostile, description of several meetings in a later complaint to the governor and General Court. See Timothy Prout of Scarborough, Petition to Gov. Spencer Phips and the General Court, May 27, 1752, William Southgate Collection, folder 5, MeHS.

49. May 20, 1720, Scarborough Proprietors Records, n.p., but first page in book, MeHS.

50. June 22, 1721, Scarborough Proprietors Records, p. 13, MeHS.

51. Timothy Prout of Scarborough, Petition to Gov. Spencer Phips and the General Court, May 27, 1752, William Southgate Collection, folder 5, MeHS. For John Libby and his almost innumerable progeny, see Libby, *The Libby Family in America*, 20, and, for early generations, 17-33. Thirty-four male Libbys of the first four generations remained in Scarborough to their deaths.

52. Timothy Prout of Scarborough, Petition to Gov. Spencer Phips and the General Court, May 27, 1752, William Southgate Collection, folder 5, MeHS, which describes Prout and other proprietors protesting proceedings in town in 1722; Falmouth Town Records, 1:12-13, MeSA.

53. The Petition of Bartholomew Flagg of Boston, Blacksmith, February 26, 1727/8, NYMP, 1:66.

54. Boston Conference with Kennebec and Penobscot Delegates, January 16, 1713/14, in *NET*, 153.

55. John Penhallow Diary, July 15, 1725, MHS; *Conference* [1732], 8; *Conference* [1742], 6; *Conference* [1753], 21.

56. Figure derived from above two notes, in addition to Day, *Identity of the St. Francis Indians*, 34; and Haefeli and Sweeney, *Captors and Captives*, 227n33.

57. Estimates of village sizes come from Begon a Monseigneur, September 25, 1715, MG1 C11A F-35, f109, f112, f114, LAC; Samuel Shute, "An Answer to the First Query Propos'd by the Rt. Honble the Lords of Trade etc. Referring to the Province

of Massachusetts Bay" February 17, 1719/20, in *DHSM*, 10:108; Wenogganet, Quera-
banawit, Nodagombewit, Owanabbemit, and Pear Exces to Gov. Joseph Dudley,
February 12, 1713/14, in *NET*, 157, for a Penobscot self-warrior count of "170 men";
Memorial of Father Loyard: Upon the Present Condition of the Abnaquis (Missionary
at the village of Meductic, in New Brunswick, in 1722), in *JR*, 67:121 for a figure of
500 warriors in Meductic, Norridgewock, Penawabskik, St. Francis, and Becancour
Memoir on the present Condition of the Abenaquis [1724] by Sieur de Louvigny, in
NYCD, 9:939, advances an identical number. For a lower count of 300 Kennebecs at
Norridgewock (60 warriors), see Joseph Heath Map of Norridgewock Fort and Kennebec River, 1719, PPP, MeHS, coll. 61, Mss Map 50. For a map of the villages, see Carte
pour les hauteurs des Terres, et pour server de limitte, suivant in Paix, Entre la France
et l'Angleterre, suivant les Memoires du R. P. Aubry, Jesuiste, 1715, LAC, National Map
Collection, 6364.

58. Ghere, "The 'Disappearance' of the Abenaki," 193–207; Ghere, "Abenaki Factionalism," 142–47.

59. Portsmouth Conference with Wabanaki Delegates, July 11–15, 1713, in *NET*,
137–38.

60. "Memoire sur les Limites de l' Acadie, envoye de Quebec a Mgr le Duc d'orleans,
Regent, par le Pere Charlevoix, Jesuit, October 19, 1720, in *CMNF*, 3: 50–51; Belmessous, "Wabanaki Versus French and English Claims," 108–9.

61. "Memoir sur les Limites de l'Acadie . . . Octobre 19, 1720," in *CMNF*, 3:52–53.

62. Pulsipher, "Gaining the Diplomatic Edge," 34–37.

63. Pritchard, *In Search of Empire*, 400–401, 413–20.

64. Casco Conference with Wabanaki Sagamores to Ratify Treaty, July 21, 1713, in
NET, 142.

65. "Sewall's Journey to Arrowsick," in Sewall, *Diary*, 2:1125.

66. Ghere, "Abenaki Factionalism," 161–64.

67. Indians to Governor Samuel Shute, July 28, 1721, MAC, 31:103.

68. *George Town* [1717], 8.

69. Ghere, "Abenaki Factionalism," 25–26, 30–31.

70. Portsmouth Conference with Wabanaki Delegates, July 11–15, 1713, in *NET*, 137.

71. Portsmouth Conference, July 23–28, 1714, in *NET*, 166.

72. *George Town* [1717], 7. For French approval of Wiwurna, see Rapport de Monsieur de Vaudreuil Au Conseil, Quebec, October 31, 1718, in *CMNF*, 3: 31.

73. *George Town* [1717], 10.

74. "Journal of the Reverend Baxter," 48.

75. *George Town*, [1717], 9.

76. For Jordan's capture, see Penhallow, *History*, 5–6; for Bean, Deposition of
Joseph Bane [Bean] August 13, 1736, HKM, vol. 40, item 14; see also testimony printed
in *Defence of the Remarks of the Plymouth Company* [1754], 25. Gyles wrote an account
of his experience, *Memoirs of Odd Adventures, Strange Deliverances etc.*

77. John Gyles to Lt. Gov. Dummer, March 15, 1726/7, MAC, 31: 142. For his subsequent activities as spymaster, see John Gyles Memorial St. Georges River, February
27, 1726/7, and March 3, 1726/7, MAC, 52:329–30; John Gyles expense account for the
year July 31, 1735 to July 1736, August 2, 1736, MAC, 31:197; John Gyles Memorandum
on Disbursements on the Indians, August 28, 1740, MAC, 31:284; John Gyles Account
for Disbursements on the Indians, June 1740 to June 1741, MAC, 31:377.

78. Thomas Bannister to the Council of Trade and Plantations, July 15, 1715, in *CSP*, vol. 28, doc. 521.

79. David Ghere argued John Gyles "consistently mistranslated official treaty negotiations for over a quarter of a century from 1725 to 1752," in "Abenaki Factionalism," 174n20. Ghere provided no citations for this claim in the dissertation, but in "Mistranslations and Misinformation," 7, he cited an erroneously dated version of the Bannister claim, which he attributed to Kenneth Morrison's *Embattled Northeast*, 170-71. Morrison in turn acknowledged Lord, Sexton, and Harrington's *History of the Archdiocese of Boston*, 1:3, for the citation, although the page does not refer to this document at all. Christopher Bilodeau's "Economy of War," 397, contains the correct citation and argues that other forces besides deliberate mistranslation may have been at work in Anglo-Wabanaki diplomacy.

80. For example, see R. P. Lauverjeat [Lauverjat] to Monsieur le Marquis de Vaudreuil, August 27, 1727, in *CMNF*, 3:136.

81. Sebastian Rasles to Capt. Samuel Moody, February 7, 1720, in *Pioneers*, ed. Baxter, 96-104, quotation on 99.

82. Lord, Sexton, and Harrington, *History of the Archdiocese of Boston*, 1:117-18.

83. For the senior Saint-Castin, see Stanwood, "Unlikely Imperialist." For Joseph and Barenos, see *DCB*, vol. 3, see "Abbadie de Sainte-Castin, Joseph D', Baron de Saint-Castin," by Georges Cerbelaud Salagnac.

84. Quotation from Messieurs de Beauharnois et Dupuy to Ministre, October 20, 1727, in *CMNF*, 3:138R. P. Lauverjat to R. P. de La Chasse, July 8, 1728, 3:143-44.

85. Lord, Sexton, and Harrington, *Archdiocese of Boston*, 1:144.

86. Memorandum of a Conference Held at Richmond, October 28, 1740 [copy], Maine Historical Manuscripts Scrapbooks, 1:73, MeHS. They "pawned" their honor no fewer than three times at that conference.

87. Samuel Denny to Edward Hutchinson, November 5, 1766, Hutchinson Family Papers, folder 9 [1766], MHS.

88. Boston Conference with Kennebec and Penobscot Delegates, January 16, 1713/14, in *NET*, 155.

89. David Ghere and Alvin Morrison pointed this distinction out, but without further comment in "Searching for Justice on the Maine Frontier," 382.

90. For full bill, see August 8, 1736, in Governor's Council Executive Records, GC3 327 #5, vol. 10, pp. 47-48, MSA; Governor Belcher to Duke of Newcastle, August 5, 1736, in *CSP*, vol. 42, doc. 375.

91. *George Town* [1717], 6.

92. *George Town*, [1717], 5.

93. Portsmouth Conference, July 23-28, 1714, in *NET*, 166.

94. Williamson, *History of Maine*, 2: 88-90; "Copy of a Letter to the Rev. Baxter to Invite Him Eastward" [ca. 1717], Doggett Family Papers, box 1, folder 9, Minot Family Correspondence, MeHS.

95. Portsmouth Conference, June 7, 1716, in *NET*, 171-72.

96. *George Town* [1717], 9-10.

97. *George Town* 1717], 12.

98. *George Town* [1717], 12.

99. For the riverine dimension of this strategy, see Bennett, "A Means of Removing Them Further from Us."

100. The Committee's Report [of Eastern Claims], May 27, 1715, PPP, MeHS, vol. 1, pp. 38–39.

101. For origins of the Muscongus claim and the formation of the proprietors, see Lincolnshire Company Records, 1–24, MHS.

102. Fayerweather Diary, May 5, 1720, Bangor Public Library.

103. Fayerweather Diary, May 5, 1720, Bangor Public Library

104. Fayerweather Diary, May 16, 1720, Bangor Public Library. For Moody in Falmouth, see esp. Petition of the Proprietors and Settlers of the Town of Falmouth, 1718, MAC, 6:472–73; *Joseph Moody et al. v. Joseph Bayley and Phillip Hodgkins*, YCCPCF, box 36, file 2, vol. 8, p. 94, MeSA.

105. Shute to Penobscots Supporting John Leverett's Claims, July 19, 1720, in *NET*, 193.

106. Fayerweather Diary, July 29, 1720, and August 11–12, 1720, Bangor Public Library.

107. Fayerweather Diary, August 13, 1720, Bangor Public Library.

108. For violence, see complaint by Adam Winthrop and Edward Hutchinson, November 5, 1719, in *HJ*, 2:176.

109. Report of William Tailier, William Dudley, and John Stoddard, [of a January 1720 conference], in *DHSM*, 23:83–84.

110. Treaty with the Maine Indians, Georgetown, July 20th, 1721, in *Saltonstall Papers*, ed. R. Moody, 1:330–31.

111. Deposition of John Minot. Boston, November 27, 1719, in *Pioneers*, ed. Baxter, 279–80. For others, see Deposition of Lewis Bane, of York, Esq., December 2, 1719, in *Pioneers*, ed. Baxter, 279; Jeremiah Dummer to Council of Trade and Plantations, January 25, 1719/20, in *CSP*, vol. 31, doc. 578; *DHSM*, 23:84.

112. See, for example, Letter from the Indians to the Governor [but written by Rasles], Translated 1720, MAC, 31:97–100; Sebastian Rasles to Capt. Samuel Moody, February 7, 1720, in *Pioneers*, ed. Baxter, 96–104.

113. Gyles to Lt. Gov. Dummer, May 19, 1727, MAC, 52:376.

114. Eckstorm, "Attack on Norridgewock," 559–60; Bilodeau, "Economy of War," 349–50.

115. Messrs. de Vaudreuil and Begon to Louis XV, October 8, 1721, in *NYCD*, 9: 903; Rasles to "My Reverend Father," August 23, 1724 [August 12 Old Style], in *Pioneers*, ed. Baxter, 251–52; quotation from Joseph Heath and John Minot to Gov. Shute, May 1, 1719, in *DHSM*, 10:447.

116. Morrison, *Embattled Northeast*, 182–84; Georgetown Conference and Treaty, 1720, in *NET*, 199–205; Rapport du Monsieur le Marquis de Vaudreuil et Begon au Ministre, October 8, 1721, in *CMNF*, 3:57.

117. Rapport du Monsieur le Marquis de Vaudreuil et Begon au Ministre, October 8, 1721, in *CMNF*, 3:58.

118. Indians to Governor Shute, July 28, 1721 [New Style], MAC, 31:101–5, quotation on 103. The letter calls the river "Pi8akki," or "Pigouakki." The village of Pigwacket lay on the Saco River. The map by the Jesuit Joseph Aubrey locates the village of "Pigouakki" on the Saco River and does not give the river a name, making it likely that Rasles called the river "Pigouakki" in this letter (see Joseph Aubry [Aubrey], "Carte pour les hauteurs des Teres, et pour server de limitte, suivant in Paix, Entre la France et l'Angleterre: suivant les Memoires du R. P. Aubry, Jesuiste, 1715," LAC, rec. no. 40136).

119. Morrison, *Embattled Northeast*, 184; Father Sebastian Rasles to His Nephew, October 15, 1722, from Nanrantsaouak, in *JR*, 67:107.

120. MAC, 31:105.

121. August 21 and September 1, 1721, in *HJ*, 3:89, 106–7.

122. August 14–15 and 24–25, 1721, Baxter, "Journal," 55–58; *NYCD*, 9:905.

123. *HJ*, 3:117, 156.

124. November 17, 1721, in *HJ*, 3:158–59.

125. Morrison, *Embattled Northeast*, 185; Lord, *History of the Archdiocese of Boston*, 1:129–30; Bilodeau, "Economy of War," 374–75.

126. For other factors, see Ian Saxine, "Properties of Empire," 140–44.

127. Seven of 29 members of the council in 1720 held Maine land shares, another independently owned land in Arundel, and another was related to Maine speculators. Samuel Brown, Thomas Fitch, and Samuel Thaxter were Muscongus Proprietors, and Thomas Hutchinson was a Pejepscot Proprietor. Charles Frost claimed one-eighth of a large tract around Wiscasset. John Wheelwright was an absentee landowner in Arundel. For Muscongus membership, see Lincolnshire Company Records, MHS, 14–24; for Pejepscot Proprietors membership, see Wharton Heirs Quitclaim, February 9, 1714, PPP, MeHS, 1:29–31. For Frost, see *Maine Historical and Genealogical Recorder* 7 (1893): 73–74. For John Wheelright's land in Arundel, see January 8, 1732–3, Arundel Town Records, p. 101, MeSA. Two other Muscongus Proprietors would have sat on the council had Shute not vetoed their selection due to their association with his rival, Elisha Cooke (see veto of John Clark and Nathaniel Byfield, in *HJ*, 2:232). Both are mentioned in Jonathan Waldo Deed to Samuel Waldo, March 20, 1727/8, HKM, vol. 40, item 3. Three Boston assemblymen were Muscongus Proprietors: Elisha Cooke, Oliver Noyes, and William Clark (see *HJ*, 2:227, and Lincolnshire Company Records, pp. 14–20, MHS).

128. That wording was Shute's on July 13, 1720 (*HJ*, 2:236).

129. *HJ*, 1:226 and 2:270.

130. See, for example, *HJ*, 2:248–49, 270; and Sewall, *Diary*, 2:942.

131. Vaudreuil and Begon to the Council of Marine, October 17, 1722, in *NYCD*, 9:910–12; Penhallow, *History*, 86.

132. Samuel Shute, Proclamation against the Eastern Indians, July 25, 1722, MAC, 31:106–8.

4 / Breaking—and Making—the Peace, 1722–1727

1. Norridgewock described in Joseph Heath, "Norridgewock Fort and Kennebec River, 1719," MSS Map #50, PPP, MeHS, coll. 61. For English descriptions of the fighting, see Harmon's report, as printed in *Boston News Letter*, August 20–27, 1724, 2. For earlier reports on the engagement, see *Boston Gazette*, August 17–24, 1724, 2; and *New England Courant*, August 17–24, 1724, 2. French accounts of surviving Indians' reports in Monsieur le Marquis de Vaudreuil to Ministre, October 25, 1724, in *CMNF*, 3:108–10.

2. Sewall, *Diary*, 2:1021.

3. *The Rebels Reward: Or, English Courage Display'd.*

4. Dummer's War has been the most popular label for the conflict, referring to the acting governor of Massachusetts and his role in it (Bourque, *Twelve Thousand Years,*

186). Other scholars, like John Grenier, label the conflict Father Rasles' War, after the Jesuit missionary (see *The First Way of War,* 47); scholars of the Western Abenakis call the conflict Gray Lock's War, after a prominent leader there (Calloway, *The Western Abenakis of Vermont,* chap. 6); descendants of Maine colonists often called the struggle Lovewells' War, after a famous scalp hunter slain in 1725 (see, for example, Bourne, *The History of Wells and Kennebunk,* 326).

5. Penhallow, *History,* 127.

6. For the Bay Colony's long quest to secure Indian allies, especially the Iroquois, see Johnson, "The Search for a Useable Indian," 623–51. For Iroquois diplomatic involvement and the participation of a trio of Mohawks, see Bourque, *Twelve Thousand Years,* 193–94.

7. Messrs. de Vaudreuil and Begon to the Council of Marine, October 17, 1722, in *NYCD,* 9:911; Louis XV to Messrs de Vaudreuil and Begon May 30, 1724, in *NYCD,* 9:936; Yves F. Zoltvany, *Vaudreuil,* 149–50.

8. Grenier, *The Far Reaches of Empire,* 46–73; Calloway, *The Western Abenakis of Vermont,* 113–31.

9. See Alexander Hamilton's Journal in Baxter, ed., *Pioneers,* 320, 323, 327; Baker and Reid, "Amerindian Power in the Northeast," 98–99, 101; Zoltvany, *Vaudreuil,* 196.

10. Baker and Reid, "Amerindian Power in the Northeast," 79, 96–97. For excellent use of Indian actions as text for determining strategy, see Dowd, *War under Heaven,* chap. 4, esp. 114–15.

11. For 1722 assaults, see Penhallow, *History,* 86, 95–96; John Penhallow to Gov. Shute, July 4, 1722, in *DHSM,* 10:150–51; Captain Thomas Westbrook to Gov. Shute, September 23, 1722, in *Letters of Colonel Thomas Westbrook,* ed. Trask, 8–9; Messrs. de Vaudreuil and Begon to the Council of Marine, October 17, 1722, in *NYCD,* 9:910–11. For 1723–24 Penobscot activity, see Penhallow, *History,* 99, 103; William Coyne for Lieutenant William Canady [Kennedy], Account of Attack on St. Georges Fort, [21–23] July 1724, in *Letters of Colonel Thomas Westbrook,* ed. Trask, 66–68. For Kennebecs and Canadian Wabanakis, see Penhallow, *History,* 99, 101; Trask, ed., *Letters of Colonel Thomas Westbrook,* 56–57, 65–68; Williamson, *History of the State of Maine,* 2:123. Many accounts did not identify Indian raiders, but the timing and location of the small-scale attacks suggest many of them were conducted by local Pigwackets and Androscoggins rather than more distant groups who had an abundance of targets closer to hand. David Ghere notes that during the 1740s and 1750s, Wabanakis based in Canada preferred to raid between late April and early June, and between October and November. Small parties of Indians attacked Berwick, Falmouth, Arundel, and Saco (Biddeford) outside of these seasons (David L. Ghere, "The 'Disappearance' of the Abenaki in Western Maine: Political Organization and Ethnocentric Assumptions," *American Indian Quarterly,* ser. 2, 17 [1993]: 201–2). For raids outside of this time frame, see Williamson, *History of the State of Maine,* 2:122–23; Penhallow, *History of the Wars of New England,* 99, 102; *DHSM,* 10:182; and *Letters of Colonel Thomas Westbrook,* ed. Trask, 63–64.

12. Thayer, "Transient Town of Cork," 240–65; O'Brien, "The Lost Town of Cork, Maine," 175–84.

13. Ghere, "Abenaki Factionalism, 38–40; Hoffman, "Ancient Tribes Revisited," 16–21. Armstrong Starkey discusses this phenomenon for most Eastern Woodlands Indians in *European and Indian American Warfare,* 24–26.

14. Penhallow, *History*, 86; William Coyne for Lieutenant William Canady, July 21, 1724, in *Letters of Colonel Thomas Westbrook*, ed. Trask, 65–68.

15. *Boston News Letter*, July 9–16, 1724, 2. For a broader view of Wabanaki maritime military activity, see Bahar, "People of the Dawn," 401–26.

16. Sebastian Rasles, undated, unfinished letter taken from Norridgewock, August 12, 1724, MAC 52:15–16 [contemporary translation].

17. *Boston News Letter*, August 20–27, 1724; *Boston Gazette*, August 17–24, 1724; *New England Courant*, August 17–24, 1724.

18. Lt. Gov. Dummer to the Council of Trade and Plantations, March 31, 1725, in *CSP*, vol. 34, doc. 558.

19. Lt. Gov. John Wentworth to the Lords Commissioners for Trade and Plantations, September 12, 1724, in *DHSM*, 10:222.

20. Penhallow, *History*, 127–28.

21. Symmes, *Lovewell Lamented*; Sewall, *Diary*, 2:1030; Rev. William Waldron to Richard Waldron, May 17, 1725, Richard Waldron Papers, vol. 1, folder 7, New Hampshire Historical Society.

22. Capt. Samuel Jordan's Declaration, May 28, 1725, in *Pioneers*, ed. Baxter, 375–83; Zoltvany, *Vaudreuil*, 200–201; Note du Ministre sur les Depeches de L'anne Derniere, May 2, 1725, and Memoire du Roi aux Sieurs Marquis de Beauharnois et Dupuy, May 14, 1726, in *CMNF*, 3:126–28.

23. Joseph Heath to Governor Dummer, April 13, 1727, MAC, 52:351.

24. Rapport De Longeuil et Begon au Ministre, October 31, 1725, in *CMNF*, 3:126.

25. Ghere, "The 'Disappearance' of the Abenaki," 195.

26. Samuel Thaxter and William Dudley, Journal of the Commissioners to Canada, May 26, 1725, in *Pioneers*, ed. Baxter, 351; *CSP*, vol. 34, doc. 740 xxx.

27. M. Begon to Count de Mourepas, April 21, 1725, in *NYCD*, 9:943.

28. *NYCD*, 9:944.

29. French and British accounts differ on the scope of the desired atonement (*CSP*, vol. 34, doc. 740 xxx; *NYCD*, 9:944–45.

30. Penhallow, *History*, 117–18.

31. John Penhallow Diary, July 15, MHS.

32. John Penhallow Diary, July 16, MHS.

33. Lt. Gov. Dummer to Gov Joseph Talcott, December 1, 1724, and Talcott to Dummer, December 22, 1724, in *Pioneers*, ed. Baxter, 359–64.

34. Sewall himself had been writing to the Connecticut governor (Samuel Sewall to Gurdon Saltonstall, January 15, 1721/2, and July 16, 1722, in Sewall, *Letter Book*, 2:139–42).

35. John Minot to Col. Stephen Minot, October 4, 1725, MAC, 52:294. For Stephen Minot, see Minot, *A Genealogical Record of the Minot Family*, 16–17. Compare Minot's arguments with Samuel Sewall to Gov. Gurdon Saltonstall, January 15, 1721/22 in Sewall, *Letter Book*, 2:140–42. In 1718 Sewall wrote to Stephen Minot as a "long and intimate Acquaintance" and stayed with him at Georgetown in 1717 (Sewall to Minot, February 28, 1717/8, in Sewall, *Letter Book*, 2:92–93). Proprietors Thomas Hutchinson and Adam Winthrop were also members of the SPG with Sewall, and Winthrop took over Sewall's duties as treasurer in 1724 (Sewall, *Diary*, 2: 970–71; *SHG*, 4:213).

36. Penhallow, *History*, 128.

37. Penhallow, *History*, 2.

38. Dummer, *Defence*, 12–13.

39. Dummer, *Defence*, 9.

40. See *HJ*, 6:217–18, for the list of council members in 1725. For Muscongus membership, see Lincolnshire Company Records, 14–24, MHS.

41. Boston Meeting, Massachusetts Governor's Council and Penobscots, July 28–August 2, 1725, in *NET*, 276–77.

42. *NET*, 278.

43. *NET*, 277.

44. *NYCD*, 9:955.

45. Boston Conference with the Wabanakis, November 11–December 2, 1725, in *NET*, 282–83.

46. The clerk recorded Saugaaram's's name first when listing the delegates, and Saugaaram affixed his mark first when the Indians signed the treaty draft, indicating he led the four-man delegation that also included Arexis, Francois Xavier, and Weguanumba (*NET*, 283; Boston Treaty with Wabanakis, December 15, 1725, in *NET*, 294).

47. For variety of spellings, see *DCB*, vol. 3, s.v. "Sauguaaram," by Kenneth M. Morrison; for meaning, see MacDougall, *Penobscot Dance*, 83, 85.

48. *Conference* [1726], 3; *Conference* [1727], 4. Loron's statements indicate that his Catholicism probably went beyond mere baptism. He told Dummer his people kept the Sabbath (*Conference* [1726], 6) and told Governor Jonathan Belcher the French priests "show us the way to heaven," (Indian Conference, August 25, 1740, in *DHSM*, 23:207–8).

49. Falmouth-Casco Conference, July 10–August 11, 1726, in *NET*, 309. For evidence of a "Laurent" living at Pentagoet in 1708, see Pierre La Chasse, Manuscript Census of Acadia, 1708, Ayer Ms 751, pp. 34–35, Newberry Library.

50. Loron first appeared in the records at a conference held in October 1720 as "Capt. Looraw," an Anglophone pronunciation of his name (Georgetown Meeting, October 12, 1720, in *NET*, 198). For Wabanaki leadership qualities, see Morrison, "Dawnland Decisions," 47, 54, 58–65.

51. *Conference* [1742], 14.

52. St. Georges Conference, August 19–24, 1751, in *NET*; for "Gun-powder," 672; for "manured," 673.

53. For oratory and ritual knowledge, see Calloway, *Pen and Ink Witchcraft*, 17–18. Wenongonet led the Penobscots after Madockawando's departure until his death in 1724. His successor, Wenemouet, led the Penobscots until his death in 1730, although he assumed his predecessor's name in 1726. Edewakenk was the last man mentioned as chief of all the Penobscots before 1763, with Massachusetts governors mentioning him until 1742. During the subsequent turmoil of the 1740s and 1750s, the Penobscots do not appear to have coalesced around a single leader (MacDougall, *Penobscot Dance*, 75–76, 82–84). MacDougall claims Loron succeeded Wenemouet, but no records indicate this was in fact the case (*DCB*, vol. 2, s.v. "Wenemouet," by Frank T. Siebert Jr.). For Edewakenk as chief, see *Conference* [1732], 1 (Loron is listed as "one of his Chief Captains"); and *Conference* [1742], 3.

54. *DCB*, vol. 2, "Wenemouet," by Frank T. Siebert Jr. For illness, see *Conference*, [1726], 8, also in *NET*, 302. The name "Wenemouet" meant "weak war chief" (MacDougall, *Penobscot Dance*, 82).

55. *Conference,* [1726], 3.

56. Boston Conference with the Wabanakis, November 11, December 2, 1725, in *NET,* 282; Ghere, "Abenaki Factionalism," 50–52.

57. For Pejepscot Proprietors, see Ephraim Savage Indenture to the Pejepscot Proprietors, November 5, 1714, PPP, MeHS, vol. 7, box 5, folder 7, pp. 351–60; for Muscongus Company, see Lincolnshire Company Records, bound volume, pp. 14–20, MHS. Winthrop also held shares in the Pemaquid Proprietors by the time they began attempts to colonize their claim (Meeting of Pemaquid Proprietors on August 31, 1743, Pemaquid Proprietors Book of Records, 1:1, AAS).

58. For the Pejepscot copy, see Report of the Committee of Council, November 17, 1725, PPP, MeHS, vol. 4, box 2, folder 16, pp. 325–28. For the official copy, see MAC, 6:5–11, discussion of Muscongus and Pejepscot Patents on pages 5 and 8.

59. MAC, 6:6–7.

60. MAC, 6:8.

61. MAC, 6:11.

62. The first few days centered on establishing responsibility for a Canadian Wabanaki raid, and Massachusetts reading proposed terms of Native political "submission," although, as Loron's later testimony indicates, the record of those terms appears heavily doctored, as it records no Indian response, while all previous and future stated claims of Wabanaki submission met with vehement protest, indicating the terms were never actually read to the Indians, or at least not translated as such (Boston Conference with the Wabanakis, November 11–December 2, 1725, in *NET,* 284–86).

63. *NET,* 286.

64. *NET,* 286.

65. *NET,* 286.

66. *NET,* 287.

67. *NET,* 287.

68. *NET,* 288.

69. *NET,* 288.

70. *NET,* 288.

71. *NET,* 289.

72. *NET,* 289.

73. July 15, 1725, John Penhallow Diary, MHS.

74. *NET,* 289.

75. *NET,* 289.

76. *NET,* 290.

77. *NET,* 290.

78. Draft Treaty for Boston Conference [November 1725], in *NET,* 291–92.

79. Boston Treaty with Wabanakis, December 15, 1725, in *NET,* 293.

80. Boston Treaty with Wabanakis, December 15, 1725, in *NET,* 292.

81. Boston Treaty with Wabanakis, December 15, 1725, in *NET,* 293.

82. Loron and Lauverjat to Lt. Gov. Dummer, January 28, 1726 (N.S.), MAC, 29:250–51.

83. For claims of authority, see Boston Conference with Wabanakis, in *NET,* 282–84, 288.

84. Calloway, *Pen and Ink Witchcraft,* 17–18, 23; David Ghere, "Mistranslations and Misinformation," 4–5.

85. *NET*, 288.

86. David Ghere argues this was the case in "Mistranslations and Misinformation," 7 and passim.

87. December 22, 1725, in *HJ*, 6:431–32.

88. *DHSM*, 10:354.

89. Bilodeau, "Economy of War," 397–98; *DCB*, vol. 3, s.v. "Lauverjat, Étienne," by Thomas-M. Charland; Lord, Sexton, and Harrington, *History of the Archdiocese of Boston*, 1:135–36; Zoltvany, *Vaudreuil*, 167. For Lauverjat's encouragement of the confrontational faction, see R. P. Lauverjeat [Lauverjat] to Monsieur le Marquis de Vaudreuil, August 27, 1727; and R. P. Lauverjat to R. P. de La Chasse, July 8, 1728, in *CMNF*, 3:136, 143–44.

90. Edmund Mountfort to Lt. Gov. Dummer, February 18, 1725/6, in *DHSM*, 10:239–40.

91. John Gyles to Lt. Gov. Dummer, April 8, 1727, MAC, 52:347. True to form, Gyles's addendum to the message blamed the Jesuits for this acquired mistrust. By this time Wenemouet had taken the name Wenongonet (Gyles spelled it as "Wenogge-nett" and "Wenengenit" at various times), in honor of one of his predecessors. For notice of the change, see Wenengenit to Lt. Gov. Dummer, October 4, 1726, in *DHSM*, 23:365–66. See also *DCB*, vol. 2, s.v. "Wenemouet," by Frank T. Siebert Jr.

92. For those hopes verbalized, see *Conference* [1726], 6.

93. *Conference* [1726], 1–8; for Wenemouet's illness, 8.

94. *Conference* [1726] 6, 15, for Wainwright as clerk.

95. *Conference* [1726], 9.

96. *Conference* [1726], 9.

97. *Conference* [1726], 9.

98. *Conference* [1726], 9.

99. *Conference* [1726], 10. Thanks to Bruce Bourque for helping clarify Madocka-wando's eastward origins.

100. Morrison, *Embattled Northeast*, 130–31.

101. *Conference* [1726], 10. Ghere ("Mistranslations," 8) interprets this as a sign that the Penobscots were unaware of Massachusetts's other, more expansive claims. While this is possible, I argue that, with regard to the St. Georges region, the Penobscots never acknowledged the Madockawando sale, and so the issue at hand was the land occupied by the two blockhouses the Muscongus Company had built there, making that land the "small Tract" disputed, which they tried to minimize for the sake of peace.

102. *Conference* [1726], 11; Seventeenth-Century Wabanaki to English Deeds Shown at the Casco Conference, in *NET*, 314–16, quotations on 315.

103. *NET*, 316.

104. *NET*, 316.

105. *Conference* [1726], 12.

106. *Conference* [1726], 12.

107. *Conference* [1726], 13.

108. *Conference* [1726], 13.

109. *NET*, 307–13.

110. John Gyles to Lt. Gov. Dummer, March 27 and April 8, 1727, MAC, 52:339, 345–47; Joseph Heath to Dummer, April 13, 1727, MAC 52:351; Gyles to Dummer,

228 / NOTES TO PAGES 98-100

April 28, 1727, MAC, 52:362-63; Memoire du Roi Aux Siurs Marquis de Beauharnois et Dupuy, April 29, 1727, in *CMNF*, 3:130-31; Abstract of Dispatches from Canada, with the Minister's recommendation, approved by the King, March 17, 1728, in *NYCD*, 9:990-91.

111. John Gyles Memorial, St. Georges River, February 27, 1726/7, and March 3, 1726/7, MAC, 52:329-30; Gyles to Dummer, April 25, 1727, MAC, 52:358-60.

112. Loron qtd. in Gyles to Dummer, May 4, 1727, MAC, 52:364. For Penobscot peacekeeping efforts, see also Gyles to Dummer, May 19, 1727, and May 26-27, 1727, MAC, 52:376, 375.

113. Lauverjat complained about the efforts by Joseph and Barenos Saint-Castin on behalf of the peace faction in Penawabskik and accused them of only tepid support for the war effort from the start (R. P. Lauverjat to R. P. de La Chasse, July 8, 1728, in *CMNF*, 3:143-44).

114. For reports on Wabanaki factions in Canada, see Heath to Dummer, June 12, 1727, MAC, 52:584; Gyles to Dummer, June 22, 1727, MAC, 52:388a.

115. At the beginning of the conference, the Penobscots asked for Jordan to "Interpret to us, because we understand him plainest, and the other two [Gyles and Bean] will stand by (*Conference* [1727], 5; for interpretation, *Conference* [1727], 13-14).

116. *Conference* [1727], 13-14.

117. Ghere, "Mistranslations," 9.

118. *DCB*, vol. 2, s.v. "Wenemouet," by Frank T. Siebert Jr.; "A Memorial to the Honoured Wm. Dummar Esqr. Etc of a Confurance held at St. Georges River by Gyles and Chiefs of Panobcut and auther tribes and Jesuitt," June 27, 1727, in *NET*, 348.

119. "Confurance," in *NET*, 348. Gyles's suspicion is doubly revealing, considering his own activities.

120. "Confurance," in *NET*, 348. Captain Thomas Smith, future truckmaster at Saco, helped Gyles read the treaty, written in "an unknown hand." Perhaps Smith also helped Gyles craft an interpretation that would satisfy the Indians as well.

121. For ongoing French hopes for war, see Memoire du Roi Aux Siurs Marquis de Beauharnois et Dupuy, April 29, 1727, in *CMNF*, 3:130-31; Zoltvany, *Vaudreuil*, 200-201.

122. "Confurance," in *NET*, 349.

123. *Conference* [1727], 7, 21. The Pigwackets, at least, may have been present in the St. Francis (the British called them "Arresaguntacooks") delegation, including "Suzack, Son of Beawando (Aidewando/Atecuando) and Saaroom (*DCB*, vol. 2, s.v. "Atecouando [fl. 1710-26]," by Gordon M. Day; Brian D. Carroll, "'Savages' in the Service of Empire: Native American Soldiers in Gorham's Rangers, 1744-1762," *NEQ* 85 [September 2012]: 395n19).

124. *Conference* [1727], 7-12, quotation on 9.

125. *Conference* [1727], 12.

126. *Conference* [1727], 12-13.

127. *Conference*, [1727], 28-29.

128. Hutchinson, *History of Massachusetts*, 2:241.

129. Hutchinson specifically referred to the province's erection of regulated truck houses on the frontier in response to Wabanaki requests, neglecting the issue of lands. Nevertheless, his straightforward assessment that Massachusetts had broken its pledges before 1727 was accurate (*History of Massachusetts*, 2:241).

130. For the later Kennebec statements indicating their views on the treaties, see St. Georges Conference and Related Documents, September 20-29, 1753, in *NET*, 719-20. For Penobscot views on the legality of conquest, see their statements printed in Samuel Waldo, *A Defence of the Title*, 12.

131. Parker, "Early Modern Europe," in *The Laws of War*, ed. Howard, Andeopoulos, and Shulman, 40-58.

132. *Conference* [1727], 9.

133. Abstract of Dispatches from Canada, March 17, 1728, in *NYCD*, 9:993.

134. David Ghere in particular. For his allegations of Massachusetts deception, see "Mistranslations and Misinformation," 7 and passim.

135. David L. Ghere and Alvin H. Morrison point out this distinction but do not investigate why Massachusetts officials did this in "Searching for Justice on the Maine Frontier," 382.

136. For full bill, see August 8, 1736, in Governor's Council Executive Records, GC3 327 #5, vol. 10, pp. 47-48, MSA; Governor Belcher to Duke of Newcastle, August 5, 1736, in *CSP*, vol. 42, doc. 375.

137. Traite de Paix entre les Anglois et les Abenakis, 1727, in *CMNF*, 3:134-35. Alexandre le Borgne De Belisle, husband of Anastasie D'Abbadie Saint-Castin, daughter of the elder Baron Saint-Castin and Pidianske, also signed the document.

138. R. P. Lauverjat to R. P. de La Chasse, July 8, 1728, in *CMNF*, 3:143-44.

139. Indian Explanation of the Treaty of Casco Bay, in *NYCD*, 9:966-67.

140. Kenneth Morrison goes even further, implying Loron spoke for the Wabanakis as a whole in this letter (Morrison, *Embattled Northeast*, 190). Herald Prins depicts Loron delivering this statement at the treaty signing in 1727 near Falmouth but includes no evidence in "The Crooked Path of Dummer's Treaty," 373-74. This unusual letter has bedeviled other careful scholars besides Prins. Daniel Mandell's annotated anthology of northeastern Indian treaties is the current gold standard. Mandell places the document in 1727, labeling it the "Penobscot View of Boston and Casco Conferences," and tracing its origins in E. B. O'Callaghan's well known nineteenth-century documentary collection (cited in the above note). But Mandell places the document *before* the 1727 Falmouth ratification in his collection (*NET*, 316-18).

141. *Conference* [1726], 3.

142. *George Town* [1717], 6-7.

143. For the full sequence of events from the French perspective, see Memoire des Sieurs Beauharnois et Hocquart au Roi, October 13, 1735; Memoire du Roy aux Sieurs de Beauharnois et Hocquart, May 15, 1736; Memoire du Roy aux Sieurs de Beauharnois et Rocquart, May 10, 1737; Memoire du Roy aux Sieurs de Beauharnois et Hocquart, May 15, 1738, in *CMNF*, 3: 173-74, 178, 182, 184. These events are discussed more fully in chapter 5.

144. See Abstract of Dispatches from Canada, with the Minister's recommendation, approved by the King, March 17, 1728, in *NYCD*, 990-95.

145. Scholars of the Jesuits took early notice of British deception. See, for example, Lord, Sexton, and Harrington, *History of the Archdiocese of Boston*, 1:137. David Ghere argues Loron's letter, and the Lauverjat/Castin statement, together reveal the true Penobscot version of events, in "Mistranslations and Misinformation," 8-10. Ghere mistakenly argues that many Penobscot leaders signed the Lauverjat/Castin letter. He insists that the "excluseive use of Gyles or Bean at every subsequent

conference from 1727 to 1752" requires a critical reading of all statements but does not extend this scrutiny to French translations. For Ghere's criticism of Gyles and the other translators, see "Mistranslations and Misinformation," 7; Ghere, "Abenaki Factionalism," 174n20; and Ghere and Morrision, "Searching for Justice," 381–83. Morrison shares Ghere's assessment of the British translators and points to growing Wabanaki wariness about French motives but never questions Lauverjat's translations in *Embattled Northeast*, 188–90. Christopher Bilodeau, in contrast, points out the prominent role Lauverjat played and argues "had there been widespread differences in the treaties, no doubt more Indians would have complained," in "Economy of War," 397–98.

146. Boston Conference with Penobscots and Norridgewocks, December 9, 1727–January 3, 1728, in *NET*, 373–81. The conference concerned the prices of trade goods and continuing violence around Nova Scotia involving the Mi'kmaqs.

147. *Conference*, [1726]; *Conference*, [1727]; quotation in 1726 treaty, 13.

148. *Conference* [1726], 14–15, 22.

149. November 18, 1717, in *HJ*, 1:251. Massachusetts was not the first colony to publish Indian treaties for public consumption. New York published *An Account of the Treaty between His Excellency Benjamin Fletcher Captain General and Governour in the Province of New York, etc. and the Indians of the Five Nations* in 1694.

150. *George Town* [1717], cover.

151. *Conference* [1726], 23.

152. *Conference with the Eastern Indians* . . . [1726], this copy in KPP, box 13, folder 3, MeHS. On the first page is written "Belcher Noyes 1752/Josiah Little." Little's name is written in a different hand, in darker ink, indicating he acquired the treaty later. For Noyes's assumption of the role of company clerk from Winthrop, see his notation on the back of a copy of a 1687 John Parker sale of land to Silvanus Davis in PPP, MeHS, vol. 7, box 5, folder 13, p. 465a.

153. *Conference* [1727], KPP, box 14, folder 2. Henry Gibbs wrote his name—now faded—on the first page. Josiah Little's name is in newer, bolder ink lower on the page.

154. See, for example, *A Conference of His Excellency Jonathan Belcher with . . . Indian Tribes at Falmouth in Casco Bay, July 1732*, KPP, box 13, folder 3. This copy has Josiah Little's name written on the first page.

155. Nathan Dane Papers, box 6, folder 4, Book No. 1 "General Statement of the Title and Posession of the Kennebec Proprietors of the Kenebec Purchase, from the Late Colony of New Plymouth[,] Nathan Dane." p. 16, MHS.

156. Deposition of John Gyles, June 7, 1754, PPP, MeHS, vol. 10, box 6, folder 2, pp. 4–5.

157. Testimony of Mary Varney, June 5, 1795, Sheepscot Manuscripts, vol. 2, p. 92b, MeSL.

158. Belcher Noyes to Enoch Freeman, November 12, 1763, PPP, MeHS, vol. 5, box 3, folder 4, p. 77.

159. Deed of Warumbee, Darunkin, and other Indians to Richard Wharton [copy] July 7 1684, PPP, PEM, series 1, box 1, fol. 1; see also PPP, MeHS, vol. 1, box 1, p. 15.

160. Pejepscot Proprietors Answer to North Yarmouth Petition to the General Court, July 1741, [draft by Adam Winthrop], PPP, MeHS, vol. 6, box 4, folder 12, pp. 352–53.

161. *Conference with the Eastern Indians . . .* [1726], KPP, box 13, folder 3. Noyes highlighted passages on pages 6, 7, 9, 10, 11, 12, and 13. Quotation on p. 12, which, along with p. 13, emphasizes equal treatment for the Wabanakis and colonists.

162. *Conference* [1727], KPP, box 14, folder 2, pp. 9, 12.

163. "Extract from the Conference Held at Falmouth 1754," PPP, PEM, series I, box 1, folder 2, Documents Relating to Title, 1714–1796.

164. Williamson, *History of the State of Maine,* 2:151. Williamson estimates about two hundred killed and captured, with about one-third of the total made prisoner.

165. Cotton Mather tallied the costs in human and financial costs of the fighting in *Observable Things* and *Duodecennium Luctuosum.*

166. Nicolar, *Life and Traditions of the Red Man,* 138–39; Speck, "Eastern Algonkian Wabanaki Confederacy," 497–99, 505–6, quotation on 499.

167. Wicken, *Mi'kmaq Treaties on Trial,* 29, 55, 61–64, 90, 110–27; Plank, *Unsettled Conquest,* 79–81; Lennox, *Homelands and Empires,* 47–48, 85–89.

168. In the only systematic study of Wabanaki demographics in the years following 1725, David Ghere argues postwar Wabanaki warrior counts explode myths of large-scale Indian casualties during Dummer's War (Ghere, "Myths and Methods," 528). For 1725 as a decisive year, see also Baker and Reid, "Amerindian Power in the Early Modern Northeast," 104.

5 / In Defiance of the Proprietors, 1727–1735

1. Smith, *Smith Journals,* ed. Willis, 46.

2. Willis, *History of Portland,* 332.

3. Smith, *Smith Journals,* ed. Willis, 49.

4. Willis, *Smith Journals,* 7–11, 49, 53, 67n2, for Smith's land purchase. Falmouth Town Records, 1:120, 124, MeSA.

5. March 26, 1728, Falmouth Town Records, 1:214, MeSA; Smith, *Smith Journals,* ed. Willis, 67.

6. Smith, *Smith Journals,* ed. Willis, 68.

7. Inhabitants of North Yarmouth to the Committee in Boston, April 17, 1731, in NYMP, 1:116.

8. Scarborough Town Records, March 9, 1729/30, 1:80, July 10, 1732, 1:88, MeHS.

9. Brunswick Town Records, October 16, 1744, p. 21, MeSA.

10. Baker, *Clarke & Lake Company,* 81–82nn21 and 29.

11. Sheepscot chain of title in Sheepscot Manuscripts, Memorial by Samuel Wittemore, 3:168; meetings and further activity around 1738 in Sheepscot Manuscripts, 2:72a, 2:77a–d, 3:148a, 3:152a, all in MeSL.

12. Job Averell to Samuel Whittemore August 8, 1739, Sheepscot Manuscripts, 1:37a; Deposition of Patrick Rogers, October 3, 1768, Sheepscot Manuscripts, 4:199a–b, all in MeSL.

13. Chase, *Wiscasset in Pownalborough,* 38–41.

14. Chushman, *A History of Ancient Sheepscot and Newcastle,* 101–2, 113; Meeting of Pemaquid Proprietors, August 31, 1743, Pemaquid Proprietors Book of Records No. 1, 1:1, AAS.

15. Williamson, *History of Maine,* 2:165–67.

16. David Dunbar Deed to David Cargill, May 10, 1732, box III–1 folder 1, Pownalborough Courthouse Collection, MeHS.

17. *DHSM*, 10:445–47, quotation on p. 447. For ongoing Penobscot suspicion, see *CSP*, vol. 37, doc 533.

18. Dunbar to Lt. Gov. William Dummer, December 4, 1729, in *DHSM*, 10:452–53.

19. *CSP*, vol. 36, doc. 1045; Colonel Dunbar to Mr. Secretary Popple, December 10, 1729 in *DHSM*, 10:455.

20. See, for example, *A Memorial, Humbly Shewing, the Past and Present State of the Land . . . in New England in America*; and Moody, "Three Documents Concerning a Proposal to Establish a Province of Georgia in New England."

21. Williamson, *History of Maine*, 2:172.

22. For Belcher's dislike of the Irish, see Richard Waldron Papers, Belcher to Richard Waldron, June 2, 1735, box 1, vol. 2, p. 125; and Belcher to Richard Waldron, August 18, 1735, box 1, vol. 2, p. 177, NHHS; Belcher to Richard Waldron, November 14, 1739; and Belcher to Messrs. Partridge and [Andrew] Belcher, December 24, 1739, both in BL, reel 6, MHS.

23. Belcher to William Sharp, October 29, 1731; Belcher to Richard Waldron, November 29, 1731; Belcher to Richard Waldron, November 20, 1732, all in BL, reel 2, MHS.

24. Williamson, *History of Maine*, 2:169–72. Several of these companies did not yet keep official records, but their founders complained about Dunbar's colony. Joseph Roberts, Samuel Whittemore, and Samuel Loring claimed land along the Sheepscot River from Nathaniel Draper and in 1738 became the Sheepscot Proprietors (see Sheepscot Manuscripts, 3:148a for first meeting; 3:168, 173a for Draper claim explanation, all in MeSL). The Pemaquid Proprietors, holding under the Drowne Claim, had their first recorded meeting in 1743, but Shem Drowne was active in opposing Dunbar (Pemaquid Proprietors Book of Records, vol. 1, p. 1, Pemaquid Proprietors Papers, AAS).

25. *CSP*, vol. 37, docs. 528 and 528.

26. *CSP*, 37, vol. doc. 533.

27. Samuel Waldo to Thomas Paine, December 22, 1729, in *Saltonstall Papers*, ed. Moody, 1:366; Samuel Waldo to Elisha Cooke, March 3, 1729/30, in *Saltonstall Papers*, ed. Moody, 1:367–68; Williamson, "Brigadier General Samuel Waldo," 80–81.

28. Copy of Adam Winthrop Petition "To the Right Honorable the Lords Commissioners for Trade and Plantations," Pejepscot Proprietors Papers, series 1, box 1, folder 2, PEM.

29. P. Yorke and C. Talbot, August 11, 1731, in *DHSM* 11:118.

30. Quotations from Thomas Coram to Lords Commissioners for Trade and Plantations, November 28, 1729, in *DHSM*, 10:436–37; James Alford's Affidavit, January 28, 1731, in *DHSM*, 11:105–6.

31. P. Yorke and C. Talbot, August 11, 1731, in *DHSM*, 11:124, 128. For the full debate and hearing, see *DHSM*, 11:97–134.

32. HKM, vol. 40, item 81, Declaration of John Campbell, February 26, 1746/7.

33. See the following in HKM, vol. 40: item 29, Petition of St. Georges Settlers to Samuel Waldo, April 12, 1738; item 79, Declaration of Thomas Henderson, February 18, 1746/7, item 80, Declaration of William Burns, February 26, 1746/7.

34. Dunbar to Secretary Popple in 1731, qtd. in Robert E. Moody, "The Maine Frontier," 330.

35. See, for example, September 20, 1727, Scarborough Proprietors Records, 18, MeHS.

36. Martin, *Profits in the Wilderness*, 283–87.

37. Scarborough Town Records, 1:80, 88, 91, MeHS.

38. NYMP, 1:115–17.

39. They referred to An Act for Regulating of Townships, Choice of Town Officers, and Setting Forth Their Power, November 16, 1692, in *Acts and Resolves*, 1:64–68.

40. Petition of the Ancient Proprietors of Falmouth, [n.d., but written in 1728], MAC, 6:487–88.

41. Petition to Gov. Belcher and the House of Representatives, Lewis Family Papers, box 2 folder 1, MeHS. Although unsigned, the petition is written in John Smith's poorly spelled style and refers to the holdings of both Powell and Smith in the first person. The letter was almost certainly written in response to the town complaint about the committee (NYMP, 1:123) received by the House on July 15, 1732.

42. November 11, 1731, Falmouth Proprietors Records, 1:11.

43. May 11, 1730, Falmouth Town Records, 1:432–35; "Copy of what was don at the Meeting of the antient proprietors of Falmouth May 20 1730," Falmouth Proprietors v. John East, January 1731/2, YCCPCF, box 44, file 13, vol. 9, p. 96. A notice posted by the New Proprietors on March 15, 1731, further indicates the shared interests of the town and New Proprietors. It advertised the formation of a proprietors' committee formed to sell common lands "to defray the charges of the town" (Andrew Hawes Papers, box 2, folder 10).

44. "A Legal [Old] Proprietors Meeting," May 6, 1731, Falmouth Proprietors v. John East, January 1731/2, YCCPCF, box 44, file 13, vol. 9, p. 96.

45. "Copy of what was don at the Meeting of the antient proprietors of Falmouth May 20, 1730," Falmouth Proprietors v. John East, January 1731/2, YCCPCF, box 44, file 13, vol. 9, p. 96; Falmouth Proprietors Records, 3 vols., May 13, 1730, 1:2, and October 29, 1730, 1:4, MeSA.

46. Scarborough Proprietors Records, September 20, 1739, 30–31, MeHS.

47. The Scarborough Proprietors, aware of the dubious legality of their meetings, did not keep complete records of early 1720s proceedings. However, Boston merchant Timothy Prout provided a detailed, if hostile, description of several meetings in a later complaint to the Governor and General Court (Timothy Prout of Scarborough, Petition to Gov. Spencer Phips and the General Court, May 27, 1752, William Southgate Collection, folder 5, MeHS).

48. June 22, 1720, Scarborough Proprietors Records, 16, for residency requirements, see September 20, 1727, Scarborough Proprietors Records, 18, MeHS. Although their records did not detail the Proprietors' methods for voting—as it was illegal—Timothy Prout and other dissenters lodged frequent protests over the practice (Scarborough Town Records, July 1, 1732, 1: 89, MeHS; July 26, 1750. in Scarborough Proprietors' Record Book, Libby Family Papers, box 4 vol. 1, p. 37, MeHS; August 13, 1750, Scarborough Proprietors Records, p. 186, MeHS).

49. Garrisons listed in Petition to Lt. Gov. William Dummer by William Scales and Peter Weare on behalf of the "Inhabitants and Proprietors of North Yarmouth," April 4 1723, North Yarmouth Proprietors Records, 1:34.

50. North Yarmouth Proprietors Records, 1:18, MeHS.

51. North Yarmouth Proprietors Records, 1:26–36, MeHS.

52. Petition to the Committee for the Resettlement of North Yarmouth, January 10 1728/9, NYMP, 1:78. For list of tenants, see NYMP, 1:62.

53. Petition of the Proprietors residing in North Yarmouth, May 28, 1729, NYMP, 1:81.

54. Copy, Petition of Nonresident Proprietors to Governor Jonathan Belcher, January 15 1731, NYMP, 1:112.

55. Agents of Falmouth Answer to the Petition of the Ancient Proprietors, September 1730, MAC, 6:498–99.

56. Petition to Governor and General Court on Behalf of North Yarmouth, May 28, 1740, MAC, 303:32; see also Petition on behalf of North Yarmouth. . . . , March 26, 1741, MAC, 114:650–52.

57. Timothy Prout to the Gentlemen of the Plimouth Company, December 7, 1754, Kennebeck Purchase Company Records, Manuscripts and Archives Division, NYPL.

58. Allen and Moody, eds., *Province and Court Records of Maine,* 5:65–66.

59. Inhabitants of North Yarmouth to the Committee in Boston, April 17, 1731, NYMP, 1:115.

60. Petition of the Ancient Proprietors of Falmouth, [n.d., but written in 1728], MAC, 6:487–88.

61. Petition of the Resident Proprietors of Falmouth, June 28, 1728, MAC, 6:486.

62. July 10, 1732, Scarborough Town Records, 1:89, MeHS.

63. Copy of a notice sent from Boston, September 9, 1729, Scarborough Town Records, 1:77, MeHS.

64. An Act Directing How Meetings of Proprietors of Lands Lying in Common May Be Called, March 25, 1713, in *Acts and Resolves,* 1:704.

65. Timothy Prout of Scarborough, Memorial to Gov. Spencer Phips and the General Court, May 27, 1752, William S. Southgate Collection, folder 5, MeHS.

66. Samuel Libby copy of Scarborough Proprietors' Book, Libby Family Papers, box 4, vol. 1, p. 37. As proprietors clerk, Libby copied Prout's dissent, entered after a meeting held on July 26, 1750. The dissent is written in Prout's style, but the signature and bottom of the complaint is cut off. This is possibly a copy of a separate piece of paper attached to the original book (which Libby had made a copy of, after a vote directing him to do so on February 13, 1753—see Scarborough Proprietors' Records, MeHS, 205).

67. Colley, *Britons: Forging the Nation,* chap. 2.

68. Christopher Toppan to Lt. Gov. Dummer, January 13, 1726/7, MAC, 52:328.

69. Petition of the Ancient Proprietors of Falmouth [n.d., but 1728], MAC, 6:487.

70. See Charles T. Libby, *The Libby Family in America. 1602–1881* (Portland, ME: B. Thurston & Co., 1882), 22–23. For the descent of Prout's claim from the Cammock Patent, see the evidence presented in Prout v. Fly, YCCPCF, October 1728, box 32, file 26, vol. 8, p. 51.

71. Willis, *Smith Journals,* 49.

72. Petition of the Ancient Proprietors of Falmouth [n.d., but 1728], MAC, 6:488.

73. Petition of Nonresident Proprietors to Jonathan Belcher January 15, 1731, NYMP, 1:112.

74. For an overview of the practice of law in Maine, see Allen, "Law and Authority to the Eastward," 273–312.

75. All quotations taken from Petition of Moses Pearson September 1753, MAC, 43:744–45. Corroborating testimony in Declaration of Fergus Hagens, November 26,

1753, MAC, 43:747; and Andrew Fanueil Phillips Deposition, December 19, 1753, MAC, 8: 283. See also Declaration of Samuel Small Jr., November 26, 1753, MAC, 43:747.

76. Enoch Greenleaf to the Judges of the Superior Court, May 3 1722, in *Saltonstall Papers*, ed. Moody, 1:346.

77. Quotation from Timothy Prout Petition to Lt. Gov. Spencer Phips and the General Court, May 27, 1752, MAC, 43:535; see also Petition of Timothy Prout, read in Gen. Court, November 22 1752, MAC, 46:273–74; and Timothy Prout Petition Copy, May 27, 1752, William Southgate Papers, folder 5, MeHS.

78. The Answer of Daniel Fogg and Samuel Libbee to the Petition of Timothy Prout, November 22, 1752, MAC, 43:538.

79. Timothy Prout to the Gentlemen of the Plimouth Company, December 7, 1754, Kennebec Company Purchase Records, Manuscripts and Archives Division, NYPL.

80. Timothy Prout to the Gentlemen of the Plimouth Company, December 7, 1754, Kennebec Company Purchase Records, Manuscripts and Archives Division, NYPL.

81. Sir Ferdinando Gorges to George Cleeve and Richard Tucker, January 12, 1636, in Joseph Moody et al. v. Joseph Bayley and Phillip Hodgkins, October 1729, YCCPCF, box 36, file 2, vol. 8, p. 94.

82. See depositions of John Lane and Josiah Walters, August 25, 1727, Deposition of Moses Felt, March 29, 1728, and Deposition of Benjamin Gallop, March 22, 1728/9, all in Joseph Moody et al. v. Joseph Bayley and Phillip Hodgkins, October 1729, YCCPCF, box 36, file 2, vol. 8, p. 94.

83. Bayley and Hodgkins successfully appealed in May 1730 but then lost in a final judgment in May 1731 (see Bayley et al. v. Moody et al., May 1730, SCJRB, reel 4, folio 313; Moody et al. v. Bayley et al., May 1731, SCJRB, folio 102–3).

84. Quotation from Proprietors of Falmouth v. John East, January 1731/2, YCCPRB, vol. 9, p. 97. Evidence in YCCPCF, Falmouth Proprietors v. John East, January 1731/2, YCCPCF, box 44, file 13, vol. 9, p. 96.

85. For Prout's suspicions, see Timothy Prout Petition to Lt. Gov. Spencer Phips and the General Court, May 27, 1752, MAC, 43:535; Timothy Prout to Gentlemen of the Plimoth Company, December 17, 1754, Kennebeck Purchase Company Records, Manuscript and Archives Division, NYPL. Prout v. Fly, October, 1728, YCCPCF, box 32, file 26, vol. 8, p. 51. Other case is Prout v. Grafton, October 1728, YCCPCF, box 32, file 27, vol. 8, p. 51. The cases defy easy explanation, however. In Prout v. Fly, Prout managed to produce not only deeds but a witness—Hannah Halum—challenging Fly's claim to uninterrupted possession. Prout also bested Grafton, who claimed title under the Scarborough Proprietors that had excluded Prout, Grafton won an appeal and the case went all the way to the Superior Court before Prout prevailed (see Grafton v. Prout, SCJRB, May 1730–1731, folio 103).

86. See Prout v. Harmon, January 1735/6, YCCPCF, box 61, file 17, vol. 10, p. 296; Prout v. Harmon, July 1737, YCCPCF, box 68, file 5, vol. 11, p. 7; Prout v. Harmon, June 1741, SCJRB, reel 7, folio 109; Prout v. Trickey, July 1740, YCCPCF, box 84, file 3, vol. 12, p. 210; Prout v. Trickey, June 1741, SCJRB, reel 7, folio 109; Prout v. James Libby, October 1748, YCCPCF box 105, file 15, vol. 13, p. 299; Prout v. John Libby et al., October 1748, YCCPCF, box 105, file 16, vol. 13, p. 301; Prout v. Samuel Libby et al., June 1750, SCJRB, reel 8, folio 17–18; Prout v. Misservy, June 1750, SCJRB, reel 8, folio 18. For mutual accusations of bad blood and malfeasance between Prout and his neighbors, the extensive Libby family and their allies, see the series of petitions and

evidence stemming from a 1752 hung jury in Prout v. Libby in a 1752 Superior Court case, MAC, 43:534–39; 46: 273–74, 276–77, 296–99, 301, 305.

87. For Alger heirs, see Sybil Noyes, Charles Thornton Libby, and Walter Goodwin, eds., *Genealogical Dictionary of Maine and New Hampshire* (Baltimore: Genealogical Publishing Co., 1972), s.v. "Andrew Alger" and "John Milliken," 61, 481. For the sale, see Declaration of Jane the Indian of Scarborough, September 19, 1659, in Milliken v. Fabins et al., April 1736, YCCPCF, box 61, file 37, vol. 10, p. 306. For the Millikens losing cases against grantees from the Scarborough Proprietors, see, for example, Milliken v. Haines, April 1736, YCCPCF, box 61, file 38, vol. 10, p. 307; Milliken v. Haines, June 1737, Supreme Court of Judicature Suffolk Files, reel 5, folio 96; Milliken v. Haines, June 1741, MSA, SCJRB reel 7, folio 100; Milliken et al. v. Haines and Scammon, February 1736/7, YCCPCF, box 65, file 24, vol. 10, p. 431. A York County jury also found in favor of the Millikens' neighbors holding land from the Scarborough Proprietors in Milliken et al. v. Roberts, February 1736/7, box 65, file 23, vol. 10, p. 430, but this was reversed in the Superior Court (see Milliken et al. v. Roberts, June 1737, SCJRB, reel 5, folio 96).

88. Milliken et al. v. Jewett et al., May 1731, SCJRB, folio 104; Milliken v. Roberts, June 1737, SCJ reel 5, folio 96. Writing about various Maine land titles in 1795, James Sullivan noted of the Alger claim, "The Courts always adjudged the title to be good" (Sullivan, *History of the District of Maine*, 151).

89. Zuckerman: *Peaceable Kingdoms*; Fischer, *Albion's Seed*, 189–96.

90. August 16, 1739, in North Yarmouth Town Records, 1:75–76, MeHS.

91. Cook, *The Fathers of the Towns*.

92. September 18, 1727, in Smith, *Smith Journal*, ed. Willis, 53. Among the "gentlemen" to whom Smith referred were John Powell, Job Lewis, and Edward Shove (although the town records indicate he was accepted on August 17) (see 1:120, 1:124 in Falmouth Town Records, MeSA).

93. March 24, 1730/1, Falmouth Town Records, 1:8, MeSA. For Moulton's life, see Burrage and Stubbs, *Genealogical and Family History of the State of Maine*, 1:413–14.

94. October 6, 1735, North Yarmouth Town Records, 1:24, MeHS.

95. See November 18, 1729, Falmouth Town Records, 1:344–46 and May 16, 1731, Falmouth Proprietors Records, 1:9, both MeSA.

96. See Falmouth Town Records, 1:335–37 (no specific date recorded but entered after March 28, 1729, and before September 13, 1729) for agreement; see November 14, 1729, 1:342 for his leadership of a town meeting to advance local interest, see August 17, 1727, 1:120, December 14, 1727, 1:151 for his earlier opposition to the town admitting new grantees, all in Falmouth Town Records, MeSA.

97. October 16, 1737, Scarborough Proprietors Records, 26, MeHS.

98. Willis, *Smith Journals*, 77.

99. September 22, 1732, Falmouth Proprietors Records, 1:14–17, MeHS.

100. December 11, 1734, Falmouth Proprietors Records, 1:30–31, MeHS. See also 1:33–40.

101. Smith, *Smith Journals*, ed. Willis, 77.

102. Petition to the Committee for the Resettlement of North Yarmouth, 10 January 1728/9, NYMP, 1:78.

103. For Falmouth, see Falmouth Proprietors Records, vol. 1, pp. 9, 15, 18, MeSA. For Scarborough, see Scarborough Town Records, vol. 1, p. 77, MeHS.

6 / The Rightful Owners Thereof, 1735–1741

1. See Waldo Petitions of July 5, 6, 26, and 27, 1736, in *DHSM*, 10:156–72; and Waldo, *A Defence of the Title*.

2. Affidavits of Thomas Gregg, Samuel Boggs, Andrew Momford, Henry Alexander, and Thomas Kilpatrick, May 13, 1738, in the "St. Georges Affidavit," HKM, vol. 40, item 11.

3. Affidavit of Samuel Boggs, May 13, 1738, HKM, vol. 40, item 11.

4. *CSP*, vol. 42, doc. 365 ii,

5. These events are discussed briefly in Bourque, *Twelve Thousand Years*, 196–97; Ghere, "Mistranslations and Misinformation," 12; and Batinski, *Jonathan Belcher*, 126. For more detailed analysis, see Saxine, "Performance of Peace."

6. Batinski, *Jonathan Belcher*, 8.

7. Batinski, *Jonathan Belcher*, 69–71; Jonathan Belcher to Col. John Stoddard, March 31, 1732, BL, reel 2; Belcher to Mr. Seicombe, February 25, 1737, BL, reel 5; Belcher to Mr. Seicombe, April 22, 1737, BL reel 5. For the failure of the missionaries Belcher sent, see Belcher to John Gyles, February 28, 1735, BL, reel 4; and Belcher to Mr. Dalrymple, July 30, 1737, BL, reel 5.

8. *SHG*, 4:437, 442.

9. Batinski, *Jonathan Belcher*, 71–2. See also Belcher to William Sharp, September 19, 1732, BL, reel 2.

10. Belcher to Reverend Christopher Toppan, August 14, 1732, BL, reel 2.

11. Vaughn, "From White Man to Redskin."

12. Belcher to Lord Edgemont, August 1, 1737, BL, reel 5; Kawashima, *Puritan Justice and the Indian*.

13. Belcher to Col. William Blakeney, September 15, 1740, BL, reel 6.

14. Bourque, *Twelve Thousand Years*, 196.

15. For complaints, see Belcher to Col. Thomas Westbrook [from Sec. Willard, draft], September 7, 1736, MAC, 52:542; and Conference with Polin & Indians of Presumpscot, August 10 and 13 1739, in *DHSM*, 23:257–62.

16. Belcher to John Gyles, October 23, 1736, BL, reel 5.

17. Morrison, *Embattled Northeast*, 28–32.

18. Belcher to Capt. Thomas Smith, October 30, 1734, BL, reel 4. A captain's commission was worth £10 per year, and a lieutenancy £6, "to continue seven years."

19. See, for example, the John Minot Ledger, 1731–1736, [Fort Richmond], and John Minot Account Book for Fort Richmond, both in the Pejepscot Historical Society, Brunswick, Maine. Fort Richmond was the truck house for the Kennebecs. Entries in the Ledger on pages 52–53 and 56 list "Premegan an Indian on Allowance," "Pepeguoant an Indian," "Quenois an Indian," and Packanambemet an Indian" all receiving payments. See also entries in the Account Book on pages 18, 31, 39, 73, 80–81. For Penobscot rejections, see Boston Conference, Massachusetts Governor, Penobscots, and Norridgewocks, 1738, in *NET*, 412. For Loron's rejection, see Belcher to John Gyles, February 28 1735/6, BL, reel 4. The only three Penobscots who took the commissions were "Col. Lewis, Espequit and Ninent."

20. Muscongus (Lincolnshire) Patent in Lincolnshire Company Records, pp. 1–13, MHS.

21. Williamson, "Brigadier General Samuel Waldo," 79–80.

22. "The Plymouth Company lands at Muscongus in which Samuel Waldo was a great Proprietor," vol. 26, Lincoln Family Papers, AAS. Early company activity and copies of founding deeds are in Lincolnshire Company Records, pp. 1–32, MHS. See also a valuable history kept by Belcher Noyes in Pejepscot Company Deeds, 1764, p. 77, MHS. Waldo's inheritance in Deed to Samuel Waldo, March 20, 1727/8, HKM, vol. 40, item 3. Waldo later gained half of all the company land as a reward for his lobbying efforts in England in 1730–31 (see Noyes above; and Williamson, "Samuel Waldo," 80–81).

23. Petition of Richard Fry to Jonathan Belcher [June 22, 1739], MeHS, Maine Historical Manuscripts Scrapbook, 1: 87.

24. Petition of Thomas Westbrook to General Court, January 13, 1737/8, MAC, 41:232–37.

25. Barry and Peabody, *Tate House*, 20–21. The body was located in 1976 during an archaeological dig.

26. "Samuel Waldo's Interview with the Indians," November 2 and 11, 1735," in *Saltonstall Papers*, ed. Moody, 1:390.

27. For examples of European colonists and terms of agreement, see in Patent, July 7, 1735, HKM, vol. 40, item 10; Waldo's agreements with John Bryson, July 27, 1753, Archibald Anderson, July 17, 1753, and John Millen, July 20, 1753, all in Henry Knox Papers, MeHS, box 21, folder 4; Francis Shaughnessy Indenture from Samuel Waldo, 1736, and Jeremiah Voss Indenture from Samuel Waldo, January 26, 1743, both in Henry Knox Papers, box 22, folder 4, MeHS.

28. Waldo, *Samuel Waldo of Boston, Merchant, Intending with All Possible Expedition . . .*

29. Waldo, *Whereas since my return from St. Georges*, 1–2.

30. Waldo, *A Defence of the Title*, 12. His original account claimed the Indians asked for a conference "by Espiquiett, their Second Chief" (Waldo, *Whereas since my return from St. Georges*, 1). The language is unclear about whether Espequent attended in person or was merely represented by others.

31. Elisha Cooke to Middlecott Cooke, May 21, 1735, in *Saltonstall Papers*, ed. Moody, 1:388.

32. Patent, July, 7, 1735, HKM, vol. 40, item 10.

33. See, for example, Belcher to Richard Waldron June 2, 1735, Richard Waldron Papers, box 1, vol. 2, p. 125, and Belcher to Richard Waldron, August 18, 1735, Richard Waldron Papers, box 1, vol. 2, p. 177, New Hampshire Historical Society. For "Eastern Trampoorer," see Belcher to Richard Waldron, December 3, 1736, BL, reel 5; for "Bogland," see Belcher to Waldron, June 2, 1735, box 1, vol. 2, Richard Waldron Papers, New Hampshire Historical Society.

34. Waldo, *A Defence of the Title*, 11; Belcher to John Gyles, April 14, 1735, BL, reel 4.

35. Waldo included a copy of Middlecott Cooke's deposition about the incident in his *Defence of the Title*, 36–37. The text of Cooke's deposition was similar, but not identical to, an anonymous report of "Samuel Waldo's Interview with the Indians, November 2 and 11 1735" found in the *Saltonstall Papers*, written in an "unknown hand" to editor Robert E. Moody, who collected many of Middlecott Cooke's letters. This anonymous report departed from Cooke's submitted testimony by including the detail that Loron had told Waldo that "those People . . . were but a few of their

tribe and had no order to act or do anything but that they were now the whole tribe not only acted for themselves but for all the tribe around" (Moody, ed., *Saltonstall Papers*, 1:388–91, quotation on 389). Even if Cooke did not write this anonymous report, his deposition clearly drew from it, though Cooke neglected to mention Loron's rejection of the authority of any of the Indians meeting with Waldo in the spring. The following description of the conference uses both accounts, keeping these facts in mind.

36. Waldo, *A Defence of the Title*, 36, Moody, ed., *Saltonstall Papers*, 1:389.

37. Moody, ed., *Saltonstall Papers*, 1:389; Waldo, *A Defence of the Title*, 36.

38. Waldo, *A Defence of the Title*, 36–37.

39. Moody, ed., *Saltonstall Papers*, 1:389, Waldo, *A Defence of the Title*, 37.

40. Belcher to John Gyles, February 28, 1735, BL, reel 4.

41. This letter can be found in Waldo, *A Defence of the Title*, 12; and in *CSP*, vol. 42, doc. 365 i.

42. Quotation from Belcher to John Gyles, February 28 1735, BL, reel 4. For a previous claim by Lieutenant Governor William Dummer that he could not tamper with private property rights, see *Conference* [1726], 9–10. See also statements by a Massachusetts commission at a 1752 conference at St. Georges in *NET*, 690.

43. Deposition of Jane and Ann Woodside, May 14, 1738, HKM, item 31.

44. Waldo, *A Defence of the Title*, 12.

45. For an explanation of lineage leaders in Wabanaki society, see Ghere, "Abenaki Factionalism," 48–52.

46. Waldo, *A Defence of the Title*, 12. Among the other signers were names that seldom, if ever, appeared on conference records or treaties, including Pate, Papadowit, Chaouset, and Joseph Akasunhawk.

47. Waldo, *A Defence of the* Title, 12. David Ghere argues that as a result of tensions over the Waldo incursion, Espequet was demoted, and possibly banished, as he was living with the Passamaquoddy for a time in the late 1730s (Ghere, "Abenaki Factionalism," 176). Loron alluded to this when speaking to Belcher in 1738 (see Boston Conference, Massachusetts Governor, Penobscots and Norridgewocks, 1738, in *NET*, 413).

48. Waldo, *A Defence of the Title*, 12.

49. Waldo, *A Defence of the Title*, 12.

50. *CSP*, vol. 42. doc. 375 ii, a and b, www.british-history.ac.uk.

51. For Espequent's commission, and Loron's refusal, see Belcher to John Gyles, February 28, 1735, BL, reel 4. Of the fifteen commissions Belcher sent to the Penobscots, only "Lewis, Espequit, and Ninent" accepted.

52. *HJ*, 14:70–71, 79.

53. Qtd. in Waldo, *A Defence of the Title*, 13, also in *NET*, 408. The copy in the *Calendar of State Papers* contains the full record of the hearing, which also dealt with the price of beaver (see *CSP*, vol. 42, doc. 375, ii).

54. Waldo, *A Defence of the Title*, 14.

55. Waldo, *A Defence of the Title*, 14.

56. Waldo, *A Defence of the Title*, 14.

57. Waldo, *A Defence of the Title*, 14. The large paper with a seal was probably a copy of the Plymouth Patent of 1629. See Lincolnshire Company Records, MHS, 1–3.

58. Waldo, *A Defence of the Title*, 14.

59. Baker, "Scratch with a Bear's Paw," 245–47; Nash, "Abiding Frontier," 196–97.

60. William Coyne for Lieutenant William Canady, July 21, 1724, "Account of Indian Attack on St. Georges Fort," in *Westbrook Letters*, ed. Trask, 67.

61. Waldo, *A Defence of the Title*, 14.

62. *CSP*, vol. 42, doc. 365 ii,

63. Report in *CSP*, vol. 42, doc. 375 ii f; also in Waldo, *A Defence of the Title*, 16.

64. *HJ*, 14:91–93.

65. *CSP*, vol. 42, doc. 365 ii.

66. Belcher to Messrs. Partridge and [Andrew] Belcher, December 24, 1739, BL, reel 6.

67. Peabody, *An Essay to Revive and Encourage Military Exercises*.

68. For committee membership, see *HJ*, 14:81. For Stoddard's suggestion that Massachusetts employ dogs against the Wabanakis, see John Stoddard to Lt. Gov. William Dummer, March 27, 1724, MAC, 51: 391; and William Shirley to Col. John Stoddard, May 14, 1746, William Shirley Papers, folder 4 [1746], MHS, which references Stoddard's "proposals respecting the use of Dogs in seeking and pursuing the Indians."

69. *HJ*, 15:33; Belcher to Lords of Trade, July 11, 1737, BL, reel 5, MHS.

70. Waldo, *A Defence of the Title*, 12.

71. *HJ*, 14:94. The House did not record the breakdown of most votes, including these. Cooke had brought up the 1725 conference between Dummer and four Penobscot delegates, where the forts on the St. Georges had been discussed, and Dummer insisted on the province's right to keep the forts. No mention had been made, however, about an expansion of towns.

72. These members were Samuel Thaxter, Anthony Stoddard (cousin of John Stoddard on the joint committee), and John Jeffries. All three were part of the "20 Associates" who each held one-thirtieth part of the remaining 100,000 acres of the Muscongus Patent not held by Waldo (see Lincolnshire Company Records, pp. 14–24, MHS; for council membership, see *HJ*, 14:7).

73. *HJ*, 14:102–3; Belcher qtd. in *CSP*, vol. 42, doc. 365 ii. For bill for gifts, see August 8, 1736, in Governor's Council Executive Records, GC3 327 #5, vol. 10, pp. 47–48, MSA.

74. Affidavit of Nicholas Byram, August 24, 1736, HKM, vol. 40, item 15.

75. *CSP*, vol. 42, doc. 365 ii.

76. Affidavit of Samuel Boggs, May 13, 1738, HKM, vol. 40, item 11.

77. William McIntire Affidavit, May 13, 1738, HKM, vol. 40, item 11.

78. Waldo, *A Defence of the Title*.

79. Waldo left no record of this exchange, probably because Belcher and most members of the General Court wanted him to give up. But the journey is referenced in item 29, Petition of St. Georges Settlers to Samuel Waldo, April 12, 1738; and item 11, Affidavit of Samuel Boggs, May 13, 1738, both in HKM, vol. 40. Waldo's colonists claimed he had secured the approval of the Indians to maintain the status quo, but based on previous exchanges with the Penobscots, it is probable the speculator put the same favorable gloss on the Native position as he had in April and November 1735. A letter from Governor Belcher to John Gyles in early 1737 referred to a Penobscot complaint, delivered through Gyles, about Waldo's ongoing activities, including the meeting (see Belcher to John Gyles, February 25, 1737, BL, reel 5). Belcher also mentioned the visit in an address to the House, reported in the *New England Weekly Journal* (Boston), May 31, 1737.

80. For Waldo's evidence implicating Belcher and Gyles, see Declaration of Robert Rutherford, April 10, 1738, item 16; Declaration of William Woodside, May 10, 1738, item 30; Deposition of Jane and Anne Woodside, May 14 1738; item 31, Deposition of Theodore Atkinson, January 22, 1739, all in HKM, vol. 40. For Belcher's reaction and rebuttals to Waldo's witnesses in his private correspondence, see Belcher to Waldron, August 30, 1736; Belcher to Waldron, September 20, 1736; and Belcher to Waldron, November 22, 1736, all in Richard Waldron Papers, box 2, vol. 3, pp. 16–18, New Hampshire Historical Society. Michael Batinski, Belcher's most recent biographer, takes Waldo's claims at face value, citing the testimony of Waldo and his supporters (included above). But Batinski ignores statements from the Penobscots refuting Waldo's claims, along with evidence provided by Gyles and other frontier officers. Gyles began employing paid informers among the Indians in 1720, continuing for many years afterward. (see John Gyles to Gov. Samuel Shute, September 16, 1720, MAC, 31:96; see also John Gyles Memorial St. Georges River, February 27, 1726/7, and March 3, 1726/7, MAC, 52:329–30; John Gyles expense account for the year July 31, 1735, to July 1736, August 2, 1736, MAC 31:197; John Gyles Memorandum on Disbursements on the Indians, August 28, 1740, MAC 31:284; John Gyles Account for Disbursements on the Indians, June 1740 to June 1741, MAC 31:377). Gyles expressed further support for the imperial project in general in a 1729 letter: Gyles to Colonel Dunbar, November 14, 1729, in DHSM, 10:445–46.

81. Boston Conference, Massachusetts Governor, Penobscots, and Norridgewocks, June 28–July 6, 1738, in NET, 418.

82. Lord, Sexton, and Harrison, History of the Archdiocese of Boston, 1:153.

83. Quotation from Declaration of Robert Rutherford, April 10, 1738, HKM, item 16; see also Declaration of William Woodside, May 10, 1738, HKM, item 30.

84. Middlecott Cooke, "An Account of My Voyage to St. Georges in the Eastern Parts of the Province, in Saltonstall Papers, ed. Moody, 1:395.

85. A. R. Cutter to Governor Jonathan Belcher, December 3, 1737 [copy], HKM, item 19.

86. Memoire des Sieurs Beauharnois et Hocquart, October 5, 1734, LAC, MG1 C11A F-61, f28–f29; Memoire des Beauharnois et Hocquart au Roi, October 13, 1735, in CMNF, 3:173–74; Memoire du Roi aux Sieurs de Beauharnois et Hocquart, May 15, 1736, in CMNF, 3:178; Memoire du Roi aux Sieurs de Beauharnois et Hocquart, May 10, 1737, in CMNF, 3:182; Memoire du Roy aux Sieurs de Beauharnois et Hocquart, May 15, 1738, in CMNF, 3:184.

87. Belcher to John Gyles, February 25, 1737, BL, reel 5; see also "Boston Conference, Massachusetts Governor, Penobscots, and Norridgewocks, June 28–July 6, 1738," in NET, 410–19.

88. Petition of St. Georges Settlers to Samuel Waldo, April 12, 1738, HKM, item 40.

89. Belcher to Col. Thomas Westbrook [from Sec. Willard, draft], September 7, 1736, MAC, 52:542; Conference with Polin & Indians of Presumpscot, August 10 and 13, 1739, in DHSM, 23:257–62; Brooks and Brooks, "Reciprocity Principle," 21–22.

90. March 16, 1737/8, April 3, 1738, New Marblehead Proprietors Records, in Windham Records, vol. 1, MeHS, 1:33, 35, quotation on 35. See also Dole, Windham in the Past.

91. Goodwin, ed., Records of the Proprietors of Narragansett Township.

92. Petition of the Inhabitants of Brunswick to Maintain Fort George, April 25 1737, PPP, MeHS, vol. 10, box 6, folder 2, pp. 49–50.

93. Six Indian Sagamores Deed to Wharton, July 7, 1684, PPP, MeHS, vol. 1, box 1, pp. 11–12.

94. *Conference* [1726], 12.

95. For two examples, see York County Court of Sessions, October 1736, MeSA, Dom Rex v. Elizabeth Wilson and Dom Rex v. Macum, box 64, file 46, vol. 10, pp. 121–22.

7 / Troubled Times, 1741–1752

1. Williamson, *History of Maine*, 2:212.

2. Wood, *William Shirley*, 13–14, 35, 72–77; Schutz, *William Shirley*, 4–5, 17–20, 25–26.

3. Samuel Waldo Indenture to William Shirley, July 3, 1738, HKM, vol. 40, item 34.

4. Letter of Instructions to Benjamin Larrabee, July 18, 1737, PPP, MeHS, vol. 1, box 1, pp. 122–23.

5. Shirley to Waldo, April 15, 1739, HKM, vol. 40, item 43.

6. Foster, "Another Legend of the Province House," 193–200, 184.

7. *Conference* [1742], 2, 4. Based on the ratio of one warrior for every five people. The British counted approximately 120 warriors, and they apparently all brought their families.

8. *Conference* [1742], 6, 8, 10–13, 15–17. For a full list of colonists' complaints presented, see MAC, 31: 414–15; John Minot to Governor Shirley, February 21, 1741/2, MAC, 31:371; Loron to Governor Shirley, February 11, 1741/2, MAC, 31:437–38. For 1740, see Memorandum of a Conference Held at Richmond, October 28, 1740, Maine Historical Society Manuscripts Scrapbooks, vol. 1, p. 73, MeHS.

9. *Conference* [1742], 7.

10. *Conference* [1742], 14.

11. *Conference* [1742], 14. According to the treaty minutes, Shirley then asked if Loron would acknowledge Wenemouet as their sagamore, and the Penobscot demurred. Since Wenemouet's leadership during the 1720s is well established, this exchange can either be attributed to difficulties in translation or to Loron's refusal to admit to anything.

12. *Conference* [1742], 14.

13. *Conference* [1742], 14.

14. *Conference, * [1742], 14.

15. *Conference* [1742], 14.

16. *Conference* [1742], 3–4.

17. *Conference* [1742], 14–15.

18. *Conference* [1742], 15.

19. *Conference* [1742], 5.

20. *Conference* [1742], 6.

21. *Conference* [1742], 12.

22. *Conference* [1742], 12.

23. William Shirley to John Thomlinson, August 27, 1742, William Shirley Papers, folder 1, MHS.

24. William Shirley to Duke of Newcastle, August 30, 1742, in *NET*, 451.

25. Samuel Waldo to John Thomlinson, January 17, 1742, Letters to John Thomlinson, Edward E. Ayer Manuscript, Collection, ms 960, Newberry Library, Chicago.

26. MAC, 15A:33-39.

27. Declaration of Thomas Henderson, February 18, 1746/7, HKM, vol. 40, item 79; Declaration of William Burns, February 26, 1746/7, HKM, vol. 40, item 80; Robert Earle Moody, "The First Settlements of the Waldo Patent," manuscript, Robert Earle Moody Papers, box 1 folder 13, MeHS.

28. Ghere, "Abenaki Factionalism," 179-81.

29. Ghere, "Myths and Methods," 527.

30. Ghere, "Eastern Abenaki Autonomy," 2-3.

31. Jabez Bradbury to Shirley, June 18, 1744, MAC, 31:493.

32. A. R. Cutter to William Pepperell, Jeremiah Moulton and John Hill, June 19, 1744, MAC, 31:494; William Pepperell to Shirley, June 22, 1744, MAC 31:495; Conference between Gov. Shirley and Members of the Pigwacket Tribe, July 28, 1744, MAC, 31:501-3; Noah Sprague, Account of the Pigwacket Indians for the Year 1748, MAC, 31:632.

33. Ghere, "The 'Disappearance' of the Abenaki," 198, 203.

34. William Shirley to Jabez Bradbury, January 25, 1745, MAC, 31:520A.

35. Jabez Bradbury to Gov. Shirley, June 18, 1744, MAC, 31: 493. See also Benjamin Larrabee to Samuel Waldo, May 20, 1744; William McCleland to Samuel Waldo, May 23, 1744; Joshua Moody to Samuel Waldo, June 2, 1744, all in Samuel Waldo Papers, 1744, MHS.

36. Scalp Bounty against the Cape Sable and St. John Indians, November 2, 1744, MAC, 31:514.

37. Shirley to Jabez Bradbury, July 22, 1745, Shirley, *Correspondence of William Shirley*, ed. Lincoln, 1:253-54.

38. Isaac Hinkley to Loving Brother and Sister, May 6, 1747, Scammon Family Papers, MeHS.

39. "Journal of Occurrences in Canada, 1746, 1747," *NYCD*, 10:127.

40. Declaration of Thomas Henderson, February 18, 1746/7; Declaration of William Burns, February 26, 1746/7; and Declaration of John Campbell, February 26, 1746/7, HKM items 79-81.

41. Ghere, "Abenaki Factionalism" 188-89.

42. Banks, *History of York, Maine*, 1:335; William Pepperrell to Lt. Gov. Spencer Phips, October 9, 1750, MAC, 53:551.

43. Samuel Denny to Your Excellency, May 7, 1748, MAC, 53: 336-37; see also David Cargill to Josiah Willard, Esq., May 16, 1747, MAC, 53: 272-73; James McCobb to Governor Shirley, May 7, 1748, MAC, 53:335.

44. Wheeler, "Brunswick at the Time of Incorporation," 33-34.

45. 1739 List of lots bought in Brunswick from Benjamin Larrabee, PPP, MeHS, vol. 3, box 2, p. 72. For lot prices and a list of those who did pay in cash, see "Pejepscott Account Book, 1740," in PPP, PEM, series III, box 2, folder 3, p. 1.

46. October 29, 1740, PPP, MeHS, vol. 3, box 2, p. 84.

47. An Account of the Proceedings of Mssrs Noyes and Skinner in Their Late Voyage to the Eastward, March 28, 1750, PPP, MeHS, vol. 7, box 5, folder 11, p. 431.

48. An Account of the Proceedings of Mssrs Noyes and Skinner in Their Late Voyage to the Eastward, March 28, 1750, PPP, MeHS, vol. 7, box 5, folder 11, p. 431. For Larabees in the region, see North Yarmouth Proprietors Records, pp. 4-16, 39-41, 86-89, MeHS; Southgate, *History of Scarborough*, 153; March 14, 1726/7, Falmouth Town Records, 1:91, MeSA.

49. Notes in the margin of "List of the Inhabitants of Lotts at Topsham as receiv'd from Capt Benjamin Larrabee, April 9, 1746," PPP, MeHS, vol. 3, box 2, p. 35. Marginal notes from Noyes dated "anno 1749" and "Sept: 19 1749."

50. An Account of the Proceedings of Mssrs Noyes and Skinner in Their Late Voyage to the Eastward, March 28, 1750, PPP, MeHS, vol. 7, box 5, folder 11, p. 432.

51. An Account of the Proceedings of Mssrs Noyes and Skinner in Their Late Voyage to the Eastward, March 28, 1750, PPP, MeHS, vol. 7, box 5, folder 11, p. 432.

52. An Account of the Proceedings of Mssrs Noyes and Skinner in Their Late Voyage to the Eastward, March 28, 1750, PPP, MeHS, vol. 7, box 5, folder 11, p. 434.

53. Douglass, *A Summary*, 1:390.

54. Falmouth Conference, September 27–October 17, 1749, *NET*, 622–34 passim. This had been the basis upon which the Wabanakis had agreed to arrive (see Boston Conference with Penobscots and Norridgewocks, June 23–27, 1749, in *NET*, 618–19).

55. *DCB*, vol. 3, s.v. "Sauguaaram," by Kenneth M. Morrison.

56. "Journal of Occurrences in Canada; 1746, 1747," in *NYCD*, 10:127.

57. Penobscots and Norridgewocks to Shirley on Conference, September 7–8, 1749, in *NET*, 622; Falmouth Conference, September 27–October 17, 1749, in *NET*, 624, 626.

58. Indian letter to Gov. William Shirley, November 17, 1749, in *DHSM*, 23:322; *NET*, 621.

59. Samuel Denny to Governor, December 9, 1749, in *DHSM*, 23:338–39. The alias is from SCJRB, June 1751, reel 8, folio 237–8, Dom Rex v. Ledite, MSA.

60. Letter from Loron of the Penobscots to Governor Phips, April 17, 1750, in *DHSM*, 23: 328; Letter from "Woorrenock Men" written on behalf of "Asserromo Chief of the Worenock Indians, Spring 1750, in *DHSM*, 23: 329; Jabez Bradbury to John Wheelwright, April 16, 1750, MAC, 32:13.

61. Accounts of Wiscasset from Ghere and Morrison, "Searching for Justice," 378–399; Thayer, "A Page of Indian History," 81–103.

62. Fox to Governor, January 1, 1750, in *DHSM*, 23:349.

63. Jeremiah Moulton to Lt. Gov. Phips, January 11, 1750, in *DHSM*, 23:350.

64. SCJRB, June 1751, Reel 8, folio 237–8, Dom Rex v. Ledite.

65. Ghere, "Abenaki Factionalism," 202–3, 206–7; Ghere and Morrision, "Searching for Justice." 389–90.

66. Bradbury to Commanding Officer at Pemaquid, September 7, 1750, MAC, 53: 524; Williams to Moulton, September 10, 1750, MAC, 53:528. For wider Native American practices of restrained violence, see Lee, "Peace Chiefs and Blood Revenge," 701–41.

67. Thomas Henderson to Lt. Gov. Phips, April 11, 1751, MAC, 54:22.

68. Petition from North Yarmouth to "Spencer Phipps, Esq, Commander in Chief for the Time Being," September 19, 1750, MAC, 53:533; Petition to Lt. Gov. Phips "in behalf of the Rest of the Inhabitants on the Frontiers in the Eastern Parts" September 26, 1750, MAC, 53:538; Samuel Denny and others to Lt. Gov. Phips, September 27, 1750, MAC, 53:539–40.

69. Enoch Freeman to Lt. Gov. Spencer Phips, June 8, 1751, MAC, 54:35.

70. Capt. Alexander Nichols to Capt. Jabez Bradbury, April 18, 1751, MAC, 54:21.

71. Lt. Gov. Phips to Capt. Alexander Nichols, May 1, 1751, MAC 54:23.

72. See, for example, Thomas Fletcher to [?], August 2, 1750, MAC, 53:517; Jabez Bradbury to Commanding Officer at Pemaquid, September 7, 1750, MAC, 53:524; Col.

Israel Williams to Jeremiah Moulton, September 10, 1750, MAC, 53:528; Capt. William Lithgow to Lt. Gov. Phips, October 6, 1750, MAC, 53:548-49; Bradbury to Phips, October 10, 1750, MAC, 53:552; William Lithgow to Phips, July 9, 1751, MeHS Special Collections, misc. box 146/2.

73. Lt. Gov. Phips to Col. Ezekiah Cushing, September 14, 1750, MAC, 534-35; Proclamation, September 3, 1751, in *NET*, 674-75.

74. Lincolnshire Company Records, bound volume, 6-7, MHS.

75. Schutz, *William Shirley*, 137-68.

76. This occurred in two conferences at St. Georges (St. Georges Conference, August 19-24, 1751, and Conference at St. Georges, October 13-21, 1752, in *NET* 668-74 and 685-97). Phineas Stevens also traveled to Montreal to meet with the St. Francis Wabanakis, mediated by the governor of Canada and the Canadian Iroquois (Montreal Conference, July 1752, in *NET* 680-83).

77. See Ghere, "Eastern Abenaki Autonomy," 9.

78. St. Georges Conference, 19-24 August 1751, in *NET*, 670. Conference at St. Georges, October 13-21, 1752, in *NET*, quotation on 691, land and complaints 688, 690-91.

79. Instructions for Massachusetts Commissioners to St. Georges Conference, August 15, 1751, in *NET*, 668.

80. *NET*, 672.

81. *NET*, 670-71.

82. All treaties and British correspondence between the death of Wenongonet in 1730 and the outbreak of war in 1744 refer to Edewakenk as the leader of the Penobscots, and Loron as "captain" (see *Conference* [1732], 1; Samuel Waldo's Interview with the Indians, November 2 and 11, 1735, in *Saltonstall Papers*, ed. Moody, 1:389; John Gyles, Account for Disbursements on the Indians at Fort St. Georges, June 1740-June 1741, MAC, 31:377; and *Conference* [1742], 4).

83. *Conference* [1742], 7.

84. For "hearty," see *NET*, 671; for "quelled all the rest," see *NET*, 672.

85. Journal of the Proceedings of Two Conferences Begun to be Held at Falmouth, June-July 1754, in *NET*, 743.

86. *NET*, 690.

87. Wendell continued to hold shares in the company until 1757. See November 9, 1757, KPP, vol. 6, p. 136.

8 / Contrary to Their Own Laws, 1749-1755

1. Allen, ed., *Province and Court Records of Maine*, 5:65.

2. Kershaw, *Kennebeck Proprietors*, 26-27.

3. Kershaw, *Kennebeck Proprietors*, 7-27.

4. Kershaw, *Kennebeck Proprietors*, 26-27

5. A brief State of the Kennebeck Proprietors Title to the Kennebeck Purchase from the late Colony of New Plymouth [1772?], KPP, vol. 1, Letter Book 1766-1809, p. 65.

6. Milford, *The Gardiners*, 25; see also Bowen, *Elites, Enterprise, and the Making of the British Overseas Empire*, 104-13.

7. Kershaw, *Kennebeck Proprietors*, 53.

8. Kershaw, *Kennebeck Proprietors*, 45-45; Belcher Noyes, "Remarks on the Conduct of the Plymouth Proprietors" Pejepscot Company Deeds, p. 10, MHS.

9. Waldo, *A Defence of the Title*, 11.

10. Robert Temple, William Bowdoin, and Silvester Gardiner to Mr. Nelson, May 11, 1752, KPP, box 1, folder 8.

11. Anonymous, n.d., [but Florentius Vassal to Joseph Sharpe], likely ca. 1755, Gentlemen of the Plymouth Company to Florentius Vassal, March 29, 1755, both in Kennebeck Purchase Company Records, Manuscripts and Archives Division, NYPL.

12. Florentius Vassal to Joseph Sharpe, July 31, 1755, Kennebeck Purchase Company Records, NYPL.

13. Robert Temple, William Bowdoin, and Silvester Gardiner to Mr. Nelson, May 11, 1752, KPP, box 1, folder 8.

14. Qtd. in Kershaw, *Kennebeck Proprietors*, 135.

15. Milford, *Gardiners of Massachusetts*, 32; Kershaw, *Kennebeck Proprietors*, 162–64.

16. Language taken from document heading "List of Persons who in the years 1750–51 made written applications . . ." in folder 3, 1744–1757, Nathan Dane Papers, MHS.

17. Location of towns and count of petitioners in "Petition from the Inhabitants within the Limits of the Plymouth Purchase, May 8, 1751," in "Thwing and Haven Family Papers," bound volume, Thwing Family Papers, MHS; for numbered petitions for grants in 1751, see KPP, box 9, folder 4, which includes Charles Snipe Petition for Grant, May 8, 1751.

18. May 4, 1750 Proprietors Meeting, bound vol. 3, company records, 1661–1753, KPP, p. 28.

19. Committee of Plymouth Proprietors (Kennebeck) to the Selectmen of the Town of Newcastle on Shepscott River May 11, 1750, box 3, folder 7, Dogget Family Papers, MeHS.

20. For examples, see "Certificates of Impowerment," all signed by Samuel Goodwin, of various individuals, followed by dates, all in box 1, folder 4, KPP; of John Beath, January 24, 1750/1; to Thomas Young and John Pearce, January 26, 1750/1; of Mr. Henry Little, February 22, 1750/1.

21. May 8, 1751, Proprietors Meeting, KPP, bound vol. 3, pp. 66–67.

22. Samuel Goodwin Grant to Samuel Denny, Esq., March 9, 1750/1, KPP, box 1, folder 5; Protest of the Pejepscot Proprietors, February 2, 1737, PPP, MeHS, vol. 7, box 5, folder 9, p. 405.

23. Capt. Jonathan Williamson to Thomas Hubbard, February 19, 1750/1, box 3, folder 7, Wiscasset Company Papers in Doggett Family Collection, MeHS.

24. See meetings on September 22, 1749, and January 21, 1762, in Pemaquid Proprietors Papers, vol. 1, pp. 22–23, AAS.

25. Record Book of Wiscasset Company Meetings, box 3, folder 3, pp. 27–28, Doggett Family Collection, MeHS. For Draper heirs, see Job Averell to Samuel Whittemore, May 21, 1753, Sheepscot Manuscripts, 2:65a, MeSL; Job Averell to Samuel Whittemore, September 18, 1760, Sheepscot Manuscripts, 2:61a–b; Job Averell to Samuel Whittemore, March 17, 1762, Sheepscot Manuscripts, 3:174a, Job Averell to Samuel Whiteemore, July 7, 1762, Sheepscot Manuscripts, 3:175a; see also Taylor, "A Kind of Warr," 17.

26. Sewall, *Diary*, 2:970–71; *SHG*, 4:213; John Minot to Col. Stephen Minot, October 4, 1725, MAC, 52:294.

27. *SHG*, 8:235–39; for shares, see Pejepscot Company Deeds, MHS, pp. 7, 86–88; Application for a Meeting of the Pejepscot Proprietors, November 5, 1751, in PPP, MeHS, box 6, folder 10, vol. 7, pp. 435–36.

28. *Conference with the Eastern Indians* . . . (Boston, 1726), copy held in KPP, box 13, folder 3. On the cover is written "Belcher Noyes 1752" followed by, in a different hand and darker ink, indicating a later date "/Josiah Little." Quotation from p. 12, other highlighted portions are on pp. 6, 7, 9, 10, 11, 13. Little was a Pejepscot Proprietor active in the 1760s and later. The highlighted portions of the document match the color and darkness of Noyes's signature rather than Little's.

29. Pejepscot Company Deeds, 82, MHS.

30. Belcher Noyes to Enoch Freeman, November 12, 1763, PPP, MeHS, vol. 5, box 3, folder 4, p. 77

31. Application for a Meeting of the Pejepscot Proprietors, November 5, 1751, PPP, MeHS, vol. 7, box 5, folder 11, p. 435; *Pursuant to a Warrant to me directed* . . . (Boston, 1751), and Belcher Noyes to Governor Benning Wentworth, November 30, 1751, PPP, MeHS, vol. 6, box 5, folder 11, 439–40.

32. Advertisement, July 9, 1750, PPP, MeHS, vol. 10, box 6, folder 10, p. 179.

33. Quotation from Belcher Noyes to Adam Hunter, PPP, MeHS, box 2, folder 8, vol. 4, p. 99. For cost, see "Projection for selling Topsham (in Noyes's handwriting), August 21, 1752, PPP, box 2, folder 8, vol. 4, p. 99; Belcher Noyes to Adam Hunter, May 12, 1753, PPP, MeHS, box 2, folder 8, vol. 4, p. 101.

34. December 14, 1752 Meeting of the Pejepscot Proprietors, PPP, MeHS, box 2, vol. 3, p. 160.

35. *An Answer to the Remarks of the Plymouth Company*, 7.

36. *At a Meeting of the Proprietors of the Township of Brunswick*, n.p.

37. *At a Meeting of the Proprietors of the Township of Brunswick*, n.p.

38. *An Answer to the Remarks of the Plymouth Company*, 5.

39. *An Answer to the Remarks of the Plymouth Company*, 14.

40. *An Answer to the Remarks of the Plymouth Company*, 15.

41. *An Answer to the Remarks of the Plymouth Company*, 14.

42. *An Answer to the Remarks of the Plymouth Company*, 14.

43. *An Answer to the Remarks of the Plymouth Company*, 14.

44. Deposition of John Gyles, June 7, 1753, PPP, MeHS, box 6, folder 2, vol. 10, pp. 4–5.

45. Kershaw, *Kennebeck Proprietors*, 30–31. No known copy of the seal survives.

46. Gentlemen of the Plymouth Company to Florentius Vassall, March 29, 1755, Kennebeck Purchase Company Records, Manuscripts and Archives Division, NYPL.

47. *A Defence of the Remarks of the Plymouth Company*, 2.

48. *A Defence of the Remarks of the Plymouth Company*, 46. For the full text of the law, see "An Act to Prevent and Make Void Clandestine and Illegal Purchases of Lands from the Indians," June 26, 1701, in *Acts and Resolves*, 1:471–72.

49. *A Defence of the Remarks of the Plymouth Company*, 47.

50. *A Defence of the Remarks of the Plymouth Company*, 20–21.

51. For the Pejepscot Proprietors pointing out Temple's association with the Kennebeck Proprietors, see *An Answer to the Remarks of the Plymouth Company*, 18. For Temple's pretense, see *A Defence of the Remarks of the Plymouth Company*, 19.

52. Alan Taylor. "A Kind of War"; for continuation after the Seven Years' War, see Taylor, *Liberty Men and Great Proprietors*.

53. Robert Temple, William Bowdoin, and Silvester Gardiner to Mr. Nelson, May 11, 1752, KPP, box 1, folder 8.

54. "Exact Copys of two Letters, lately Received by Peter Chardon, of Boston, from the French Settlers at Frank Fort, at the Eastward," dated November 2, 1752, KPP, box 1, folder 8; Plymouth Company Appointment of a Committee to Govern Frankfort, August 10, 1752, KPP, box 1, folder 8; June 27, 1753 meeting, KPP, Company Records. 1753-1768, vol. 6, p. 27; November 2, 1757, meeting, p. 132, ibid; Kershaw, *Kennebeck Proprietors*, 63-74, 105-7, 111-12.

55. William Lithgow to Lt. Gov. Phips, March 26, 1753, MAC 32:341.

56. For quotation, see Samuel Moody Reports Wabanaki Complaints of Trespass, March 23, 1753, MAC 32:338; Penobscots Complain of English Trespasser, April 25 and May 13, 1753, MAC, 32:353, 359; see also MAC, 32:363.

57. December 14 and 30, 1752, *HJ*, 29:84, 112.

58. April 7, 1753, *HJ*, 29:151-52.

59. April 12, 1753, *HJ*, 29:165.

60. Proclamation by Lt. Gov. Spencer Phips, April 13, 1753, MAC, 32:379; MAC, 32:362 and 364.

61. Committee Report, June 6, 1753, MAC, 32:364.

62. Seventeenth-Century Wabanaki to English Deeds Shown at Casco Conference, in *NET*, 315.

63. James Otis, John Winslow, Gamaliel Bradford, Samuel White, and William Taylor to Kennebeck Proprietors, 1761, KPP, box 2, folder 9; William Pepperrell and Thomas Hubbard, along with other investments, each held one-sixty-fourth of the Wiscasset Company claim ("Shares of the Proprietors of the Wiscassett Company," Doggett Family Collection, box 3, folder 6, MeHS).

64. The commission had earlier met with the Penobscots and had no trouble reaffirming peace, especially after they announced the province had removed the Mantinicus squatters. The separate meetings appear to have been accidental, although the commission did not mention the deeds to the Penobscots (St. Georges Conference and Related Documents, September 20-29, 1753, in *NET*, 709-10; Ghere, "Abenaki Factionalism," 218-19).

65. St. Georges Conference and Related Documents, in *NET*, 716.

66. The most relevant deeds were by Agebedosset and Kennebis to Christopher Lawson, October 10, 1649, Agebedossett and Kennebas to Lawson, Spencer, and Lake, May 4, 1653, and Wassamack to Thomas Lake and Roger Spencer, June 25 1653, all for land along the Kennebec River. Deeds are numbered 12-14, Seventeenth-Century Wabanaki to English Deeds Shown at Casco Conference, in *NET*, 315.

67. *NET*, 718

68. *NET*, 719-20.

69. *NET*, 720.

70. *NET*, 720.

71. *NET*, 721.

72. November 7, 1753, Proprietors Meeting, KPP, vol. 6, pp. 45-46.

73. Kennebeck Proprietors to Samuel Goodwin, February 27, 1754, KPP, box 1, folder 10.

74. Ghere, "Abenaki Factionalism," 220-21.

75. Ghere, "Abenaki Factionalism," 221–24; Ghere, "Eastern Abenaki Autonomy," 10–12; Lord, Sexton, and Harrington, *History of the Archdiocese*, 1:81, 186.

76. William Shirley to the General Court of Massachusets, March 28, 1754, in Shirley, *Correspondence of William Shirley*, ed. Lincoln, 2:37–38.

77. Shirley to the Earl of Holderness, April 19, 1754, and Shirley to Sir Thomas Robinson, May 8, 1754, in Shirley, *Correspondence of William Shirley*, ed. Lincoln, 2:52–60, 62–68, quotation on 67.

78. General Court of Massachusetts to Shirley, April 9, 1754, in Shirley, *Correspondence of William Shirley*, ed. Lincoln, 2:50.

79. April 3 and 17, 1754, KPP, vol. 6, pp. 57–58, 62.

80. Kershaw, *Kennebeck Proprietors*, 134–35; Schutz, *William Shirley*, 177–79; KPP, vol. 9, p. 4.

81. Milford, *The Gardiners of Massachusetts*, 32.

82. Coppy [sic] of Governour Shirley's Letter to the Lords Commissioners for Trade, December 31, 1754, Kennebeck Purchase Company Records, NYPL.

83. Florentius Vassal to Joseph Sharpe, April 2, 1755, Kennebeck Purchase Company Records, NYPL.

84. *Journal of the Proceedings at Two Conferences* [1754], 7.

85. Douglass, *A Summary*, 1:390; Ghere, "Myths and Methods," 527.

86. Journal of the Proceedings at Two Conferences [June and July 1754], in *NET*, 739, 744–45.

87. *NET*, 743.

88. *NET*, 748.

89. See esp. *NET*, 749.

90. Shirley to Sir Thomas Robinson, August 19, 1754, in *Shirley Correspondence*, ed. Lincoln, 2:74–75; Lord, Sexton, and Harrington, *History of the Archdiocese of Boston*, 1:187–93.

91. *NET*, 753–59.

92. Ghere, "Eastern Abenaki Autonomy," 12–13; Ghere, "Abenaki Factionalism," 229–31; Lt. James Howard to Gov. Shirley, October 11, 1754, MAC, 54:190.

93. House of Representatives, June 9, 1755, in *DHSM*, 24:30.

94. Jabez Bradbury to Gov. Shirley, June 27, 1755, in *DHSM*, 24:35–36.

95. Penobscots to Shirley, June 27, 1755, in *DHSM*, 24:34.

96. James Cargill's Memorandum Relating to the Killing of Indians, in *DHSM*, 24:36–37.

97. Benjamin Moggaridge to Jeremiah Powell, July 19, 1755, folder 3, Jeremiah Powell Papers, MeHS.

98. Action of the House, August 8, 1755, DHSM, 24:46–47; Phips to Penobscots, August 18, 1755, in *DHSM*, 24:52.

99. Action of the House, November 1, 1755, in *DHSM*, 24: 62; A Proclamation by Spencer Phips, November 3, 1755, in *DHSM*, 24:63.

100. *A Strange Account of . . . a Great Bubble*, 4, 9, 5–6. For authorship, see Milford, *The Gardiners*, 33.

101. Hutchinson, *History*, 3:20.

Conclusion. Treaties Buried and Lost

1. "Journal of the Voyage of Gov. Thomas Pownall," 373.
2. "Journal of the Voyage of Gov. Thomas Pownall," 369. For identity of Wabanaki participants, see 370.
3. "Journal of the Voyage of Gov. Thomas Pownall," 370, 372.
4. Day, "Oral Tradition as Compliment."
5. Bourque, *Twelve Thousand Years*, 202–4; Ghere, "Abenaki Factionalism," 256–75; Ghere, "Myths and Methods in Abenaki Demography," 525; Day, "Oral Tradition as Compliment."
6. Leamon, *Revolution Downeast*. 6.
7. Bartlet, ed., *Frontier Missionary*, 83–84.
8. McBride and Prins, "Molly Ockett," 329–30.
9. Leamon, *Revolution Downeast*, 6; Clark, *Eastern Frontier*, 336.
10. Conrad, ed., *They Planted Well*, 9. For a comparison of New England and Nova Scotian townships, see Mancke, "Corporate Structure and Private Interest," 161–77.
11. Bartlet, ed., *Frontier Missionary*, 88.
12. Samuel Ford to Edward Hutchinson, February 14, 1764, folder 9, Hutchinson Family Papers, MHS.
13. Belcher Noyes to anonymous [probably Enoch Freeman], October 24 1763, PPP, MeHS, vol. 4, box 2, folder 11, p. 180.
14. Thomas Wilson [and others in Topsham] to Noyes, November 9, 1762, and Thomas Wilson to Belcher Noyes, November 16, 1762, PPP, MeHS, vol. 4, box 2, folder 10, pp. 150, 151.
15. Thomas Wilson [and others in Topsham] to Noyes, November 9, 1762, PPP, vol. 4, box 2, folder 10, p. 150.
16. Pejepscot Proprietors Writ against Wilsons and Douglasses for Trespass, September 5, 1763, vol. 4, box 2, folder 10, p. 175; Pejepscot Proprietors v. William Wilson, Lincoln County Court of Common Pleas Record Book [hereafter LCCPRB], September 1763, box 1, pp. 39–40, reel 1, MeSA; Pejepscot Proprietors v. Thomas Wilson, LCCPRB, September 1763, box 1, p. 40, reel 1; Belcher Noyes to Enoch Freeman, June 17, 1767, PPP, MeHS, vol. 4, box 2, folder 13, p. 215.
17. Petition of Capt. Thomas Wilson to the General Court, June 7, 1771, PPP, MeHS, vol. 4, box 2, folder 13, p. 253.
18. "Journal of the Voyage of Gov. Thomas Pownall," 382.
19. Taylor, *Liberty Men and Great Proprietors*, chap. 7 passim.
20. Countryman, "Out of the Bounds of the Law"; Taylor, "'A Kind of Warr'"; Bellesiles, *Revolutionary Outlaws*; Taylor, *Liberty Men and Great Proprietors*.
21. Banner, *How the Indians Lost Their Land*, 104–11.
22. Sullivan, *The History of Land Titles in Massachusetts*, iv–v.
23. Sullivan, *History of the District of Maine*, 131–35; *The History of Land Titles*, 23.
24. Sullivan, *History of the District of Maine*, 140. Sullivan himself did speculate, and was the major proprietor of Limerick, Maine (Taylor, *Liberty Men and Great Proprietors*, 216).
25. Sullivan, *History of the District of Maine*, 136–37.
26. Sullivan, *History of the District of Maine*, 131.
27. Sullivan, *History of the District of Maine*, 135.

28. John Winthrop, "General Considerations for the Plantations in New England, with an Answer to Several Objections," in *Winthrop Papers*, 2:120.

29. Sullivan, *The History of Land Titles in Massachusetts*, 29.

30. Sullivan, *History of the District of Maine*, 138–39.

31. Banner, *How the Indians Lost Their Land*, 150–90.

32. Onuf, *Jefferson's Empire*; Bowes, *Land Too Good for Indians*.

33. MacDougall, *Penobscot Dance*, 94–95.

34. Calloway, *American Revolution in Indian Country*, chap. 2; Montgomery, "Projecting Power in the Dawnland," chap. 5.

35. MacDougall, *Penobscot Dance*, for refugees, 158; for treaties, 107–24.

36. Pawling, ed., *Wabanaki Homeland*, 6–18, 53–53, 277–78.

37. Reid, "Maritime Colonies, and the Supplanting of Mi'kma'ki/Wulstukwiuk, 1780–1820."

38. Battiste, ed., *Living Treaties*, 4–5.

39. MacDougall, *Penobscot Dance*, 26.

40. MacDougall, *Penobscot Dance*, 30.

41. Patterson, *Eighteenth-Century Treaties*.

42. Palmater, "Living M'kmaw Treaties"; Wicken, *Mi'kmaq Treaties on Trial*; Nicholas, "Mascarene's Treaty of 1725."

43. Francis Flisiuk, "Maine Has Its Own Standing Rock"—The Penobscot River Fight Explained," *Portland Phoenix*, October 1, 2017.

44. "Journal of the Voyage of Gov. Thomas Pownall," 372.

Bibliography

Manuscript Sources

American Antiquarian Society, Worcester MA

Curwen Family Papers
Lincoln Family Papers
Belcher Noyes Diaries
Pemaquid Proprietors Papers

Bangor Public Library, Maine

Thomas Fayerweather Diary

Raymond H. Fogler Library Special Collections, University of Maine, Orono

Fannie Hardy Eckstorm Papers

Library and Archives of Canada, Ottawa, ON

CIIA
National Map Collection. Carte pour les hauteurs des Terres, et pour server de limitte, suivant in Paix. Entre la France et l'Angleterre, suivant les Memoires du R.P. Aubry, Jesuiste, 1715 NMC 6364.

Lincoln County Courthouse, Wiscasset, ME

Lincoln County Deeds

Maine Historical Society, Portland

Bowdoin, Flucker, and Knox Papers
Dogget Family Papers
John S. H. Fogg Collection
Gorham Records
Andrew Hawes Papers
Dominicus Jordan Estate Papers
Jordan Family Papers
Kennebec Proprietors Papers [Plymouth Company Papers]
Henry Knox Microfilms
Henry Knox Papers
Lewis Family Papers
Libby Family Papers
Maine Historical Society Manuscripts Scrapbooks
John Minot Account Book
Robert Earle Moody PapersNorth Yarmouth Maine Papers—David Shepley
    Collection
North Yarmouth Proprietors Records
North Yarmouth Town Records
Moses Pearson Papers
Pejepscot Proprietors Papers
Jeremiah Powell Papers
Pownalborough Courthouse Collection
Timothy Prout Legal Documents
Scammon Family Papers
Scarborough Papers
Scarborough Proprietors Records
Scarborough Town Records
William Southgate Collection
Samuel Waldo Papers
Richard Wharton Indian Deed, 1684, Misc. Box 61/6, MS00277
William Henry Woodward Papers
Windham Records

Maine State Archives, Augusta

Arundel Town Records
Berwick Town Records
Biddeford Town Records
Brunswick Town Records
Falmouth Proprietors Records
Falmouth Town Records
Gorham Proprietors Records

Kittery Town Records
Lincoln County Court of Common Pleas and Court of Sessions Records
Topsham Town Records
Wells Town Records
York County Court of Common Pleas and Court of Sessions Records and Case
    Files

Maine State Library, Augusta

Sheepscot Manuscripts

Massachusetts Historical Society, Boston

Jonathan Belcher Letterbooks
Nathan Dane Papers
David Stoddard Greenough Family Papers
Hutchinson Family Papers
Lincolnshire Company Records
Pejepscot Company Deeds
John Penhallow Diary, 1723
Quincy, Wendell, and Upham Family Papers
Thomas Saunders Papers [reel P-775]
William Shirley Papers
Cyprian Southack LettersThwing Family Papers
Samuel Waldo Papers, 1744

Miscellaneous Large Manuscripts
Joseph Bean. Manuscript map of Rivers in York County, Maine, February 1741

Miscellaneous Manuscripts
Joseph Heath Letter to Jabez Bradbury, December 19, 1738

Massachusetts State Archives, Boston

Governor's Council Executive Records
Massachusetts Archives, Collections
Suffolk County Probate Records
Superior Court of Judiacature Records

Newberry Library, Chicago

Edward E. Ayer Manuscript Collection
Theodore Atkinson Letters, ms 39Benjamin Pollard Letters, ms 732
Samuel Waldo Letters, ms 960

New Hampshire Historical Society, Concord

Richard Waldron Papers
Waldron/Belcher Papers
Journal of Samuel Willard, 1725

New York Public Library, Manucripts and Archives Division

Kennebeck Purchase Company Records

North Yarmouth Historical Society, North Yarmouth, ME

Town of North Yarmouth Records

Pejepscot Historical Society, Brunswick, ME

John Minot Ledger
Belcher Noyes Deed to Thomas Wilson, 1763

Phillips Library of the Peabody Essex Museum, Salem, MA

Pejepscot Proprietors Papers

Newspaper Sources (Colonial)
American Weekly Mercury (Philadelphia)
Boston Gazette
Boston News Letter
New England Courant (Boston)
New England Weekly Journal (Boston)

Newspaper Sources (Modern)
Portland Phoenix

Online Databases
America's Historical Newspapers
Early American Imprints, Series I: Evans, 1639–1800, Readex
Early English Books Online (EEBO)
Eighteenth Century Collections Online (ECCO)

Printed Document Collections
Acts and Resolves, Public and Private, of the Province of the Massachusetts Bay: To Which Are Prefixed the Charters of the Province. With Historical and Explanatory Notes, and an Appendix. Boston, 1869–1922.

Allen, Neal, and Robert Earl Moody, eds. *Province and Court Records of Maine.* Portland: Portland Historical Society, 1928–1975.

Baxter, James P., ed. *Christopher Levett of York: The Pioneer Colonists in Casco Bay.* Portland, ME: Gorges Society, 1893.

———, ed. *The Pioneers of New France in New England with Contemporary Letters and Documents.* Albany, NY: J. Munsell's Sons, 1894.

Calendar of State Papers: Colonial America and West Indies, 1574–1739. 44 vols. London: Her Majesty's Stationary Office, 1860–1994. Accessed at British History Online, www.british-history.ac.uk

Calloway, Colin, ed. *Dawnland Encounters: Indians and Europeans in Northern New England.* Hanover, NH: University Press of New England, 1991.

Goodwin, William F., ed. *Records of the Proprietors of Narragansett Township, no. 1, Now the Town of Buxton, York County, Maine, From August 1st, 1733 to January 4th, 1811.* Concord, NH, 1871.

Hull, John T., ed. *York Deeds.* Portland, ME: B. Thurston & Co., 1887.

Massachusetts Historical Society. *Journals of the House of Representatives of Massachusetts.* Boston, 1919–90.

Mandell, Daniel, ed. *New England Treaties, North and West: 1650–1776.* Vol. 20 in *Early American Indian Documents: Treaties and Laws, 1607–1789,* edited by Alden Vaughan. Washington, DC: University Publications of America, 2003.

Moody, Robert M., ed. *The Saltonstall Papers.* Collections of the Massachusetts Historical Society, ser. 6, vol. 80, 2 vols. Boston: Massachusetts Historical Society, 1972.

O'Callaghan, E. B., ed. *Documents Relative to the Colonial History of the State of New York; Procured in Holland, England and France.* 15 vols. Albany: Weed, Parsons and Company, 1856–87.

Shirley, William. *Correspondence of William Shirley, Governor of Massachusetts and Military Commander in America, 1731–1760.* Edited by Charles H. Lincoln. 2 vols. New York: Macmillan, 1912.

Thwaites, Reuben Gold, ed. *The Jesuit Relations and Allied Documents: Travels and Explorations of the Jesuit Missionaries in New France, 1610–1791.* 73 vols. Cleveland: Burrows Brothers Company, 1896–1901.

Trask, William, ed. *Letters of Colonel Thomas Westbrook: and Others Relative to Indian Affairs in Maine, 1722–1726.* Boston: Littlefield, 1901.

Van Der Beets, Richard, ed. *Held Captive by Indians: Selected Narratives, 1642–1836.* Knoxville: University of Tennessee Press, 1973.

Vaughan, Alden, ed. *Early American Indian Documents: Treaties and Laws.* 20 vols. *1607–1789.* Washington, DC: University Publications of America, 1979–2003.

Webster, John Clarence, ed. *Acadia at the End of the Seventeenth Century, Letters, Journals, and Memoirs of Joseph Robineau de Villebon, Commandant* of Acadia, 1690–1700 and Other Contemporary Documents. St. John: New Brunswick Museum, 1934.

Published Indian Treaties

An Account of the Treaty between His Excellency Benjamin Fletcher Captain General and Governour in the Province of New York, etc. and the Indians of the Five Nations . . . Beginning the 13th day of August, 1694. New York: 1694. Evans Collection, ser. 1, no. 702.

The Conference with the Eastern Indians, at the Ratification of the Peace, Held at Falmouth in Casco-Bay, in July and August, 1726. Boston, 1726. Evans Collection, ser. 1, no. 2751.

The Conference with the Eastern Indians, at the Ratification of the Peace, Held at Falmouth in Casco-Bay, in July and August, 1726. Boston, 1754. Evans Collection, ser. 1, no. 7216.

The Conference with the Eastern Indians at the Further Ratification of the Peace, Held at Falmouth in Casco-Bay, in July 1727. Boston, 1727. Evans Collection, ser., no. 2885.

A Conference of His Excellency Jonathan Belcher with. . . . Indian Tribes at Falmouth in Casco Bay, July 1732. Boston, 1732. Evans Collection, ser. 1, no 3554.

A Conference Held at the Fort St. George's in the Country of York, the Fourth Day of August . . . 1742 between his Excellency William Shirley, Esq . . . and the Chief Sachems and Captains of the Penobscott, Norridgewock, Pigwaket or Amiscogging or Saco. St. John's Bescommonconty or Ameriscongging and St. Francis Tribe of Indians. Boston, 1742. Evans Collection, ser. 1, no. 4976.

A Conference Held at St. George's in the County of York . . . 1753. Boston, 1753. Evans Collection, ser. 1, no. 7025.

George Town and Arrowsick Island, Aug. 9th, 1717, Annogue Regni Regis Georgii Magna Britannia, &c. A Conference of His Excellency the Gouvernour, With the Sachems and Chief Men of the Eastern Indians. Boston, 1717. Evans Collection, ser. 1, no. 1894.

Journal of the Proceedings at Two Conferences Begun to be held at Falmouth in Casco Bay in the County of York. Boston, 1754. Evans Collection, ser. 1, no. 7222.

Other Published Primary Sources

An Answer to the Remarks of the Plymouth Company. Boston, 1753. Evans Collection, ser. 1, no. 6976.

An Appeal to the Men of New England, with a Short Account of Mr. Randolph's Papers. Boston: 1689. Evans Collection, ser. 1, no. 455.

At a Meeting of the Proprietors of the Township of Brunswick in the County of York . . . Boston: 1753. Evans Collection: ser. 1, no. 40647.

Blackstone, William. *Commentaries on the Laws of England.* 4 vols. London, 1766.

Bulkley, John. "The Right of the Aboriginal Natives to the Lands." Introduction to *Poetical Mediations, Being the Improvement of Some Vacant Hours,* by Roger Wolcott. New London, CT, 1725. Evans Collection, ser. 1, no. 2722.

Chadwick, Joseph. "An Account of a Journey from Fort Pownal—Now Fort Point—Up the Penobscot River to Quebec, in 1764." *Bangor Historical Magazine* 4 (1889): 141–48.

Coke, Sir Edward. *The First Part of the Institutes of the Lawes of England. Or, a Commentarie upon Littleton, Not the Name of a Lawyer Onely, but of the Law it selfe.* London, 1628.

A Defence of the Remarks of the Plymouth Company, on the Plan and Extracts of Deeds Published by the Proprietors of the Township of Brunswick. Boston, 1753. Evans Collection, ser. 1, no. 6988.

Defence of the Remarks of the Plymouth Company, On the Plan and Extracts of Deeds published by the Proprietors (as they term themselves) of the Township of Brunswick. Boston, 1754. Evans Collection, ser. 1, no. 7098.

Douglass, William. *A Summary, Historical and Political, of the First Planting, Progressive Improvements, and Present State of British Settlements in America.* 2 vols. Boston, 1749. Accessed on ECCO.

Dummer, Jeremiah. *A Defence of the New England Charters.* Boston, 1721. Evans Collection, ser. 1, no. 2216.

Gyles, John. *Memoirs of Odd Adventures, Strange Deliverances etc., in the Captivity of John Gyles, Esq., Commander of the Garrison on St. George River, in the District of Maine.* In *Held Captive by Indians: Selected Narratives, 1642–1836,* edited by Richard Vanderbeets. Knoxville: University of Tennessee Press, 1973.

Johnson, Samuel. *A Dictionary of the English Language.* London, 1755–56. Accessed on ECCO.

Josselyn, John. *An Account of Two Voyages to New England.* London, 1674. Accessed on EEBO.

"Journal of the Reverend Joseph Baxter of Medfield, Missionary to the Eastern Indians in 1717." *New England Genealogical and Historical Register* 21. Boston: New England Historic-Genealogical Society, 1847–. 45–60.

"Journal of the Voyage of Gov. Thomas Pownall, From Boston to Penobscot River. May 1759." *CMeHS* 5 (1857): 363–89.

Keayne, Robert. "The Apologia of Robert Keayne." Edited by Bernard Bailyn. *WMQ,* 3d ser., 7, no. 4 (October 1950): 568–87.

Maillard, Antoine Simon. *An Account of the Customs and Manners of the Micmakis and Maricheets Savage Nations . . . From an Original French Manuscript-Letter, Never Published . . .* London, 1758.

Mather, Cotton. *Decennium Luctuosum: An History of Remarkable Occurrences, in the Long War, Which New-England hath had with the Indian Salvages, From the Year, 1688. To the Year 1698.* Boston, 1699. Accessed on EEBO.

———. *Duodecennium Luctuosum: The History of a Long War with Indian Salvages, And Their Directors and Abettors; From the Year, 1702. To the Year, 1714.* Boston, 1714. Accessed on ECCO.

———. *Observable Things: The History of Ten Years Rolled away under the Great Calamities of A WAR with Indian Salvages: Repeated and Improved, In a Sermon, at Boston Lecture.* Boston, 1699. Accessed on EEBO.*A Memorial, Humbly Shewing, the Past and Present State of the Land lying Waste and Uninhabited between Nova Scotia, and the Province of Main in New England and America.* London, 1721. Evans Collection, ser. 1, no. 2261.

Moody, Joseph. *Handkerchief Moody: The Diary and the Man.* Edited and translated by Philip McIntire Woodwell. Portland, Me: Colonial Offset Printing Co., 1981.

Moody, Robert E., ed. "Three Documents Concerning a Proposal to Establish a Province of Georgia in New England." *NEQ* 14, no. 1 (March 1941): 113–20.

Moody, Samuel. *The Debtors Monitor, Directory & Comforter: or, The Way to Get & Keep out of Debt. In Three Sermons.* Boston, 1715.

Palmer, John. *The Present State of New England Impartially Considered, in a Letter to the Clergy.* Boston, 1689. Accessed on EEBO.

Pawling, Micah A., ed. *Wabanaki Homeland and the New State of Maine: The 1820 Journal and Plans of Survey of Joseph Treat.* Amherst: University of Massachusetts Press, 2007.

Peabody, Oliver. *An Essay to Revive and Encourage Military Exercises, Skill and Valor among the Sons of God's People in New England.* Boston, 1732. Copy in Library of the Society of the Cincinnati, Washington, DC.

Penhallow, Samuel. *The History of the Wars of New England with the Eastern Indians.* Boston, 1726. Reprint, Edward Wheelock Williamstown, MA: Corner House, 1924, 1973.

Pursuant to a Warrant to me directed . . . Boston, 1751. Evans Collection, ser. 1, no. 40599.

Rasles, Sebastien. *A Dictionary of the Abnaki Language in North America.* Edited by John M. Pickering. Memoirs of the Academy of Arts and Sciences, n.s., 1. Cambridge, MA, 1833.

Raudot, Antoine Denis. *Relation par lettres de l'Amérique Septentrionale, Années 1707–1710.* Edited by Camile de Rochemonteix. Paris: Letouzey et Ané, 1904.

Rawson, Edward. *The Revolution in New England Justified, and the People There Vindicated from the Aspersions Cast upon Them by Mr. John Palmer.* Boston, 1691. Evans Collection, ser. 1, no. 575.

The Rebels Reward: Or, English Courage Display'd. Being a full and true Account of the Victory obtain'd over the Indians at Norrigiwock, on the Twelfth of

August last, by the English Forces under Command of Capt. Johnson Harmon. Boston, 1724.

Sewall, Samuel. *The Diary of Samuel Sewall, 1674–1729*. Edited by Thomas M. Halsey. New York: Farrar, Straus and Giroux, 1973.

———. *Letter Book of Samuel Sewall. CMHS*, 6th ser., 2 (1888).

———. "A Memorial Relating to the Kenebeck Indians." *Collections of the Maine Historical Society*, ser. 1, vol. 3 (1853): 350–53.

Smith, Reverend Thomas. *Journals of the Reverend Thomas Smith, and the Reverend Samuel Deane, Pastors of the First Church in Portland: With Notes and Biograpical Notices: And a Summary History of Portland*. Edited by William Willis. Portland, ME: Joseph S. Bailey, 1849.

A Strange Account of the Rising and Breaking of a Great Bubble. Boston, 1767. Evans Collection, ser. 1, no. 10778.

Symmes, Thomas. *Lovewell Lamented. Or, A Sermon Occasion'd by the Fall of the Brave Capt. John Lovewell and Several of His Valiant Company, in the Late Heroic Action at Piggwacket, Prounounc'd at Bradford, May 16, 1725*. Boston, 1725. Evans Collection, ser. 1, no. 2705.

Vanderbeets, Richard, ed. *Held Captive by Indians: Selected Narratives, 1642–1836*. Knoxville: University of Tennessee Press, 1973.

Waldo, Samuel. *A Defence of the Title of the late John Everett, Esq, to a Tract of Land in the Eastern Parts of the Province of Massachusetts Bay, Commonly Called Muscongus Lands, Lying upon St. George's, Muscongus, and Penobscot Rivers*. Boston, 1736. Evans Collection, ser. 1, no. 4098.

———. *Samuel Waldo of Boston, Merchant, Intending with All Possible Expedition* . . . Boston, 1735. Evans Collection, ser. 1, no. 4088.

———. *Whereas since my return from St. Georges River in the eastern parts of this province* . . . Boston, 1735. Evans Collection, ser. 1, no. 40087.Winthrop, John. *Winthrop Papers* (Boston: Massachusetts Historical Society, 1931)

Published Oral Historical Sources

Harrington, M. Raymond. "An Abenaki 'Witch-Story.'" *Journal of American Folklore* 14, no. 54 (July–September 1901): 160.

———. "An Abenaki 'Witchcraft Story.'" *Journal of American Folklore* 15, no. 56 (January–March 1902): 62–63.

All Other Secondary Sources

Adelman, Jeremy, and Stephen Aron. "From Borderlands to Borders: Empires, Nation States, and the Peoples in between in North American History." *American Historical Review* 104, no. 3 (June 1999): 814–41.

Akagi, Roy H. *The Town Proprietors of the New England Colonies: A Study in Their Development, Organization, Activities and Controversies, 1620–1770*. Philadelphia: University of Pennsylvania Press, 1924.

Albion, Robert G. *Forests and Sea Power: The Timber Problem of the Royal Navy, 1652–1862.* 1926. Reprint, Annapolis, MD: Naval Institute Press, 2000.

Allen, Neal, Jr. "Law and Authority to the Eastward: Maine Courts, Magistrates, and Lawyers, 1690–1730." In *Law in Colonial Massachusetts, 1630–1800,* edited by Daniel R. Coquillette, 273–312. Boston: Colonial Society of Massachusetts, 1981.

Anderson, Chad. "Rediscovering Native North America: Settlements, Maps, and Empires in the Eastern Woodlands." *Early American Studies* 14, no. 3 (Summer 2016): 478–505.

Anderson, Virginia DeJohn. *Creatures of Empire: How Domestic Animals Transformed Early America.* New York: Oxford University Press, 2004.

Armitage, David. *The Ideological Origins of the British Empire.* Cambridge: Cambridge University Press, 2000.

Arneil, Barbara. *John Locke and America: The Defence of English Colonialism.* Oxford: Clarendon, 1996.

Aron, Stephen. "Pigs and Hunters: Rights in the Woods." In *Contact Points: American Frontiers from the Mohawk Valley to the Mississippi, 1750–1830,* edited by Andrew R. L. Cayton and Frederika J. Teute. Chapel Hill: University of North Carolina Press, 1998.

Attwood, Bain. "Law, History and Power: The British Treatment of Aboriginal Rights in Land in New South Wales." *Journal of Imperial and Commonwealth History* 42, no. 1 (2014): 171–92.

Bahar, Matthew. "People of the Dawn, People of the Door: Indian Pirates and the Violent Theft of an Atlantic World." *JAH* 101, no. 2 (September 2014): 401–26.

Baker, Emerson W. *The Clarke & Lake Company: The Historical Archaeology of a Seventeenth-Century Maine Settlement.* Augusta: Maine Historical Preservation Commission, 1985.

———. "Finding the Almouchiquois: Native American Families, Territories, and Land Sales in Southern Maine." *Ethnohistory* 51, no. 1 (Winter 2004): 73–100.

———. "Formerly Machegonne, Dartmouth, York, Stogummor, Casco, and Falmouth: Portland as a Contested Frontier in the Seventeenth Century." In *Creating Portland: History and Place in Northern New England,* edited by Joseph A. Conforti. Lebanon, NH: University of New Hampshire Press, 2005.

———. "A Scratch with a Bear's Paw: Anglo-Indian Land Deeds in Early Maine." *Ethnohistory* 36, no. 3 (1989): 235–56.

———. "Trouble to the Eastward: The Failure of Anglo-Indian Relations in Early Maine." PhD diss., College of William and Mary, 1986.

Baker, Emerson, Edwin A. Churchill, Richard D'Abate, Kristine L. Jones, Victor A. Conrad, and Herald E. L. Prins, eds. *American Beginnings: Exploration,*

Culture, and Cartography in the Land of Norumbega. Lincoln: University of Nebraska Press, 1994.

Baker, Emerson W., and John G. Reid. "Amerindian Power in the Early Modern Northeast: A Reappraisal." *WMQ* 61, no. 1 (2004): 77–106.

———. *The New England Knight: Sir William Phips, 1651–1695*. Toronto: University of Toronto Press, 1998.Banks, Charles E. *History of York, Maine. Successively Known as Bristol (1632), Agamenticus (1641), Gorgeana (1642), and York (1652) in Three Volumes*. Boston: Calkins, 1931–35.

Barry, William David. *Tate House: Crown of the Maine Mast Trade*. With Frances W. Peabody. Portland: National Society of Colonial Dames of America in the State of Maine, 1982.

Batinski, Michael C. *Jonathan Belcher, Colonial Governor*. Lexington: University of Kentucky Press, 1996.

Battiste, Marie, ed. *Living Treaties: Narrating Mi'kmaw Treaty Relations*. Sydney, Nova Scotia: Cape Breton University Press, 2016.Beck, Harold P. *The American Indian as a Sea Fighter in Colonial Times*. Mystic, CT: Marine Historical Association, 1959.

Bellesilles, Michael A. *Revolutionary Outlaws: Ethan Allen and the Struggle for Independence on the Early American Frontier*. Charlottesville: University Press of Virginia, 1993.

Belmessous, Saliha, ed. *Native Claims: Indigenous Law against Empire*. Oxford: University Press, 2011.

Bennett, Zachary M. "A Means of Removing Them Further from Us: The Struggle for Waterpower on New England's Eastern Frontier." *NEQ* 90, no. 4 (December 2017): 540–60.

Benton, Lauren. *Law and Colonial Cultures: Legal Regimes in World History, 1400–1900*. Cambridge: Cambridge University Press, 2002.

Benton, Lauren, and Richard Ross. *Legal Pluralism and Empires, 1500–1850*. New York: New York University Press, 2013.

Bilodeau, Christopher J. "Creating an Indian Enemy in the Borderlands: King Philip's War in Maine, 1675–1678." *Maine History* 47, no. 1 (January 2013): 11–42.

———. "The Economy of War: Violence, Religion, and the Wabanaki Indians in the Maine Borderlands." PhD. diss., Cornell University, 2006.

———. "Understanding Ritual in Colonial Wabanakia." *French Colonial History* 14, no. 1 (2013): 1–31.

Bishop, Charles A. "Territoriality among Northeastern Algonquians." *Anthropologica* 28, no. 1–2 (January 1986): 37–63.

Bourne, Edward E. *The History of Wells and Kennebunk from the Earliest Settlement to the Year 1820, at Which Time Kennebunk Was Set Off, and Incorporated*. Portland, ME: B. Thurston & Co., 1875.

Bourque, Bruce J. "Ethnicity on the Maritime Peninsula, 1600–1759." *Ethnohistory* 36, no. 3 (Summer 1989): 257–84.

————. *Twelve Thousand Years: American Indians in Maine*. Lincoln: University of Nebraska Press, 2001.

Bowen, H. V. *Elites, Enterprise, and the Making of the British Overseas Empire, 1688–1775*. London: Macmillan, 1996.

Bowes, John P. *Land Too Good for Indians: Northern Indian Removal*. Norman: University of Oklahoma Press, 2017.

Breen, T. H. *The Character of the Good Ruler: A Study of Puritan Political Ideas in New England, 1630–1730*. New Haven, CT: Yale University Press, 1970.

Brooks, Lisa T. *The Common Pot: The Recovery of Native Space in the Northeast*. Minneapolis: University of Minnesota Press, 2008.

Brooks, Lisa T., and Cassandra M. Brooks. "Reciprocity Principle and Traditional Ecological Knowledge: Understanding the Significance of Indigenous Protest on the Presumpscot River." *International Journal of Critical Indigenous Studies* 2, no. 2 (2010): 11–28.

Burrage, Henry S. *The Beginnings of Colonial Maine, 1602–1658*. Portland: Printed for the State, 1914.

Burrage, Henry S., and Albert Roscoe Stubbs. *Genealogical and Family History of the State of Maine*. 4 vols. New York: Lewis Historical Publishing, 1909.Bushman, Richard L. *From Puritan to Yankee: Character and the Social Order in Connecticut, 1690–1765*. Cambridge: Harvard University Press, 1967.

Calloway, Colin. *The American Revolution in Indian Country*. Cambridge: Cambridge University Press, 1995.

————. *Pen and Ink Witchcraft: Treaties and Treaty Making in American Indian History*. Oxford: Oxford University Press, 2012.

————. *The Western Abenakis of Vermont, 1600–1800: War, Migration, and Survival of an Indian People*. Norman: University of Oklahoma Press, 1990.

Campbell, William J. *Speculators in Empire: Iroquoia and the 1768 Treaty of Fort Stanwix*. Norman: University of Oklahoma Press, 2012.

Carroll, Brian D. "'Savages' in the Service of Empire: Native American Soldiers in Gorham's Rangers, 1744–1762." *NEQ* 85 (September 2012): 383–429.

Cayton, Andrew R. L., and Frederika J. Teute, eds. *Contact Points: American Frontiers from the Mohawk Valley to the Mississippi, 1750–1830*. Chapel Hill: University of North Carolina Press, 1998.

Chase, Fannie S. *Wiscasset in Pownalborough: A History of the Shire Town and the Salient Historical Features of the Territory between the Sheepscot and Kennebec Rivers*. Wiscasset, ME: Southworth-Anthoensen Press, 1941.

Chmielewski, Laura M. *The Spice of Popery: Converging Christianities on an Early American Frontier*. Notre Dame, IN: University of Notre Dame Press, 2012.

Churchill, Edwin. "Too Great the Challenge: The Birth and Death of Falmouth Maine, 1624–1676." PhD diss., University of Maine, 1979.

Clark, Charles E. *The Eastern Frontier: The Settlement of Northern New England 1610–1763*. New York: Knopf, 1970.

Colley, Linda. *Britons: Forging the Nation, 1707–1837*. New Haven, CT: Yale University Press, 1992.

Conforti, Joseph A., ed. *Creating Portland: History and Place in Northern New England*. Lebanon, NH: University of New Hampshire Press, 2005.

Conrad, Margaret, ed. *They Planted Well: New England Planters in Maritime Canada*. Fredericton, New Brunswick: Acadiensis, 1988.

Cook, Edward M., Jr. *The Fathers of the Towns: Leadership and Community Structure in Eighteenth-Century New England*. Baltimore: Johns Hopkins University Press, 1978.

Cook, Sherbourne F. "Interracial Warfare and Population Decline among the New England Indians." *Ethnohistory* 20, no. 1 (Winter 1973): 1–24.

Cooper, John. "Is the Algonquian Family Hunting Ground System Pre-Columbian?" *American Anthropologist*, n,s., 41, no. 1 (January–March, 1939): 66–90.

Coquillette, David R., ed. *Law in Colonial Massachusetts, 1630–1800*. Vol. 62. Boston: Colonial Society of Massachusetts, 1981.

Countryman, Edward. "'Out of the Bounds of the Law:' Northern Land Rioters in the Eighteenth Century." In *The American Revolution: Explorations in the History of American Radicalism*, edited by Alfred Young. DeKalb: Northern Illinois University Press, 1976.

Crawford, William. "Northeast Plants." In *Handbook of North American Indians*, vol. 3.

Cray, Robert E., Jr. "'Weltering in their Own Blood': Puritan Casualties in King Philip's War." *Historical Journal of Massachusetts* 37, no. 2 (Fall 2009): 107–23.

Cronon, William. *Changes in the Land: Indians, Colonists, and the Ecology of New England*. New York: Hill and Wang, 1983.

Cushman, David Quimby. *A History of Ancient Sheepscot and Newcastle, Including Early Pemaquid, Damariscotta, and Other Contiguous Places, From the Earliest Discovery to the Present Time ,Together with the Genealogy of More Than Four Hundred Families*. Bath, ME: Upton & Son, 1882.

Day, Clarence Albert. *A History of Maine Agriculture*. Orono: University of Maine Press, 1954.

Day, Gordon M. *The Identity of the St. Francis Indians*. Ottawa: National Museums of Canada, 1981.

———. "Oral Tradition as Complement." *Ethnohistory* 19, no. 2 (Spring 1972): 99–108.

———. "The Ouragie War: A Case History in Iroquois-New England Relations," In *Extending the Rafters: Interdisciplinary Approaches to Iroquoian Studies*, edited by Michael K. Foster, Jack Campisi, and Marianne Mithun. Albany: State University of New York Press, 1984.

———. "The Western Abenaki Transformer." *Journal of the Folklore Institute* 12 (1976): 77–84.

de Vries, Jan. *The Industrious Revolution: Consumer Behavior and the Household Economy, 1650 to the Present.* New York: Cambridge University Press, 2008.

Demeritt, David. "Agriculture, Climate, and Cultural Adaptation in the Prehistoric Northeast." *Archaeology of Eastern North America* 19 (Fall 1991): 183–202.*Dictionary of Canadian Biography.* www.biographi.ca.

Dole, Samuel Thomas. *Windham in the Past.* Windham Historical Society, 1916.

Drinnon, Richard. *Facing West: The Metaphysics of Indian-Hating and Empire-Building.* Minneapolis: University of Minnesota Press, 1980.

Dunn, Shirley W. *The Mohicans and Their Land, 1609–1730.* Fleischmanns, NY: Purple Mountain, 1994.

Eckstorm, Fannie Hardy. "The Attack on Norridgewock, 1724." *NEQ* 7, no. 3 (September 1934): 541–78.

Emery, Geoffrey Alexander. *Ancient City of Gorgeana and Modern Town of York (Maine) from Its Earliest Settlement to the Present Time.* Boston: G. A. Emery, 1874.

Fischer, David Hackett. *Albion's Seed: Four British Folkways in America.* New York: Oxford University Press, 1989.

Foster, Michael K., Jack Campisi, and Marianne Mithun, eds. *Extending the Rafters: Interdisciplinary Approaches to Iroquoian Studies.* Albany: State University of New York Press, 1984.

Foster, Stephen. "Another Legend of the Province House: Jonathan Belcher, William Shirley, and the Misconstruction of the Imperial Relationship." *NEQ* 77, no. 2 (June 2004): 179–223.

Ghere, David L. "Abenaki Factionalism, Emigration and Social Continuity: Indian Society in Northern New England, 1725 to 1765." PhD diss., University of Maine, Orono. 1988.

———. "The 'Disappearance' of the Abenaki in Western Maine: Political Organization and Ethnocentric Assumptions." *American Indian Quarterly,* ser. 2, 17 (1993): 193–207.

———. "Eastern Abenaki Autonomy and French Frustrations, 1745–1760." *Maine History* 34, no. 1 (Summer 1994): 2–21.

———. "Mistranslations and Misinformation: Diplomacy on the Maine Frontier, 1725 to 1755." *American Indian Culture and Research Journal* ser. 4, 8 (1984): 3–26.

———. "Myths and Methods in Abenaki Demography: Abenaki Population Recovery, 1725–1750." *Ethnohistory* 44, no. 3 (Summer 1997): 511–34.

Ghere, David L., and Alvin H. Morrison. "Sanctions for Slaughter: Peacetime Violence on the Maine Frontier, 1749–1772." In *Papers of the Twenty-Seventh Algonquian Conference,* edited by David H. Pentland. Winnipeg: University of Manitoba, 1996.

———. "Searching for Justice on the Maine Frontier: Legal Concepts, Treaties, and the 1749 Wiscasset Incident." *American Indian Quarterly* 25, no. 3 (Summer 2001): 378–99.

Grant, Charles S. "Land Speculation and the Settlement of Kent, 1738–1760." *NEQ* 28, no. 1 (March 1955): 51–71.

Greenblatt, Stephen. *Marvelous Possessions: The Wonder of the New World.* Chicago: University of Chicago Press, 1992.

Greene, Jack P. *Pursuits of Happiness: The Social Development of Early Modern British Colonies and the Formation of Early American Culture.* Chapel Hill: University of North Carolina Press, 1988.

Greer, Alan. "Commons and Enclosure in the Colonization of North America." *AHR* 117, no. 2 (April 2012): 365–86.

———. *The People of New France.* Toronto: University of Toronto Press, 1997.

———. *Property and Dispossession: Natives, Empires, and Land in Early Modern North America.* Cambridge: Cambridge University Press, 2018.

Grenier, John. *The Far Reaches of Empire: War in Nova Scotia, 1710–1760.* Norman: University of Oklahoma Press, 2008.

———. *The First Way of War: American War Making on the Frontier, 1607–1814.* New York: Cambridge University Press, 2005.

Greven, Philip J. *Four Generations: Population, Land, and Family in Colonial Andover, Massachusetts.* Ithaca, NY: Cornell University Press, 1970.

Griffin, Patrick, ed. *Experiencing Empire: People, Power, and Revolution in Early America.* Charlottesville: University of Virginia Press, 2017.

Grumet, Robert S., ed. *Northeastern Indian Lives, 1632–1816.* Amherst: University of Massachusetts Press, 1996.

Haefeli, Evan, and Kevin Sweeney. *Captors and Captives: The 1704 French and Indian Raid on Deerfield.* Amherst: University of Massachusetts Press, 2005.

Hallowell, A. Irving. "The Size of Algonkian Hunting Territories: A Function of Ecological Adjustement." *American Anthropologist*, n.s., 51, no. 1 (January–March 1949): 35–45.

Hardesty, Jared. *Unfreedom: Slavery and Dependence in Eighteenth-Century Boston.* New York: New York University Press, 2016.

Heyrman, Christine Leigh. *Commerce and Culture: The Maritime Communities of Colonial Massachusetts, 1690–1750.* New York: Norton, 1984.

Hinderaker, Eric. *Elusive Empires: Constructing Colonialism in the Ohio Valle: 1673–1800.* New York: Cambridge University Press, 1997.

Hirsch, Adam J. "The Collision of Military Cultures in Seventeenth-Century New England." *JAH* 74, no. 4 (March 1988): 1187–212.

Hixon, Walter L. *American Settler Colonialism: A History.* New York: Palgrave Macmillan, 2013.

Hodson, Christopher. "Rethinking Failure: The French Empire in the Age of John Law." In *Experiencing Empire: People, Power, and Revolution in Early America*, edited by Patrick Griffin, 127–46. Charlottesville: University of Virginia Press, 2017.

Hoffman, Bernard G. "Ancient Tribes Revisited: A Summary of Indian Distribution and Movement in the Northeastern United States from 1534 to 1779. Parts I–III." *Ethnohistory* 14, no. 1/2 (Winter–Spring 1967): 1–46.

———. "Souriquois, Etechemin and Kwedech—A Lost Chapter in American Ethnography." *Ethnohistory* 2, no. 1 (Winter 1955): 65–87.Holland, Kathryn E. *Deerskins and Duffels: The Creek Indian Trade with Anglo-America, 1685–1815.* Lincoln: University of Nebraska Press, 2008.

Horsman, Reginald. *Race and Manifest Destiny: Origins of American Anglo-Saxonism.* Cambridge: Harvard University Press, 1981.

Howard, Michael, George J. Andreopoulos, and Mark R. Shulman, eds. *The Laws of War: Constraints on Warfare in the Western World.* New Haven: Yale University Press, 1994.

Hutchinson, Thomas. *The History of the Colony and Province of Massachusetts-Bay.* 3 vols. Edited by Lawrence Shaw Mayo. Cambridge: Harvard University Press, 1936, Reprint, New York: Kraus Reprint Co., 1970.

Hutton, Ronald. *Stations of the Sun: A History of the Ritual Year in Britain.* Oxford: University Press, 1996.

Innes, Stephen. *Creating the Commonwealth: The Economic Culture of Puritan New England.* New York: Norton, 1995.

———. *Labor in a New Land: Economy and Society in Seventeenth-Century Springfield.* Princeton, NJ: Princeton University Press, 1983.Jennings, Francis. *The Invasion of America: Indians, Colonialism, and the Cant of Conquest.* Chapel Hill: University of North Carolina Press, 1975.

Johnson, Richard. "The Search for a Useable Indian: An Aspect of the Defense of Colonial New England." *JAH* 64 (December 1977): 623–51.

Kars, Marjorine. *Breaking Loose Together: The Regulator Rebellion in Pre-Revolutionary North Carolina.* Chapel Hill: University of North Carolina Press, 2002.

Kawashima, Yasuhide. *Puritan Justice and the Indian: White Man's Law in Massachusetts, 1630–1763.* Middletown, CT: Wesleyan University Press, 1986.

Kershaw, Gordon E. *The Kennebeck Proprietors, 1749–1775: "Gentlemen of Large Property & Judicious Men."* Portland: Maine Historical Society, 1975.

Kim, Sung Bok. *Landlord and Tenant in Colonial New York: Manorial Society, 1664–1775.* Chapel Hill: University of North Carolina Press, 1978.

Konig, David. *Law and Society in Puritan Massachusetts: Essex County, 1629–1692.* Chapel Hill: University of North Carolina Press, 1979.

Leach, Douglas Edward. *The Northern Colonial Frontier, 1607–1763.* New York: Holt, Rinehart and Winston, 1966.

Leamon, James S. *Revolution Downeast: The War for American Independence in Maine.* Amherst: University of Massachusetts Press, 1993.

Leavenworth, Peter S. "'The Best Title that Indians Can Claime': Native Agency and Consent in the Transferal of Penacook-Pawtucket Land in the Seventeenth Century." *NEQ* 72, no. 2 (June 1999): 275–300.

Leavitt, M. Robert, and David A. Francis, eds. *Wapapi Akonutoakonol: The Wampum Records, Wabanaki Traditional Laws*. Fredericton: University of New Brunswick, 1990.

Lee, Wayne. "Peace Chiefs and Blood Revenge: Patterns of Restraint in Native American Warfare, 1500–1800." *Journal of Military History* 71, no. 3 (July 2007): 701–41.

Lennox, Jeffers. *Homelands and Empires: Indigenous Spaces, Imperial Fictions, and Competition for Territory in Northeastern North America, 1690–1763*. Toronto: University of Toronto Press, 2017.

Lepore, Jill. *The Name of War: King Philip's War and the Origins of American Identity*. New York: Knopf, 1998.

Libby, Charles T. *The Libby Family in America. 1602–1881*. Portland, ME: B. Thurston & Co., 1882.

Little, Anne M. *Abraham in Arms: War and Gender in Colonial New England*. Philadelphia: University of Pennsylvania Press, 2007.

Little, Elizabeth. "Three Kinds of Indian Land Deeds at Nantucket, Massachusetts." In *Papers of the 11th Algonquian Conference*, edited by William Cowan, 61–70. Ottawa: Carleton University, 1980.

Lockridge, Kenneth A. *A New England Town: The First Hundred Years in Dedham Massachusetts, 1636–1736*. New York: Norton, 1985.

Lord, Robert, John E. Sexton, and Edward T. Harrington. *History of the Archdiocese in the Various Stages of its Development, 1604 to 1943 in Three Volumes*. New York: Sheed and Ward, 1944.

Lovejoy, David S. *The Glorious Revolution in America*. Hanover, NH: University Press of New England, 1972.

Lynn, John A. *Battle: A History of Combat and Culture from Ancient Greece to Modern America*. Philadelphia: Westview, 2003.

MacDougall, Pauleena. *The Penobscot Dance of Resistance: Tradition in the History of a People*. Durham: University of New Hampshire Press, 2004.

MacFarlane, Alan. *The Origins of English Individualism: The Family Property and Social Transition*. London: Wiley-Blackwell, 1991.

Macmillian, Ken. *Sovereignty and Possession in the English New World: The Legal Foundations of the English New World*. Cambridge: Cambridge University Press, 2006.

Malone, Joseph J. *Pine Trees and Politics: The Naval Stores and Forest Policy in Colonial New England, 1691–1775*. Seattle: University of Washington Press, 1964.

Mancke, Elizabeth. "Corporate Structure and Private Interest," In *They Planted Well: New England Planters in Maritime Canada*, edited by Margaret Conrad, 161–77. Fredericton, New Brunswick: Acadiensis, 1988.

Martin, John Frederick. *Profits in the Wilderness: Entrepreneurship and the Founding of New England Towns in the Seventeenth Century*. Chapel Hill: University of North Carolina Press, 1991.

McBride, Bunny, and Herald E. L. Prins. "Walking the Line: Molly Ockett, Pig-wacket Doctor." In *Northeastern Indian Lives, 1632–1816*, edited by Robert S. Grumet, 321–47. Amherst: University of Massachusetts Press, 1996.

McClellan, Hugh D. *History of Gorham, Maine*. Portland, ME: Smith & Sale, 1903.

McConville, Brendan. *These Daring Disturbers of the Public Peace: The Struggle for Property and Power in Early New Jersey*. Ithaca, NY: Cornell University Press, 1999.

McHugh, P. C. "'A Pretty Government!': The 'Confederation of United Tribes' and Britain's Quest for Imperial Order in the New Zealand Islands during the 1830s." In *Legal Pluralism and Empires, 1500–1850*, edited by Lauren Benton and Richard Ross, 233–60. New York: New York University Press, 2013.

McKinley, Albert Edward. *The Suffrage Franchise in the Thirteen English Colonies in America*. Philadelphia: Ginn and Co., Selling Agents, 1905.

Milford, T. A. *The Gardiners of Massachusetts: Provincial Ambition and the British-American Career*. Durham: University of New Hampshire Press, 2005.

Minot, Joseph Gratton. *A Genealogical Record of the Minot Family in America and England*. Boston: privately printed, 1897.

Montgomery, Alexandra. "Projecting Power in the Dawnland: Colonization Schemes, Imperial Failure, and Competing Visions in the Gulf of Maine World." PhD diss., University of Pennsylvania. 2019.

Moody, Robert E. "The Documents Concerning a Proposal to Establish a Province of Georgia in New England." *NEQ* 14, no. 1 (March, 1941): 113–20.

———. "The Maine Frontier, 1607–1763." PhD diss., Yale University, 1933.

Morrison, Alvin H. "Dawnland Decisions: Seventeenth-Century Wabanaki Leaders and Their Responses to Differential Contact Stimuli in the Overlap Area of New France and New England." PhD diss., SUNY Buffalo, 1974.

Morrison, Kenneth M. *The Embattled Northeast: The Elusive Ideal of Alliance in Abenaki-Euramerican Relations*. Berkeley: University of California Press, 1984.

———. "The Mythological Sources of Abenaki Catholicism: A Case Study of the Social History of Power." *Religion* 11 (1981): 253–63.Nash, Alice. "The Abiding Frontier: Family, Gender and Religion in Wabanaki History, 1600–1763." PhD diss., Columbia University, 1997.

Nicholas, Andrea Bear. "Mascarene's Treaty of 1725." *University of New Brunswick Law Journal* 43 (1994): 3–20.

Nicolar, Joseph. *The Life and Traditions of the Red Man*. Bangor, ME: C. H. Glass and Co., 1893.

Nobles, Gregory H. *Divisions throughout the Whole: Politics and Society in Hampshire County, Massachusetts, 1740–1775*. Cambridge: Cambridge University Press, 1983.

Noyes, Sybil, Charles Thorton Libby, and Walter Goodwin Davis, eds. *Genea-*

logical Dictionary of Maine and New Hampshire. Baltimore: Genealogical Publishing Co., 1972.

O'Brien, M. J. "The Lost Town of Cork, Maine: The Early Attempt by Robert Temple and Emigrants from Ireland to Establish a Settlement in the Kennebec Wilderness." *Journal of the American-Irish Historical Society* 12 (1913): 175–84.

Onuf, Peter S. *Jefferson's Empire: The Language of American Nationhood*. Charlottesville: University of Virginia Press, 200.

Owen, Daniel E. *Old Times in Saco: A Brief Monograph of Local Events*. Saco, ME: Biddeford Times, 1891.

Pagden, Anthony. *Lords of All the World: Ideologies of Empire in Spain, Britain, and France, c. 1500–1800*. New Haven, CT: Yale University Press, 1995.

Palmater, Pamela. "My Tribe, My Heirs and Their Heirs Forever: Living Mi'kmaw Treaties." In *Living Treaties: Narrating Mi'kmaw Treaty Relations*, edited by Marie Battiste, 24–41. Sydney, Nova Scotia: Cape Breton University Press, 2016.

Parker, Geoffrey. "Early Modern Europe." In *The Laws of War: Constraints on Warfare in the Western World*, edited by Michael Howard, George J. Andreopoulos, and Mark R. Shulman, 40–58. New Haven, CT: Yale University Press, 1994.

Patterson, Stephen. "Eighteenth-Century Treaties: The Mi'kmaq, Maliseet, and Passamaquoddy Experience." *Native Studies Review* 18, no. 1 (2009): 25–52.

Pencak, William A., and Daniel K. Richter, eds. *Friends and Enemies in Penn's Woods: Indians, Colonists, and the Racial Construction of Pennsylvania*. University Park: Pennsylvania State University Press, 2004.

Pierce, Josiah. *A History of the Town of Gorham, Maine, Prepared at the Request of the Town*. Portland, ME, 1862.

Plane, Anne Marie. *Colonial Intimacies: Indian Marriage in Early New England*. Ithaca, NY: Cornell University Press, 2000.

Plank, Geoffrey. *An Unsettled Conquest: The British Campaign against the Peoples of Acadia*. Philadelphia: University of Pennsylvania Press, 2001.

Powell, Sumner Chilton. *Puritan Village: The Formation of a New England Town*. Middletown, MA: Wesleyan University Press, 1963.

Preston, David L. "Squatters, Indians, Proprietary Government, and Land in the Susquehanna Valley." In *Friends and Enemies in Penn's Woods: Indians, Colonists, and the Racial Construction of Pennsylvania*, edited by William A. Pencak and Daniel K. Richter. University Park: Pennsylvania State University Press, 2004.

———. *The Texture of Contact: European and Indian Settler Communities on the Frontiers of Iroquoia, 1667–1783*. Lincoln: University of Nebraska Press, 2009.

Prins, Herald E. L. "Chief Rawandagon, Alias Robin Hood: Native 'Lord of Misrule' in the Maine Wilderness." In *Northeastern Indian Lives, 1632–1816*, edited by Robert S. Grumet. Amherst: University of Massachusetts Press, 1996.

———. "Children of Gluskap: Wabanaki Indians on the Eve of the European Invasion." In *American Beginnings: Exploration, Culture, and Cartography in the Land of Norumbega*, edited by Emerson A. Baker et al. Lincoln: University of Nebraska Press, 1994.

———. "The Crooked Path of Dummer's Treaty: Wabanaki Diplomacy and the Quest for Aboriginal Rights." In *Papers of the 33rd Algonquian Conference*, edited by H. C. Wolfart, 360–77. Winnipeg: University of Manitoba, 2002.

———. *The Mi'kmaq: Resistance, Accommodation, and Cultural Survival.* Fort Worth: Harcourt Brace College, 1996.

Pritchard, James. *In Search of Empire: The French in the Americas, 1670–1730.* Cambridge: Cambridge University Press, 2004.

Pulsipher, Jenny Hale. "'Dark Cloud Rising from the East': Indian Sovereignty and the Coming of King William's War in New England." *NEQ* 80, no. 4 (December 2007): 594–95.

———. "Gaining the Diplomatic Edge: Kinship, Trade, Ritual, and Religion in Amerindian Alliances in Early North America." In *Empires and Indigenes: Intercultural Alliance, Imperial Expansion, and Warfare in the Early Modern World*, edited by Wayne Lee, 19–48. New York: New York University Press, 2011.

———. *Subjects unto the Same King: Indians, English, and the Contest for Authority in Colonial New England.* Philadelphia: University of Pennsylvania Press, 2005.

Ray, Roger B. "Maine Indians' Concept of Land." *Maine Historical Society Quarterly* 13, no. 1 (1973): 28–51.

Reid, John G. *Acadia, Maine, and New Scotland: Marginal Colonies in the Seventeenth Century.* Toronto: University of Toronto Press, 1981.

———. "Empire: The Maritime Colonies, and the Supplanting of Mi'kma'ki/ Wulstukwiuk, 1780–1820." *Acadiensis* 38, no. 2 (Summer/Autumn 2009): 78–97.

———. *Essays on Northeastern North America, the Seventeenth and Eighteenth Centuries.* Toronto: University of Toronto Press, 2008.

———. *Maine, Charles II, and Massachusetts: Governmental Relationships in Early New England.* Portland: Maine Historical Society, 1977.

Richter, Daniel K. *The Ordeal of the Longhouse: The Peoples of the Iroquois League in the Era of European Colonization.* Chapel Hill: University of North Carolina Press, 1992.

Robinson, Aileen Moreton. *The White Possessive: Property, Power, and Indigenous Sovereignty.* Minneapolis: University of Minnesota Press, 2015.

Rowe, William Hutchinson. *Ancient North Yarmouth and Yarmouth, Maine, 1636–1936.* Yarmouth, ME: New England History Press, 1937.

Russell, Howard S. *A Long, Deep Furrow: Three Centuries of Farming in New England*. Hanover, NH: University Press of New England, 1976.

Saxine, Ian. "Performance of Peace: Indians, Speculators, and the Politics of Property on the Maine Frontier, 1735–1737." *NEQ* 87, no. 3 (September 2014): 379–411.

———. "Properties of Empire: Indians, Colonists, and Land Speculators on the Maine Frontier, 1713–1763." PhD diss., Northwestern University, 2016.

Schusky, Ernest L., ed. *Political Organization of Native North Americans*. Washington, DC: University Press of America, 1980.

Schutz, John A. *William Shirley, King's Governor of Massachusetts*. Chapel Hill: University of North Carolina Press, 1961.

Seed, Patricia. *Ceremonies of Possession in Europe's Conquest of the New World, 1492–1640*. Cambridge: Cambridge University Press, 1995.

Sibley, John Langdon, and Clifford K. Shipton. *Sibley's Harvard Graduates: Biographical Sketches of Those Who Attended Harvard College*. 17 vols. Cambridge: Harvard University Press, 1873–1975.

Simonoff, Faren R. *Crossing the Sound: The Rise of Atlantic American Communities in Seventeenth-Century Eastern Long Island*. New York: New York University Press, 2004.

Smith, S. D. *Slavery, Gentry, and Capitalism in the British Atlantic: The World of the Lascelles, 1648–1834*. Cambridge: Cambridge University Press, 2010.

Snow, Dean. "The Ethnographic Baseline of the Eastern Abenaki." *Ethnohistory* 23, no. 3 (Summer 1976): 291–306.

———. "Wabanaki 'Family Hunting Territories.'" *American Anthropologist*, n.s. 70, no. 6 (December 1968): 1143–51.

Snow, Dean, and Kim Lanphear. "European Contact and Indian Depopulation in the Northeast: The Timing of the First Epidemics." *Ethnohistory* 35, no. 1 (Winter 1988): 15–33.

Southgate, William S. *The History of Scarborough, From 1633 to 1783*. In *Collections of the Maine Historical Society*, vol. 3. Portland: Published for the Society, 1853.

Speck, Frank G. "Abenaki Clans—Never!" *American Anthropologist*, n.s., 37, no. 1 (July–September 1935): 528–30.

———. "The Eastern Algonkian Wabanaki Confederacy." *American Anthropologist*, n.s., 17, no. 3 (July–September 1915): 492–508.

———. "The Family Hunting Band as the Basis of Algonkian Social Organization." *American Anthropologist*, n.s., 17, no. 2 (April–June 1915): 289–305.

Stackpole, Everett. *Old Kittery and Her Families*. Lewiston, ME: Press of Lewiston Journal Co., 1903.

Stanwood, Owen. *The Empire Reformed: English America in the Age of the Glorious Revolution*. Philadelphia: University of Pennsylvania Press, 2011.

———. "Unlikely Imperialist: The Baron of St. Castin and the Transformation of the Northeastern Borderlands." *French Colonial History* 5 (2005): 43–61.

Starkey, Armstrong. *European and Native American Warfare, 1675–1815*. Norman: University of Oklahoma Press, 1998.

Stern, Philip J. "'Bundles of Hyphens': Corporations as Legal Communities in the Early Modern British Empire." In *Legal Pluralism and Empires, 1500–1850*, edited by Lauren Benton and Richard Ross, 21–48. New York: New York University Press, 2013.

Sturtevant, William C., ed. *Handbook of North American Indians*. Washington, DC: Smithsonian Institution Press, 1978–.

Sullivan, James. *History of the District of Maine*. Boston, 1795. Reprint, Augusta: Maine State Museum, 1970.

———. *The History of Land Titles in Massachusetts*. Boston, 1801.

Taylor Alan. "'A Kind of Warr': The Contest for Land on the Northeastern Frontier, 1750–1820." *WMQ*, 3d ser., 46, no. 1 (January 1989): 3–26.

———. *Liberty Men and Great Proprietors: The Revolutionary Settlement on the Maine Frontier, 1760–1820*. Chapel Hill: University of North Carolina Press, 1990.

Thayer, Henry O. "Fort Richmond, Maine." *CMeHS*, 2d ser., 5 (1894): 129–60.

———. "Ministry on the Kennebec: Period of the Indian Wars." *CMeHS*, 2d ser., 10 (1899): 263–81.

———. "Transient Town of Cork." *CMeHS*, 2d ser., 4 (1893): 240–65.

Thompson, E. P. "The Moral Economy of the English Crowd in the Eighteenth Century." *Past & Present* 50 (February 1971): 76–136.

Vaughan, Alden T. "From White Man to Redskin: Changing Anglo-American Perceptions of the American Indian." *American Historical Review* 87 (October 1992): 917–53.

Vickers, Daniel. "Competency and Competition: Economic Culture in Early America." *WMQ*, 3d ser., 47, no. 1 (January 1990): 3–29.

———. *Farmers and Fishermen: Two Centuries of Work in Essex County*. Chapel Hill: University of North Carolina Press, 1994.

Walker, Willard, Gregory Buesing, and Robert Conkling. "A Chronological Account of the Wabanaki Confederacy." In *Political Organization of Native North Americans*, edited by Ernest L. Schusky, 41–84. Washington, DC: University Press of America, 1980.

Watson, Stephen Marion, ed. *The Maine Historical and Genealogical Register*. Portland: S. M. Watson, 1886.

Wheeler, George A., and Henry W. Wheeler. *History of Brunswick, Topsham, and Harpswell, Maine*. Boston: A. Mudge, 1878.

Wheeler, Henry W. "Brunswick at the Time of Incorporation." *Collections of the Pejepscot Historical Society* 1 (1889): 21–45.

Wicken, William. *Mi'kmaq Treaties on Trial: History, Land, and Donald Marshall Junior*. Toronto: University of Toronto Press, 2002.

Williamson, Joseph. "Brigadier-General Samuel Waldo, 1696–1759." *CMeHS*, ser. 1, 9 (1887): 75–94.

Williamson, William D. *The History of the State of Maine; From Its First Discovery, A.D. 1602, to the Separation, A.D. 1820, Inclusive.* 2 vols. Hallowell, ME: Glazier, Masters & Smith, 1939.

Willis, William. *The History of Portland, from 1632 to 1864: With a Notice of Previous Settlements, Colonial Grants, and Changes of Government in Maine.* Portland: Bailey and Noyes, 1865.

Wilson, Jon. *The Chaos of Empire: The British Raj and the Conquest of India.* London: Simon and Schuster, 2016.

Wiseman, Frederick Matthew. *The Voice of the Dawn: An Autohistory of the Abenaki Nation.* Hanover, NH: University Press of New England, 2001.

Wood, George. *William Shirley, Governor of Massachusetts, 1741–1756: A History.* New York: Columbia University Press, 1920.

Yirush, Craig. *Settlers, Liberty, and Empire: The Roots of Early American Political Theory, 1675–1775.* Cambridge: Cambridge University Press, 2011.

Young, Afred, ed. *The American Revolution: Explorations in the History of American Radicalism.* DeKalb: Northern Illinois University Press, 1976.

Zoltavny, Yves F. *Philippe de Rigaud de Vaudreuil, Governor of New France, 1703–1725.* Toronto: Mclelland and Stewart, 1974.

Zuckerman, Michael. *Peaceable Kingdoms: New England Towns in the Eighteenth Century.* New York: Norton, 1978.

Index

About the Author

Ian Saxine is Assistant Professor of History at Bridgewater State University. His work has previously appeared in the *New England Quarterly*, winning the 2013 Whitehill Prize in Early American History.